Tanzania
The Limits to Development from Above

Kjell J. Havnevik

Nordiska Afrikainstitutet, Sweden 1993
in cooperation with
Mkuki na Nyota Publishers, Tanzania 1993

Indexing terms
Development models
State intervention
Structural adjustment
Agricultural production
Dams
Hydroelectric power
Tanzania
Rufiji District
Stiegler's Gorge

Cover: Adriaan Honcoop. Drawing based on a photo taken by Marianne Giske of the Rufiji Flood Plain during the 1979 flood.
Copyediting: Susanne Ljung Adriansson
Language editing: Madi Gray

Printed in Sweden by
Motala Grafiska AB, Motala 1993

ISBN 91-7106-335-8 (Sweden)
ISBN 9976-973-19-5 (Tanzania)

For Marianne, Anna, Ella,
Jonatan and Gustav Giske
and Herman Musahara

What we call the beginning is often the end
And to make an end is to make a beginning.

(Excerpt from Little Gidding by
T.S. Eliot)

Contents

List of Tables

8

List of Figures and Maps

Abbreviations and Acronyms

BRALUP	Bureau of Resource Assessment and Land Use Planning (presently the Institute of Resource Assessment, IRA)
CATA	Cashewnut Authority of Tanzania
CCM	Chama cha Mapinduzi (The Revolutionary Party)
cumex	Cubic metres per second (measurement of water flow)
DKB	Deutsche Kolonial Buch
EIA	Environmental Impact Assessment
ERP	Economic Recovery Programme
F	Female
f.o.b.	Free on board
FAO	Food and Agricultural Organisation, specialized agency of the UN
FFYP	First Five Year Plan
ft	Feet
GAPEX	General Agricultural Products Export Corporation
GDP	Gross domestic product
ILO	International Labour Office
KNCU	Kilimanjaro Native Cooperative Union
KNPA	Kilimanjaro Native Planters' Association
M	Male
m.	Million
MOPROCO	Morogoro Oil Processing Company
MW	Megawatt
NDC	National Development Corporation
NHL	Norwegian Hydrodynamic Laboratories
NMC	National Milling Corporation
NORAD	Norwegian Agency for International Development
RDA	Ruvuma Development Association
RTC	Regional Trading Company
RUBADA	Rufiji Basin Development Authority
SIDA	Swedish International Development Authority
SIDO	Small Industries Development Organisation
TAFICO	Tanzania Fishing Corporation
TANESCO	Tanzania Electrical Supply Company
TANU	Tanganyika African National Union
TCA	Tanzania Cotton Authority
TFNC	Tanzania Food and Nutrition Centre
Tsh.	Tanzanian shilling
UFI	Ubungo Farm Implements Factory
UNDP	United Nations Development Programme
URT	United Republic of Tanzania
US	United States
USAID	United States Agency for International Development
UWT	Umoja wa Wanawake Tanzania (The national women organisation of CCM)

A note on currency and exchange rates

Before 1905 the German colonial government used rupees, Indian currency also used in Zanzibar. The value of rupees fluctuated in terms of German marks, until it was fixed in 1905 at three rupees for four marks. From 1905 to 1914 one mark exchanged for one shilling in Kenya or Uganda, and 20 shillings equalled one East African Pound (EAP equal to one British pound). During the British period and up to 1967 one EAP continued to be exchanged for one British pound.

The Tanzanian currency is based on the shilling (Tsh.), divided into 100 cents. The official and parallel foreign exchange rates (Tsh. per US $) is shown below for the period 1967–1992.

Official and parallel foreign exchange rates (Tsh. per US $)

Year	Official rate	Parallel rate	Apparent overvaluation
1967–74	7.0	n.a.	n.a.
1975–79	8.0	n.a.	n.a.
1980	8.2	21.0	156.1 %
1981	8.3	27.5	231.3 %
1982	9.3	32.6	250.5 %
1983	11.1	39.6	256.8 %
1984	15.3	60.0	292.2 %
1985	17.5	100.0	471.4 %
1986	32.7	170.0	419.9 %
1987	64.3	180.0	179.9 %
1988	97.2	195.0	100.6 %
1989	145.0	250.0	72.4 %
1990	194.2	300.0	54.5 %
1991	219.0	366.0	67.1 %
1992	300.0	450.0	50.0 %

Sources: Coulson, 1982; Ministry of Foreign Affairs/Danida, 1992; Bagachwa et al., 1992; EIU Tanzania Country Report No. 3, 1992 and Ofstad, 1992

Acknowledgements

This book is based on investigations and analyses which have been carried out intermittently since the mid-1970s. Many institutions and people have contributed to its realisation.

Without the support of the Institute of Resource Assessment (IRA) (formerly BRALUP), the University of Dar es Salaam, during 1978–80, the undertaking of field work and the first phase of analysis could not have materialised. I am thankful to the former director of IRA, Adolfo Mascarenhas, and my colleagues there, Deborah Bryceson, Finn Kjærby, Han Bantje, A. Kapele, J. Sayana and S. Kajula. For documentation, invaluable support was rendered by the Dar es Salaam University Library and its Africana section and the Tanzania National Archives. Other Tanzanian institutions which assisted included SIDO, the Ministry of Natural Resources at central, regional and district level, GAPEX, NMC, CATA, TCA, TAFICO, RTC, RUBADA, The Census office and UWT (all acronyms are explained in the list of abbreviations). The NORAD Office in Dar es Salaam and its representatives, Olav Myklebust and Jorun Mæhlum assisted at various stages. In Rufiji District the peasants provided the main contribution by taking time to inform and show us under what conditions their wide range of production activities are carried out. Thanks are also due to R.P.G. Lambourn, Mr. and Mrs. Mainwaring, all missionaries in Rufiji District, and A.S.J. Temba, F.R. Mwaisaka, E.J. Luanda, M.J.L. Msaki, I.J. Mkwera, Mr. Roma, Mr. Pazi, all working in the district administration in the late 1970s, and Abdul Sheriff, Department of History, University of Dar es Salaam, and the late C.T. Thomas of SIDO and the Ministry of Industries.

In Norway, during the first half of the 1980s, the major support for the work was provided by the Chr. Michelsen Institute — ASU and its resourceful library. Its former director, Just Faaland, supported it throughout. Assistance at various stages was rendered by Kirsti Hagen Andersen, Sidsel Blegen, Astrid Blom, Ole David Koht Norbye and Jan Isaksen. A subsequent stage of the work was carried out at the Centre for Development Studies (CDS), the University of Bergen. CDS members Gunnar Sørbø, Eldar Bråten and Eyolf Jul-Larsen all provided valuable support. The very competent secretarial assistance

12

rendered by Gerd Handal and Anne Kari Håving was also much appreciated.

At the Scandinavian Institute of African Studies in Uppsala, the work was supported by research colleagues and the library staff. During the Uppsala period I am particularly grateful for the inspiration and support from Yusuf Bangura, Shadrack Gutto, Bertil Odén, Peter Gibbon, Kenneth Hermele and Håkan Gidlöf.

A major part of this book is based on my Ph. D. thesis at the Project Planning Centre, the University of Bradford. My supervisor, Andrew Coulson, provided efficient and constructive guidance. He made writing the thesis a challenge as well as a constructive learning process. John Weiss and Steve Curry, Project Planning Centre staff, also assisted in different stages.

During long periods of the research work and thesis writing I have benefited from discussions and support from Rune Skarstein. Our cooperation on studies related to Tanzania has been of great value to me. Likewise my long-term cooperation with Peter Gibbon, Finn Kjærby, Thorvald Gran, Cheryl Payer, Even Heien, Berit Aasen, Tore Linné Eriksen, Jalibu Mwene-Milao, and Samuel Wangwe has meant a lot at various stages of the research work. At later stages constructive comments were provided by Juhani Koponen, Phil Raikes, Jannik Boesen, Andrew Kiondo, C.S.L. Chachage and Björn Lunöe.

Through his commitment and tireless work, Herman Musahara, presently with the College of Business Education, Dar es Salaam, a research assistant in the Rufiji survey work, bears an important responsibility for the completion of that work. As a friend and commentator during later stages of the work his contribution has been highly appreciated. My wife Marianne Giske participated and supported both during the field work period in Rufiji District and throughout the period of analysis and writing. Her assistance has been of great importance to me.

In the last phase the work has improved considerably through the professional language editing by Madi Gray. I am also grateful for the support from Mai Palmberg and Susanne Ljung Adriansson, both in the publication unit of the Scandinavian Institute of African Studies.

Maps 1–4 were drawn by Anchy de la Garza and 5–6 by the Department of Geography, University of Dar es Salaam. All photographs were taken by Marianne Giske.

The publication of this book has been made possible by economic support from the Norwegian Research Council for Science and the Humanities (Norges Almenvitenskapelige Forskningsråd, NAVF), for which I am grateful.

Uppsala, April 1993   *Kjell J. Havnevik*

Map 1. Tanzania; roads, railways and main cities

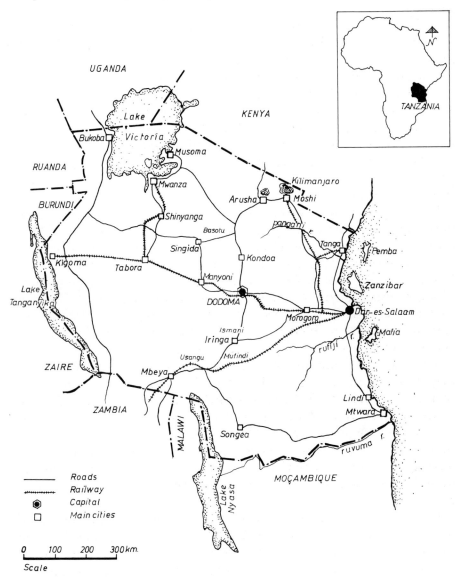

Roads
Railway
Capital
Main cities

0   100   200   300 km.
Scale

Map 2. *Tanzania; administrative division 1986*

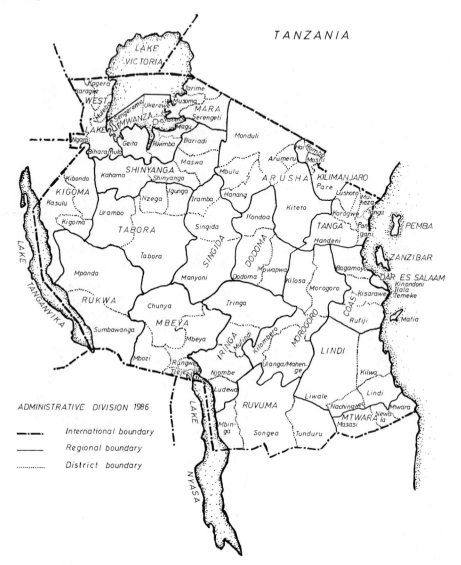

ADMINISTRATIVE DIVISION 1986

- —·—·— International boundary
- ————— Regional boundary
- ············ District boundary

Map 3. *Tanzania; mountains, highlands and rivers*

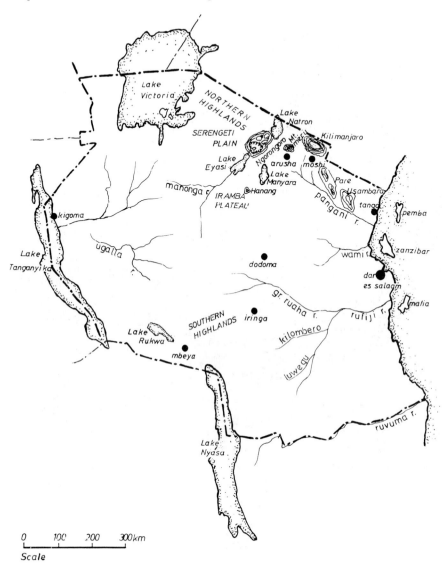

Map 4.   *Tanzania; annual rainfall (average)*

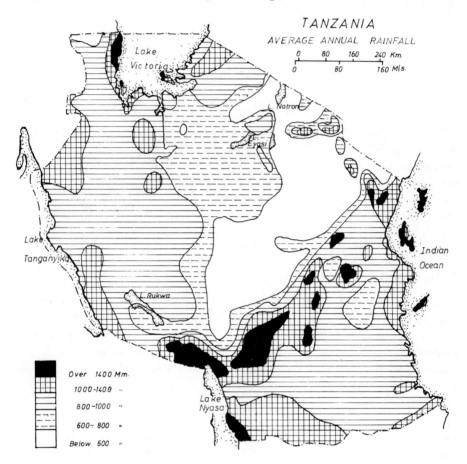

TANZANIA

AVERAGE ANNUAL RAINFALL

1. Introduction

The people of colonial Tanganyika and post-colonial Tanzania have been subjected to a development premised on multifaceted interventionist policies which have affected nearly all areas of society. This development from above, often implemented by force by the colonial- and the post-colonial state and pushed by external donor agencies, the IMF and the World Bank in the last two decades, has resulted in a state-dominated, externally dependent and undemocratic society.

THE LIMITS TO DEVELOPMENT FROM ABOVE

This book aims at documenting and understanding historical and contemporary processes associated with development from above. The intention is to do this by investigating the content, implementation and effects of major interventionist policies and mechanisms. Such an analysis must, however, rest on a thorough knowledge of the social structures, the productive systems and the environmental terrain over which the intervention is enforced or pushed. The outcome of the intervention will not only derive from the policies themselves, but will also depend upon the nature of human responses to and ecological impact of such policies. It is the analysis of the various responses, by producers, social groups or movements, that most clearly reveals the limits to development from above.

The book analyses issues related to the limits to development from above in four parts, each with a different emphasis, but nevertheless interconnected.

The first part, which focuses on *the post-colonial model*, integrates an analysis of the last part of colonialism with the first decades of of post-colonial rule, i.e. the period from around 1950 to the mid-1980s.

The second and major part provides a broad and at times detailed regional study to understand *state intervention and peasant response* in Rufiji District, Coast Region.

The third part investigates the initiation and planning of a major hydro-power project, *the Stiegler's Gorge Project*, located at the western edge of Rufiji District. The project illustrates the role and intervention of external donors and international consultants, alongside the Tanzanian state, in pushing a major unviable project, which would have had tremendous economic, social and ecological effects.

Part four focuses on external intervention by the IMF and the World Bank through the policies of *Structural Adjustment*, launched throughout Africa during the 1980's. The emphasis is on the content and effect of structural adjustment on the agricultural sector in Tanzania.

THE POST-COLONIAL MODEL

The analysis of the post-colonial model in Tanzania is located in a broader African perspective. It focuses on the model's emergence, development and breakdown and the transition between these phases. In a historical perspective the period investigated represents a bridge between colonial reign in Africa and the structural adjustment regime of the 1980s and 1990s.

The nature and development of the post-colonial model cannot be understood apart from the political, social, regional and economic structures of the colonial regime from which it emerged. The post-colonial model is analysed with respect to the social forces forming the broad anti-colonial alliance, the changes in the relative power of these forces after independence and how the post-colonial state related both to the external sphere and internal political, economic and social developments. The growing role of external assistance and its implications for the post-colonial model, its character and survival, is also investigated. An understanding of the post-colonial model also provides important insights into the constraints and problems facing the implementation of structural adjustment policies in Tanzania and Africa. Part I of the book thus provides a framework for an analysis of the interventionist policies in its subsequent parts. These parts will in turn contribute to a deepening and/or extension of the analysis of the post-colonial model.

STATE INTERVENTION AND PEASANT RESPONSE

In many economies where agriculture is dominant, the national strategy for development has been to undertake several transitions simultaneously, like a transition both to socialism and an industrial society. Implicit in these strategies was a third transition, the transformation of agriculture, often from feudal social relations and traditional methods of cultivation, to a collective production organisation with improved or mechanised means of production (Saith, 1985). In many countries aiming for socialism and industrialisation, this proved difficult to realise in spite of extensive state intervention. The dominance of agriculture in the national economy made the extraction of surplus from this sector the only conceivable basis for the development of industry and other sectors, as well as for financing a growing bureaucracy to administer the state apparatus. Under such conditions the state not only has an objective interest in controlling the agricultural surplus, but also in influencing, or increasing its size. Most development strategies based on parallel transitions hence turned out to be extremely ambitious. They opposed the theories of sequential socialist transformation, i.e. first industrialisation and capitalism, then socialism, and overlooked the experiences of transformation of many presently industrialised countries. A prerequisite for industrialisation was often a prior continuous increase of the productivity of agricultural labour, which ensured a growing surplus for appropriation.

Hence the size, growth and control of the agricultural surplus are issues that were relevant during history, at different times for various social formations. The analysis of rural class forces and the role of the state were central elements in the debates of these issues.

The debate on agricultural transformation has increased in vigour also in Africa. In many countries the limited growth of a proletarianised class due to the abundance of land and limited industrial development has caused problems in delineating class forces and determining the character of the state. The transition from the colonial to the "independent" state has added to the complexity of an analysis of the state in African social formations.

State intervention most directly aimed at appropriating the agricultural surplus takes place in the sphere of circulation, where financial regulations, price policies and marketing arrangements are important elements. In many African countries as well as in Tanzania this is illustrated by major state intervention and reorganisation of agricultural marketing over recent decades, as well as an active use of price policies to influence the terms of trade between the agricultural and the nonagricultural sectors. A state monopoly of the marketing of agricultural produce has been commonly used to get access to the agricultural surplus.

While intervention at the level of circulation aims for access to what is already produced, intervention at the level of production has the objective of influencing the size of the surplus. Such intervention can either occur in terms of technology support and input packages to improve production and productivity, or through attempts by the state to influence or change the social relations of production and thereby unleash productive forces. State intervention at the level of production can also aim at controlling the conditions of peasant production through legislation on minimum acreages, land use or directives related to settlements. Both the colonial and the post-colonial state in many African countries have utilised different modes and combinations of interventions, such as, on the one hand, support for the improvement of the productive conditions and, on the other, appropriation through various mechanisms of the increase in the agricultural surplus. A major problem for long-term agricultural development occurs when the state appropriates greater resources than it channels into agricultural cultivation and improvement of rural welfare.

The state may in the short run be able to intensify its appropriation of the agricultural surplus, but it risks undermining the ability of peasants to invest in technology and land improvement and thus alienating them from the state and pushing them into other production lines or non-productive activities. (For a more theoretical discussion of the concept of agricultural surplus and development, see Appendix 1.)

The second and major part of this book focuses on state intervention and peasant responses during the colonial- and post-colonial era in Rufiji District, Coast Region. The history and features of this district, including the demarcation of ecological and agro-economic zones, are presented in Chapter 3. The analysis deals primarily with four major mechanisms of state intervention in agricultural and rural areas: agricultural marketing, agricultural price policies, villagisation, and legal and coercive mechanisms. Knowledge about the character, timing and enforcement of these mechanisms and the responses by peasants are important for understanding the character of the state and state–peasant relations, in the colonial- and post-colonial regimes.

In order to draw conclusions about the impact of state intervention on production there is, however, also a need to isolate the physical and climatic conditions of the agricultural system. The Rufiji agricultural system is particularly complex, due to its flood-dependent character. Historical records and more recent surveys are made use of to arrive at an understanding of the physical properties of the system (Chapter 4). A major emphasis in analysing peasant responses is the observation that peasants are not only agriculturalist, but also work on non-agricultural production, like fishing, forestry including charcoal production, and various lines of handicrafts. Documentation and analysis of these aspects are based on a major survey of Rufiji District and presented in Chapter 5. A review of major forms of state intervention in rural production on both the national and Rufiji District level is presented in Chapter 6. Chapter 7 ties together the analysis of the four preceding chapters and adds relevant historical and empirical material which focuses on the effects of state intervention. In order to trace these effects on agricultural production there is a need to analyse the whole range of peasant production activities and other responses and at the same time to isolate factors linked to physical properties, climate and floods. This is the type of analysis embarked upon in Part II of the book. Chapters 3–6 may be read independently of each other, while it is of benefit to have these previous chapters as a base when reading Chapter 7.

HYDROPOWER VERSUS THE PEOPLE; THE STIEGLER'S GORGE PROJECT

Development from above has often taken the form of joint intervention by the state and external donors, in particular after the launching of the Arusha Declaration in 1967. Total external assistance to Tanzania increased from US $ 51 million in 1970 to around US $ 700 million in 1981, making the country increasingly more dependent on aid in spite of the proclamation of the policies of self-reliance.

The Nordic countries provided an important share of the external assistance to Tanzania. There is a strong element of self-interest in the development cooperation of the Nordic countries, as of other donors. This is reflected in the tying of aid and as well in the rapid increase of Nordic aid employing domestic resources and personnel from sectors affected by the global economic stagnation which unfolded in the 1970s. The large-scale and highly capital-intensive development projects which emerged in Tanzania and elsewhere in Africa during the 1970s can only be properly explained against the background of donor self-interest. But on the other hand, recipient governments, more interested in the implementation and status of large projects, than with their subsequent viable operation, had no objection to this type of assistance. Governments, including the Tanzanian, were becoming increasingly dependent upon a continuous aid flow for the expansion of the state apparatus and the parastatal companies. Thus a common ground existed in the 1970s for western donors and African governments to pursue the planning and implementation of large scale development projects. This is also the background to the Stiegler's Gorge Project where Norwegian eagerness to employ domestic competence in hydro-power development was matched by the appetite of the Tanzanian bureaucracy for large-scale development projects.

An analysis of the planning of this major project is the focus of the third part of this book. The Stiegler's Gorge hydropower project would require construction of a large dam at the western edge of Rufiji District which would mean an end to the flood-adapted agricultural system of the area. The production of electricity would be of such a magnitude that the economics of the project, as seen in the late 1970s, would require the build-up of a number of capital-intensive industries, including aluminium industries, or electricity exports to neighbouring countries. The analysis of the planning of this project also shows there was disregard for both the people and the ecology of Rufiji District, including the major lines of production, agriculture and fisheries. The Tanzanian government attempted to implement this project in close cooperation with external donors and international consultant companies in spite of the emergence of the severe economic crisis, yet it failed. The experience of the planning of the project provides a clear illustration at project level of the breakdown of the post-colonial model and at the same time it is a sign of the crisis of development aid.

STRUCTURAL ADJUSTMENT AND AGRICULTURE

The 1970s had also witnessed an increase in the political and economic bargaining power of the Third World in relation to the western countries, reflected in rising prices for basic commodities (oil and minerals, but also some agricultural products), more intense divisions among the superpowers and the victory of national liberation movements, like in Africa where former Portuguese colonies gained political freedom. This enhanced bargaining power of the Third World was expressed in the UN declaration of a New International Economic Order in the mid-1970s and in the efforts by the superpowers to influence the Third World through increased levels of public lending directed mainly to Africa and private lending channeled primarily to Latin-America.

The global economic stagnation which intensified in the late 1970s and the debt crisis which followed on its tracks, exposed the weakness of the rising Third World influence during the decade. The economic growth attained contributed, in particular for African countries, neither to economic consolidation nor to resistance to the new strategies of control which emerged in the leading western countries.

The latter now ceased to be concerned with buying into the "success" of Third World countries as this had evaporated. Instead western countries and international financial institutions became increasingly concerned about repayment of the huge loans they had handed out to the Third World countries. This is the background for the initiative taken in the early 1980s by the USA, assisted by Great Britain, Germany and Canada, to promote "aid coordination", a concept which first emerged in the OECD in 1981. Two years later the DAC -members of OECD agreed to a system where the World Bank, UNDP and other leading agencies, i.e. the IMF, would direct the donor community in order to attain consistency between donor policies and programmes, and the recipient governments' overall and sectoral development objectives and needs (Gibbon, Havnevik & Hermele, 1993).

"Aid coordination" thus resulted in a unified front facing recipient countries, directed by the IMF and supported by the World Bank and major western bilateral donors. This also led to a rising influence of the IMF and the World Bank and a simultaneous growth in the interest of the major western powers in the specific development policies of these institutions. The merging of interests between major western powers and the IMF and the World Bank was clearly confirmed by the US undersecretary of state for Africa in November 1991. He underlined that the structural adjustment policies pursued by the international financial institutions coincided with the US policies vis à vis the Third World (statement made at the annual conference of the African Study Association in St. Louis, November 1991).

In the 1980s structural adjustment programmes designed by the World Bank were introduced, mainly to unwilling recipient governments in the Third World, by employing the mechanism of "aid coordination". There was no longer an escape route for these governments. This fact was painfully experienced by Tanzania when the Nordic countries in November 1984 closed the door on the country's strategy of relying on the more sympathetic like-minded countries for the expansion of development assistance.

Structural adjustment programmes include a series of elements of which the main ones are: producer price reforms, removal of subsidies, liberalisation of internal and external trade, new foreign exchange regimes usually including severe devaluations, the introduction of cost-sharing for state-supplied services, privatisation and contraction and restructuring of government institutions. Some of these reforms were unavoidable and would have had to be implemented by governments of any orientation. Others, however, reflect both in theory and practice, the new ideology which emerged in the most powerful western countries during the late 1970s and early 1980s.

The central premises of the policies of structural adjustment for African agriculture were cited in the World Bank's major 1981 report (World Bank, 1981a). Firstly the policies which had been pursued by African governments had been pro-industrial, emphasising import substitution including a high degree of protection and rationing of imports. This led to a rise in the prices of agricultural inputs and consumer goods. Government investment in agriculture tended to decline and the major share of it was channeled to import dependent state farms. Secondly, the presence of an excessive state apparatus was associated with heavy taxation of farmers and particularly with depressed producer prices. Thirdly import substitution was linked to overvaluation of local currencies which constituted an additional taxation of agriculture.

The most important element of the "new" agricultural strategy developed by the World Bank to combat the situation of neglect and exploitation of agriculture was a focus on smallholder production. It was claimed that these producers commanded a vast untapped potential, their location in impoverished rural areas implied that this would be the best option for enhancing basic needs and lastly it would be the cheapest way for governments to raise output in agriculture.

Within this framework several important qualifications were related to the position of larger farmers in the promotion of smallholder agriculture. Closer scrutiny of the strategy, clearly allows for the reading of its design as one that gives priority to commercial medium- and larger scale export oriented farmers, who would introduce new methods and whose achievements would trickle down to the less prosperous smallholders. To support these production-level changes, the distribution and trading activities linked with agriculture ought also to be privatised and commercialised. The strategy further emphasises the concentration of productive investment on high potential regions and areas, thus opening the way to increased regional differentiation.

The objective of Part IV of this book is, within this framework, to analyse developments in Tanzania with emphasis on agriculture. World Bank led structural adjustment programmes were initiated in Tanzania in 1986. This part thus represents a continuation of the macrohistoric analysis of Part I and the regional study of Part II and takes the investigation of Tanzanian agriculture and state–peasant relations up to the early 1990s. By integrating the analysis of Part IV with that of the break-down of the post-colonial model, the limits to structural adjustment from above are more clearly revealed.

CONCLUSION

In conclusion, this book represents an attempt to analyse historical and contemporary processes associated with development from above in Tanzania and its limitations. The documentation and analysis is pursued through a broad macrohistoric framework (Part I), an in-depth regional study (Part II), an analysis of a major project (Part III) and by investigating developments on sectoral level (Part IV). The hope is that these approaches and their interconnections can contribute to an understanding of important processes of Tanzanian development. An additional objective is the documentation in concrete ways of the real conditions on a local level facing peasants, craftsmen and craftswomen and fishermen.

Each of the four parts of this book represents an entity and can be read independently. The reading of more or all parts will hopefully add to the understanding of the history and complexity of Tanzanian development and as well to the limits of a model premised on development from above.

FUTURE PERSPECTIVES

According to the documentation and analyses presented in the four parts of this book, the regime of interventionist policies in colonial- and post-colonial Tanzania have not contributed to a broadly based development. After a brief period of popular support, even the policies of the Arusha Declaration met with problems of mobilising people for state-led national development. During the last two decades an increasing divide has materialised between the state bureacracy and the people, which eventually resulted in the loss of political legitimacy by the Party (CCM) and the state. The increased dependence of the state on external donors, the IMF and the World Bank is also likely to have generated a growing distrust among people for the development solutions promoted by these institutions.

The implication of the structural adjustment policies, implemented in Tanzania since 1986, is to structure the external relations of the economy to the needs of the world market. The results attained so far, after six to seven years of rapid increases in external assistance, are discouraging. Growth in the major sector, agriculture, seems to be linked more to increased resource availability and improved weather conditions, than to lasting productivity improvement. A sustainable industrial growth has failed to materialise in spite of sizeable increases in foreign exchange to the sector.

An alternative perspective for the future could be to structure the external relations of Tanzania to the needs of the country as reflected in a sound basis for long-term sustainable development. Attempts at such a shift of development paradigm will, however, come up against strong resistance both externally and internally. A movement in such a direction may, however, emerge through a process of genuine democratisation at all levels of society. The end result of this process could be a government responsible and accountable to its people, rather than to external financial institutions and donor agencies. The process of democratisation in Tanzania is, at the time of writing, in its infancy, but its results will be of major importance to the development of the country and its people, because it might also imply an end to development from above.

PART I

The Post-Colonial Model

2. The Emergence, Development and Breakdown of the Post-Colonial Model in Tanzania

The objective of this chapter is to identify and analyse central features of the post-colonial model in Tanzania. Particular focus will be on understanding the model as it emerges, its subsequent phases and underpinnings and its breakdown in the late 1970s/early 1980s.

The emergence of a post-colonial model is intimately tied to the development of the nationalist movement in the 1950s. The period 1961–67 contains two major features: modernisation of the economy and consolidation of the post-colonial state. The Arusha Declaration (AD) of 1967 and the period to 1972/73 represents an important modification of the post-colonial model, which emphasises its social profile and, through nationalisation of parts of the economy, creates space for Africanisation on a grand scale. Hence the policies of the Arusha Declaration represent an attempt to meet the aspirations and demands of the social base of the nationalist movement.

The third stage, from 1973 to 1978/79, is one in which authoritarian state leadership is strengthened and gradually becomes predominant. This is the period of development of fully-fledged statism, of which the seeds had been sown in earlier periods. Authoritarianism develops in response to problems of implementation of the Arusha policies, negative external economic developments and increased stagnation in the domestic economy. These developments are, however, at least partly, offset by considerable increases in foreign assistance. This enables the state to maintain the social profile of the post-colonial model up to 1976/77. In relation to agriculture the state resorts to more coordinated mechanisms for surplus appropriation resulting in peasants withdrawing their labour from export crop production and increasingly channeling their labour and production to non-state controlled areas and markets.

During 1978/79 to 1983/84 the model breaks down. The state is increasingly challenged from both inside and outside and has to accept fundamental changes in policies, i.e. signifying the breakdown of the post-colonial model. Important features include the decline of the social profile, reduced state intervention and control, i.e. reform and liberalisation of government and the economy. The breakdown of the post-colonial model opens the way for an agreement between Tanzania and the IMF in August 1986 and a systematic programme is designed in close cooperation with the World Bank to set Tanzania on the road to development following the principle of structural adjustment.

The argument is that it is possible to identify a single basic post-colonial model which undergoes several modifications because of economic, political and social responses and pressures. The Chapter will attempt to focus on the central features of the various stages as well as to analyse the transition between them.

Central concerns include modernisation, the economic and social structure, the development and character of the state and the relation between the state and civil society. The analysis rests on a series of hypotheses about the nationalist project and its attempts to create a nation state, which are seen as underlying the post-colonial model.

EMERGENCE AND CENTRAL FEATURES OF THE POST-COLONIAL MODEL

The economic, social and regional structures, which developed in Tanganyika in the pre-independence period, provide a background for understanding the social forces heading and promoting the nationalist movement and the central features of the development model which it promoted.

Background

In the most important economic sector, agriculture, British colonial policy comprised two main phases between 1945 and 1961. The first, which lasted until the mid-1950s, emphasised soil conservation to rehabilitate agricultural land which had suffered from soil erosion due to excessive exploitation during British colonial rule, up to and including World War II. Such rehabilitation was only thought to work if backed by legal compulsion and enforced by the Native Authorities (Iliffe, 1971:34 and Pratt, 1976:25). This period saw major development schemes undertaken, like the Sukumaland Scheme (opening up new land, bush clearing and water development) from 1947, the Uluguru Land Usage Scheme initiated in 1949 (bench terracing), the Mbulu Development Plan of the same year (destocking of cattle and land opening) and compulsory cattle dipping which started in 1954 in Iringa Region.

Vast amounts of administrative energy went into implementation of these and other schemes, and some major objectives were met. The high degree of coercion and compulsion, however, met with widespread resistance from the peasants and during the second half of the 1950s this policy and its attendent schemes were abandoned. The political consequences of the widespread unrest were directed against the colonial regime and undermined the position of the Native Authorities and the chiefs, who were closely associated with them. This discontent helped open up a space for the nationalist movement in the rural areas (Pratt, 1976:28 and Iliffe, 1971:35).

From the mid-1950s the focus of colonial agricultural policy shifted from the peasants to the wealthier African farmers. It was thought to be likely to accelerate a transition from subsistence-like cultivation to a more commercialised agriculture, while enhancing political stability. The colonial state saw political stability as an important precondition for attracting external capital "once it was accepted that it was unwise to continue to finance development from profits on the sale of African-grown cash crops" (Bowles, 1980:181). An integral part of this policy was to replace the customary land tenure system with individual freehold (Iliffe, 1971:37). By 1956 the total area of alienated land had reached 3 million acres, an increase of over 50 per cent from 1949. Though not all of it was for agriculture, the significance of the land alienation stands out when compared to the total land under African cultivation, estimated at 4.5 million acres in 1956. The number of holders of the alienated land was a little less than 1,500, and a sizeable proportion of it was not used (29 per cent in 1961) (Bowles, 1980:184).

Throughout the colonial period the administration attempted to improve plantation agriculture, especially the sisal estates in the eastern part of the country. In 1949–51 sisal alone constituted more than 50 per cent of the total value of exports from Tanganyika (Bowles, 1980:183). More remote areas were compelled to supply migrant labour to plantations, throwing the burden of subsistence cultivation on women and children. Cash crop cultivation in the labour reserves was prohibited in order to obstruct alternative income generation to purchase basic commodities and to pay taxes. Areas with high cash and export crop potential, like coffee and tea, were not faced with such restrictions. The result of this agricultural policy, and the infrastructural investments which accompanied it, was increased regional imbalances in economic and social terms. Much of the western and the southern parts of the country were sinking deeper into underdevelopment.

This pattern was also reflected in the educational system. For instance in the coffee-growing Kilimanjaro area, the Chagga Council was allowed to levy a special tax on coffee, and most of the money was spent on building schools. Outside Kilimanjaro it was hardly possible to get a Western education unless pupils enrolled in Christian mission schools. By contrast, in the Muslim areas of the coast and the south, Christian missionary opposition prevented government recognition of Muslim schools. By 1956 only 20 students were studying for degrees and another 59 were in different non-degree courses at universities or professional institutions. In Coulson's words, "It was a tiny number from which to draw the high-level manpower to run a country" (Coulson, 1982:90).

The industrial sector did not constitute an alternative source for growth and employment. By the late 1950s there existed only about 30 companies in the country with more than five employees. Total employment reached only about 20,000 and the sector contributed only 3–4 per cent of the gross domestic product (Coulson, 1982:79). The main reason for this extremely low degree of industrialisation was that the British colonial investment in East Africa was channeled into Kenyan industry. In 1927 Tanganyika formally joined the Kenyan/Ugandan customs union, which entailed that the goods of the more industrialised Kenya could enter the other two countries free from any tariff (Coulson, 1982:73). In fact, Tanganyika's economy, as Bowles has shown, was treated as an integral and peripheral part of the larger British economy. The principle of the doctrine of comparative advantage was "even expressed sometimes as the duty of the colonies to make sacrifices for the good of the industrial centres, and the praise of the sterling area as a mutual benefit society." (Bowles, 1980:186).

Developments in civil society in Tanzania during the 1950s were significant for several reasons. The labour movement, which had been created from below during the 1940s, collapsed after a major riot in 1950 (Iliffe, 1979:537). The next phase of the organisation of labour was to come from above and in 1955 the Tanganyika Federation of Labour (TFL) was launched. Union membership increased from 13,000 in 1956 to about 200,000 in 1961 while the number of registered unions rose from 25 to 40 during the same period. By 1961, 42 per cent of the country's workers were unionised compared with 12 per cent in Uganda and only 8 per cent in Kenya. Between 1956 and 1958 the number of industrial disputes trebled, from 54 to 153, while man-days lost increased from around 60,000 to 297,000 (Iliffe, 1979:538–39 and Coulson, 1982:138). The constitution of TFL asserted the independence of the labour movement from political control, hence TFL did not affiliate to TANU. The political aims of the TFL were "to encourage workers to register and vote, to exercise their full rights and responsibilities of citizenship, and to perform their rightful part in the political life of the nation" (Iliffe, 1979:538). At the time of independence the Tanganyikan labour movement was the best organised and strongest force in civil society.

The cooperatives were also growing rapidly in the 1950s. In 1952 188 cooperative societies existed with 153,000 members. By 1957 these figures had risen to 474 and 305,000 respectively. According to Coulson, "by 1959 there were 617 societies, and the cooperatives were effectively marketing all the cotton produced in the country, the coffee produced by African farmers, much of the paddy and cashew nuts, and were beginning to make inroads into the marketing of maize and oil-seeds. Their membership had risen to 325,000 out of a population of approximately two million farm families, which, although still only a minority, included most of the prosperous kulak farmers who were rapidly increasing their production of export crops in the 1950s" (Coulson, 1982:116). The cooperative movement aimed at greater control of trade and marketing for the African population, hence it was struggling against both the private Asian traders and the colonial government.

German colonisation was associated with the establishment of a pattern in which most local traders were Asian, while the export/import business was arranged by European trading companies and Asian merchants. During this period Asian traders were established in most towns and in the rural areas, hence it was difficult for Africans to enter trade even at the lowest level. Later the British colonial state actively discouraged Africans from commercial operations. The Credit to Natives (Restriction) Ordinance of 1931 "insisted that an African must have specific government permission before he could even request a bank to lend him money" (Coulson, 1982:60-1). Hence cooperatives became the vehicle through which Africans could protect their production and trade. By the end of the 1950s the cooperative movement had enabled farmers to obtain higher prices. It further operated as a means of attaining power and influence. In turn, this created the basis for ambitious and educated Africans to become involved in crop production (Coulson, 1982:69 and Iliffe, 1971:40).

In spite of the development of some social differentiation among African growers and interest groups, the basic class divide coincided with the major ethnic divisions; the white minority was entrenched in the colonial state apparatus/plantation agriculture and the export/import business, while the Asians had control over the major part of trade and commerce, crop purchases and sales and other intermediary positions. Africans constituted the bulk of the agricultural producers, workers and a small group of educated people in civil service, the education system and the cooperative movement. Issues related to tribe did not play a significant role in Tanganyika. According to Iliffe, "Tanganyika's pre-colonial units had been so numerous, ill-defined, and situational that colonial aggregation was equally confused. This helped to prevent most tribal improvement societies from achieving anything significant, which in turn made their members more receptive to nationalist politics. Moreover, nationalists were fortunate that Tanganyika had no dominant tribe". Furthermore, "like townsmen, political leaders saw their various units and organisations situationally: the tribal union was for local affairs, the wider organisation was for larger problems. Even TANU's founders provided for tribal unions to affiliate to the nationalist party. Only in the late 1950s did the nationalist movement elevate itself above other political organisations and demand exclusive loyalty to the nation" (Iliffe, 1979:490).

Nationalist consciousness developed primarily in the mass movements of trade unions and cooperatives and as well in clubs for African civil servants and teachers, from one of which the first political party, TANU, would eventually emerge (Coulson, 1982:102). The young and well educated nationalists, who entered the scene in the 1950s and were to lead the movement, carried with them motivations blending idealism with the desire for personal improvement (Pratt, 1976:23). The common overall objectives of the nationalist movement were modernisation and attainment of majority African rule, including Africanisation of government and state institutions. The means to be employed to meet these objectives as well as the time perspective for attaining them were, however, the basis for considerable discussion and disagreement. In spite of this, certain central elements of policy developed with a high degree of continuity which constituted the central features of the post-colonial model. Against the background sketched above I will analyse developments in the late colonial and early post-colonial period in order to identify these elements.

Central features of the post-colonial model

Tanganyika neared the end of colonial rule with a social structure of limited differentiation, in spite of growing social division in some areas. As TANU membership grew, its social basis became increasingly diverse, and according to Iliffe, "no one social group dominated, but certain patterns of support recurred" (Iliffe, 1979:523). Hence no African social group was sufficiently dominant economically to aspire to the leadership of the nationalist movement. It was a small group of educated Tanzanians with the teacher Julius Nyerere at the forefront who took the initiative to form TANU and stayed on as its leaders. A small, but well organised labour force and a large mass of poor farmers, constituted the social base of the nationalist movement (Kiondo, 1989:11). The motto of the first TANU government, "Freedom and Development", reflected this social reality.

As TANU moved to the rural areas it did not, however, exploit the hostility which had developed over the Native Authorities' role in implementing the rules and orders linked to colonial agricultural policy. In fact the national leadership of TANU neither endorsed nor encouraged resistance to this policy and its development schemes. Nyerere and his colleagues were disturbed by vigorous and possibly violent local protests which they neither initiated nor could control. In the quest for modernisation and wishing to present a responsible image to the colonial state, they tended to accept uncritically the judgement of professionally qualified officers on such technical issues as the need for cattle-culling, tie-ridging and terracing (Pratt, 1976:34).

The national issue which cemented support for TANU throughout Tanganyika was the attempt by the colonial state to give disproportionate political power to the European and Asian minorities within the political institutions of post-colonial Tanganyika. "The attempt to impose 'multiracialism' at the District level dramatized this issue in terms immediately comprehensible to the rural masses. Opposition to multiracialism became the cause in 1957 and 1958 which united the rural African and the educated and political active town dweller. This issue aroused deep-rooted African fears that Tanganyika might yet be dominated by Asian and European minorities" (Pratt, 1976:28).

As chairman of TANU Nyerere did his utmost to establish ethnic and tribal unity in the struggle for independence. In the negotiations over constitutional issues with the colonial government Nyerere argued, "that the interracial cooperation and the intertribal unity which TANU had generated and was sustaining were political and social assets of enormous value. They would be threatened if Africans came to feel that they would have to fight for their independence" (Pratt, 1976:52).

TANU's consensus generating role, though important, had clear limitations. Firstly, the consensus centered around the major objectives of modernisation and nationalism. By placing the nation as the framework for modernisation, the nationalist movement and later the post-colonial state, came to repress and undermine cultural and religious variations as well as certain important ways to make a livelihood in the country. For instance, many of the major pastoralist groups, including the Maasai, had their land alienated by both encroaching agriculturalists, and the post-colonial state which appropriated pastoral land for the creation of conservation areas, wildlife parks and state farms. The forced movement of pastoralists into nucleated villages during the 1970s and 1980s further undermined the conditions for the pastoral way of living.

Not much is known about the relationship between indigenous re-

ligions and nationalism. Many religious practitioners did not participate in politics, while others seemingly considered TANU a threat to
the indigenous order. In the Mbulu Highlands indigenous religious
influence was probably opposed to the nationalist movement.
Traditionalists, however, usually lacked the skills of the modern politicians and "TANU leaders were modernists who, like Nyerere, habitu-
ally spoke of indigenous religions with an embarrassed smile"
(Iliffe,1979:550).

Christian attitudes to nationalism varied. Christian churches and
missions were extensively intertwined with the colonial state. The colonial state paid nine-tenths of mission teachers' salaries. The Christian
churches were also linked to the critics of the colonial society. For instance, many of the TANU leaders had been trained in mission and
church schools, including Nyerere and Oscar Kambona, the secretary
of TANU. These leaders transferred an ideology of Christian altruism
to TANU which differed from indigenous ethics (Iliffe, 1979:547).
But to place all Christian religious movements in the nationalist camp,
is according to Ranger a serious error. In his review of religious politics
of Christian churches and movements in Sub-Saharan Africa, he concludes that, "...we can begin to construct a much more complex pattern
of religious politics. This was sometimes anti-colonial, and sometimes
allied to movements of nationalism, but so far from taking these connections for granted we need to treat them as problematic, as needing
explanation, just as all other kinds of social and political implications of
religious movements need explanation" (Ranger, 1986:51).

Discussing the Muslim response to nationalism, Iliffe contends that
"Muslim reactions to TANU were probably more completely positive
than those of Christians" (Iliffe, 1979:551). Muslim activists helped to
establish TANU and Muslim brotherhoods provided significant support to the nationalist movement due to their predominantly African
membership and regional extension. Nearly every strand of Muslim
opinion supported TANU, though there were exceptions, notably
among conservative coastal leaders. For instance, the National Union
of Tanganyika, mainly based in Dar es Salaam suggested in 1959 that
independence should wait until Muslims had attained the same educational level as Christians. But TANU, using its strength, mobilised a
number of sheikhs to fight this idea (Iliffe, 1979: 552).

A recurring tendency among nationalist modernisers in Sub-Saharan Africa is the selective cooptation and employment of traditional
cultural values and phenomena, elevating them to symbols of the new
national state (MacManus 1991:50). This attempt to provide the modernisers with links to traditional values and culture, aims at preempt-
ing the growth and opposition of traditional cultural and religious

movements not leaning towards modernisation. TANU and the post-colonial state in Tanzania were able to minimize cultural tension and thereby give the post-colonial model some basic cultural cohesion. This was mainly achieved by the continued promotion of Swahili as a national language, as opposed to English, and the launching of the policies of ujamaa, i.e. brotherhood, in the Arusha Declaration of 1967, when major modifications were made to the post-colonial development model. Elements of ujamaa policies could already be found in the early stages of the post-colonial model, but then more strictly linked to the paradigm of modernisation.

In the early post-colonial period, the policy of modernisation was strongly associated with continued dependence on the colonial power, Great Britain, both for civil service manpower and investments. This was partly due to the lack of development of a domestic bourgeois class, the low level of education and weak and externally dependent economic structures. The First Three Year Development Plan, covering 1961–64, prepared by British civil servants, was largely a compilation of individual capital projects collected from various Ministries. The emphasis was on modernisation through development of import substituting industries, a policy which was further underlined in the Second Development Plan (1964–69). Modernisation of agriculture was to be pursued through continued support for progressive farmers and mechanisation, but also through the establishment of highly capitalised nucleated villages. Investments for modernisation was expected to come from the British state and from private sources, both foreign and local (Pratt, 1976: 97). Small farmers were left to fend for themselves. Of greatest importance to them was the expansion of the cooperative movement.

The cooperative movement solidly supported the nationalist policies and immediately after independence the government made great efforts to spread the movement to non-cash crop producing areas. The objectives were both to increase the marketed agricultural output, and to reduce the dominant role played by the Asian ethnic minority as intermediaries in trade and crop purchasing. Government regulation of agricultural marketing increased steadily, and by the end of 1966 twelve national agricultural boards had been established with either regulatory or advisory or monopoly functions (Wagao, 1982:5). A three-tier agricultural marketing system constituted by these boards, primary societies and regional cooperative unions was designed as the only legal channel of agricultural marketing, entailing strong government control and regulation in this area.

Government control and regulation of the agricultural sector was to increase further. Already in 1966 the government appointed a Special

Committee of Enquiry into the cooperative movement, which concluded that it was suffering from basic defects and problems. The
Committee argued that these were caused by uninformed membership, shortage of qualified manpower, absence of democracy at union
level and political interference (United Republic of Tanzania 1966:9–
10). A later report (Kriesel et al., 1970) confirmed these findings, but
while it recommended more independence for societies doing well,
the original Committee argued for the need for "a greater degree of
central responsibility and central accountability" (Havnevik, 1988:44).
These recommendations opened the way for increased government
interference into the cooperative movement.

The post-colonial state's agricultural policies illustrate most clearly
the general nature of its interventions. While these policies were intended to modify the ethnic and regional imbalances of commercial
agriculture by promoting progressive farmers and mechanisation,
they simultaneously increased social differentiation in the rural areas.
This differentiation was fuelled by the larger farmers' increased control of the cooperative movement.

The expectations and aspirations of the broad masses of peasants,
workers, civil servants and others who supported the nationalist movement in its anti-colonial struggle included provision of social services,
better education, employment opportunities and higher incomes in
the post-colonial situation. Failure by the government to meet these demands after independence was bound to create and strengthen divis-
ive forces in society. According to Jamir Amal, a nationalist of Asian
background, "In the short run, the success of leadership will depend
on the ability to deal sucessfully with these contending forces. In the
long run it will depend on the rate of economic and social progress.
The critical test is one of being able to reconcile the short-term
priorities with the long-term objectives" (Jamal quoted in Pratt, 1976:1,
see also Lonsdale, 1981:196).

The TANU leadership's policy of continuing to depend on the
former colonial power, Britain, set clear limitations on the speed of Africanisation of national institutions. The major share of senior government positions, the police and the military were in the hands of the
former colonial masters, and trade and business in the early independence period were mainly conducted by non-Africans. In addition,
British economic assistance fell way below expectations. Hence, when
pressures mounted for Africanisation from within the social base of
the nationalist movement itself, the leadership had to retreat, though
not wholly, from this dependency policy.

The post-colonial government tried to meet popular demand in
some areas. This was mainly done by raising minimum wages in both

1961 and 1963. This meant a significant improvement in the position of poor workers, but it also implied a more general rise of wage rates. However, the Africanisation measures and the social profile of the post-colonial modernisation were insufficient to stem popular demands. The demands of the autonomous and well organised labour unions came to represent a threat to the post-colonial state.

To contain all these developments the post-colonial state from 1962 onwards took initiatives to subjugate the civil society, which had developed, and promoted the nationalist movement to power. Attacks were mainly focussed on the labour movement. Legislation to disarm individual labour unions, to ban participation of senior civil servants in trade unions and drastically limit the right to strike were introduced in June 1962. A few months later the Preventive Detention Act was passed and this power was used against trade union leaders and traditional chiefs who challenged the nationalist policies (Pratt, 1976:187). In February 1964 the National Union of Tanganyika (NUTA) was established creating a single national union affiliated to TANU. The labour union thus lost the autonomous position it had opted for in the anti-colonial struggle. The creation of NUTA followed the January 1964 army mutiny, which was related to trade union demands for Africanisation and higher wages, and which was quelled by British troops called in by the nationalist government (Coulson, 1982:140).

In July 1965 a new one-party state Constitution was introduced. The underlying assumption of this Constitution was "that the nation is harmonious and united and that the elections involve the choice of trusted individuals who will then legislate on the nation's behalf" (Pratt, 1976:207). This "state for the people" ideology envisaged the state as a unifying factor and a provider of "each and everything to all people equally, while protecting them from external exploitation, manipulation and/or domination" (Kiondo, 1989:12 and Coulson, 1982:329). Coulson continues, "It is a small step from this to Nyerere's modernization theory, which rejects the past (as 'traditional') and inherited patterns of production (as destructive and backward, despite the evidence to the contrary). Ultimately this viewpoint is authoritarian and implies social engineering (or 'management' by the state apparatus) rather than democracy, although Nyerere himself does not take the logic that far, at least in his writings" (Coulson, 1982:329).

Kiondo argues that the increasing predominance of authoritarianism over democracy led to the emergence of a specific form of 'statism' in Tanzania. Statism is understood by Kiondo (with reference to Holmquist) as a simultaneous expansion and centralisation of state economic activities and dimunition of avenues of popular participation (Holmquist, 1983:23 quoted in Kiondo, 1989:41). According to

Kiondo it can be traced to the struggles in the early independence period between the newly created post-colonial state and labour unions. Pratt, writing in 1976, was unwilling to draw conclusions about the longer-term consequences of what he calls the "Tanzanian democratic one-party system". He argued that "in its early manifestation as well as in its original purposes it was intended to provide and did provide an effective popular check upon authoritarian tendencies within the TANU leadership" (!) (Pratt, 1976: 208). Nevertheless, Pratt conceded as well that "the electoral system could easily be adapted to a more authoritarian style of leadership" (ibid.).

Despite elements of authoritarianism it is more realistic to regard the significant features of the post-colonial state in the early independence period as the pursuit of modernisation and development via a variety of channels. Some democratic institutions and channels of popular expression were closed but even when increasing government interference in the cooperative movement took place, it was still an autonomous organisation and in industry the state actively promoted the private sector. A tendency to regard post-colonial rule as a trade-off between developmentalism and modernisation on the one hand and democracy and pluralism on the other certainly existed. Nyerere himself on several occasions returned to the "analogy between a wartime coalition government in a constitutional democracy and the need for a united effort in Tanganyika to achieve stable government and rapid economic development. The 'war against poverty, ignorance and disease' required a national effort similar to the effort needed to win a war against an enemy power" (Pratt, 1976: 68). A one-party system was seen as a both proper and genuinely democratic response to a national crisis. Yet, it also sowed the seeds for a more systematic authoritarian rule.

The result of the developmentalist strategy was, however, growing economic and social differentiation. The undermining of civil society through the politicisation of government institutions further weakened the division between the state/Party and civil society. Political power made it possible for economic control and the regulatory mechanisms employed by the government to be used for personal enrichment by those in authority. Already in the early years of independence Nyerere was of the opinion, "that the unity and commitment to the common good which he had seen as a central feature of TANU in the years of political struggle were being destroyed by the scramble of party members for status, income and personal power" (Pratt, 1976:117). Hence in the early years there were manifestations of a growing divide between the TANU leaders and the bureaucracy on the one hand and the social base of the nationalist movement, poor peasants and workers on the other. The demands and aspirations of these groups for independence had not been met.

The above observations and analysis provide some basis for summarising and interlinking the policy elements which relate to and constitute what can be termed the post-colonial model. Major ongoing policies of the post-colonial government include the quest for modernisation and development.

The post-colonial state also took important regulatory initiatives in the early independence period, aimed at both ethnic issues and regional imbalances and related particularly to the agricultural sector. The regulatory aspects were also to some extent linked to the consensus generating policies of the nationalist movement and the post-colonial state. A nation with important ethnic divisions and large regional, economic and social imbalances was seen by the leaders to need a common ground for sustaining its long-term development. Some kind of consensus about important policies was thus seen to be required. But the common ground for consensus was limited to the modernisation perspective, which was further diminished by excluding the social forces which threatened the consolidation of the post-colonial state, in particular the trade union movement.

Another set of post-colonial policies included what I call secondary trade-offs or compromises between the leaders of the nationalist movement and its social basis. This implies that they did not in themselves constitute a major policy line, but were incorporated in the more generally specified post-colonial model sketched above. One policy of this character linked to the modernisation perspective was the pursuance of economic and technical dependence of the former colonial empire, Britain, and on reliance on private capital, external and internal, for investments for modernisation. This policy, however, required early modifications due to limited external responses.

A different strand of post-colonial policies was related to the demands and aspirations of the social base of the nationalist movement. These demands implied that the post-colonial state was faced with some kind of responsibility for meeting the basic needs of the population, i.e. improvement in social service, education and water supply, etc. Increased employment opportunities, higher incomes and Africanisation also constituted part of these demands. The developmentalist policies pursued, however, led to increased differentiation and inequality and hence could only to a limited extent satisfy these expectations. The social profile of the post-colonial policies had been given low priority in the early post-independence period, resulting in a gradual loss of legitimacy of the post-colonial state.

The post-colonial state's legitimacy was further weakened because

the developmentalist emphasis emerged at the expense of a democratic and pluralistic civil society and included exclusion or forced
cooptation of social groups that threatened the consolidation of the
post-colonial state.

The overall result was a marked limitation of the common ground
that provided the basis for consensus about the path of national development. This reflected that Tanzania was on its way to a more
capitalist organised society, contrary to the ideas for societal development launched by president Nyerere in the early post-independence
years. A bridging of the divide between TANU and its social base, required a re-emphasis of the social and distributionist profile of the
post-colonial model and the introduction of policies to check or halt
capitalist development. Such important modifications came about
with the launching of the Arusha Declaration in 1967.

THE MODIFICATION OF THE POST-COLONIAL MODEL; THE ARUSHA DECLARATION AND SUBSEQUENT DEVELOPMENTS

The Arusha Declaration was based on Nyerere's ideas and visions and
was adopted by the National Executive Committee of TANU in late
January 1967. The Declaration stated that TANU would build a
socialist society. The major principles of such a society were to include
individual human rights, including freedom of expression, and an interventionist role for the state. It was declared that the state needed effective control of the means of production in order to ensure economic
justice and prevent "accumulation of wealth to an extent which is in-
consistent with the existence of a classless society" (Coulson,
1982:176).

The longest part of the Arusha Declaration dealt with the policy of
self-reliance. It admitted the government was unable to provide the social services demanded by people. It further underlined the dangers
of relying on foreign assistance, emphasised rural development and
agriculture and de-emphasised industrial and urban development. It
was stated that the only basis for development was hard work by the
people. Shortly after its publication on February 5, 1967, two other
Presidential Papers were issued, "Education for Self-Reliance", and
"Socialism and Rural Development". The latter promoted the concept
and policy of ujamaa, which implied a commitment to a more collective
way of rural production, life and society.

Interpretations of the Arusha Declaration are many and varied. Issa
Shivji has argued that it provided the emerging class of bureaucrats,
the bureaucratic bourgeoisie, with an economic basis through the

nationalisation of some industry, trade, the banks and the insurance companies (Shivji, 1976). The centrality of state control of the economy in the Arusha Declaration is also emphasised by Kiondo who sees the launching of the Declaration as the take-off of statism proper (Kiondo, 1989:12).

At this point in Tanzanian development, it seems too early to launch this analytical class category. In my assessment such categorisation is unnecessary for understanding the basis for and objectives of the Arusha Declaration (refer also to discussions in Lonsdale, 1981, pp. 199–200 and 203–4). I prefer to argue that the Arusha Declaration was based on a broader nationalist paradigm and its primary aim was to change the direction of societal development so that the TANU leadership, the bureaucrats and the social base of the nationalist movement would grow closer together. The simultaneous introduction of the leadership code was aimed at controlling the misuse of political powers by party and government. The policies of the Arusha Declaration emphasised equity and self-reliance and reopened a space for a consensus which was in danger of disappearing. The Declaration's language is not only economic and political, but echoes certain religious and cultural chords (see, for instance, Frostin, 1988:30-1). This selective cooptation of traditional elements in the policies of the Arusha Declaration could have appeal even for people and social groups which did not share the modernisation perspective.

The intention of extending state control over the economy can thus be seen as a means to reestablish consensus or unity within society. The policies were meant as an effective check on capitalist development in agriculture, industry, banking and trade. On the other hand, the nationalisations also opened the way for major increases in the employment of middle and higher ranking Africans and hence laid the foundations for a major expansion of the African middle class. This allayed the misgivings of those who demanded more Africanisation, about other elements of the policies of the Arusha Declaration, including its socialist rethoric focusing on equality and ascetic leadership. Not only Tanzanian leaders, but also those in other Sub-Saharan African countries, were faced with a similar challenge to balance the demands of the nascent petit-bourgeoisie with the reproduction of the supply of basic needs to meet the demands of the broad masses (Bangura, 1989). The Arusha Declaration tried to strike a balance between these two concerns.

An analysis of Tanzanian development after the Arusha Declaration and up to 1972/73 indicates that the authoritarian tendencies in the state apparatus were toned down and attempts to implement some of the major Arusha policies occurred in a basically benevolent way. State intervention in rural production and society during the period 1967–72 was characterised by a major initiative to move people into nucleated villages and to promote communal farming. At the time these policies were clearly anti-capitalist, involving state appropriation of land and restrictions on the use of hired labour. During the implementation of the ujamaa strategy, however, a more concrete plan for such a transformation could not be produced by the party and the government. Many of the personnel of state institutions and the party did not understand the significance of the strategy, nor how they should deal with the peasantry. Yet, at least in some of the early ujamaa campaigns, including the very first one in Rufiji District, Coast Region, discussion and persuasion were the main methods of implementation. Those who wished to employ force to move peasants were stopped by directives from above, at least once by the President himself. Even though implementation was benevolent, it was riddled with confusion and the result was a slow movement of people into new villages and negligible success in terms of communal cultivation. (Havnevik, 1988. See also Chapter 6.)

In the area of basic needs provision, the movement of people into nucleated villages was accompanied by large scale programmes to improve and expand health-, water- and education facilities. These programmes constituted an integral part of ujamaa policies, the argument being that people had to live in villages in order for the government to reach them with these services. Important progress was made in terms of improving social services and education in the rural areas during the early post-Arusha period.

Nonetheless, as early as 1969, contradictions started to appear. In that year the party banned the Ruvuma Development Association (RDA), an autonomous organisation created in the early 1960s acccording to the ujamaa principles which Nyerere had formulated. In 1967 it included 17 settlements and about 400 families (Coulson, 1982:265). But on September 25 , 1969, the headline of *The Nationalist* informed readers: "TANU to run all Ujamaa villages". This decision had been made by the TANU Central Committee on the grounds that it was necessary to create uniformity in the developments of ujamaa villages. "The Committee felt that because socialism in villages is TANU's policy, the Party should be fully involved with the development of all Ujamaa villages" (ibid.). The police were immediately sent to all the RDA villages to remove all of RDA's property. The expatriates who had assisted the organisation left the country within a few days. In this case the paternalistic and authoritarian face of the party reemerged.

Up to the Arusha Declaration, the private sector had been regarded as the main vehicle for the development of Tanzania. The number of parastatals at independence was negligible and increased to only 64 by 1967 (Coulson, 1982:272). The new policy of direct state control of the economy accelerated the speed of the creation of parastatal companies. By 1974, 139 parastatals had been established and the number was increasing. According to Coulson the parastatal sector was intended to perform three roles: to reduce the transfer of profits out of the country, to expand investment in productive sectors and to strengthen productive infrastructure (Coulson, 1982:274). To control profit transfers it was necessary for the state to control a wide range of financial institutions. In spite of increasing state intervention in the economy through the parastatal sector, Helleiner, writing in the early 1970s, observed that, "Price controls, licensing systems, quota restrictions are conspicuous by their scarcity in this aspiring socialist state" (Helleiner, 1971, quoted in Kiondo, 1989:69). The creation of the Standing Committee on Parastatal Organisations (SCOPO) in 1967, the Tanzania Audit Corporation (TAC) in 1968 and The National Board of Accountants and Auditors (NBAA) in 1972 was an attempt to provide a better environment for the parastatals, rather than a framework for total state economic control as some observers claimed.

The tendency for implementation of the Arusha policies to go less than smoothly affected not only the agricultural sector but also industry. The TANU Guidelines of February 1971 emphasised the vanguard role of the party and stated that, "The time has now come for the Party to take the reins and lead all the people's activities", and at the same time it was argued that, "There must be a deliberate effort to build equality between the leaders and those they lead". The Guidelines were used most spectacularly, however briefly, as a worker's charter against oppressive and arrogant leaders of parastatal companies. From February 1971 to September 1973, thirty-one strikes directed mainly against the abuses of managers and bureaucrats were reported in the press (Coulson, 1982:286). But from August 1972, when the government crushed a strike in Dar es Salaam by dismissing workers, and other employers followed suit, it was clear that the workers could not count on government support for such strikes (Mapolu, 1973:32).

Important government policy initiatives aimed at the rural areas, through villagisation and supply of social services, and at increasing state direction of industry, banking and trade emerged from the early post-Arusha period, 1967 to 1972/73. There is evidence of important gains in the supply of social services and education, and only limited force was employed in the villagisation campaign, though the picture is contradictory. To some extent the divide between the leaders of the nationalist movement and its social base was reduced. With regard to the parastatals, there are indications that factions in the TANU leadership wanted to control the abuses of managers and waste in these companies. Strikes were permitted for some time with a basis in the TANU Guidelines. But the contradictory emphases in the implementation of the Arusha policies indicate that disagreement had emerged in TANU's leadership, and that those pushing for more authoritarian policies and implementation had been strengthened. In my assessment, 1972/73 illustrates the dawn of a period of authoritarian rule in Tanzania.

DEVELOPMENTS IN THE AUTHORITARIAN PERIOD, 1972/73–1978/79

As Table 2.1 shows, there was little in the overall economic situation in the early post-Arusha period to give rise to concern. The annual rate of growth of GDP per capita was 2.5 per cent between 1967 and 1973. However, some negative signals were already emerging. Growth rates in agriculture and industry started to drop at the end of the 1967–73 period and the trade balance began a continuous negative drop (Bank of Tanzania, undated, Table 13). From 1971, at times massive grain imports started. The State Trading Corporation (STC), set up to manage the nationalised import and wholesale trade activities, began to collapse by mid-1971. Virtually unlimited borrowing by STC started to strain the entire financial system and problems began to affect other parastatals. Shortages emerged in the supply of foodstuffs, industrial inputs and durable consumer goods (Resnick, 1981:108–109).

The gradual increase in authoritarianism is not directly related to the decline of economic indicators. While economic advisors to the government tried to make it aware of the negative trends, the course of development in the early 1970s was still politically driven. The increased authoritarianism should rather be seen as a response by the party to the lack of progress in the implementation of major Arusha policies, in particular villagisation. By 1973 the President himself had swung to the authoritarian side, a signal which was registered by the party and government. From this point, government control and expansion accelerated in all economic sectors, including industry and agriculture, and over what remained of civil society. While the initial spurt of authoritarianism was politically driven, subsequently these tendencies were fuelled by negative developments in the external and domestic economy. Hence political and economic forces pulled in the same direction and, as the seeds had been sown earlier, the road was now open for what Kiondo and Holmquist denote as statism. The increase in development assistance during this period made it possible

Table 2.1.   *Tanzania: Economic indicators for 1967–1984*

	1967–73	1974–78	1979–81	1982–84
Growth rate of real GDP	5.2	2.5	2.1	0.6
Growth rate of GDP per capita	2.5	-0.9	-1.1	-2.9
Ratio of investment to GDP	20.8	20.6	22.2	16.4
Ratio of net exports to GDP	-2.6	-9.6	-11.4	-7.1
Ratio of current account deficit to GDP	-2.9	-9.7	-11.7	-7.4
Ratio of debt to exports	120.6	187.1	261.1	513.1
Ratio of debt service to exports	5.6	6.6	9.4	12.1
Growth rate of real output in agric.	2.3	4.7	-1.0	1.8
Growth rate of real output in ind.	7.8	4.7	-10.2	-9.9
Growth rate of exports	3.6	-6.8	7.1	-16.7
Growth rate of imports	3.6	2.8	14.3	-8.4

Source: Lele, 1989, p. 25

for the state to bring about a major expansion of the state apparatus and continue the expansion of social services, in spite of the underlying economic stagnation. Hence, some of the basic policies of the post-colonial model persisted, albeit in an authoritarian framework.

Around 1973, following a strengthening of regional administration (the 'decentralisation' of 1972), state intervention in the rural areas took a new turn. Between 1973 and 1976 intensive implementation of villagisation was undertaken. The concept of ujamaa was dropped, as was the emphasis on communal production. Persuasion was frequently replaced by the outright use of force as evidenced in reports from Morogoro Region (Lwoga, 1978:12-13), from Mara (Matango, 1975:17), from West Lake (Boesen et al., 1977), from Maasailand (Parkipuny, 1976:154-5), from Mwanza and Shinyanga (Mwapachu, 1976:119) and from Iringa (deVries and Fortmann, 1979:130-1). In November president Nyerere was quoted in the government paper *Daily News* saying, "to live in villages is an order" and "there was a need for every Tanzanian to change his mode of life if rapid progress was to be achieved. People who refused to accept development changes were stupid, if not ignorant or stubborn" (*Daily News*, November 7, 1973). The modernisation message could not be clearer.

The results of the more authoritarian implementation of the villagisation policies were spectacular. From 1972 to March 1973 the population in registered villages had barely increased, from 1,980 to 2,028 million. By January 1974, the population in villages had increased to 2,560 million (Coulson, 1982:241). From then on, as villagisation campaigns gained momentum, the speed of movement accelerated dramatically. By June 1975 the number of people living in villages had reached 9.1 million and by January 1977 about 13 million (Nyerere, 1977). In his report to the TANU National Executive Committee in January 1977, ten years after the Arusha Declaration, Nyerere stated that these results were a tremendous achievement by the party and government leaders in cooperation with the people of Tanzania (Nyerere, 1977). About 70 per cent of the rural population had been resettled in the course of about three years .

Villagisation was accompanied by the increased use of bye-laws to regulate agricultural practices and other aspects of rural life. Bye-laws had been used extensively by the colonial state from around 1946 to the mid-1950s (see above), but had been allowed to lapse during the 1960s. Their revival occurred in 1974 and 1975 (Fimbo, 1977:13, Coulson, 1982:256 and Havnevik, 1988:98–106). On the 13th of August 1974, this revival was explained by the *Daily News* in the following way, "Bye-laws requiring people to cultivate the land and care for their farms have been operating in the country for many years. After independence their enforcement was somehow neglected. They are now being revived in many parts of the country to combat laziness and drunkenness" (See also Chapter 6).

New agricultural producer price policies were introduced in 1973, aimed at influencing the composition of agricultural production. One objective of these policies was to increase the production of food crops to enhance national food sufficiency. This was reflected in pan-territorial prices and an increase in producer prices of food crops relative to those of export crops. Prices were fixed centrally on an annual basis, and farmer organisations had no say in price determination. A fundamental aspect of this price policy was a considerable transfer of financial surplus from the peasantry to the state. This was brought about by the fixing of producer prices at a level far below the level of general price increases, in particular for export crops, and by the increasing overvaluation of the Tanzanian shilling. In an analysis of state–peasant tranfers in the 1970s, Frank Ellis estimates the value of such transfers as 4.66 billion Tsh. representing an average implicit tax of 26.6 per cent on peasant crop income. "The incidence of surplus transfer was progressive through time so that if 1970 is taken as a base year net additional resource transfers out of agriculture had reached a level of nearly 1 billion Tsh. per annum by 1980" (Ellis, 1983:235).

Agricultural marketing also saw major and drastic new initiatives by the Tanzanian state. From 1972/73 onwards government crop authorities began to be established. When the implementation of the villagisation was finalised in 1976, the government simply banned the cooperative unions. Instead an agricultural marketing system was established in which each registered village acted as a primary society while the crop authorities were given sole responsibility for crop purchases, processing and sales. The intention was to create one crop authority for each of the major export crops, while another authority, the National Milling Corporation (NMC), was given the responsibility for domestic food crops. Even though the government had already restricted the autonomy of cooperatives earlier, this change meant that the state had appropriated direct control of agricultural marketing from a movement of large and small scale farmers. The economic and political significance of this intervention was great and the problems it led to haunted the agricultural sector and state finances for a long time.

One effect of the creation of crop authorities and villages as primary units of purchase was a drastic increase in the unit cost of handling the various crops. In 1970 Kriesel et al. had already shown that unit costs of handling would decrease by increasing the size of the primary cooperative units (Kriesel et al.,1970). An additional cost increase occurred because, while most crop authorities were establishing branches throughout the territory, production of their specific crop(s) had begun to fall. For instance, the Cashewnut Authority's purchases fell from around 140,000 tonnes in 1973 to only 44,000 tonnes in 1978/79 (Havnevik,1988). The causes for this particularly dramatic decline were partly associated with villagisation (peasants were moved far from their trees) and partly with the introduction of the 1973 price policies which hurt export crops, particularly cashew nuts. The state tried to force peasants back to cashewnut production through the introduction of bye-laws, but only succeeded to a limited extent, in spite of imposing fines and prison sentences (Havnevik, 1988). Instead, where possible, peasants diverted their labour to more remunerative non-agricultural activities, like charcoal production. In Rufiji District the state then attempted to control and restrict this activity by forcing a ban on charcoal burning. Peasants responded by stopping the marketing of charcoal, but still produced for stock. When the ban was lifted, marketing of charcoal increased dramatically (Havnevik, 1988:266–272). Rather than retreating into subsistence as some observers argue (i.e. Hyden, 1980), in face of stagnation and increased state intervention, the peasants seem to have opted for market oriented diversification, including non-agricultural production lines. In some areas these changes have set in motion new processes of accumulation and growing social differentiation (Kjærby, 1987:59).

The direction and character of state intervention in agriculture in the period after 1972/73, as reflected in villagisation, agricultural marketing and producer price policies, and a recourse to legal and coercive methods like the bye-laws, clearly denote both a gradual increase in state authoritarianism and a more coordinated approach to intervention. This coordination seems to have been viewed as a means of increasing state control of the agricultural surplus, which was becoming increasingly necessary due to the need to finance a rapidly increasing state bureaucracy in the face of an underlying economic stagnation. This stagnation had become openly manifested in 1974/75 and then again after 1977. An important observation related to the balance of payments imbalances of 1974/75 is their correction through additional borrowing from external sources (Meyers, 1985: 25 quoted in Kiondo, 1989:191). This corrective measure was not available in the 1980s.

Kiondo describes the proliferation of the state sector, in particular from the early 1970s onwards. The number of parastatals increased from 64 in 1967 to 149 in 1977, then to 380 in 1981 (Kiondo, 1989:75). The activities of the parastatals now embraced all types of economic production, services, tourism and trade both in terms of imports, exports and internal distribution. Acts, committees and various types of squads all proliferated during the 1970s in order to guide, regulate and control the parastatals. They included the Parastatal Supervision of Funds and Financial Control Act of 1974; the Sub-Committee of the Central Committee of the party which had the sole purpose of keeping track of the performance and problems of the parastatals; the Parliamentary Sub-Committee on Parastatal Accounts; and the Anti-Corruption Squad that emerged from the Prevention of Corruption Act of 1970 (Kiondo, 1989:70).

The expansion of state control of the economy took place parallel with the further undermining of civil society. Workers' channels of protest were partly blocked in 1973 and closed completely in 1977 when the affiliation of the National Union of Tanzanian Workers to TANU was modified and it was completely incorporated into the newly created party, Chama cha Mapinduzi (CCM). The cooperative movement, to some extent still an autonomous farmers' organisation, had been banned the previous year. In the process the institutions of civil society in which the movements' social base was organised were scrapped. One important, but often overlooked, consequence of this was the elimination of internal accountability. Kiondo observes, "Both processes (i.e. state expansion and undermining of civil society, KJH) are mutually reinforcing in the sense that the control of the civil society enables the state to create a state sector free from public accountability and use it to further control the public" (Kiondo, 1989:76).

The growth of unaccounted expenditure in the parastatal sector, and in particular in the crop authorities, eventually took on such proportions that it posed a threat to vital activities covered in the government budget. In April 1980 the government had to issue a special circular (Government Circular No. 4, 1980) which directed the parastatals to adhere to recommendations and directives drawn up by responsible committees of the party and government. It stated that the lack of response to decisions taken in these committees was an abuse which had to be rectified. At the same time the audit committee of Parliament instructed the ministries to assist the parastatal companies to improve on their miserable performance as to financial control and accounting (*Daily News*, April 23, 1980). The committee noted that most parastatal companies did not employ internal auditors. Of the 188 companies which were investigated by the committee, 85 had recorded considerable losses. It was further detected that some of the parastatals completely lacked operational directives and procedures which implied that financial transactions and accounting activities were carried out in a haphazard way (*Daily News*, July 22, 1979 and April 23, 1980).

The tendencies towards agricultural stagnation in Tanzania during the 1970s were only the most serious of the economic problems emerging. Yet even these tendencies were not statistically clear at the time. Table 2.1 (2nd column) shows a growth rate of real output in agriculture from 1974 to 1978 of 4.7 per cent annually. This 'increase' was, however, based on the assumption that 'subsistence' production (50 per cent of the total) was increasing by 6.8 per cent per annum. This increase was supposed to occur at the same time as official producer prices and purchase guarantees were first introduced for food crops, including traditional subsistence crops like sorghum, millet and cassava, in 1973. Annual government purchases of these crops increased from 16,000 to 77,000 tonnes during the 1970s (calculated on the basis of three year annual averages). During the same period official purchases of export crops dropped from 635,000 tonnes to 403,000 tonnes while cereals (maize, rice and wheat) went down from 239,000 tonnes to 216,000 tonnes (Ellis, 1982 and Marketing Development Bureau, 1980 and 1985).

Thus the overall tendency for marketed agricultural output was one of decline and stagnation accompanied by a marked increase in crops which traditionally belong to the 'subsistence fund'. The growth rate of total agricultural output of 4.7 per cent annually as indicated in Table 2.1 is probably therefore inflated due to overestimation of subsistence production. On the other hand, some underestimation of export crop production may have occurred due to smuggling. This is of particular relevance for coffee, maize and rice. A more likely estimate for total agricultural growth from 1973 to 1978 is in the range of 3 to

3.5 per cent, i.e. about the same rate as the population growth (Havnevik and Skarstein, 1982). The major change in agricultural production during this period is consequently a change in the composition of production, from export to food crops. This analysis, coupled with Ellis' finding of a progressive transfer of financial surplus from the peasants to the state during the decade, indicate that the state mechanisms for surplus appropriation, though effective for some period, could not be sustained. Crops marketed through state channels provided too little remuneration for the producer to allow the system to be reproduced. As a consequence, the growth of parallel, illegal marketing, accelerated from the end of the 1970s and led to further undermining of the state budget (see Chapter 9).

Alongside agricultural stagnation, another important factor came to force the Tanzanian state to rely on new sources for financing its own expansion and maintaining the social profile of the development model. This was the adverse development in the international economy, in particular the oil price increases in 1973 and 1979. From the mid-1960s Tanzania had sought to scale down its dependence on Britain for external assistance. The introduction of the Arusha policies generated a new sympathy for Tanzanian development, and donor response emerged from the Nordic countries and the World Bank, some other countries in west and east Europe and, not least, China. Foreign aid as a share of GDP increased from 7.2 per cent annually in the early 1970s (three year average 1970–73) to 12.4 per cent at the end of the decade (average 1977–79). As a share of total imports foreign aid accounted for 9.6 per cent and 34.6 per cent at the beginning and end of the decade respectively (Havnevik et al., 1988:125).

A major share of the assistance was invested in the expansion of social infrastructure and education and increasingly during the decade in the expansion of industry and government institutions. Estimates of the sectoral distribution of foreign aid according to donors' commitments show an increase in the percentage share to industry from 8 per cent annually in the period 1974–76 to 29 per cent in 1977–80, while that for social services went up from 9 to 11 per cent (Collier, 1987 and Havnevik et al., 1988:129). Substantial support for the industrial sector after introduction of the Tanzanian basic industry strategy in the mid-1970s was linked to the industrial depression in the western world and the favourable international liquidity situation based on the recycling of petrodollars. Agriculture received a decreasing share of foreign aid, registering a drop from 18 to 11 per cent during the same period.

The increased attention to industrial development at the expense of agriculture by both the Tanzanian state and its donors was an integral part of the continuing trend of statism. Eventually it fuelled the Tanzanian crisis, once external factors had triggered it in the late 1970s. During the 1970s, the share of manufacturing in total investments increased from 10–15 per cent to 35–40 per cent (Svendsen, 1986:66). But the capacity created was hardly utilised, because of the increasing and acute shortages of foreign exchange which developed after 1977, when a short spell of import liberalisation and a drastic fall in coffee prices occurred simultaneously. At the same time employment in the industrial sector grew as if the increased capacity was being utilised. The effect was a dramatic decline in productivity of labour and capital in Tanzanian industry (Skarstein and Wangwe, 1986). Manufacturing and community services both saw very substantial increases in employment (86 per cent and 75 per cent respectively), during the period 1974 to 1982. This rapid growth in non-agricultural employment was facilitated by a large fall in real wages (Svendsen, 1986:69). Real wages in both industry and government started to fall from around the mid-1970s, and by the late 1980s as much as 80 to 90 per cent of the real wage in 1975 had been lost.

An important contributory factor was agriculture's inability either to generate sufficient foreign exchange for imports of spare parts and raw materials, or to supply domestic processing factories with raw materials. For instance, the eleven cashewnut processing factories which were established with World Bank and Italian support in the 1970s had a rated annual capacity of processing 103,000 tonnes. This was below actual collection figures at the time that the expansion was initiated. By the end of the decade agriculture could only provide about 40,000 tonnes of cashewnuts annually, which implied that six of the eleven factories never processed any cashew nuts at all (Havnevik, 1988:32). In spite of this failure, Tanzania had to repay the World Bank loans extended for these factories, otherwise other sources of international assistance and loans would dry up. As Table 2.1 shows, the ratio of debt to exports increased substantially from the period 1967–73 to 1974–78, from 120.6 to 187.1. The considerably lower increase of the ratio of debt service to exports, from 5.6 to 6.6, reflects the fact that many of Tanzania's loans were on concessional terms, as well as that already Tanzania was not repaying all its loans according to agreed schedules.

Health and education indicators report a continuous positive development from 1960 to around 1980, when a negative trend was initiated. Life expectancy at birth increased from 42 to 52 years, then dropped to 50 years in 1985. The infant mortality rate (under 1 year) fell from 155 to 103 and subsequently increased to 110. The child mortality rate (1–4 years) went down from 32 to 20 (1977) and then rose to 22 in 1985. Population per physician fell from 21,000 to 18,500 (1977) before subsequently increasing to 26,200 in 1984 while the population per nurse declined from 8,300 to 3,300 (1977), then went up to 8,100 in 1984. In the mid-1970s about 40 per cent of the population had access to safe water while the percentages of relevant age groups enrolled in primary schools increased continuously from 28 (1960), to 70 (1976) and 87 (1984) (Havnevik, 1982 and World Development Reports, various issues). Statistics made available in the early 1990s show, however, a drastic drop in primary school attendance rates during the 1980s (see Chapter 9).

Due to lags in investment and implementation, it was to be expected that the share of total government expenditure on health and education should have started falling at an earlier stage. Statistics indicate that the government's share of expenditure on health peaked in 1973/74 at 9 per cent of total expenditure, then dropped to 5.2 per cent as an annual average in the period 1978/79–1981/82 (Havnevik et al., 1988:171) and further to 4.9 per cent in 1985 (World Development Report). The share of the government's expenditure on education seems to have begun declining somewhat earlier, in 1972, when 17.3 per cent of total government expenditure was allocated to that sector, a figure which had dropped to 7.2 per cent by 1985 (World Development Report).

The rapid increase in foreign assistance to Tanzania during the 1970s, as shown in Table 2.2, had the effect of compensating for the underlying tendency of economic stagnation and strengthened authoritarian statism, which became the dominant trend from around 1973. The priorities of external aid coincided with those of the Tanzanian state, i.e. the expansion of industry and state institutions as well as the maintainance of the social profile of the development model. Thus the expectations of both the bureaucratic class and the social forces, which had supported the nationalist movement, could continue to be met, at least to some extent. During the latter half of the 1970s, however, the quantity and the quality of the health services, water provision and education started to deteriorate.

Parallel to this an erosion of real wages in industry and government service and of peasant incomes set in. The squeezing of the peasantry and wage earners was accompanied by increased state authoritarianism, increasing inefficiency and a growth in unaccounted expenditure in government and parastatals. These trends gave rise to an increasing loss of political legitimacy on the part of the state and the party. Thus, when external events triggered off the economic crisis in 1978/79, the crisis which emerged also had clear social and political dimensions.

Table 2.2. *Foreign aid disbursements to Tanzania. US $ m.*

Year	Net loans*	Total grants	Total aid	Grants as % of total foreign aid	Technical coopera- tion grants	Tot. aid net of techn. cooper. grants	Techn. cooper. grants as % of total aid
1970	23.7	27.5	51.2	53.7	21.3	29.9	41.6
1971	31.8	30.6	62.4	49.0	23.8	38.6	38.1
1972	16.6	44.5	61.1	72.8	34.7	26.4	56.8
1973	35.4	64.9	100.3	64.7	41.3	59.0	4 1.2
1974	63.1	99.4	162.5	61.2	47.6	114,9	29.3
1975	114.4	187.9	302.3	62.2	60.2	242.1	19.9
1976	71.3	195.7	267.0	73.3	76.7	190.3	28.7
1977	124.7	215.4	340.1	63.3	80.2	259.9	23.6
1978	-32.5	456.6	424.1	107.7	106.0	318.1	25.0
1979	101.2	487.0	588.3	82.8	138.2	450.1	23.5
1980	8.5	657.7	666.2	98.7	172.6	493.6	25.9
1981	193.4	508.5	701.9	72.5	176.4	525.5	25.1
1982	193.8	490.2	684.0	71.7	181.2	502.8	26.5
1983	164.0	429.9	593.9	72.4	173.9	420.0	29.3
1984	128.3	429.5	557.8	77.0	138.7	419.1	24.9
1985	78.9	408.0	486.9	83.8	135.6	351.3	27.8
1986	n.a.	n.a.	680.0	n.a.	260.0	420.0	38.2

* Concessional loans less principal repayments.
Source: OECD: *Geographical Distribution of Financial Flows to Developing Countries*, Paris, several editions up to 1987. Figures for 1986 are from UNDP/Tanzania office; *Development Cooperation Report 1986*, Dar es Salaam, 1987

The period from 1973 to 1978 saw the rise of statism. The state had taken control of the major areas of the economy and effectively closed all avenues for popular opposition and participation. The weakening of the economy created some, however limited, room for liberalisation of the external economy, as well as more space for the private sector towards the end of the period, especially in 1977. This was the first instance of the state conceding to such pressures, though only for a limited period. External and internal pressures for liberalisation intensified during the subsequent period which signified the break-down of the post-colonial model of Tanzania.

CRISIS AND BREAKDOWN OF THE POST-COLONIAL MODEL, 1978/79–1983/84

The crisis developing from 1978/79 reflected adverse external developments and pressures and, most importantly, domestic structural imbalances (fuelled by external aid) and the increasing social divisions generated by statism. The nature and depth of the crisis entailed a breakdown of the post-colonial model. Developmentalism was discredited, along with its abused regulatory mechanisms and the space for consensus generation consequently narrowed. The changing external environment provided no option for a new compromise capable of both maintaining statism and restoring social service delivery. Internal and external forces during this period moved onto the offensive against statism, pushing for a rolling back of the state, a stronger emphasis on the market, and privatisation and liberalisation of all sectors of the economy. The new development model which emerged from this struggle made no allowance for a social profile of development.

The important external shocks which set the Tanzanian crisis in motion worked at different levels. The break-up of the East African Community in 1977 meant that Tanzania had to establish new structures for civil aviation, harbour administration, railways as well as central services for posts and telecommunications. Investments in these areas contributed strongly to an increase in imports. Coupled with the import liberalisation in 1977 an immediate effect was a near doubling of the value of imports between 1976 and 1978, resulting in an external deficit of US $ 675 million, or about 60 per cent of total imports, in the latter year. The doubling of oil prices in 1978/79 added a further US $ 150 million per year to the import bill. Tanzania's terms of trade started to fall from 1977 onwards. From a level of 143 in that year they dropped to 88 in 1981 (1980=100). The problems of agricultural stagnation were accentuated by bad weather in the early 1980s. The overall result was an accumulated balance of payments deficit of about US $ 530 million during 1978-81 (Havnevik et al., 1988:115).

The war against Amin's Uganda, which commenced in November 1978, caused further disruption in agricultural production and transport services and a large increase in the import of military equipment and fuel. In 1978/79, the war brought about an increase in defence spending of Tsh. 1,845 million or 137 per cent, corresponding to an increase in defence's share of total government expenditure from 12.3 per cent in 1976/77 to 24.4 per cent in 1978/79 (Skarstein et al., 1988: 68).

Sectoral level performance clearly indicated an abrupt downward turn of the economy. Between 1979 and 1981 industrial production registered a negative growth rate of 10.2 per cent, barely improving to minus 9.9 per cent in the period 1982–84 (see Table 2.1, Columns 3 and 4). Agricultural output also declined (minus 1 per cent per annum) during the period 1979–81, before improving to 1.8 per cent per annum during the following three year period. (The problem of agricultural statistics has been discussed earlier and will not be repeated here.) The ratio of debt to exports increased from 187.1 in 1974–78 to 261.1 in 1979–81 and then doubled to 513.1 in 1982–84. In spite of this, the debt service ratio only doubled for the entire period 1974–78 (6.6) to 1982–84 (12.1). The growing imbalance between debt levels and export growth clearly showed that the debt crisis could not be solved by an increase in agricultural exports alone. The growth rate of GDP continued to decline, to 2.1 per cent in 1979–81 and then to 0.6 per cent in 1982–84. This meant that GDP per capita for these respective periods amounted only to about minus 1 and minus 3 per cent respectively.

The effects of declining overall growth and the lower priority accorded to health and education emerge in health indicators and observations on education and water supplies. The health indicators previously referred to reflect a worsening situation from the late 1970s onwards. Deterioration in the supply of safe water exacerbated this. Observations indicate that an increasing number of water schemes were out of operation or were not being implemented even before the onset of the economic crisis in 1978/79 (Mujwahusi, 1978). In analysing the rural water supply sector, Therkildsen reports that in 1984 "probably less than 20 per cent of the rural population is regularly drawing water from improved water sources" (Therkildsen, 1986:293). If existing schemes had been working, nearly twice as many people would have been supplied with water. Furthermore, water schemes under construction in the early 1980s required four to five years to be completed, while during the 1970s one to two years were sufficient.

The quality of education deteriorated after the introduction of universal primary education in 1976. From the early 1980s onwards, lack of school books, pupils' desks, teachers' housing and poor school maintenance eroded much of what Tanzania had gained during its first two decades of independence.

From the early 1980s most rural health stations had only a very limited supply of medicine to offer, if any at all.

The deepening crisis was also reflected in commodity scarcities, both consumer goods and basic inputs for production, like agricultural implements (Mothander et al., 1989). Strict confinement policies for basic inputs were introduced in order to reduce leakages to private trading channels. The poor liquidity of many of the government-run

village shops meant, however, that even in cases where farm implements reached regional centres they could not be distributed to the villages. This implied that farmers in need of ploughs and hoes and with
cash to buy them were not able to do so, hence conditions for production deteriorated further.

Rising unemployment, in particular among urban youth, and lack
of opportunities for income generation posed a growing threat of
political instability. In 1983, in response to scarcity problems and rising unemployment, the state took refuge in the use of extra-legal force
which set aside the whole judicial system provided for in the Constitution.

The Economic Sabotage (Special Provisions) Act (No. 9 of 1983)
constituted the government's campaign to fight hoarding, overpricing
and other types of economic sabotage. Special tribunals were set up to
try economic sabotage offences. No legal representation was allowed,
neither was bail permitted. All rules of evidence and procedure were
set aside and police were given extensive powers of search, investigation and detention (Shivji, 1988:49–50).

The passing of the Human Resources Deployment Act (No. 6 of
1983) gave the Minister of Labour a free hand to deal with the problem
of rising unemployment in the cities and towns. According to Shivji the
Minister was "permitted to take a census of all people, identify 'unemployed' and 'non-productive' labour and 'make arrangements
which will provide for a smooth, co-ordinated transfer and subsequent
employment of unemployed residents'." The Minister was also, according to Shivji, given a blank cheque under which he could arrange
for the relocation of persons chargeable with or previously convicted
of being 'idle and disorderly' persons and 'rouges and vagabonds'
(Shivji, 1988:24).

The objectives of these Acts were to give the state powers to deal with
tendencies of political instability and threats from social groups unin-
corporated within existing mechanisms of state surveillance and control–the unemployed and members of the commercial bourgeoisie.
These Acts set aside the judicial system and massively violated the
rights of people belonging to these social groups. These developments
also contributed to a further breakdown in popular respect for the
legal system in general.

The implementation of these Acts further exposed the authoritarian character of the state. It soon became clear that the state would not
allow the Acts to be used against its own bureaucratic class. Higher
government officials were exempted and those who were detained
were released. The mass arrests during the economic sabotage campaign at the end of March and during April 1983 led to the detention

of 1,139 persons of which 1,072 were businessmen (Kiondo, 1989:237). When popular pressure mounted for turning the Economic Sabotage Act against the state bureaucracy, the official campaign weakened and then died. Meanwhile young people and the unemployed, who were rounded up and sent back to their home areas under the Human Resources Deployment Act, had no hope of finding employment there.

For the state the passing and implementation of these two Acts resulted in a further loss of political legitimacy. It appeared that opposition was more widespread than anticipated. In particular, despite the campaign, the commercial bourgeoisie was gaining in confidence and challenging the state to retreat in various ways. In the agricultural sector the state was pressed to reintroduce cooperatives. A new Cooperative Act was passed in 1982, but the restoration of the movement required considerable time. The party was, moreover, not willing to let the cooperatives become completely autonomous, and hence retained control of the apex of the movement. A National Agricultural Policy (NAP) was launched alongside the 1982 Structural Adjustment Programme. NAP opened the way for an element of private ownership of land, attempted to encourage an atmosphere more conducive to private investment in agriculture and advocated the liberalisation of various aspects of agricultural marketing. These policy changes were clearly a retreat on the part of the state, signalling a partial acknowledgement that excessive state intervention and control of the agricultural sector was one of the major causes for its dismal performance.

To improve the flow of external resources to fight the crisis, Tanzania entered into an agreement with the IMF for a standby credit in 1979. Relations with the IMF were, however, broken in 1980 because Tanzania failed to observe agreed credit ceilings, mainly due to overexpenditure on the current budget. Tanzania then attempted to come to an agreement with the World Bank, without IMF involvement, an arrangement rejected by the Bank in 1981. Tanzania was then offered an IMF structural adjustment programme, which it rejected due to its lack of compatibility with the Tanzanian development model. The impact of this falling out with the international financial institutions was, as shown in Table 2.2, reflected in a decline in the overall flow of external assistance to Tanzania, from US $ 702 million in 1981 to US $ 487 million in 1985.

The Tanzanian government then went about designing its own programme for national survival (NESP). This programme aimed at reviving agricultural exports and increasing the utilisation of capacity in industry. But NESP was formulated in a hurry, the targets were not realistic and "it did not articulate ways of mobilizing people and resources in order to achieve the targets. There was little discussion even among policy makers themselves. At the end of the period most targets of the NESP were not achieved. If anything, most variables (e.g. exports, industrial output) moved in the opposite direction to the one projected" (Wangwe, 1987:151). The NESP experience is one among many which shows that by the early 1980s the state had become incapable of mobilising popular support for critical objectives. Indeed, the 1981 CCM Guidelines included "failure or inability of the party to mobilise peasants and workers" as one of its four major challenges. The other challenges related to a hostile international environment, declining agricultural production and the expansion of local capitalism (Kiondo, 1989:234).

The next major attempt of the state to regain control over the overall crisis was linked to the work of the Technical Advisory Group (TAG) in early 1982. World Bank President, Robert McNamara, had earlier shown sympathy for the poverty focus and social profile of the Tanzanian post-colonial development model. A friendship between McNamara and Nyerere had developed and at this stage it was translated into the idea of establishing an independent group of knowledgeable persons (TAG), respected by both the World Bank and the Tanzanian state, to design a programme for structural adjustment. In contrast to the IMF structural programme offer in 1981, TAG recommended "retention of the subsidy on maize-meal and an increasing relative emphasis on government recurrent spending on basic needs and infrastructural rehabilitation at the expense, largely, of military spending" (Loxley, undated mimeo: 7 quoted in Kiondo, 1989:137). But in the end neither the Bank nor the Fund accepted the TAG recommendations. While the Tanzanians rejected TAG's acceptance of devaluation, the World Bank regarded the recommendations as insufficient to bring about the necessary adjustment. The result was that the Structural Adjustment Programme of 1982 failed to command sufficient external support and funding.

The next tactic of the Tanzanian government was to seek increased financial support from sympathetic states, particularly the Nordic countries and the Netherlands, aid that was not tied to the harsh conditions set by the IMF. However, in November 1984, during a joint Nordic/Tanzania government sponsored conference, the Nordic countries jointly conveyed the message to the Tanzanian leadership that there was no opening for an expansion of Nordic assistance without a Tanzanian agreement with the IMF. Hence the Nordic countries also aligned themselves with the IMF conditions. There was no attempt to develop an alternative understanding of the Tanzanian crisis or of measures which could help the country to ease or to overcome it. The door was closed. Foreign aid continued to fall in 1983 and 1984 and reached a low point of US $ 487 million in 1985 (see Table 2.2).

Hence the message was clear. Unlike the situation in the mid-1970s, there existed no external sources of support for a state driven development model with a social profile in the early 1980s. Furthermore, the donor community were collectively not only deemphasising the social profile of development, they were also seeking a reduced role for the state sector or its complete roll-back. External forces hence came to boost the domestic commercial bourgeoisie in its struggle against statism.

Kiondo argues that certain political reforms of the period 1978–83 represented a reduction in the span of direct centralised state control which had been built up during the 1960s and 1970s. Particularly important was the separation of party and government at regional and district level in 1982, which created greater room for manoeuvre for private capital at the local level (Kiondo, 1989:176). The balance of power between the state bourgeoisie and the private commercial bourgeoisie had tilted in favour of the latter (Kiondo, 1989:179). But the major breakthrough for the commercial bourgeoisie came with the launching of the 1984/85 budget. Recurrent expenditure for agriculture was more than doubled from the 1983/84 budget, agricultural producer prices were raised significantly, a large devaluation was announced as well as the removal of subsidies on maize meal (the urban staple food) and agricultural inputs. The budget also considerably weakened the emphasis on social services and education. The development budget for social services was reduced and school fees were introduced. The budget incorporated a significant retreat by the state bourgeoisie and in essence it contained major concessions to the policies promoted by the IMF and the World Bank. Thus the budget signified a new path of development and the breakdown of the post-colonial model. It gave the signal for rapprochement between Tanzania and the international financial institutions and soon new discussions ensued, which would reroute Tanzania's development path along the lines of IMF/World Bank guided structural adjustment principles.

The post-colonial model promoted by Nyerere and the nationalist movement could not overcome the challenge posed by domestic crises and pressures as well as a hostile external environment. The developmentalism of the nationalist movement became discredited because of overt state regulation and control of a basically inefficient and undynamic character. The trade-off between developmentalism and the absence of democracy had not worked. In the end the people were left with neither development nor democracy. In turn this initated a process, albeit gradual, in which people started to organise by themselves. This development related to social groups involved in the modernisation project, and was also embodied in certain traditional forms of social organisation which started to reappear. In Mwanza, the Sungu Sungu traditional defense networks, reemerged in the early 1980s. Their objectives were to protect villages and fight cattle thefts. In other regions similar traditional organisations sprang up. Indications are that religious movements were also becoming more active.

Perhaps the most significant development in the last years of Nyerere's rule was the erosion of popular support for the continuation of any form of nationalist based development model. It appears that the nature of the present political and economic structures and factional struggles is such that the state is unable even to mobilise support for a development strategy which includes priority for a social profile. Hence, the post-colonial state has come to a point where it has become completely separated from its social base. This, more than anything else, explains the breakdown of the post-colonial model.

This breakdown and the adoption of a new transitional development path also implied that there no longer existed a role for Nyerere. In 1985 he withdrew from the Presidency, but retained the chairmanship of the party until 1990 when he resigned. His main function during those last five years was to see that the transition from the old to the new, still undefined, development model was peaceful.

Remains of the old model linger and some struggles against the new policies of structural adjustment and the free market continue. New contenders on the arena are the social and religious groups which did not support the modernisation paradigm or were not included in it. It remains to see whether these groups will be able to exert any influence on the future development model, which is likely to be a model beyond that of IMF/World Bank led structural adjustment.

PART II

State Intervention and Rural Production in Rufiji District

Map 5. *Rufiji District; ecological and agro-economic zones*

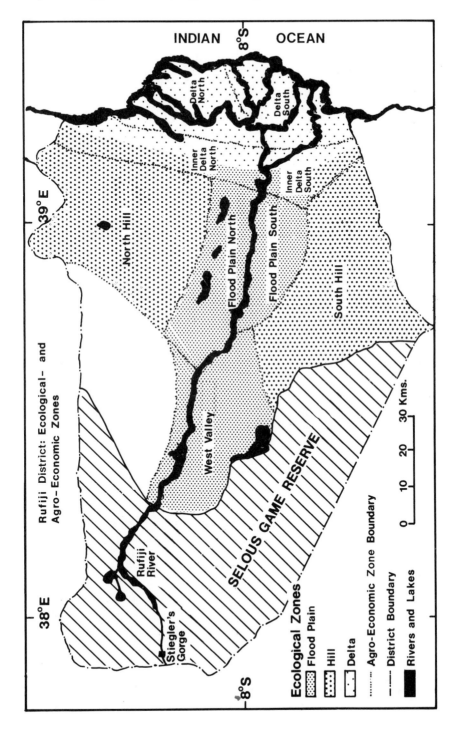

Map 6. *Rufiji District; villages and road network*

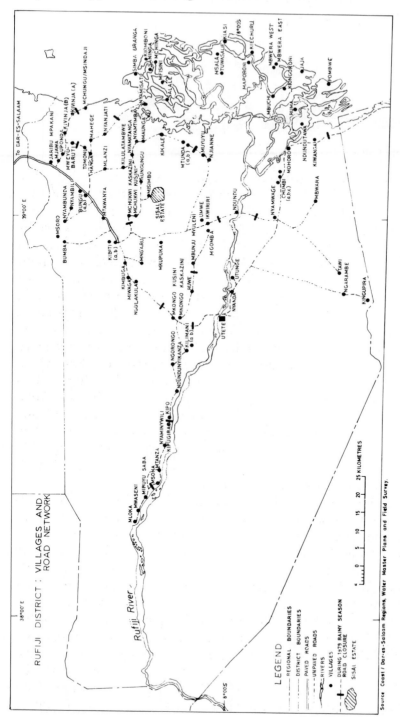

Source: Coast/Dar-es-Salaam Region, Water Master Plans and Field Survey.

3. The History, Location and Features of Rufiji District

THE HISTORY OF RUFIJI DISTRICT

The history of what is presently Rufiji District is intimately tied to the development of the coastal Swahili culture based on nearly two thousand years of trading connections between Arab countries and the East-African coast (Bull, 1973). This trade was made possible by the monsoon winds which carried Arab dhows to the East African coast. After a more "recent" Portuguese intervention which collapsed in 1670, an interregnum period of 100 years "allowed the process of local independence and economic growth to reassert itself" (Sheriff, 1971). From around 1730 the Omani intervention in East Africa took on a form of sustained commercial and territorial expansion. The Omani merchants "traded in the less ostentatious but perhaps more important commodities in the age-old commerce between East Africa on the one hand and Arabia and the Persian Gulf on the other, such as grain and mangrove poles in exchange for dates, dried fish and Muscat cloth. It was probably these commodities, and slaves, which initially attracted and sustained the attention of the Arabs to East Africa. The Arabian coastline is deficient in foodstuffs and timber" (Sheriff, 1971:39). There were three major areas for mangrove poles, of which one was the Rufiji delta (Sheriff, 1971:40).

Towards the end of the 17th century the island of Zanzibar increasingly asserted its importance as the centre of the commercial empire of the Omani sultanate which was based on trade in slaves and ivory. In 1840 a branch of the Omani sultanate established itself permanently on Zanzibar. Simultaneously, the cultivation of cloves spread rapidly on Zanzibar, displacing traditional crops such as coconuts and rice. At the same time, the population of Zanzibar increased rapidly, mainly due to the influx of slaves, who could no longer be reexported as before. Restrictions on the slave trade were initiated by the Moresby Treaty of 1822, which prohibited the export of slaves to the south of Cabo Delgado. The Hamerton Treaty of 1845 made exports of slaves to the north of Lamu illegal (Sheriff, 1971:452). The combination of increased labour absorption in clove cultivation on Zanzibar and the restrictions on the slave trade transformed the structure of the commercial empire of Zanzibar.

The coastal areas of East Africa, the so-called *Mrima*, the stretch from Rufiji in the south to Vanga (in present-day southern Kenya) in the north, came to take on an increasingly important role in supplying Zanzibar with grains. According to the sultan of Zanzibar, Seyyid Said, the *Mrima* was the area "from whence Zanzibar receives the greater part of its revenue, and it bore the heaviest tax burden". The highest rate of duty, was levied on Nyamwezi ivory, copal and grains from this part of the coast, amounting to between a fifth and a third of their value at the coast. This duty decreased to as low as 5 per cent with increased distance from Zanzibar in both north- and southwards directions (Sheriff, 1971:314). The climatic factor facilitated Zanzibar's control of the *Mrima*, since this area is at the edge of the monsoonal system. It allowed longitudinal communication between East Africa and Arab countries, and it also permitted lateral communication as dhows could tack between Zanzibar and the *Mrima* coast as far south as Rufiji throughout almost the whole year (Sheriff, 1971:294).

Loarer, who travelled in Rufiji in the 1840s, observed the role of agriculture in the area:

> Le riz d'Oufidji (Rufiji) est après celui Momfia (Mafia) le plus estimé de la côte orientale d'Afrique, on en exporte de grande quantité pour Zanguebar (Zanzibar). Le riz se vend toujours en paille à Oufidji, les habitants trop occupés de la culture de leur terre, n'ont pas le temps de le peler. C'est dans cet êtat que l'acheteur les marchandise Zanguebar, on a, suivant les années 30 à 40 kilos de riz en paille pour une piastre et de plus on paye prèsque toujours en hammi americain ou de Cutch. On cultive aussi beaucoup le maïs à Oufidji. En un mot, cette petite region est un des grenier les plus riches de Zanguebar (Loarer, 1849).

These observations indicate that rice and maize were major crops of the Rufiji flood plain, and that a labour constraint existed in the agricultural system, as there was no time for dehusking rice before exporting or selling it.

In the 1870s Elton crossed the lower parts of the Rufiji valley and observed:

> The fertility of the lands lying between the Mahoro and Rufiji is extraordinary. Maize, rice, millet, ground-nuts and peas are largely cultivated, and heavy crops are garnered every year, the periodical inundations bringing fresh life to the soil. Sheep, cattle, and goats are in sufficient numbers to be bought for export and shipped at either Murengu or Samanga. In fact, from the Mahoro to the Rufiji was a three hours' march through a land of plenty (Elton, 1898:97).

Ziegenhorn also observed the export of large quantities of beans, maize, rice and sesame seeds from Rufiji to Zanzibar (Ziegenhorn, 1890). "Little Calcutta", (Calcutta *mdogo*), was used by some to refer to

Rufiji because of the importance of rice exports (Kjekshus, 1977a:32 and DKB, 1893:495).

In 1880 the Sultan of Zanzibar sent William Beardall and 15 armed men to explore the Rufiji river by boat. He reported:

> The country along the lower part of the Rufiji, from the coast up to the neighbour-hood of the first falls, presents few of striking features. All the region on the south side of the river is a low flat plain (flooded during rains). ...the soil being very fertile, and growing splendid crops of rice, which is the chief product. The natives also cultivate maize, tobacco, pumpkins, sugar-cane, and a little cassava and sweet potatoes where the soil is light. Cotton would, I believe, grow exceedingly here (Beardall, 1881:646).

Beardall further observed that the country close to the river was well inhabited for that part of Africa, "both banks (of the river) being fairly lined with small straggling villages" (Beardall, 1881:646). The villages were said to be very much alike, the huts were thatched with palmetto leaves and their sides made from mere grass screens. The reason being that during the rainy period the country is under water. "The people then go about in canoes, sleep on high bedsteads built in the roof of the hut, and do their cooking on a small platform of sticks thickly plastered over with clay, and raised on stakes above flood-level" (Beardall, 1881:646).

Towards the end of the 19th century the sultanate of Zanzibar lost its hegemony, due to German colonisation of Tanganyika. From 1885 to 1890 the German East African Company was responsible for the administration of the territory and from 1891 this responsibility passed into the hands of the German state (Iliffe, 1969:11). It was the Germans who introduced cotton on a large scale to the lower Rufiji valley in 1902. The Germans wanted the African peasants to grow cotton as a *Volkskultur*. Forced cotton growing, including much brutality, interfered with and threatened local agriculture. A rebellion started in the southern Rufiji hills at the onset of the 1905 cotton season. This rebellion, called *Maji Maji*, was one of the largest peasant uprisings in Africa. It spread through the southern part of Tanganyika and lasted for two years. Altogether 75,000 Africans were killed during the war (Temu, 1980:119).

The forced cultivation of cotton in Rufiji did, however, demonstrate the suitability of Rufiji soils for this crop. After *Maji Maji*, cultivators in Rufiji planted large acreages under their own control (Iliffe, 1969:167). In addition, the Germans established ten cotton plantations along the Rufiji river between 1907 and 1910 (Iliffe, 1969:100). Cotton was grown in Usukuma and Rufiji and three other areas emerged as centres of tropical crops for the European market (Iliffe, 1969:167). The major crops of the Rufiji valley agricultural system, rice, maize and cotton, were thus introduced before the onset of the First World War.

Another major change introduced by the colonial powers, was taxes. The first tax ordinance was issued by the Germans in 1897. This so-called hut tax was first intended to be educational and to force Africans to accept paid labour and grow cash crops. The educational objectives were soon subordinated to an increased need for current revenue (Iliffe, 1969:160). After the First World War Tanganyika was given as a League of Nations' mandate to Great Britain, which took over the German tax system. Tax collection became one of the major tasks of the colonial district organisation. For instance in 1935 the local district commissioner writes: "Tax has been mentioned in almost every paragraph of this report. It remains a regrettable fact that Native Administration is entirely dominated by this question. The time of Administrative Officers which should be devoted to better causes, is largely monopolized by the necessity of re-inforcing the effort of the Native Collectors. Out of 200 days spent on tours in the year by the Assistance District Officers, 136 were in connection with tax matters plus 27 days in part of the District Officer."

The records of colonial tax collection also show intra-district differences in ability to pay taxes. For instance in the District Annual Report for 1943 it is stated that, "500 of the taxes of 2,333 paid in West (Mtanza and Kwangwazi, i.e. West Valley) were 'alien' taxes paid in Dar es Salaam Township, it being quite impossible for these people either to feed themselves or to obtain their tax locally" (DAR, 1943).

The District Annual Reports of Rufiji for the 1930s and 1940s repeatedly mention that people from Rufiji go to Dar es Salaam, Zanzibar, Mafia or to sisal estates along the Central Line in search for work. The colonial adminstration did its best to promote labour migration, in particular during the war period, to increase production of agricultural raw materials. For instance, in 1941 a labour camp where migrants could sleep was established at Mohoro. In 1942, this camp was visited by 1,950 persons of whom 110 were labourers, 585 women and 328 children. 80 per cent of the total number of travellers used the camp during the dry season, from September to December (DAR, 1942). The number of migrants using the labour camp increased during the war years and the colonial administration in the district recommended that additional camps should be established (DAR, 1943).

Another area of concern to the colonial administration was transportation, in particular of agricultural crops from Rufiji District. Around 1910 the Germans introduced a regular steamer service with the sternwheeler "Tomondo". After about 20 years it was retired. The river was looked upon as the major potential transport system, but the

The Rufiji river entering the flood plain below Stiegler's Gorge

Road condition in Rufiji valley before onset of flood, January 1980

Preparation for charcoal burning, North Hill

Storage of mangroves by water channel, Delta South

Canoes are an important means of transport for fishermen as well

Local boat (mashua), Delta South

Tailor

Bicycle repair

Mat-makers

Nyungo maker

colonial administration encountered increasing difficulties in keeping it open. A major reason for this seems to have been increasing silting of the river.

In 1929 the African Wharfage Company acquired "Tomondo" and some lighters. They were "anxious to run powered transport on the Rufiji to collect the produce of the fertile valley and take it down to the coast at the Delta mouth from where it would go by coastal craft to the main East African ports". "Tomondo" was reconditioned, but unfortunately in the harvest season the river was too shallow even for the shallow-draft "Tomondo" (Morgan, 1959:33). Morgan, a sea captain, then suggested that the colonial administration should take steps to force the river into a single channel in order to increase its depth. A method for this called "bandalling" had been used on the Tigris in Mesopotamia in the 1914–1918 war. The colonial administration supplied material and the transport company boats and personnel, but the experiment failed (Morgan, 1959:34). Thus dhows and canoes remained the major means for moving produce along the river to the delta mouth. Larger dhows had for centuries been the sole transporters of mangrove poles from the Rufiji delta to Zanzibar and the Arab and Persian countries and were to remain so. As their cargo was collected in the delta, these dhows did not need to penetrate up-river where the problems of navigation became increasingly acute.

Information from historical records does indicate, however, that navigation on the Rufiji river was far easier in the early colonial period compared to its later phase. This indicates that silting of the river took place over a long period and has also continuously enlarged the outer delta area.

Apart from agricultural crops, mangroves and coconuts were the major products of the Rufiji delta. Mangroves were exploited through the handing out of concessions. The district annual reports from various years state that it was a recurrent problem for the concessionaires to hire local Rufiji labour for cutting the mangroves. At times labour simply had to be brought in from outside to undertake this job (cf. Chapter 5). It was also reported that the Rufiji people were reluctant to engage in wage labour on plantations in the area, be they sisal or cotton. One reason could be that such work would interfere with the labour needs of the households. Another vaguer explanation was that the Rufiji people rejected such work because it resembled the earlier type of labour organisation on plantations using slave labour.

Because of low wages and lack of security in the plantation system in Tanganyika, Africans only engaged in such work temporarily, maintaining their membership in their rural-based kinship group (Rweyemamu, 1973:22). Many plantations during the post-slave period did not offer permanent jobs at all. With the legal abolition of slavery and the British administration of Tanganyika, the slave-based Arab plantation system disappeared. Attempts by Europeans to engage in plantation agriculture along the coast, including Rufiji, did not meet with success. Only a few Greek and Asian capitalists managed to conduct such activities over a period, including the operation of cotton ginneries.

Several writers claim that the period between 1800 and 1900 was crucial for the development of the Swahili culture (Reeves, 1979:41). During this period the coastal culture penetrated inland areas from a small number of coastal centres, which includes places like Mbwera and Mohoro in the Rufiji District. This diffusion seems to have been due to several factors including the caravan trade and the later development of the export-oriented plantation system. The spread of Swahili culture and its dominant religion, Islam, also took place through the exclusive use of muslim *akidas* as officials at lower levels in the German colonial administration (Reeves, 1979) and through the activities of the Muslim brotherhoods (Nimtz, 1980).

The spread of Islam was particularly rapid in the first four decades of the colonial period, from 1890 to 1930, but it is important to note that the influence of Islam on traditional African religions and ways of life is an extremely complex issue. Most scholarly works depict the influence of Islam on African society as a continuous one-way process through which African culture is transformed through an interaction with Islam into an ultimate synthesis (Trimingham, 1968:44). Others claim, however, that the Africanisation of Islam is much more of a two-way process in which African culture in turn influences Islam so that the ultimate result is an African synthesis of Islam. Some go as far as to state that, "Islam in many respects has become as African as African traditional religions" (Eile, 1985:1). Nevertheless, the norms and values of coastal Islam are important parameters for understanding economic processes of change. The interrelationship between culture, religion and economy may pose constraints or offer potentials for overall development, in particular, constraints on accumulation, expanded reproduction and redistributive effects. A full understanding of these aspects would require a thorough field study, and can be dealt with in this book only through the use of secondary material.

THE LOCATION AND FEATURES OF RUFIJI DISTRICT

The Rufiji District is located in the south of the Coast Region, one of 20 regions in mainland Tanzania. The district extends approximately 180 km from Stiegler's Gorge in the west to the Rufiji delta to the east and is about 110 km at its widest point from north to south. From the major trading village of the district, Kibiti, to Dar es Salaam, the capital, the distance is about 150 km. A tarmac road extending as far as this village was finished in 1968. The district is intersected from west to east by the Rufiji river, the major Tanzanian river, which has a catchment area of about one fifth of the country's territory. There are three main tributaries, the Luwego, the Kilombero and the Great Ruaha rivers which merge to form the Rufiji river before it cuts through the edge of the higher inland plateau at Stiegler's Gorge (cf. Map 3).

The flood plain below Stiegler's Gorge constitutes one of the three ecological zones of the district (cf. Map 5). This river valley has a major agricultural potential. Due to natural annual floods, the agricultural system is very complex. The peasants farming in the zone have adapted their agricultural practices to this system in various ways. The annual flooding of the river seriously constrains vehicle transport over the plain and traffic on barges across the river during the rainy season. Yet, conditions are improved for transport using local means, the canoe.

The Rufiji delta, starting 150 km from Stiegler's Gorge and extending for about 30 km, constitutes a second ecological zone. Here the impact of river floods are felt much less than in the river valley, due to the fanning out of the river in a wide delta. More reliable rainfall along the coast, compared to inland, is advantageous for agricultural cultivation, while the intrusion of tidal waters leads to soil salinity. The Rufiji delta hosts one of the major mangrove forests of the East African coast.

The hill areas of Rufiji District, to the north and south of the flood plain, constitute the third ecological zone of the district. Here floods have no impact, agriculture is purely rain-fed. This zone has a rich and varied forest vegetation (cf. Map 5).

Dividing the district into three ecological zones is a first step towards identifying the characteristic features of the major agricultural systems. For a thorough analysis, one of the intentions of this part, a more detailed sub-division of the district into agro-economic zones is required.

An overall survey of the district and observations made there in the period 1978–1980 provided three major criteria for demarcating these zones. Since agricultural cultivation is the major base for productive activities, responses to state intervention will to some extent depend on the features of agriculture. Hence, each zone has more or less uniform conditions for agricultural cultivation. Demarcation on the basis of this criterion only, corresponds to dividing the district into ecological zones. The second criterion is related to transport or access. Access to raw materials, inputs and markets is of critical importance for the ability of peasants to take up new production activities. Accordingly it was stipulated that each zone should have similar conditions in this respect. This criterion leads to a further division of the ecological zones, mainly because access conditions vary substantially from the north to the south of the Rufiji river. The river is thus a major demarcation line for agro-economic zones. Floods may obstruct transport lines for major economic activities for up to six months a year.

The third criterion for the demarcation of agro-economic zones is based on the finding that conditions for productive activities change gradually when moving westwards from the delta area. Between the major ecological zones, the delta to the east, the flood plain and the hill areas to the west, there are borderline areas, which have very uneven conditions for agriculture. These areas, however, had very uniform features regarding peasants' participation in non-agricultural production. The range of activities is more varied in the borderline areas, as peasants can engage in production activities which are characteristic of the delta area as well as of the hill- and valley areas. This borderline zone runs in north-south direction between the major ecological zones and is divided into north and south due to intersection by the Rufiji river.

In the delta area there is no such clear intersections, as the river fans out into numerous channels in which the water level is affected by ocean tides. The north/south distinction in this area is based on the fact that the northern channels, the main outlets of the Rufiji river, are permanently navigable by fair sized dhows and mashua (local boats). In the south water transport is obstructed by the variations of the tide in shallow channels and canoes are the main means of transport.

Here an agro-economic zone is defined as a part of the district in which conditions for productive activities have similar dominant features. This will provide the basis for a careful analysis of the peasants' responses to state intervention. The concept of an agro-economic zone may also be of value for planning purposes, as conditions for productive activities may be sufficiently similar in each agro-economic zone to warrant the adoption of a unified policy for agriculture, crafts and small industries, fishing and forestry. This definition differs somewhat from others which mainly concern a planning strategy focusing on agriculture. In the following section a brief characterisation of the agro-economic zones of the district will be presented (cf. Maps 5 and 6).

North Hill, the major agro-economic zone in terms of both area and population, is located between the northern Rufiji flood plain and the Kiserawe District border. The zone is part of the hill ecological system, which has a rain-fed and potentially limited agricultural system and has easy access to Dar es Salaam. This has affected the types of non-agricultural activities taken up in response to ecological stress and state intervention, and in particular, has led to an intensification of forest exploitation. This has come to be by far the most important activity in terms of the generation of cash incomes. Other important non-agricultural activities are mat making, coconut-oil production, thatching, basketry and pottery. The total population of the agro-economic zone in 1978 was 36,821 in 24 villages (Population Census, 1978).

The agro-economic zone, *West Valley*, is located west of Ngorongo village in the northern flood plain, and also belongs to the flood plain ecological system. Relocation in 1969 (Operation Rufiji) of the homesteads of the population from the south-of-river flood plain to the elevated northern edge of the flood plain, led to a severe curtailment of the agricultural capacity of the area (Sandberg, 1973). An improved road built on the northern edge along the river provided better access to markets and raw materials, but could in no way compensate for the loss of agricultural production due to inaccessibility of fields during the flood season (Bantje, 1979 and 1980a). Low spots on the road make it prone to flooding and thus has reduced the improved accessibility of that part of the zone located to the west of the village of Kipo. Participation in non-agricultural activities in the zone is low, the major ones being mat making, fishing, basketry, honey collection, making wooden beds and pottery. The total population of the zone was 11,891 distributed in 9 villages (Population Census, 1978).

Flood Plain North is immediately north of the Rufiji river, borders on North Hill and in the west on West Valley, and stretches eastwards to and include Muyuyu village. This zone has a good agricultural potential and the villages are located close to the river flood plain. It has relatively easy access to Dar es Salaam, to the flood plain and the Rufiji river. The western part of the zone may, however, be cut off in years of high flood as in 1974 and 1979 respectively. The major non-agricultural activities include mat making, fishing, charcoal production, embroidery, making wooden beds and basketry. The zone has 7 villages with a population of 31,971 (Population Census, 1978).

The border-line zone of *Inner Delta North* extends from the Rufiji river in the south to the Indian Ocean in the north, bordering in the east on the Rufiji delta and in the west on the agro-economic zones of Flood Plain North and North Hill. Conditions for agricultural production are not completely uniform, as the zone stretches between different ecological zones. The population enjoys access to the major resources of the delta area, notably mangroves, fish and coconuts, and the forest resources of North Hill and Flood Plain North. The varied and rich resource base is reflected in the non-agricultural activities. Of major importance is mat making, coconut-oil production, fishing, salt production, mangrove cutting and charcoal production. The zone has 9 villages with a total population of 10,708 (Population Census, 1978).

Inner Delta South is the southern part of the border-line agro-economic zone. It extends from the Rufiji river in the north to the district border in the south. In the west it borders on Flood Plain South and the southern hill areas, in the east on the Rufiji delta. Like Inner Delta North, agricultural conditions vary somewhat within the zone. There is an abundance of forests, which partly compensated for reduced agricultural cultivation after relocation of villages. The location south of the Rufiji river obstructs access to the major markets to the north. Consequently forest-based activities are mainly for local markets. The composition of non-agricultural activities reflects the access to forest resources in the west and the fishing grounds in the east. The major activities are mat making, fishing, making wooden beds, carpentry and saw mills, charcoal production and thatching. The zone contains 3 villages with 8,884 people (Population Census, 1978).

Delta North and Delta South are agro-economic zones with a varied resource base. The flow of the river makes rice growing possible in some areas even in the dry season. Coconut trees create a basis for extended economic activities, the production of coconut oil, thatching and copra (dried coconut meat). Cattle rearing in coconut areas further diversifies the resource base. Fishing activities are mainly concentrated to shallow waters off the delta, which are very rich in prawns. Major means of transport are canoes and local boats.

Different conditions for navigation led to a division of the area into two agro-economic zones, Delta North and Delta South. Permanent navigation in Delta North and the road to Dar es Salaam from the village Nyamisati, provide this zone with better access than Delta South. The main route to Dar es Salaam is by boat to Nyamisati or Kisiju and from there by road. The most important non-agricultural production is similar for Delta North and Delta South, the major activities being coconut oil production, mangrove cutting, mat making, fishing, salt production and thatching. Delta North has a population of 3,620 and comprises 6 villages, while Delta South has 12 villages with a total population of 16,732 (Population Census, 1978).

According to the 1978 Census, the population of Rufiji District was 135,334. In that year 95 per cent of the population lived in about 80 registered villages. The sex ratio of the district was 90 in 1978, i.e. there were 90 males for every 100 females. This was the lowest recorded for the whole country. The average sex ratio for the Coast Region as a whole was 96. Population growth has been low, but variable. For the period 1948–1957 the average annual growth rate of Rufiji District was 1.4 per cent, for 1957–1967 it fell to 0.2 per cent and for 1967–1978 it increased to 1.9 per cent. These growth rates are below those of other districts of the Coast Region as well as those of the country as a whole, which recorded a growth rate of 3.3 annually in the latter period (Population Census, 1978). The population growth rates and the sex ratios indicate that there is a high out-migration, particularly of males, from Rufiji District.

4. Physical Features and the Agricultural System

The objective of the first part of this chapter is to describe and analyse over time the physical features, rainfall, and floods, in order to provide a sound basis for the subsequent analysis of the agricultural system of Rufiji District. The latter places emphasis on understanding the three different farming systems of the district, their strength and vulnerabilities, and how these relate to the physical features. A major effort is made by the use of historic material to identify the changes in composition over time of agricultural production. The history of famines and responses to them by peasants and authorities are also analysed. Other aspects of relevance to the agricultural system that are taken up include techniques employed in cultivation, issues related to land tenure and the division of labour as well as the use of hired labour.

PHYSICAL SEASONAL FACTORS, RAINFALL AND FLOODS

In most African countries there is a certain marked seasonality that affects production. The degree of seasonality is a major factor affecting the understanding of the multifaceted character of peasant production. The reasons for these cyclical trends in production cannot be traced only to climatic factors, but have to be understood in the context of the historical development of Africa. Lack of development of the productive forces left most African countries including Tanzania at the mercy of natural variations. The lack of a buffer between nature, i.e. rainfall, floods, temperature and wind, and conditions for rural production has entailed that production systems are sensitive to and directly affected by such variations. The strength and survival of these production systems depend upon their ability to adapt to physical variations. As the timing and strength of these changes are not entirely predictable, such an adaptation must include options which can deal with sudden and unexpected, but not unlikely, variations in nature. This aspect is particularly relevant in areas prone to flooding by major rivers.

Table 4.1. *Average monthly rainfall in Rufiji District (in millimetre)*

	Mtanza (west)	Utete (middle)	Mohoro (east)
January	110.5	108.8	119.6
February	56.9	101.9	105.7
March	135.1	154.5	159.8
April	140.0	193.0	269.2
May	63.2	71.8	102.1
June	2.5	11.1	10.9
July	1.5	6.4	6.4
August	6.9	6.6	15.0
September	13.0	14.1	12.3
October	24.6	30.5	37.8
November	31.8	86.1	98.7
December	111.5	100.4	158.5
Total	697.5	885.2	1096.0
	Average of 4 years	Average of 38 years	Average of 21 years

Source: M. Yoshida, 1974

The role of rainfall

Average annual rainfall varies considerably between different areas of Rufiji District, the main characteristic being a declining average rainfall further away from the coastal areas. The historical data presented above shows that Mohoro, located in east of the Rufiji valley, close to the coast, has an annual average rainfall of 1,096 mm; Utete, in the middle section of the flood plain, 885 mm; and Mtanza, in the western valley, 697.5 mm (Table 4.1). Data from the Meteorological Department shows that the area west of Utete receives the least rainfall in the Coast Region, an annual average of between 600 and 800 mm.

For agricultural production, however, it is not the average annual rainfall which matters the most, but its seasonal pattern. As can be inferred from Table 4.1 there exists in Rufiji District both the "short rains" which usually start in November and peak in December/January; and the "long rains" which fall mainly during March and April. Corresponding to this pattern, the agricultural season starts in October. The distribution of rainfall during October and November is

Table 4.2.   *Annual rainfall at Utete for the agricultural years (September–*
             August) 1972–73 to 1980–81

Year	Rainfall (millimetre)
1972–73	878
1973–74	826
1974–75	988
1975–76	766
1976–77	542
1977–78	851
1978–79	1,246
1979–80	784
1980–81	883

Source: Bantje and Niemeyer, 1984, p. 377

most critical, as it determines when field preparations can start and the
success of early crops. Average rainfall during the short rains at Utete
(in the centre) is 219 mm (52 year average for the months of September–December), but in one out of every 3 years rainfall is extremely low, i.e. below 150 mm during the same period (Bantje,
1980a).

The next critical period in relation to rainfall, for most of East Africa, is the length of the dry spell between the short and the long rains.
In Rufiji District it may last up to two months, but in some years the
rain may fall continuously, merging the two rain periods.

During the long rains, the combination of floods and rains is of relevance for agricultural cultivation, fishing and other non-agricultural
activities, and transport. The complexities of the system will become
clearer after the properties of the floods have been discussed. But first,
let me present variations in rainfall for the more recent years, 1972 to
1981, which is of particular relevance to this study.

In Table 4.2 annual rainfall at Utete indicates the variation in the
rainfall situation in the district from 1972 to 1981.

The statistics for these nine years show that average annual rainfall
varies from 542 mm in 1976–77 to 1,246 in 1978–79 and that two out
of these nine years were "dry", i.e. rainfall in the range of 600–800
mm, while one year (1976–77) was a "drought", i.e. below 600 mm.
This compares fairly well with the rainfall data for Utete over 52 years,
which show that three in ten years are "dry" and one in ten a
"drought".

Figure 4.1. *Means and standard deviation of rainfall 1972–81, Utete, Rufiji District*

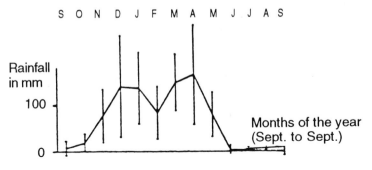

Source: Bantje and Niemeyer (1984), p. 387.

The variation in rainfall for the period 1972–1981 clearly emerges from Figure 4.1 showing means and standard deviation of rainfall on a monthly basis.

Floods

The function of floods

The Rufiji river enters Rufiji District through Stiegler's Gorge at the western edge of the district. It is Tanzania's largest river with a catchment area extending over one fifth or 68,500 square miles of the mainland territory, including parts of Mbeya, Iringa, Morogoro, Dodoma, and Lindi Regions. This entails that flooding in the Rufiji river is mainly connected with the level of rainfall and run-off conditions in areas other than Rufiji.

The floods have various roles in the Rufiji valley, delta and the adjacent coastal waters. These roles are linked to both ecological factors and production conditions and are:

- To compensate for shortage of rainfall for agriculture in the wet season. This compensatory function is particularly important in the area from Utete westwards, where rainfall is lower and more erratic than in the areas closer to the coast.
- To regenerate soil fertility through the spread of nutritious silt carried with the flood water. The importance of this function is emphasised by local peasants who say that three years without major floods will reduce yields to half.
- To create conditions for cultivation during the dry season, when

cotton and maize can be planted on inundated areas. The size of the
flood, and accordingly, the area inundated determines the
maximum acreage that can be cultivated during the dry season.
– To improve conditions for fishing. The most important fishing
  grounds in the valley are in inundated areas, where lakes are
  formed by the flood water. The floods also bring important nutrients to the fish in the valley, the delta and coastal waters.
– To help sustain a large mangrove forest in the Rufiji delta. The
  flood water helps to reduce salinity and restore the ecological balance necessary for the growth ⁄and sustenance of the mangrove
  forest.

As mentioned in Chapter 3, floods also have a significant impact on
conditions for transport in the district. Major floods obstruct road
transport and the crossing of the river by ferries, but at the same time
they improve riverine transport by canoe and dhow in the delta area.
The floods obstruct overland traffic between the south-western part of
Tanzania and the central and northern areas, including Dar es
Salaam. Hence, the area north of the river has much easier access to
the major markets of Dar es Salaam than the rest of the district.

   It is important to realise that the floods of the Rufiji river impact dif-
ferently on the various sections of the Rufiji valley and delta (cf. Maps
5 and 6). The upper section of the valley, from Mloka to Ngorongo, is
the area most badly in need of flood water compensation, but is also
hardest hit by large floods because of the regime of the river and the
topography of the flood plain. This section is consequently prone both
to droughts and destructive floods. In the centre, eastwards from
Ngorongo village to the inner delta areas, the widening of the flood
plain and the flood-dampening effect from the filling up of lakes in
the upper section make the floods more gentle. The lower section,
which includes parts of the inner delta, enjoys the least destructive
floods due to the fanning out of the river in various branches and the
flood-dampening effects of the middle- and upstream areas.

The historic development of floods

Prior to 1926 there is little reliable data for floods in the Rufiji river,
but there is some evidence of major floods in the last century. One
example occured around 1875, when a flood is said to have changed
the course of the river from the north to the south edge of the river valley in the areas north of Utete (Beardall, 1881 and Jack, 1957:6). A.S.
Stenhouse, a colonial district agricultural officer, said that floods
which occurred early this century were well remembered by people

who had attached special names to them. The flood of 1905 was called *faya*, the local name for machine gun, which was first seen by the local population during the *Maji Maji* uprising. The major flood of 1917, maybe one of the heaviest of this century, was named *ndege* (bird), as this was the year in which the first plane was seen. Another indication of the size of that flood is given by a report that the warship H.M.S. *Mersey*, engaged in a naval operation against the German war ship *Königsberg*, went as far up the river as Msomeni in February 1917 (Jack, 1957: 6–7). R. de la B. Barker, who knew the Rufiji District intimately, made the following observation about this flood: "Rufiji is unfairly denounced by collective minds influenced by the strong consensus of opinions resulting from those of many thousands of Europeans who chanced to see Rufiji during its flood period of 1917 when British troops were in that theatre of operations in the war. Normal conditions are less generally known and seasonal change gives the area months of favourable phases when visitors with guides might find much enjoyment, thrill and benefit from rambling about the riverine scenes of East Africa's most important river" (Barker, 1937).

Regular measurement of river floods was first inititated by the placing of a river gauge at Mpanganya Experiment Station in 1926. It was in use until June 1938, when river gauging started at Zombe Experimental Station 12 miles east of Mpanganya. The two gauges were set to record from the same base mark; although it is possible that there may be a slight variation in the readings because the width of the flood plain differs at the two locations (Jack, 1957:8 and Savile, 1945:70). The river is narrower at Mpanganya compared to Zombe, which means that a quick rise or fall of the river at Mpanganya was recorded as a smaller rise or fall at Zombe. Yet, steady high levels at Mpanganya resulted in a higher rise at Zombe, probably due to a flattening out of the decline of the river at or below Zombe (Savile, 1945:70). The Zombe readings were continued until 1956 when a station was established at Utete (IK4) about 25 kms downstream from Mpanganya. The level of the Utete gauge was not adjusted to those of Mpanganya and Zombe, hence these readings are not strictly comparable. Observations show, however, that the readings from Utete are about 5.5 feet higher (Bantje, 1979) and, by adjusting the Utete readings, it is possible to construct a table for timing, maximum height and duration of floods from 1926 to 1977 (see Table 4.3).

From 1954/55 alternative gauging stations for water discharge values were established. Most complete are the data from Stiegler's Gorge (1K3) and Pangani Rapids (1K3A) (Temple and Sundborg, 1973:356). After 1954/55 there are accordingly different sets of recordings for the water flow at different points of the Rufiji river. The readings at

Table 4.3. *Timing, duration and height of floods 1926–1977*

| Year | Timing | | Duration | | Max. height* |
	Month	Week	Months	Weeks	(feet)
1926	April	1st	2	0	0.0
1927	Jan.	1st	2	2	10.0
1928	Feb.	4th	3	2	9.2
1929	March	4th	1	0	9.6
1930	Jan.	4th	4	1	13.0
1931	April	1st	2	0	8.9
1932	April	1st	1	2	9.9
1933	Feb.	1st	3	1	9.3
1934	April	1st	2	0	9.0
1935	March	1st	2	0	13.6
1936	Jan.	3rd	4	2	13.7
1937	Feb.	4th	3	2	12.8
1938	April	1st	2	0	9.5
1939		n.a	n.a		11.4
1940	Feb.	4th	5	1	13.1
1941		n.a.	n.a		11.7
1942	Jan.	1st	5	3	13.4
1943	March	1st	3	4	11.2
1944	March	1st	3	1	13.7
1945	Jan.	1st	5	3	14.0
1946	April	3rd	1	2	11.3
1947	Feb.	1st	9	1	13.3
1948	Dec. (1947)	4th	4	3	10.1
1949		n.a.	n.a.		4.2
1950	Feb.	4th	3	1	12.7
1951	Jan.	4th	4	1	11.3
1952	Jan.	4th	5	1	14.3
1953		n.a.	n.a.		6.0
1954	Feb.	4th	1	0	10.1
1955	March	4th	2	0	12.8
1956	Feb.	1st	6	1	15.3
1957	March	4th	2	1	14.9
1958	Jan.	4th	5	1	17.8
1959	Jan.	4th	4	0	20.0
1960	Dec. (1959)	4th	3	2	17.6
1961	April	2nd	2	1	15.8
1962		n.a	n.a.		23.0
1963	Feb.	2nd	3	1	18.7
1964	Jan.	2nd	4	2	18.3
1965	March	3rd	2	0	16.5
1966	April	1st	1	3	15.3
1967	April	2nd	1	1	14.0
1968	Dec. (1967)	1st	8	0	19.0
1969	April	2nd	1	1	21.8
1970	Feb.	2nd	2	2	17.4

Year	Timing Month	Timing Week	Duration Months	Duration Weeks	Max. height* (feet)
1971	April	1st	1	3	16.2
1972	March	3rd	2	4	23.3
1973	Feb.	4th	3	0	14.6
1974	April	4th	1	3	22.2
1975	March	4th	2	3	15.4
1976	Feb.	4th	2	3	19.6
1977	Feb.	1st	2	1	14.6

* Maximum height indicates height over the base level in feet/inches. Example: In 1927 the flood commenced during the first week of January (column 2) and lasted for two months and two weeks (column 3) with a maximum height of 10 feet above base level.

Notes: Readings from 1926 to 1939 are taken from Mpanganya. The original readings have been reduced by 2'7" to adjust the zero level of the gauge to the average dry season level of the river (FAO, 1961 and Bantje, 1979:30). Readings from 1939 to 1955 are from Zombe and from 1955 to 1977 from Utete. The detailed flood plain readings show that some floods, in 1927, 1948, 1960, 1967 and 1977, consisted of different phases.

In 1927 the first flood period lasted for 2 weeks, then 2 months and 2 weeks went by until the next flood period. The first period started the first week of January and the second in the first week of April.

In 1948 the first flood period started in the last week of December 1947 and lasted for two weeks. The second period started the first week of February and lasted for four months and two to three days.

In 1960 the flood came in three periods, the first lasted for one month and commenced the last week of December 1947. The second period started the last week of February and lasted for one month and one week. The third period started the first week of May and lasted for one month and one week.

In 1976 the flood came in two periods. The first began in the last week of February and lasted for one month and one week. The second period started in the middle of April and lasted for one month and one week.

In 1977 the flood consisted of four periods, the first began in the first week of February and lasted for two weeks, the second started in the middle of March and lasted for one and a half week, the third started in the second week of April and lasted one week and the fourth started late April and lasted for one month.

Sources: Telford, 1929, p. 17; Jack, 1957, pp. 9–10; Savile, 1945, pp. 69–72; and Bantje, 1979, pp. 29–31

Stiegler's Gorge measure water flow in cubic metres per second (cumex), plotted for 7 day discharges. Graphs of these readings are shown in Figure 4.2.

By measuring the graphic presentation of Figure 4.2 it is possible to estimate how long the duration of the water flow was above 1,000, 2,000 and 3,000 cubic metres per second (cumex) at Stiegler's Gorge (cf. Table 4.4).

Figure 4.2. *Flood pattern in the Rufiji flood plain 1957–1979 (measured by a 7-day discharge hydrograph at Stiegler's Gorge)*

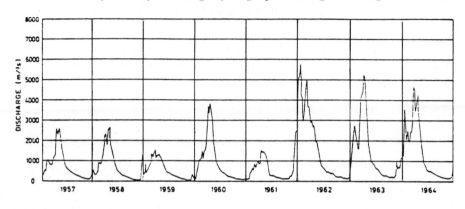

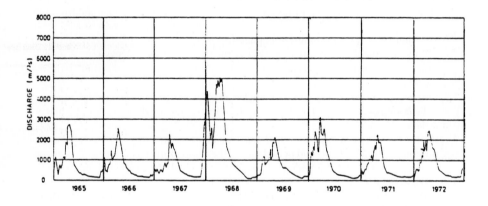

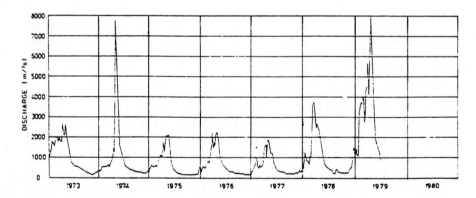

Source: Hafslund, 1980:*Stiegler's Gorge Power and Flood Control Development*. Project Planning Report. Volume 1

Table 4.4. *Water flow discharges at Stiegler's Gorge and time intervals above 1,000, 2,000 and 3,000 cumex and maximum flow (in 1,000 cumex, cubic metres per second)*

Year	>1,000 cumex months	weeks	>2,000 cumex months	weeks	>3,000 cumex months	weeks	Max. flow (cumex)
1957	2	3	1	1	0	0	2,600
1958	2	4	1	1	0	0	2,600
1959	2	1	1	1	0	0	1,500
1960	3	3	1	2	1	0	3,800
1961	1	2	0	0	0	0	1,500
1962	5	4	4	2	2	1	5,700
1963	4	3	3	1	1	3	5,200
1964	4	4	3	3	1	2	4,600
1965	2	2	1	0	0	0	2,700
1966	2	4	0	3	0	0	2,500
1967	1	3	0	1	0	0	2,100
1968	6	3	5	1	3	1	5,100
1969	2	4	0	1	0	0	2,000
1970	4	1	1	4	0	1	3,000
1971	2	4	0	1	0	0	2,200
1972	3	1	0	3	0	0	2,400
1973	5	1	1	1	0	0	2,700
1974	2	2	1	1	1	0	7,800
1975	2	2	0	2	0	0	2,100
1976	2	2	0	2	0	0	2,200
1977	1	4	0	0	0	0	1,800
1978	2	4	1	3	0	2	3,700

Source: Estimated by E. Heien on the basis of Figure 4.2, refer Hafslund, 1980, p. 23

Since measurements of the river flow started in 1926, knowledge has accumulated about the relationship between floods and agriculture. It is difficult to predict the behaviour of the river with any accuracy because flooding is related both to rainfall in the up-country basin and, as will be argued later, to socio-economic factors. R. de Z. Hall, a District Officer in Rufiji, closely investigated the relation between precipitation and the behaviour of the river (Savile, 1945:70). He found certain time lags between upper basin rainfall and the reaction of the river at the Mpanganya river gauge. The accuracy of prediction was not very high, because the behaviour of the river depended more on the duration of rainfall than on the total precipitation. This finding was supported by the 1937 flood which was well above the then average, although the rainfall in the drainage basin was 9 per cent below average. Marshland (1938:57) states that one is unable to predict the size of the flooded areas when the river reaches 13 feet in the gauge, as so many factors influence the free passage of water.

According to Savile (1945), the height of a flood alone may not be so significant in terms of the destruction of crops. This was evidenced by the 1935 flood which reached a maximum height of 13.6 feet on the gauge, but caused little damage to crops in the valley as it receded quickly. The floods in 1930, 1936, 1940, 1942 and 1944 recorded maximum levels similar to that of 1935, but the high levels prevailed for longer periods, which had dramatic effects on the crops. The reason is that the river banks are somewhat higher than the surrounding land. Thus, if flooding is to occur downstream, it can only do so after the water level has remained above the river banks for some time, so that the surrounding land is completely flooded. Savile claimed that the 10 feet mark on the gauge represented a danger point for floods, but the effect is linked to the duration of the flood.

Another significant element is the timing of the flood. Heavy floods in January and February will destroy both short rain crops and recently planted flood season crops. If heavy floods occur later, in March, April or May, they may damage rice and maize and cotton planted during the long rains. Nevertheless, the negative effects of floods should not be exaggerated as they are generally beneficial and necessary for the flood-adapted cultivation systems of the river valley.

The period following Savile's analysis shows that the maximum height of 10 feet on the gauge did not in itself represent a danger mark. Between 1945 and 1977 the maximum height was below that mark in only two years, 1949 and 1953. The most adverse and damaging floods since 1944 occured in 1945, 1952, 1956, 1962, 1968, 1974 and 1979. The 1962 and 1968 floods were characterised by high peaks, early arrival (December), and long duration. The 1974 flood had an extremely high peak, but was less damaging because of its timing and short duration. The profiles of floods from 1957 to 1979 are shown in Figure 4.2. A characteristic feature of flood patterns is the large number of heavy floods, particularly in the 1960s. The overall flows recorded range from 70 m^3/s (cubic meter per second/cumex) to 11,000 cumex in 1979. Information from the Rufiji Basin Development Authority (RUBADA) shows, however, that the 1979 flood was even higher, since it destroyed the gauges placed at a spot above the 11,000 cumex flow. The annual flow of the river ranges from 16,000 to 60,000 Mm^3 (million cubic meters). The average annual flow for the period amounts to 28,000 Mm^3, which is equivalent to 900 cumex. This excludes the 1979 flood, for which the annual measurements were incomplete. As can be seen from the figure, there is an extreme variability in the shape of the hydrograph. The major contrast is between the large volume flood of 1968 that peaked at only 5,000 cumex and the low volume, high peak, flood of 8,000 cumex in 1974 (Hafslund, 1980).

Savile raised an important issue in his 1945 article. He was concerned about the tendency for the degree of flooding to increase, for which he sought an explanation. The data available indicated that the old flood regime of heavy floods every 12 to 15 years had been superseded by a more frequent flood regime. The 1945 flood was the first in which floods occured in two consecutive years. Savile's hypothesis was that there could be two reasons for this change: either higher rainfall in the drainage basin or a marked increase in the surface run-off (Savile, 1945:71).

He went on to investigate the rainfall graphs of all relevant stations in the drainage area and came to the following conclusions:

> There has been no apparent cycle of increased rainfall during the period 1935 to 1944 which could account for the marked increase in flooding that has taken place. On the contrary, the cycle of high rainfall appears to have occurred during the period 1930 to 1936 and thereafter the average rainfall from March to June appears to have been as low, if not lower, than that of the preceding year. It would appear, therefore, that the increased degree of flooding during the last ten years is not due to a cycle of years of high rainfall.
>
> From 1934 onwards the rises and falls in the flood levels appear to have been sharper, as a rule, giving a more needle-like appearance to the flood peaks. This would seem to indicate that the rate of surface run-off has become higher in some portion, or portions, of the Rufiji basin, presumably as a result of the destruction of the natural vegetative cover. (Savile, 1945:71–72)

Savile's prediction for the future was that this tendency of increasing surface run-off is likely to continue and would "result in heavy floods becoming an annual occurrence as is now the case in the Ruvu valley" (Ibid.).

History proved Savile wrong. From 1945 to 1955 the only big flood was in 1952. Since then peak floods have been frequent, but most of them, at least up to 1962, were not very damaging to crops. This temporary change, back to infrequent major floods, might be linked to the colonial government's drive for land conservation. Such measures tend to enhance the water retention capacity of the soil and hence should reduce run-off. Perhaps an investigation of rainfall patterns in the Rufiji drainage basin and soil conservation in the same area could provide some answers as to the effectiveness of the conservation programmes measured by a change to a less flood prone regime in the Rufiji river. As such programmes were, however, linked to unpopular measures (cf. Chapter 6), they broke down around Independence. Soil erosion was no longer considered a major problem for Tanzanian agriculture (Christiansson, 1986:150). During the 1960s and 1970s the tendency towards heavy flooding in the Rufiji river recurred. In Chapter 8 I shall return to the issue of non-climatic factors as causes for floods, when I discuss the project planning reports for the Stiegler's Gorge Hydropower Project.

THE AGRICULTURAL SYSTEM

In this section focus will be on various aspects of the agricultural system. First, the properties of the sub-systems are outlined, then production series over time, and data on occurrences of famine, famine relief and nutrition are presented. Subsequently the impact of physical features on agricultural production are traced. The two last sections investigate the social relations of production in agriculture and the technical level of production.

The properties of the agricultural system

The dominant agricultural sub-system of Rufiji District is the *Rufiji river floodplain farming system* with two seasons of crops per year through natural inundation by floods. The main crops are rice, maize, cotton, cow-peas and bananas. An extension of this system, with a somewhat different ecology and conditions for production is the *Rufiji delta farming system*, also with two seasons of crops annually. It is less dependent upon floods and relies more upon rainfall. Here there are perennial groves of coconuts. The second major sub-system, the *Rufiji hill agricultural system*, consists of upland cultivation in rolling, hilly, sandy and infertile areas to the north and south of the river. The southern part is covered by forested bush. The main crops are upland rice, sesame, cassava and pigeon peas. Additional crops include mangos and bananas and groves of cashew nut and coconut trees. On the plots of permanent houses there are fruit trees, in particular oranges and pawpaws, and beans, maize and pineapples.

All systems are intensive mixed crop systems. Farming in the river valley is in a delicate balance with nature due to floods, droughts and vermin problems. Throughout history this balance has been upset by adverse floods, but large floods have seldom had a negative impact on *all* agricultural seasons. Thus the relationship between floods and agriculture is complex.

Clay soils are most common on the flood plain covering large areas and supporting tall grassland vegetation. Moisture retention capacity because of their heavy texture is high, but they suffer from poor drainage. During floods the finest and most fertile silt is deposited on these soils, due to the calmness of the water in the basins behind the river levees. *Mbaragilwa* soils are found on the elevated ground around the low river levees. These soils are medium-textured and have excellent physical properties, good water retention capacity, but are also well drained. Continuous cultivation takes place in these soils with at times up to three crops grown on the same plot each year.

The valley areas which are not reached by the floods, *gongo*, have sandy or heavy clay soils. They are water-logged in the rainy season, but may be cultivated when drying and yield about half of *mbaragilwa* soils (Sandberg, 1974a:5–7 and Cook, 1974).

The crucial factor for the fertility of soils seems to be the nutrients in the silt carried by the flood water and deposited on the top soil. If a field of *mbaragilwa* land has not been flooded for three years, the peasants estimate the yield to drop by about one half. Thus the extent and interval of flooding play an important factor in explaining the variation in land use (Sandberg, 1974a:7). A property of flood plain cultivation is, thus, that given favourable floods, cultivation can continue to produce reasonable results without the addition of artificial fertiliser.

Flood plain cultivation takes place in two main seasons, the main flood season (*mvuli*) and the dry season (*mlau*). Observations of these seasons and their relationship to the floods have been analysed by several researchers (Telford, 1929; Jack, 1957; Sandberg, 1973 and 1974a; Yoshida, 1974 and Bantje, 1980a). There seems to be agreement that in both seasons cultivation is dependent upon the floods, their timing, peak and duration, but in different ways.

To take proper advantage of the floods, *mvuli* crops must be planted prior to the occurrence of the flood, so that an optimum size of the plants exists at the onset of the flood. Planting too early often results in plants wilting because of water shortages. Crops that are planted too late may drown or be washed away by the flood. By using the knowledge accumulated through generations, peasants attempt to reap maximum rewards from the floods. An intimate knowledge of the topography and ecology of the flood plain and the planting of different breeds in different locations help peasants to minimise their losses.

The dry season (*mlau*) crops grow on previously inundated areas. Planting occurs immediately after the withdrawal of the flood water, and the roots of the plants feed on the sinking ground water. This implies that the size of the potentially cultivable area each dry season correlates with the size of the inundated area.

The above generates the hypothesis that there exists an optimal size of the flood, related to timing, peak and duration, which will promote the best total agricultural production for both seasons combined. There has been considerable discussion about the exact properties of this flood profile. One important reason is that floods have different impacts on the various sections of the flooded area: the upper part (West Valley zone), the centre (the flood plain zones) and the delta area. Most of the discussion about the optimal flood has been related to its effects on agriculture in the middle section, as this area has the greatest potential. A rule of the thumb is that a moderate flood provides relatively good harvests both in the *mvuli* and *mlau* seasons, a large flood is destructive to the crops of the *mvuli* season but creates very good conditions for the *mlau* season and for fishing, and that the worst scenario is no or very small floods that create poor conditions for cultivation in both seasons as well as for fishing. The yields of the dominant crops of the two seasons, rice (*mvuli*) and cotton (*mlau*), are often used as an indicator of the results of the respective seasons.

As indicated earlier, not only do the profiles of the floods determine the outcome of the agricultural season, but rainfall may also have a compensating effect in years of no or small floods. The compensating role of rainfall decreases with movement westwards from the coast, as the annual rainfall in the west valley only amounts to half of that in the coastal and delta areas. That is why cashew trees cannot be grown west of Kipo village. This indicates that the west valley or upper part of the flood plain has the most fragile physical conditions. In years of large floods, this area experiences the worst damage to fields and crops, and in years of low or no floods it receives the smallest degree of compensation in terms of rainfall. The central flood plain areas (Flood Plain North and South) are less negatively affected by large floods, and receive more in terms of annual rainfall.

The delta area is only marginally affected by large floods, and then mostly in a positive way. In addition, this area receives the most stable and largest annual rainfall. It is, however, dependent upon large floods at regular intervals in order to reduce the salinity of the soils caused by the penetration of the tidal waters. In the whole of the Rufiji river valley maybe the area located strategically best for cultivation is the inner delta area, where the beneficial effects of floods can still be felt, where intrusion of tidal water is less than in the outer delta area, but which still receives about the same amount of compensatory rainfall. The villagisation of this area (cf. Chapter 6) shows that when new villages were located, planners did not take these important and favourable production conditions into account and most villagers in the area were forced to move. In the outer delta area agriculture is constrained by shortage of land, sandy soils and high salinity. The sandy soils provide a good environment for coconut trees.

Table 4.5. *Time of planting and harvesting of rice, maize, cotton and pulses in the Rufiji flood plain*

Crop	Planting Early	Late	Harvesting Early	Late	Growing period (months)
Rice	January	February	June	July	6
Maize (*Mvuli*)	November	December	February	March	4
(*Mlau*)	May	June	August	September	4
Cotton	May	June	October	November	6
Pulses	May	June	October	November	6

Source: Lema, 1979. The table is also based on the author's interviews and the works of Sandberg, 1974a and Cook, 1974

Another important constraint on the agricultural system of the river valley is the supply of labour, identified by Yoshida (1974) and supported by the studies of Sandberg (1974a). The issue of labour shortages is particularly important when the harvesting of the flood season crops (*mvuli*) concurs with the recession of the flood waters, because this is exactly the time when the *mlau* season crops, like cotton, have to be planted so their roots can feed on the sinking ground water. Table 4.5, showing the time of planting and harvesting for the major crops, indicates the possibility of such overlap occuring.

Table 4.5 shows that when rice is planted early, in January, and the flood water recedes at the harvest in June, a labour constraint will occur related to the simultaneously harvesting of rice and the planting of cotton. This explains why it is difficult to raise good rice and cotton harvests in the same year. The other period of labour constraint occurs in October when cotton is still being harvested while the fields are being prepared for the next season. Labour constraints are not, however, confined to the flood plain agriculture, they affect as well upland agriculture and non-agricultural production and migration. The data for crops and non-agricultural commodities may shed some light on the priorities of the peasants. The analysis of the changes in their production priorities will be further discussed in Chapter 7.

In the upland and hill agricultural systems, both north and south of the Rufiji river, the agricultural potential is lower due to the topography and the poor quality of the soil. Conditions are most suitable for the cultivation of drought resistant crops and cashew trees. In seasons with favourable rainfall rice may be grown, in particular, in valley depressions where waterlogging occurs. Since the agricultural potential of these areas is lower, many peasants migrate to the river valley to cultivate or engage in non-agricultural production.

Agricultural production over time: composition and trends

Rice and cotton

As previously explained, the harvests of the flood-season crop, rice, and the dry season crop, cotton, are the main indicators of the success of these two seasons. My next task will thus be to present production data related to physical factors, such as rainfall and flood profiles (see Table 4.6). Regarding rainfall, it is not the amount during the calendar year which is the most relevant, but the pattern of rainfall for each annual agricultural cycle, which starts with the preparation of fields in September before the short rains and ends in August the following year.

It must be taken into account that the data has several limitations. The data for rice production does not represent total production, but the amount of rice transported from the district and sold through legal channels like licenced traders, cooperatives or government crop authorities. The rice data also includes rice originating from outside the flood plain area where, however, most of the rice is grown. Thus what peasant producers consume directly or sell for consumption within the district do not enter the statistics. As the share of the total rice harvest for local consumption may vary from year to year depending on the production of fish, for instance, one cannot infer from the figures of external rice sales the total amount harvested. The existence and varying use of parallel, non-official or non-legal, marketing channels further complicate both the estimation of total rice production over time and the relationship between flood profiles and rice harvests.

The data for cotton sales ought to more accurately represent total flood plain production. Cotton is only grown in the Rufiji river valley and inner delta areas, hence there is no problem of including production from outside the valley in the total figures for the district. Furthermore, cotton cannot be consumed and is little used for local production of clothing.

Due to the limitations of the data, the analysis must be tentative. It may have some value in checking whether it supports or calls into question some of the major hypotheses about the Rufiji valley agricultural system. The method used to check the relationship between the two series of variables is linear regression based on the least square method. Then the correlation coefficient is used to measure the degree of dependence between the relevant dependent and independ-

Table 4.6. *Rice and cotton sales in relation to prices, rainfall and floods*

Year	Rice Sales (tonnes)	Rice Price (per tonne)	Cotton Sales (tonnes)	Cotton Price (per tonne)	Rainfall mm at Utete Sept.–Aug	Floods Max height (feet and cumex)	Floods Durat. (months)	Time (months)
1920	410	-	59	10	-	-	-	-
1921	1,098	-	324	19	-	-	-	-
1922	636	-	371	16	-	-	-	-
1923	1,220	-	350	18	654.1	-	-	-
1924	316	15	506	19	799.7	-	-	-
1925	121	15	340	9	566.6	-	-	-
1926	-	19	438	8	819.8	-	2	April
1927	632	9	12	17	758.7	10.0	2 1/2	Jan.
1928	2,500	-	116	15	681.4	9.2	3 1/2	Feb.
1929	687	-	170	16	753.0	9.6	1	March
1930	317	-	140	6	989.0	13.0	4 1/4	Jan.
1931	3,000	-	48	8	864.7	8.9	2	April
1932	1,672	-	259	9	1,133.8	9.9	1 1/2	April
1933	2,888	5	443	10	783.8	9.3	3 1/4	Feb.
1934	3,235	5	304	8	1,082.4	9.0	2	April
1935	1,400	5	578	10	528.7	13.6	2	March
1936	809	5	1,167	12	982.6	13.7	4 1/2	Jan.
1937	1,899	5	2,135	9	881.3	12.8	3 1/2	Feb.
1938	1,704	5	578	8	986.5	9.5	2	April
1939	4,596	5	1,116	9	1,004.2	11.4	-	-
1940	4,000	5	1,972	10	840.4	13.1	5 1/4	Feb.
1941	3,500	7	650	9	971.0	11.7	-	-
1942	4,700	-	739	17	1,273.4	13.4	5 3/4	Jan.
1943	3,480	6	760	12	1,235.2	11.2	4	March
1944	3,321	-	950	-	950.5	13.7	3 1/4	March
1945	440	-	993	-	1,148.5	14.0	5 3/4	Jan.
1946	0,5	-	151	-	484.2	11.3	1 1/2	April
1947	3,293	-	602	-	1,192.2	13.3	9 1/4	Feb.
1948	325	-	119	-	952.0	10.1	4 3/4	Dec.
1949	37	-	298	-	657.5	6.2	-	-
1950	3,500	-	875	-	731.5	12.7	3 1/4	Feb.
1951	6,941	-	38	-	778.2	11.3	4 1/4	Jan.
1952	898	-	404	-	889.2	14.3	5 1/4	Jan.
1953	4,230	-	118	-	547.7	6.0	-	-
1954	6,000	-	270	-	667.2	10.1	1	Feb.
1955	9,600	-	245	-	1,197.0	12.8	2	March
1956	546	-	1,850	-	722.0	15.3	6 1/4	Feb.
1957	5,128	-	1,455	57	1,013.7	14.9	2 1/4	March
1958	1,223	-	1,263	57	847.0	17.8 (2,600)	5 1/4	Jan.
1959	2,350	-	548	-	664.5	20.0 (1,500)	4	Jan.
1960	3,170	15	3,917	58	824.0	17.6 (3,800)	3 1/2	Dec.

Year	Rice Sales (tonnes)	Price (per tonne)	Cotton Sales (tonnes)	Price (per tonne)	Rainfall mm at Utete Sept.–Aug	Floods Max height (feet and cumex)	Durat. (months)	Time (months)
1961	5,135	41	163	-	815.0	15.8 (1,500)	2 1/4	April
1961/62	200	-	5,981	-	1,213.0	23.0 (5,700)	6	Dec.
1962/63	-	-	5,255	-.	1,068.1	18.7 (5,200)	3 1/4	Feb.
1963/64	636	-	3,197	-	1,320.5	18.3 (4,600)	4 1/2	Jan.
1964/65	-	-	1,455	-	493.5	16.5 (2,700)	2	March
1965/66	2,845	-	1,688	-	729.0	15.3 (2,500)	1 3/4	April
1966/67	4,436	-	1,106	-	616.0	14.0 (2,100)	1 1/4	April
1967/68	3,301	-	2,522	-	990.0	19.0 (5,100)	8 3/4	Dec.
1968/69	290	-	407	-	915.5	21.8 (2,000)	1 1/4	April
1969/70	600	-	162	-	605.7	17.4 (3,000)	2 1/2	Feb.
1970/71	4,384	520	1,727	1,000	735.8	16.2 (2,200)	1 3/4	April
1971/72	3,818	520	518	1,100	817.7	23.3 (2,400)	3	March
1972/73	4,208	560	500	-	878.0	14.6 (2,700)	3	Feb.
1973/74	-	600	764	1,150	826.0	22.2 (7,800)	1 3/4	April
1974/75	58	650	3,450	1,500	988.0	15.4 (2,100)	2 3/4	March
1975/76	1,421	1,000	184	2,000	766.0	19.6 (2,200)	2 3/4	Feb.
1976/77	561	1,000	121	2,300	542.0	14.6 (1,800)	2 1/4	Feb.
1977/78	127	1,200	111	2,300	851.0	- (3,700)	-	-
1978/79	50	1,200	984	2,400	1,246.0	- (<11,000)	4	Feb.
1979/80	-	-	2,017		784.0			
1980/81	23	1,750	122		883.0			
1981/82	-	-	39		-			
1982/83	1	-	114		-			
1983/84	-	-	51		-			
1984/85	28	6,000	53		-			
1985/86			56					

Note: The notation of price per tonne is in East African Pounds (EAP) up to 1967, during which time 1 EAP exchanged for 1 UK pound. From 1967 onwards the price notation is in Tanzanian shillings (Tsh.). The Tsh. was slowly and gradually devalued up to the mid-1980s when a rapid and continuous devaluation took place. (See note on currency and exchange rates.)

Sources:

For *rice*: 1933–1939 Rufiji District Annual Report (DAR) 1939; 1976/77–1984/85 National Milling Corporation's Office (NMC) in Kibiti and the Coast Region (Dar es Salaam); otherwise Bantje, 1979

For *cotton*: Yoshida, 1974, p. 11, whose sources are: Information from the Statistics Division, Kilimo; Department of Agriculture, 1924; Annual Report of the Seed and Lint Marketing Board, 1967. 1933–39 Rufiji District Annual Report 1939; 1940–45 (except 1944) DAR 1943. Production data 1969/70 to 1985/86 Tanzania Cotton Authority ginnery at Kilimani, Rufiji District. The figures are converted from bales of pure cotton of 181 kg to seed cotton based on the assumption that 500 kg of seed cotton are required for one bale. (Information from the Kilimani ginnery manager.)

ent variables. To detect breaks or major shifts in the relationship between the variables one decade is dealt with at a time and the relevant regression coefficients are calculated.

Before presenting the results, further clarification of the relationship between floods and cotton and floods and rice is required. The crop data for the colonial period relate to the calendar year. The district annual reports providing data on rice and cotton production are usually dated early in January the year following the period investigated. After 1961 the reporting of crops harvested started to follow crop years, beginning on July 1st, and ending on June 30th the following year. As a rule rice is affected by the flood occurring during the second half of the crop year. Only in cases of late planting and harvesting varieties of rice with a growing time of 6 months will purchases in one crop year be affected by the flood of the preceding year. As many varieties of rice need less than six months to grow, harvests from late plantings may be recorded during the first half of the year, during the occurrence of the flood on which it is dependent. Cotton is, however, harvested in October or November, which means that cotton harvests in crop years starting on July 1st are dependent upon the flood occurring in the preceding crop year. As some uncertainty exists about the shift in reporting from the calendar year to the crop year, two sets of correlation coefficients are calculated for cotton during the decade 1957/58 to 1966/67.

The correlation coefficient (r_r) for rice sales and the duration of floods showed the following development: 1928–37 ($r_{r1}=-0.2$), 1938–47 ($r_{r2}=0.5$), 1948–57 ($r_{r3}=-0.8$), 1958–67 ($r_{r4}=-0.8$) and the crop years 1966/67 to 1976/77 ($r_{r5}=0.3$).

The two first decades investigated show no systematic correlation between duration of the flood and rice sales. The correlation coefficients of the subsequent two decades, r_{r3} and r_{r4} show, however, a strong negative correlation, indicating that floods of long duration have a negative impact on rice harvests. This finding supports one of the major hypotheses about the flood plain farming system, i.e. that

---

For *rainfall*: 1919/20 to 1971/72: Bantje, 1979, pp. 38–39; 1972/73 to 1980/81: Bantje and Niemeyer, 1984, p. 387

For *floods*: Telford, 1929, p. 17; Jack, 1957, pp. 9–10; Savile, 1945, pp. 69–72 and Bantje, 1979, pp. 29–31. These sources are related to gauge readings (in feet) on the flood plain itself. The discharge of water in terms of cubic meter per second (m^3/s or cumex) at Stiegler's Gorge is estimated on the basis of Figure 5.1 in Hafslund, 1980, p. 23

floods of long duration, normally floods with large volumes which come early, usually lead to the drowning of the young plants. This correlation, however, disappears completely in the next decade (1966/67 to 1976/77), when the coefficient is found to be 0.3, which suggests that the farming system practiced during the previous two decades may have been upset.

In the four decades between 1928 and 1967 the correlation coefficients for cotton sales and peak floods occurring during the same calendar year as the cotton harvest, range between 0.4 and 0.7, i.e. there is a positive correlation. The correlation coefficient for the decade 1958–67 when the cotton harvest and the flood occur during the same calendar year is 0.6. If the cotton harvest is related to the height of the flood of the previous crop year, the correlation coefficient is 0.4. This means that regardless of the change in reporting from calendar to crop years, the correlation between peak flood and cotton harvest holds. This finding supports another major hypothesis about the flood plain farming system, i.e. that the cotton crop is dependent upon the size of the area inundated during the flood. A drastic change in the value of the correlation coefficient for rice occurs again when investigating the decade of the crop years 1967/68–1976/77. The value is negative, -0.2. Cotton sales have lower correlation coefficients in relation to duration of floods, which indicates that for cotton cultivation the peak height of the flood is more important than its duration.

Several analyses of the flood plain farming system have indicated that labour constraints arise when rice has to be harvested at the same time as cotton is planted. Yoshida's analysis best documents these constraints (Yoshida, 1974). Early travellers noted that the people of Rufiji sold their rice unhusked as paddy (Loarer, 1848). This suggests that a labour constraint already existed in the agricultural system in the last century. The historical data on rice and cotton sales also suggests that there were labour constraints in the farming system. Of the 57 years (1920–85) for which rice and cotton sales are recorded, 28 years had a total sales volume for both crops combined of above 3,000 tonnes. Of these 28 years high sales of each of the crops, i.e. about 2,000 tonnes and above, were recorded only three times, in 1940, 1960 and 1967 (i.e. the rice harvest of the first half year and the cotton harvest of the second half, both dependent on the flood during the first half of the respective calender years). The complexity of the system is underlined by the finding that years of high crop sales are also years when famines are reported (cf. next section). This indicates the limited extent of famines, i.e. that flood have a different impact in different parts of the system. The West Valley zone is hardest hit both by excessive floods and droughts.

In his investigation of the nutritional status of people in the district, Bantje makes an interesting comment related to labour constraints:

> A further comment may be made here on a common feature of life in Rufiji which has mystified administrators since the beginning of the colonial days. Time and again it was observed that after a good rice harvest the peasants showed no interest in planting cotton, but instead concentrated on festivities and the consumption of their rice in an extravagant and wasteful way. In spite of all pressures it has rarely been possible to realise both a good rice crop and a good cotton crop in the same year. Our analysis contributes to the understanding of this phenomenon. Years with a good rice harvest are years with a long wet season, followed by the heavy labour of the harvest. After that people have lost so much weight and are so weakened that they need time to recuperate, and to do so they need to eat prodigious amounts. The reluctance to engage immediately in the planting of a new crop therefore results from the sound knowledge that a period of rest is very necessary to gain enough strength to be able to live through the next wet season.
>
> This observation again has wider implications. It may well be that the often observed failure of peasants to increase their productivity in response to exhortations of extension officers and politicians is not a result of laziness or other psychological attitudes, but simply of the fact that their minimal energy balance does not allow them to work harder without damage to their system in the long run. Experiments with food supplementation among labourers have shown that increased energy intake makes increased production possible (Bantje, 1980a, p. 22).

The most significant trend which appears in Table 4.6 is the decline in official sales of both rice and cotton from 1975 onwards, which cannot be explained by changes in physical factors like rainfall and floods. The drop is particularly dramatic for rice, but as rice is traded on parallel or illegal markets, the real reduction may not be as large as the officially marketed figures indicate. The reduction in cotton production cannot, however, be traced to increases in illegal marketing, as such channels do not exist. The reduction in cotton sales thus reflects real decreases in the volume of cotton harvested.

Cotton

Cotton growing in Rufiji District provided the reason for establishing three ginneries located in Logeloge (West Valley), Kilimani (Flood Plain North) and Msomeni (Inner Delta South). The ginneries were established mainly by Greek and Asian private capital. In 1943 all the ginneries were owned by the East African Cotton Company (DAR, 1943). The Logeloge and Msomeni ginneries were later bought by an Asian and were closed down in 1972. From then on ginning was carried out by the Kilimani ginnery, which was taken over by the Tanzania Cotton Authority (TCA) from Coast Industries in 1976. During part of the 1970s the TCA cultivated a farm of its own in Flood Plain North, which provided about 25 per cent of the cotton ginned in 1977/78. The TCA also distributes fertilisers and pesticides for which the cost is deducted when it buys cotton from the peasants. Peasants are reluctant to use such inputs, partly due to their high price and partly because natural fertiliser is provided by the flood water.

Cashew nuts

Cashews, a perennial crop from a tree, is well suited to the soil and the climatic conditions of the edges of the flood plain and the hill area. West of Kipu village, rainfall is too low to allow for the growing of cashew trees. After the villagisation drive in the Rufiji river valley in 1968/69, cashew nuts were identified as an important cash crop in the upland area, alongside sesame, millet and pineapple. Angwazi and Ndulu (1973), who investigated the effects of Operation Rufiji, claimed that upland cultivation in the upper and middle section on both sides of the river valley was not very successful. In the Ikwiriri area, for instance, they observed plots that were cleared for planting cashew nut trees, but trees were not planted. "This we believe is due to competition for labour between rice production in the plain and the cashew production on upland ground during the same period (rainy season) (Angwazi and Ndulu, 1973:7). They did, however, observe that richer farmers hired labourers to look after their cashew trees, with good results. Where cashew trees were planted as part of *ujamaa* agricultural activities, yields were low as peasants were more interested in tending to their own plots (Sandberg, 1974a:50 and Yoshida, 1972:14). Yoshida found that, "The extremely small labour inputs for harvesting operations for the ujamaa farms reflect the fact that the harvested amounts were almost nil this year". The data available for cashew nut production, provided by the Cashew Nut Authority of Tanzania (CATA), shows a dramatic and nearly continuous decline from 1973/74 to 1979/80. From 1979/80 to 1981/82 there is a weak, improving trend which is broken in 1982/83. There seems to be no marked correlation between price changes and changes in the levels of production.

The declining trend in cashew nut production is a national feature. In the crop year 1973/74 national collection was about 140,000 tonnes, but fell to around 40,000 in the year 1979/80. In the late 1960s Tanzania began to establish cashew nut processing plants. Earlier the whole cashew nut was exported to India where further manual pro-

Table 4.7. *Cashew nut collection and producer prices, Rufiji District*

Year	Cashew collection (tonnes)	Producer prices (Tsh./kg)
1973/74	6,500	0.95
1974/75	5,000	1.05
1975/76	5,500	1.05
1976/77	3,282	1.10
1977/78	1,276	1.15
1978/79	1,987	1.70
1979/80	1,252	1.80
1980/81	1,531	3.00
1981/82	1,863	5.00
1982/83	1,075	5.00
1983/84	2,169	7.00
1984/85	1,378	9.80

Note: Price is quoted for Cashew Nut Grade A.
Source: CATA Office, Kibiti, Rufiji District

cessing took place. The processing consists of separating the kernel from the shell. The liquid in the shell has industrial uses and thus an export value. A processing capacity of 103,000 tonnes of cashew nuts was established by 1980 at the cost of Tsh. 470 m., but by then the raw materials only sufficed for utilising about 40 per cent of that capacity (*Daily News*, May 19 1984). In the same period the world price of kernels fell relative to that for the whole cashew nut. Thus the economics of this build-up of processing capacity turned out to be very negative for the Tanzanian economy. The World Bank had supported the programme through providing loans, which had to be repaid regardless of the performance of the 11 processing plants, the majority of which never started production.

The World Bank blamed the Tanzanian government for having pursued an agricultural price policy which acted as a disincentive for the collection of cashew nuts. It is true that the producer price for cashew nuts fell drastically in real terms throughout the 1970s and more than for most other export crops.

It is unlikely that the cause of the fall in cashew production is linked to prices alone. Several hypotheses have been advanced to explain the decline in cashew nut production; let me mention some without analysing the causes in detail. The age of trees is one possible cause. Replanting has not taken place, and the yield of old trees is lower than for young ones. Poor husbandry is said to be another cause, for instance lack of weeding, hence the cashew nut weeding campaign implemented in February to June 1979. Another possible cause is the increased distance between new villages and the original cashew tree fields, due to villagisation. This argument is relevant to the hill areas of Rufiji District. In addition diseases have been mentioned as a cause for the decline in production. When interviewed in October 1979, the CATA officer in Kibiti said he expected a drop in production to 1,200 tonnes in 1979/80. Without disease, he would have expected a production increase to around 2,500 tonnes during that year.

Sisal

The first sisal estate established in Rufiji District was located at Kilimani (Flood Plain North). It went out of operation in 1952 at the time of the establishment of the Misimbo estate (North Hill, see Map 6). The initial investment was made by a Greek citizen, in 1962 the estate was taken over by Fidalhusein Company, and in 1976 by K.J. Motors of Dar es Salaam. The general decline of the sisal industry was also reflected in the development of the Misimbo estate. Hardly any new investments were made after its establishment, which explains the poor state of machinery and equipment in the late 1970s. Production figures for the period 1974–1979 are shown in Table 4.8.

The decline of the sisal industry was closely related to increased competition from substitute synthetic products based on oil. The rapidly increasing oil prices since the mid-1970s onwards have improved competitiveness for natural fibres like sisal. There are eight different categories of sisal qualities depending upon the colour and length of the fibres and a wastage of 27 per cent in converting raw sisal into fibres. In the late 1970s, the Tanzania Sisal Authority (TSA) was buying the total production of the country and most of it was exported to England, Japan and Mexico. Local processing of sisal fibres into twine and rope was limited.

In 1978 the Misimbo Sisal Estate employed an average of 60 cutters and 95 general and technical assistants, including one engineer in the factory unit (decortication) and six in management. In addition there were four other employees, a total of 165 employees. This number had been the same since 1975, a marked drop in the employment level since 1970 (240 employees).

Some of the wage labourers are hired permanently while others, between a quarter and a third of the cutters and the assisting staff, are called upon when needed by the estate. Part of the workers live in small estate owned quarters, others in Misimbo village on the outskirts of the

Table 4.8. *Production of sisal at Misimbo Estate, Rufiji District (in tonnes)*

Year	Production	Price per tonne (Tsh.)
1974	595	6,000
1975	496	4,000
1976	227	2,000
1977	570	2,000
1978	415	2,000
1979	700	n.a.

Note: The production of 700 tonnes in 1979 is a projection. Data for 1980 onwards is not available.
Source: Figures provided by the management of Misimbo Sisal Estate

estate. The average wage of the cutters was Tsh. 260 a month (February, 1979). Most of the cutters came originally from Kigoma Region and Burundi, areas which have provided most of the cutters for the Tanzanian sisal estates.

Copra

The cultivation of coconut trees, which forms the basis for *copra* production, is mainly confined to the coastal area (Rufiji delta). When the nut is ripe, it is divided and the meat is left to dry in the sun. Production and official purchases of copra improve in years of low rainfall due to better conditions for drying the nuts. A long term trend of declining yields is increasingly manifested due to the old age of the trees, insufficient replanting and recurrent diseases that affect the trees. The use of raw nuts for local production of edible oil, for both direct consumption and sale, will also affect the production of copra.

Maize

Maize has become a major preferred food in Tanzania at the expense of more drought resistent crops like millet and sorghum. It is the second most important food crop of the Rufiji flood plain, in terms of the acreage cultivated in 1978. Official marketing of maize has, however, been negligible and was nearly non-existant (one tonne only) in 1978/79. Rice and maize are the major crops for which there is a potential for unofficial or black marketeering.

Table 4.9.　*Categories of crops and acreage under cultivation in 1978, Rufiji District*

	Acres under cultivation 1978	
Export crops		
Cotton	5,930	
Cashew nuts	2,410	
Copra (dried coconuts)	1,305	9,645
Food crops		
Paddy	35,954	
Maize	7,035	
Sesame	3,106	46,095
Drought resistant crops etc.		
Cassava	26,093	
Cowpeas	3,155	
Pigeon peas	3,250	
Sorghum	2,829	
Millet	689	
Potatoes	4,060	
Sugar cane	510	
Bananas	1,508	
Fruits	1,395	
Grams	2,683	
Pumpkin	305	46,477
Total		102,217

Source:　Estimated by Agricultural District Office, Utete

Cassava

In terms of the acreage cultivated, cassava has become an important crop in Rufiji District. The amount marketed during the second half of the 1970s was negligible, which implies that cassava is important for local consumption.

Sesame

The harvest is supplied to the national oil mill industry (MOPROCO in the Morogoro Region) for further processing. The relatively large area cultivated in Rufiji District in 1978 was due to a government campaign to increase supplies to the oil mill industry, which was working at very low utilization of capacity. Relatively favourable producer prices made peasants, particularly in the western part of Rufiji, plant sesame on the elevated northern bank of the flood plain.

Other crops

Other crops cultivated are *potatoes, grams* (chick-peas) and *sorghum. Bananas* and *fruits* (mango, pawpaw, pineapple and orange) are cultivated mainly in the hill areas. They are increasingly being marketed in the various local markets, pineapples and oranges in the urban markets as well, mainly Dar es Salaam. Fruits could legally be marketed without going through the national crop authorities.

Total acreage cultivated in Rufiji District

Each year the district agricultural officers attempt to estimate the acreage of various crops planted. For 1978 the estimate is shown in Table 4.9.

Famines and Famine Relief

Due to the fragile ecological environment, production in the Rufiji valley is sensitive but also quite responsive to rapid changes in physical conditions. In a sense, the history of Rufiji District is one of adaptation to change by attempts to establish a buffer between the harsh natural environment and production. Such a buffer may contain various elements: perhaps related to the crops themselves, for instance selecting a specific variety of rice, and planting in different locations to reduce risks. Sandberg (1974a:20–21) shows that the peasants of Rufiji have developed a whole range of local varieties of rice with different growing times, and differences in terms of their resistance to floods, droughts and salinity. The buffer may consist of choosing a particular location for the houses in relation to the fields to minimise intrusion by vermin and game into the fields. Destruction by vermin is a serious problem in the district, particularly in those parts close to the Selous Game reserve, which seems to have been grossly underestimated by officials. The change in settlement patterns through villagisation in both 1969 and 1973 had the effect of laying fields open to vermin, particularly in the western valley. Another way of guarding against excessive flooding would be to plant on both the flood plain and the flood plain banks.

There is, however, one basic condition related to the agricultural systems in the Rufiji river valley and delta: they are dependent upon the natural flooding of the river in order to regenerate their fertility. Hence floods, even though excessive and damaging at times, play an important role in the long-term reproduction of this system. Yet, both the valley and the hill cultivation systems are vulnerable to drought, which has negative implications for all seasons. Hence both excessive floods and droughts play a role in the causes of famine in Rufiji District.

In a sense, if droughts are excluded, the volatile and unstable conditions created by the floods are part and parcel of the agricultural system. The instantaneous and damaging effects can be compensated by medium- and long-term beneficial impacts. The population of the Rufiji valley and delta know this better than anybody else. Maybe that helps to explain why they have been so stubborn about not moving out of the river valley and delta during the villagisation campaigns in 1968/69 and 1973, as will be illustrated in Chapter 6.

In the Rufiji valley a natural disaster, like an excessive flood, does not represent a breakdown of the ecological system, but is rather the cost of regeneration of the system in the long run. When large floods occur consecutively, it must be discussed whether the costs of continuing such a system are too high. One way of identifying the costs, and maybe their most dramatic manifestation, is to investigate the occurrence of famine, the topic to which I will now turn.

The agricultural cycle, without excessive natural distortions, has two periods where food shortages do occur. The first is in November to January, before the short rain crops have produced any yields, and the second period occurs around May, just before the harvesting of the flood season crops. This is why the short rains are so critical for the food balance. During the flood season there is the possibility, if the flood has been beneficial, to compensate for food shortages by increasing fishing efforts.

Han Bantje (1980b) has made the most systematic investigation of the occurrence of famine in Rufiji District during the century of 1880 to 1980. He recorded 20 famines. In eight cases the famines developed rapidly and in the remaining they built up slowly because of unfavourable climatic conditions during successive seasons. He identifies droughts and floods as the single cause of eight famines each. Droughts seem to come in cycles. Between 1880 and 1900 there were four serious droughts and between 1940 and 1960 eight. We have earlier in this Chapter discussed the tendency for floods to have become more serious, particularly in the 1960s and 1970s.

Due to villagisation in 1968 the acute flood hazard has been removed in the West Valley, but the price to pay is a great increase in the

drought hazard. In Table 4.10 the picture of famines in and food relief to Rufiji District will be presented. The causes of the famines are
identified and as well the modes of food relief or other initiatives taken
by the colonial- and post-colonial governments. A total of 29 incidents
are included.

Some interesting features emerge from Table 4.10's data on
famines, their causes and the famine relief supplied. It appears that
the first famine requiring large scale famine relief was in 1936. After
that major relief operations occurred quite frequently, in 1940, 1943/
44, 1946, 1949, 1953, 1956 and in the post independence period in
1962, 1967, 1968, 1971/72, 1973/74, 1974, 1976–78 and 1978/79. It
seems that there are two types of famines requiring different responses. The food shortages generally develop into famines in the
western valley due to adverse floods or drought. These localised minor
famines could be handled by the colonial government by restricting
food exports from the district and by enforcing the cultivation of
famine crops, such as cassava and bananas.

From around 1940 onwards a new pattern emerges, as, for various
reasons, increasingly famines cannot be checked. Some of the reasons
may be ascribed to the change in flood regime observed by Savile
(1945). He explained that more frequent and heavy floods occured
not because of a change in rainfall in the drainage basin of the Rufiji
river, but was most likely due to increased surface run-off, caused by
adverse agricultural practices, land degradation and soil erosion. During the 1950s, however, the flood regime appears to be more gentle,
despite Savile's prediction. This may have been the result of the colonial government's efforts to halt land degradation through conservation
programmes backed by bye-laws (cf. Chapter 6).

The first decade of the post-independence period experienced
some heavy and damaging floods, particularly in 1962 and 1968. Massive famine relief support was required. The last flood spurred the
Tanzanian government to initiate its ujamaa policy in Rufiji District.
The peasant population was moved out of the Rufiji flood plain on to
the elevated escarpments. The objectives of the government were not
only to organise a successful example of *ujamaa* living and cultivation,
but also to avert the loss of lives and reduce the heavy costs incurred by
the frequent supply of famine relief to the area.

The data indicates that the post-colonial government's intervention
has been unsuccessful in doing away with famine relief operations. On
the contrary, during the 1970s the government had to provide food
relief and other support on five occasions, at times for longer periods.
It seems that this intensification in famine relief operations cannot be
explained by climatic factors, such as dramatic droughts and floods,

Kjell J. Havnevik

Table 4.10: *Famine and food relief in Rufiji District, 1880–1980*

Year of famine	Cause	Food relief etc.
1880-81	Prolonged *drought*.	
1884	*Drought*, famine affecting the whole of Eastern Tanganyika.	
1893-95	*Drought*, locust invasion and Ngoni raids (general famine).	
1898-1900	Three successive rainy seasons failed (general famine). *Drought*.	Food distributed. First attempt at famine relief.
1905/07	Large *flood* in 1905 (faya). The *Maji Maji* war 1905-07 caused disruptions.	
1917	Extremely high *flood*.	Seeds distributed
1924-25	Flood failed in two consecutive years. *Drought*. Low rainfall (566.6 mm).	To improve local food supply, export of foodstuffs prohibited.
1929-30	*Drought* in April/May 1929 and locust damage. In 1930 high *flood* (13.0 ft/Jan/4 months). Crop failure.	Seeds distributed.
1936	Very large *flood* (13.7 ft/Jan./4 1/2 m). People bought and borrowed food from relatives in hills.	Famine relief in cash, £ 1.224 and loans £ 800 to farmers affected. Seeds distributed.
1940	Extremely high and early *flood* (13.1 ft/Jan/5m). Situation aggravated by drought. 12,000 people, mainly in West Valley affected. Even 20% of crops lost in inner delta.	Relief food distributed. Traders' prices regulated. Food exports banned.
1941	No flood recorded (11.7 ft). Long rains failed, no *mlau* cultivation. Rainfall 971 mm. *Drought*.	Exports prohibited, food shortage avoided.
1943/44	Failure of short rains. Heavy *flood* (37.7 ft/March/3 m).	70 tonnes of food distributed and partly sold. People move to Liwale in search of food.
1945	Extremely heavy *flood*. (14 ft/Jan/6 m) 75% of rice damaged, and little planting due to early *flood*. Delayed *mlau*. Serious damage in all areas.	
1946	Short rains failed and poor long rains (484.2 mm). Inadequate flood (11.3 ft/March/ 1 1/2 m). All crops very poor. Large scale smuggling of rice and cassava planting had been discontinued.	200 tonnes per month throughout the year, later free issues. Total cost estimated to £ 7,000. From September an additional 200 tonnes needed.
1949	No flood. (6.2 ft). Rains failed. (657.5 mm). *Drought* in the West Valley. No *mlau* crop. Famine towards end of year.	Food imported and distributed to 1,500 people. Another 1,500 did relief work.
1952	Heavy *flood* (14.3 ft/Jan./5 m). Crops destroyed by *flood* and *drought* (rainfall 889.2 mm). Short rains delay.	Food shortage avoided by relying on cassava and bananas.

Year of famine	Cause	Food relief etc.
1953	*Drought* continued (rainfall only 547.7 mm). No flood (6 ft). Poor crops throughout, except in the delta.	Food imported to the west valley area, but also some to Mohoro (inner delta).
1956	Heavy *flood* (15.3 ft/Feb./6 m). Both rains failed (722.0 mm). Serious famine.	Food imported to the West Valley. Government had to distribute because traders had left the area.
1958	Heavy *flood* (17.8 ft/Jan/5 m) and *drought* (847 mm rainfall). Poor crops.	Famine avoided because of cassava and bananas.
1962	Heavy rains (1,213 mm) interfered with field preparation. Extremely heavy and early *flood* (23ft/Dec. /6 m). Whole valley submerged in water. *Mlau* crops also caused some relief.	6,500 tonnes of food issued against relief labour from January onwards. Famine widespread, including valley and hills. But also on national level. Food imports from the US, of this 400 tonnes to Rufiji. Distributed by planes and dhows.
1963-64	Early and heavy rains (1,068.1 and 1,320.5 mm). Early *floods* causing crop damage (18.7 ft/ Feb./3 m and 18.3 ft/ Jan./ 4 1/2 m).	Seasonal food shortages.
1965-66	*Drought* years (493.7 and 729 mm) and small floods.	Seasonal food shortages.
1967	Late flood causing food shortages (14 ft/April/1 m).	140 tonnes of food relief distributed in West Valley.
1968	One of the heaviest *floods* ever (19 ft/ 5000m³/s (cumex)/Dec./8 m). All crops lost. Led to Operation Rufiji (villagisation).	4,000 tonnes of food distributed, included the food distributed during resettlement. Cost of food and transport Tsh. 3,798,940,-.
1971-72	*Resettlement* and *drought*.	In December food shortage in West Valley. In February 10,000 people affected. 280 tonnes of food brought to the area in early 1972. Cassava seedlings distributed at a cost of Tsh. 54,850,- (1971) and Tsh. 26,400 (1972).
1973-74	*Resettlement* and *drought*.	Food shortage developed in December 1973 in West Valley. 375 tonnes of food imported during the first months of 1974. Cassava seedlings at cost of Tsh. 30,000,-.
1974	Extreme peak *flood* hit unexpectedly (22.2 ft/7800 cumex/ April/2 m). Loss of 25 lives, crops and houses.	50,000 people were affected, in particular in Ikwiriri and Mkongo divisions. Resettlement immediately afterwards (Operation Pwani). 5,500 tonnes of food distributed every month during the campaign.

Year of famine	Cause	Food relief etc.
1976-78	*Resettlement.*	Food shortages in West Valley villages from September 1976 to June 1978. Due to reluctance of district administration to supply relief food continuously developed into famine at times. In February 1977 people too weak to work properly, in March they live on bush fruits. Outmigration to look for food and jobs. March 1978 450 kgs of food stolen from depot in Nyaminywili village. Over the whole period 1,100 tonnes of food was brought into the area. Government increasingly emphasised or demanded labour for public and communal work, including road construction, class room buildings and clearing of communal fields as a counter for provision of food. In 1977 cassava seedlings for Tsh 30,000 provided.
1978-79	Probably heaviest *flood* ever (more than 11000 m³/s/Feb./4m). The whole valley submerged in water. All crops destroyed. Due to sufficient early rains (total 1,246 mm) early crops were harvested before the onset of the flood.	388 tonnes of food imported into Utete and Mohoro between February and June.

Sources: Bantje 1980a:3–10 and 26–30, Sandberg 1974a, Hafslund 1980, Jack 1957, Telford 1929, various Rufiji District Annual Reports (DAR) and Savile 1945

except in 1974 and 1979. The decline in agricultural capacity since villagisation, Operation Rufiji in 1968 and Operation Pwani in 1973, must in some way be related to the effects of these operations and to changes in the state–peasant relations.

Agricultural techniques

Hoe cultivation

In Rufiji District, the most intensive use of hoes takes place in the flood plain. Here most of the fields have been intensively tilled for decades with double cropping annually, requiring a high and physically demanding labour input per acre. To get a better idea of the household's inventory of tools for cultivation, let me present that of an old, average household, cultivating 2 acres of cassava, pigeon-peas and cashew nuts (excluded from the acreage) on the upland terraces and rice, maize and cow peas and bananas in the flood plain. The household is located in Ikwiriri village and the husband, about 60 years old, has one wife and their children are married. One son lives nearby and helps out at times with food and labour. The inventory of tools (of 1983) includes the following: Three large tanged hoes, of which two are 6–7 years old and British made. The tang broke off on both of these, but they were repaired by local blacksmiths. The third large hoe is 15 years old. All three hoes were quite worn, a third to half the blade was worn off due to usage. The fourth hoe of the household, a tanged weeding hoe, was 20 years old and was used by the wife to weed rice in muddy clay. In addition the household had two matchets and one tanged axe. The axe was made by a local blacksmith and was two years old. By way of comparison Yoshida (1974) found that the average number of implements per household was 4.28 hoes, 1.68 matchets and 0.15 axes.

In addition to large hoes, small weeding hoes are commonly used in Rufiji District and in most other areas of Tanzania where rice is grown. In cases of slash and burn cultivation, little primary tillage nor much weeding are required, in order not to disturb the balance of nutrients in the soil. This is particularly important in areas where soils are infertile, as in large parts of the coastal areas. Because of this, a small hoe is both agronomically and technically the most appropriate implement for making small seed beds for individual plants. In areas of minimum tillage coupled with the burning of grass, fairly high average returns to labour have been obtained in comparison to systems with one annual cropping, which have become most widespread in Tanzania, after villagisation.

The above may provide some explanation for the relatively low demand for hoes in the coastal regions. The standard explanation often heard by bureaucrats, manufacturers and distributors is that the coastal people are lazy and do not want to work hard.

However, the primary tillage in the flood plain system, the *mvuli*, does require a heavy input of labour. It is unlikely that a strong adult can manage to clear more than one acre of land in these hard clay soils. Dry season cultivation does not require much labour input, as the crops are planted directly on the wet ground after recession of the flood waters. If these areas are cleared of grass before the onset of the flood, planting is particularly easy and requires little labour. This is why the labour return on cotton cultivation in the flood plain during dry season is higher than for rice in the wet season. Given that the major mode of cultivation is by manual labour using the hoe, this technique poses a severe limitation on the capacity to expand the acreage of the present farming system. This limiting factor has been observed by many. For instance in his agro-economic survey of 80 Rufiji households Yoshida (1974) found that the hoe was used in all farming operations. Draught animals did not exist and ploughing was limited to the provision of ploughing services by a few private tractor owners.

At the end of the 1970s a village survey indicated that a severe tool shortage was about to develop. Nearly all the villages which were interviewed about problems of cultivation, mentioned lack of agricultural implements. At the end of 1983 farm implements were still in short supply, even on a national level (Mothander et al., 1989). Investigations in Rufiji District showed that at the same time as peasants in the flood plain zones complained about the lack of large tilling hoes, hundreds were in store in the Regional Trading Company's (RTC) godown in Kibiti village. Yet the manager claimed that Rufiji peasants were only interested in using the small weeding hoes (Ibid.).

Mechanisation

According to Yoshida, the great depression had discouraged the British colonial government from implementing its plan for increased cultivation in Rufiji District (Yoshida, 1974:8). A new upsurge of government interest, in particular in mechanisation, came after the Second World War. Tractor ploughing was initiated to increase rice cultivation and the motives were:

– no heavy bush clearing, no need for irrigation, the existence of silt as fertiliser, and ploughing would be possible throughout the dry season;
– a desire to increase rice production and enable the peasants to increase their hoe-prepared acreages for other food crops and cotton.

In 1948 an experiment in the use of tractors with a harrow plough to prepare land for paddy fields was carried out in the dry season near Ndundu in the Flood Plain North area. The intention was to embark on large scale mechanised ploughing if the pilot scheme worked well. Initial difficulties were experienced because of the toughness of the stems of burnt grass and the hardness of the pan clays. A plot of 537 acres was ploughed. This successful demonstration led Ndundu peasants to ask for another 300 acres to be ploughed. Actually only 133 acres were ploughed and the peasants arranged to pay for this and for the allocation of land amongst themselves. The cost was calculated to be Shs. 13.50 per acre plus Shs. 1.50 in supervision charges. The Agricultural Department suggested that the price for future ploughing should be Shs. 18 per acre. The peasants had estimated that the cost of hand hoeing one acre amounted to Shs. 22 in addition to food for two men for a month. The plan for 1949 was that twenty units of 375 acres each should be ploughed for cash payment. But by the end of the year only 250 people had registered for the scheme.

The scheme was supported by £ 18,835 from the Development Loans Fund and during the period 1948–1951 a total of 10,699 acres were ploughed. To save the scheme from financial loss, ploughing charges were raised, to Shs. 23 in 1950, Shs. 40 in 1952 and to Shs. 60 in 1956. At the peak of the scheme, in 1955, a total of 7,720 acres were ploughed, but when the charges were raised to Shs. 60 an acre in 1956, only 700 acres were booked for ploughing. That year the scheme came to an end. Instead the government turned to assisting in the formation of groups of indigenous Africans to provide ploughing assistance (Yoshida, 1974; Jack, 1957:56–58; Department of Agriculture, 1956: Part I:28 and Sandberg, 1974a:13).

It seems evident that some people were able to get hold of tractors privately and to supply ploughing services in the flood plain areas. Sandberg (1974a:36) mentions that tractor services to the Msomeni area, in the Inner Delta, stopped after people there were called to move to Chumbi. At that time it was possible to get a private tractor from Mbwera (Delta North) for the cost of Tsh. 65 per acre. But it appeared that, at that price, it was more attractive to hire labour at a cost of Tsh. 40 for hoeing one acre (20–25 days work) and an additional four debes of rice for food (a debe equals one gallon) (Ibid.). KILIMO had also tried to plough with oxen, but the oxen could not move the plough because the soil was too hard (Sandberg, 1974a:25).

The next major attempt to introduce tractor ploughing was in 1969 at the time of the implementation of Operation Rufiji. A centre for hire service of tractors was based in Kibiti. In 1972 it ran into problems. In an attempt to solve them, the concept of agro-mechanisation was developed, which included functions like the spread of technical know-how and the running of demonstration farms in addition to providing ploughing services. Based on this concept a new Agro-Mechanisation Centre was established in Mkongo in 1974–75. In addition to the procurement of new machinery and equipment, 15 tractors were bought and 20 were transferred to the Centre from the ill-advised Kibiti project, many of which were in a very bad condition. At the same time the project was transferred from ministerial to regional authorities. Within three years no tractor was running. Organisation and funding were once more renegotiated. The result was a transfer back to the Ministry of Agriculture, Crop Development Division, and a decision to solicit foreign assistance to organise tractor services and run the demonstration farms. The Italian government provided 2 tractors (Fiats), a workshop and ploughing equipment, and personnel assistance, one technician and one agronomist. Excluding personnel, total assistance from the Italian government is estimated to have reached Tsh. 3 million for the period 1978–80. The Tanzanian government provided funds for another 10 Fiat tractors. In addition the Food and Agricultural Organisation (FAO) of the United Nations agreed to assist in the repair of run down tractors. Under this tractor rehabilitation programme, spares and a mechanic were provided with the expectation that at least 10 of the tractors bought in 1974–75 would be reconditioned. FAO inputs for 1978–80 is estimated to Tsh. 390,000 corresponding to a repair cost of Tsh. 35,000–40,000 per tractor. At that time this was about a third of the price of a similar new tractor (Ford) and about half of that of a new Fiat tractor. At the end of 1978 there were 35 tractors (Ford, Massey Ferguson and Same) out of order and 12 new tractors (Fiat) running.

The tractor hire services of the Centre were in great demand among peasants in the 1978–79 season. Management estimated the total demand at 14,000 acres to be ploughed at a cost of Tsh. 60 per acre. The Centre planned to plough 7,000 acres, but by February 1979 when the large flood began, only 2,000 acres had been ploughed. During the 1979/80 season the rate for ploughing one acre was raised to Tsh. 90.

Major problems faced by the Centre were lack of skilled personnel, lack of spare parts, transport during rainy season, and poor integration with the local community.

The Agro-Mechanisation Centre in Mkongo is a unique example in Rufiji District of the abundance of highly technologically advanced equipment coupled with extravagant funding. The poor results are all the more deplorable. Even though this may partly be attributed to current operations and lack of qualified personnel, the most serious cause is of a structural character; that of heavy investment in tractorisation and demonstration farming in an area prone to annual, irregular flooding. The highly unstable conditions entail risks at such high levels that investments are bound to be economically unviable when direct and indirect effects are taken into account. There is a serious need for reassessment of at least some of the major activities of the Centre, notably tractor hire services and demonstration farming. Continuation at the present scale, or more so, at the envisaged future scale of a fleet of 50 tractors, should only be allowed if conditions for production can be reasonably stabilised.

During interviews in 1979 a few villages, Kiechuru and Mbwera and Chumbi A, said that lack of access to tractor ploughing services was a major problem. The Chumbi B village had hired three tractors from the Agro-Mechanisation Centre in both 1978 and 1979. In the Ikwiriri area (Flood Plain North) five private tractor owners were charging

Tsh. 110 per acre during the 1978/79 season, almost double that of the Centre (Tsh. 60). The demand for ploughing services seemed to be correlated with the increasing shortage of implements available in the district.

Land tenure and social relations of production in agriculture

Individual households farming in the flood plain have the right to use the land they cultivate, though Yoshida, 1974), points out that the land is neither registered nor surveyed. Land use is recognised by the people in a local community and often it has fixed boundaries. Usually the land of a household is divided into the farmer's plot, the first wife's plot, the second wife's plot and so on. In Yoshida's survey of the middle and the upper flood plain harvests from the farmer's plot belonged exclusively to him, while harvests from the plot(s) of the wife(ves) were divided between the husband and wife.

In the inner delta area Sandberg (1974a) found that a new wife was given a plot of her own for food production, and in addition had to work with other wives (wife) on the husband's plot. When the crops were harvested, they normally belonged to the husband. He marketed them and spent the cash on basic commodities like paraffin, sugar, tea, salt and tinned milk. He had to buy clothes for his wife and children (at Id-El-Fitr). The head of a household also had to spend his cash income on a series of religious and social fees. This amounted to a considerable sum and placed a heavy burden on him. Sandberg found, however, that most women kept some of the harvested rice for food. Normally they hid it from their husbands and sold small quantities from time to time to buy medicine and clothes, etc. (Sandberg, 1974a:37).

In the *kidugu* land system described above, which is peculiar to the inner delta area, land has been cultivated continuously for decades without loss of fertility. From 20 to 40 people may participate in a *kidugu*, and the land of each household lies close together. Between the *kidugus* there is fallow land or river grass (Sandberg, 1974a:32). Closer to the ocean, in the delta area people live in villages which they have to leave to cultivate on scattered fields in different environments. In such settings people are extremely reluctant to engage in collective cultivation practices.

Division of labour

In the inner delta area Sandberg observed the following daily work routine which sheds some light on the division of labour between men and women:

Both husband and wife (and labourer) go out early in the morning and dig, weed, sow or harvest until the sun starts burning. Then they go to take their morning meal. After this during the hottest part of the day, as much work as possible takes place in the shade. Women pound rice and maize, or make mats. Men are engaged in the house repairs, bedrope-making, graveyard building, or small trading activities in preparation for the weekly trip to the market in Mohoro and Mbwera. When the afternoon breeze comes, they both go to the shamba to continue the work from the morning. The work goes on until dark, when the women start to prepare the evening meal while men gather to talk or play *mbao*, a popular game played with small stones. After the evening meal they go to visit neighbours or the men go fishing in the nearby rivers and lakes. For the men and older boys the night might be spent in a small hut, erected in the fields, in order to scare away pigs, hippos and birds (Sandberg, 1974a:35).

The above is the daily routine of work for a couple who live on the fields during the agricultural season. Closeness to the fields makes a rational organisation of labour possible throughout the day. Of great interest is Sandberg's observation that with increasing distances between dwelling and the fields, the "burden of work is no longer equally distributed between the sexes, but is thrown upon the women" (Ibid.). The women have to go on foot to the fields, work during the warmest part of the day and return on time to prepare the evening meal for their husbands who have remained in the village engaging in petty trading and participating in village meetings. When the distance to the fields exceeds eight km, both the husband and the wife move to the flood plain where they stay in a house, *dungu*, for the farming season. As noted by Sandberg such farming practices have disruptive impacts on the family as well as on possible ujamaa activities. For the poorer farmer the adaptation outlined is the only way to find a compromise between the call to move to ujamaa villages and the need to secure an adequate food supply and a cash income. In a survey of labour input into cultivation during 1970/71, Yoshida found that about 20 per cent of the labour time was expended on walking to and from fields (Yoshida, 1972).

In the northern flood plain area in the village of Mkongo, a male member of a cooperative gave us this picture of the gender division of labour in that part of the flood plain. In the cultivation of rice and maize he identified six processes of work: hoeing, sowing, weeding, harvesting, cutting stalks and pounding. Men and women jointly carry out two of these, hoeing and weeding. The women do three tasks on their own, sowing, harvesting and pounding, while men work alone when cutting stalks. Two of my colleagues who spent eight days in August 1979 in the northern area of the flood plain, reported that men did not work in the fields that season, but were fully occupied by trading, fishing and crafts. Only women worked in the fields. As the

1979 season was atypical because of the extremely heavy flood which created very good conditions for fishing, this observation may not contradict the above informant's perception of the normal gender division of labour in the farming season.

Children are a valuable resource on the farm, particularly before the introduction of the Universal Primary Education (UPE). Young boys take an active part in watching the fields and scaring away birds and vermin. The girls assist their mothers in the house, but go into seclusion at puberty, at least in the delta area where more people are devout muslims. Entering into seclusion does create a conflict since the introduction of UPE. When boys grow older they may begin trading activities and fishing. In 1974. when Sandberg studied the inner delta area, he reported that the school system was still controlled by the inhabitants of the delta and was adapted to the agricultural calendar. The absentee rate was low and Sandberg observed that the drift of young boys to Dar es Salaam seemed to be a lesser problem in the delta area than in the rest of the district (Sandberg, 1974a:37). During the 1980s a drastic decline in attendance rates was reported in public primary schools throughout the rural areas of Tanzania. In some areas the attendance rate was as low as 50 per cent of the pupils registered (information obtained during visits to Coast and Kigoma Regions in 1987, see also World Bank, 1991b:139). The reasons for this development are manifold. The quality of education services has deteriorated dramatically, and rural schools face severe shortages of desks, books, chalk and classrooms. Teachers lack houses and means of education, and at times payment of their salaries is long delayed. Farming households may increasingly withhold children from going to school for two other reasons. Firstly, to survive the intensified crisis of the 1980s households needed to enlarge their labour pool by employing children for various tasks. Secondly, increased expenses were related to primary schooling because of the cost of school uniforms and the introduction of school fees in the mid-1980s (see also Chapter 9).

Hired labour and job differentiation

Several observers have reported incidences of labour being hired. Angwazi and Ndulu reported that rich farmers hired people to look after their cashew trees (1973). Sandberg said that many young men in the villages of Mohoro and Chumbi could not find good land around their villages and were eager to work for others in the delta (Sandberg, 1974a:36). The only systematic study of different types of labour input in cultivation was carried out by Yoshida, who found that the input of hired labour was marginal in the 1970–71 season.

In the western valley or upstream part of the flood plain one per cent of the total labour input into cultivation was provided by hired labour, in the north and south of the centre of the flood plain it was two per cent. Most labour was hired during the months of May, June and July, primarily in the two latter months (Yoshida, 1972: Table 8). This category of labour amounts to an input of one week during June and July in the centre of the flood plain and half a week in the upper part. Yoshida's survey does not cover the delta area where the hiring of labour seems to be more common, due to a larger differentiation of incomes between households in this area. Hence the above figures underestimate to some extent the total amount of labour hired in the district as a whole, even for the early 1970s.

Villagisation also entailed prospects for increased differentiation. Those who had acquired assets, like tractors, lorries, buses etc., by the onset of villagisation moved to the newly created ujamaa villages and offered their services there. Some became politically influential and could use some of the assets of the ujamaa society for their own benefit. As crop purchasing services were officially closed to those peasants who refused to move, crop haulage for these peasants became a profitable business for the well-to-do. Sandberg mentions a lorry owner from Mkongo village (Flood Plain North) who made a profit of 3,000 bags of rice in only one harvesting season, and a tractor owner in Ikwiriri who was able to pay for his tractor in only one ploughing season (Sandberg, 1974a:49).

In the course of time, accumulation in the form of purchasing buildings in the larger villages such as Ikwiriri and Mohoro in Rufiji District and in Dar es Salaam or investing in lorries and buses may have become even more profitable than tractors. In February 1979 I was given the following picture by a lower level government employee, who travelled all around the district and was in a position to identify the number and owners of lorries and buses.

In Kibiti village two people owned three lorries between them, in Mkongo village three people had a total of four lorries, in Kilimani village one person owned five lorries and the Ginnery had two lorries. In Kikale village one person owned two buses and four lorries, which he kept in Dar es Salaam for up-country transport. In Dar es Salaam at least one Rufiji based person owned five lorries. Some of them he sent to Rufiji to collect logs for Dar es Salaam.

An interview with a lorry owner/charcoal trader from Dar es Salaam in February 1979 may indicate the prospects of profit for this category of people. The man took his lorry as far as Mkupuka (Flood Plain North) to buy charcoal. At that time prices there were Tsh. 10 per bag. Tsh. 2 were added in forest royalties when passing Kibiti. Along the road to Dar es Salaam the price per bag was Tsh. 14 hence it would have been advantageous to buy along the road because that meant less road transport and the avoidance of the poor roads of Rufiji District beyond Kibiti. The supply along the road was, however, far below the demand. In Dar es Salaam supply was also well below demand, so prices rose rapidly. The retailer paid Tsh. 27 per bag and he could sell the whole bag for Tsh. 35 or, in small quantities was able to get Tsh. 40 per bag. The transporter's cost per bag delivered in Dar es Salaam was Tsh. 17. At the gate at the entrance to Dar es Salaam there were already wholesalers and retailers bidding for the charcoal. A 7 tonne lorry can carry about 90 bags of charcoal, which means that a profit of Tsh. 900 could be made per charcoal collection trip.

The problems of keeping lorries running increased dramatically during the early 1980s as both the production of tyres and the availability of foreign exchange for spares and petrol declined seriously. Transport thus represented a serious bottleneck in the charcoal trade in the 1980s (see Chapter 5). With liberalisation and the launching of the Economic Recovery Programme (ERP) in 1986, the supply of tyres, spare parts and petrol improved. Observations in Rufiji District in August 1987 indicated that the charcoal trade had picked up again after a decline starting in 1982.

5. Non-Agricultural Production

Until the end of the 1980s the role of non-agricultural production in the rural areas had been neglected in most rural analyses. Their focus mainly on agricultural cultivation and related aspects led to a lack of understanding of important changes taking place in rural areas in terms of peasant diversification of labour away from agriculture to activities like forestry, fishing and crafts as well as trading. This limited insight into the total range of peasant labour allocation also represented an obstacle for the undertaking of fruitful analyses of the state-peasant relationship. The dominant analyses of the early 1980s rather emphasised peasant uncapturedness as a social class, its internal affective ties and its withdrawal into subsistence as a survival strategy. The narrow and at times erroneous empirical foundation of these analyses (cf. Chapter 7) barred them from detecting broader processes of change underway in the rural areas since the mid-1970s. The pattern of diversification of peasant labour of course differed between localities due to factors like unequal natural resource profiles, proximity and access to external markets and the level of local demand.

The objective of this chapter is to present the content and characteristic features of non-agricultural production in Rufiji District, Coast Region (trading activities are taken up in Chapter 7). The presentation is based on a major survey and analysis undertaken in the late 1970s/ early 1980 which clearly demonstrate the importance of non-agricultural production even at that early stage of the Tanzanian crises (Havnevik, 1980).

The first section, focusing on forestry activities, includes charcoal production, one of the major and at that time fastest growing alternative cash income source of peasants, and mangrove exploitation which is specific for the Rufiji delta area and logging. The presentation of fishing contains both the important Rufiji flood plain fisheries and the salt water fisheries immediately off the Rufiji delta which is dominated by the catching of prawns by traditional methods. As to craft production eight of the major lines undertaken in the district are investigated including blacksmithery, carpentry, saw mills, boat building, mat-making, pottery production, coconut oil production and jaggery production. (For a detailed analysis of 27 crafts identified in Rufiji District, see Havnevik, 1980.)

Table 5.1. *Charcoal production for external markets in Rufiji District*

Year	Number of bags	Producer price per bag (Tsh.)
1975	n.a	
1976	1,260	8,-
1977	8,840	10,-
1978	92,054	11,-
1979	283,602	15,-
1980	318,851	20,-
1981	349,078	30,-
1982	493,244	30,-
1983	368,377	30,-
1984	269,632	35-40,-
1985	150,937	50,-

Source: Producer prices from author's surveys

The role, conditions and integration of non-agricultural production in the district economy may be better understood through this survey and analyses of spread, production techniques, organisation of production including gender issues, training, raw material sourcing and use, product quality, return on labour and marketing and transport issues. (Methodology and definitions employed in the survey are put forward in Appendix 2.)

FORESTRY PRODUCTION

Charcoal production

The growth of charcoal production

Charcoal production for external markets, mainly that of Dar es Salaam, started in Bungu village around 1970. This followed the completion of the tarmac road from Kibiti to Dar es Salaam in 1968. Later, production spread to other villages on this major road, Uponda (1972) and Jaribu Mpakani (1973). It then expanded to Tomoni (1974), Mjawa, Kimbuga and Mkupuka (all in 1975), before 1976 saw intensification of production in the previously established producer villages, Bungu and Uponda (see Map 6). From 1977/78 onwards both expansion and intensification of production occurred and in 1978/79 charcoal production expanded to the important agricultural and fishing villages on the northern edge of the Rufiji flood plain. Table 5.1 shows the development of the production of charcoal for markets external to Rufiji in the period 1975 to 1985.

Village level data shows that nearly all charcoal production for external markets originated in 34 villages in the four divisions Mkongo, Ikwiriri, Kikale and Kibiti located in the northern and central parts of the district. These villages, in what may be termed the charcoal belt, extend over two ecological zones, the river valley and the northern hill areas (see Maps 5 and 6).

The existence of woodland and forests constituted one of the conditions necessary for the establishment of this belt. Hardwood, softer wood and bush were available. In addition to charcoal burning, the following important uses of wood locally have been identified; fuel for household use and the processing of wood by carpenters, canoe makers and saw mills to make furniture, bridges, canoes and houses. Exploitation for out-of-district use is confined to cutting logs for further processing in Dar es Salaam and to the production of charcoal. These ways of utilising the forests are complementary rather than competitive in character. The tree species *Mninga*, *Mtondoro* and *Mvule*, that are most suitable for making furniture or for export, are not good for charcoal production or local fuel. There was a risk of clearing the woodland completely if the rate of exploitation was allowed to continue at the same rate as at the end of the 1970s. The government finally realised that measures had to be taken to halt the process of deforestation. From March 1982 the royalty rate per bag of charcoal increased from Tsh. 2 to Tsh. 4 and from October 1985 it was raised to Tsh. 5. In 1985 as in 1979 the government started a campaign to prevent charcoal production.

Other factors which contributed to the rapid growth of charcoal production in these areas of Rufiji District were the villagisation campaigns, first on the northern bank of the flood plain in 1969 (Operation Rufiji) and in 1973 in the northern hill areas (Operation Pwani). When nucleated villages were established trees and forests became relatively easy to reach, in particular in the first period.

Another important factor for the creation of the charcoal belt in Rufiji District was the rapid growth of the Dar es Salaam market and the depletion of forest resources close to the city. The annual population growth of the greater Dar es Salaam area was 7.7 per cent between 1967 and 1978. The congested city area, however, probably had an annual population growth of 9–10 per cent during the same period (Sembajwe, 1979). As poorer households, relying on non-electric energy sources for fuel, constitute the bulk of this increase, the demand for charcoal was bound to rise.

A final determining factor for the growth of charcoal production was the potential for earning an income from non-agricultural activities in Rufiji District.

Characteristics of charcoal production

In the process of transforming wood into charcoal, its weight is reduced to 20–30 per cent and its volume is halved. In traditional earth kilns, the only ones in use in Rufiji District, 12 cubic metres of wood is required to produce one tonne of charcoal. The loss of energy in this process is great. While 12 cubic metres of fuelwood have a calorific value of 3.1 million K.cal., one tonne of charcoal has only 0.79 K.cal. (Openshaw, 1976).

The quality of the charcoal produced depends on the wood used. Rufiji District is well endowed with suitable trees. In 1979, such trees were becoming scarce in the charcoal belt, particularly in areas near roads. In 1987 information from people living in the charcoal belt indicated that people had started using cashew nut trees for charcoal production.

The first step in charcoal production is to fell the trees. The producers need knowledge of the availability of suitable trees. Felling the trees and chopping up their trunks is by far the most labour intensive process during which a saw and/or axe are used. A detailed survey undertaken among 20 producers in Ruwe village in the Flood Plain North zone showed that ten working days (eight hours each) were the average input of labour to fell the trees needed to produce ten bags of charcoal. This included chopping up the trunks to be stacked in an earth kiln. The average input of labour for stacking logs was one to two working days. At this stage the producer usually received some help from a friend or a family member. Cutting grass and spreading it all round the logs required two working days and covering them with earth an average of three days. The tools included a matchet, a spade and a hoe.

At the beginning of the burning process, the fire is assisted by the wind which blows into the kiln through holes in one of the short ends of the kiln. Later the holes on this end are closed while the holes at the opposite end remain open. In this way the burning takes place without oxygen, and the wood is transformed into charcoal. Average burning time was 12 days, and the labour input during this period consisted of inspection of the kiln in order to ensure that the wood was burning properly. When charcoal production takes place far from home, the time spent on walking there and back may add up to days. In Ruwe the average time spent walking to the burning site was half an hour, adding up to a total of 12 walking hours. The last part of the process is to pack the charcoal into bags. In our investigation this took five working days, including the assistance given by neighbours or family members. When ample time for inspection was added, it was calculated that the total input of labour for the production of ten bags of charcoal was 24 days. A similar study of the labour input of four producers in Mkongo village showed that the labour input for the production of ten bags was 24 working days plus three days required for walking and inspection.

The average monthly production of producers in Ruwe village was 13 bags each and in Mkongo it was ten bags. In Ruwe the average monthly production potential, i.e. if only charcoal were produced, was said to be 28 bags a month. South of Ngulakula village in the North Hill zone it was estimated that three men working hard had a potential production of 80 bags a month. Thus it is likely that the monthly production potential for individual producers does not exceed 30 bags even under very good conditions.

In most of the villages charcoal production is a part-time activity without strong seasonal fluctuations. It is complemented by some kind of agricultural production, fishing, craft or trading activity. Women charcoal producers are excluded from having fishing and trading as secondary activities. Agriculture is women's most important non-domestic form of production.

My survey of non-agricultural production activities undertaken in 1979–1980 showed that the majority of producers operated on a private, individual basis. The 20 producers in Ruwe (14 male and six female) and the four in Mkongo (three male and one female) were all private producers. Only in one village, Ngulakula, was charcoal produced on a large scale, by 160 men cooperating on an ujamaa basis. Part of their income went to the village fund for development. Since September 1984 the sale of charcoal has been taxed by village councils.

It is evident that there are elements of economies of scale in charcoal production. In felling trees, chopping the wood, stacking and inspecting it, advantages to large scale production occur which have yet to be reflected in the social organisation of production. The organisation of work entails very little division of labour, or specialisation. The productivity of labour is thus at a low level. The exclusive use of earth kilns has led to lower productivity and greater exploitation of wood than alternatives like brick kilns. Experiments have shown a standard conversion factor of six cubic metres of roundwood for each tonne of charcoal (4.2 cubic metres for mangroves) with the use of metal or brick kilns, compared to 12 cubic metres for traditional earth kilns (Openshaw, 1976).

The rapid increase in the production of charcoal in the area was bound to have a negative impact on the regeneration of woodland and forests. Only in mid-1979 were some regulations imposed on charcoal production. The efficacy of these regulations will be analysed in Chapter 7.

Mangrove exploitation

Historical background

Mangrove is a general term used for a set of plants growing in muddy swamps, creeks, deltas and sheltered areas along tropical coasts that are periodically inundated by tides (Grant, 1939). The trees forming the mangrove forests of East Africa consist of seven species with the local names of *mkoko, mkandaa, mshinzi, mchu, mlilana, msikundazi* and *mkomafi*. The total mangrove area along the coast of mainland Tanzania is estimated to be 120,000–125,000 acres of which the Rufiji delta has the main concentration (Grant, 1939 and Kjekshus, 1977).

Mangrove poles have been traded since ancient times, probably since the Arabs first set foot on the coast of East Africa. Arabs and Persians used the poles mainly for building, especially for making the ceilings and roofs of their multiple storied square houses (Grant, 1939 and Sheriff, 1971). The *boriti* (poles) of the Rufiji delta were then and still are held in high esteem because of their length, diameter, clean shape and resistance to termites.

During most of the colonial period a concession provided the right to extract mangroves from the Rufiji delta. Control of this concession was said to constitute a solid base for the accumulation of wealth. Thus the traditional rights of the local chiefs to extract mangroves were severely curtailed in the colonial period. As late as about 1899, the Sultan of Zanzibar still had the right to exploit the Rufiji delta, which he used to extract a great number of mangrove poles free of charge, despite the area being under German control. Before World War I, it was not uncommon for 40–50 dhows to call at Salale (Delta North) to load mangroves. The Germans imposed high royalty rates and the British colonialists retained them (Grant, 1939). Royalties of £ 2,500 were collected in 1922. From 1923 onwards the colonial government started to grant the Rufiji Delta Mangrove Concession to private companies giving them the right to extract mangroves from the delta. The unidentified company holding the concession from 1923 raised the price for *boriti* far in excess of the previous rates (Grant, 1939). From 1927 onwards the concession was taken over by the Rufiji Delta Trading Company, which held exclusive rights for a period of 5 years. At that time the area of the concession encompassed about 400 square miles, however, much of it was said to be unproductive (Telford, 1929).

During this period the local chief of Undengereko complained to the local authority about the introduction of rules and regulations that were hindering his people in their exploitation of the forests in order to meet their liabilities (DAR, 1931). In 1934 the concession shifted into the hands of the Liverpool Uganda Company which experienced difficulties in obtaining labour to exploit *boriti* and bark. The colonial administration came to its assistance by ensuring that "Tax defaulters in or near the Delta have been given the opportunity of working for the company for a generous wage, 30–40 Shs. a month" (DAR, 1934), a wage which eventually ended up as the delayed collection of taxes.

In 1939 it was reported that the export of poles and bark had increased, however, illicit traffic led to losses for the government of approximately Shs. 8,000 yearly (DAR, 1939). Alan Villiers, who travelled in a Kuwaiti dhow to load mangroves in the delta and stayed on board for a month, said that the dhows smuggled as much as they carried officially. Through intimate cooperation between the captain of the dhow (*nakhoda*) and the Swahili head-man, local cutters and the crew worked during the night as much as during the day, out of reach of official inspectors (Villiers, 1940). As this was the rule rather than the exception, considerable doubt is cast on official statistics of the mangrove trade (see Martin and Martin, 1978, Tables XI and XII, pp. 110–111).

1940 was reported to be the best mangrove season in ten years. Officially 600 tonnes of mangrove bark and 5,444 score (20 poles) valued at Shs. 64,585 were exported from the Rufiji delta by 53 dhows (DAR, 1940). In 1941 the lease for the concession was up for tender and was granted to Mr Ghaui of Kilwa. He brought an "unlimited supply of labour" from Kilwa (DAR, 1941). The problem of getting the people of Rufiji to accept labouring for wages to cut mangroves or do plantation work is frequently mentioned in District Annual Reports.

In the late 1940s mangroves for sleepers to expand the railways started to be extracted from the delta alongside *boriti* and bark (DAR, 1943). Exploitation accelerated considerably in the 1940s, and in 1948 the concession was reported to be a gold mine for its owner. Apart from large contracts for sleepers and bark, dhows officially collected *boriti* to the value of Shs. 250,000.

There are indications that mangrove exploitation for export declined considerably in the last decade of the colonial period. Mr Ghaui ended up by being taken to court, accused of having neglected his liabilities.

In 1962 the concession was handed to the Coast Region Cooperative Society. Cutting was mainly organised by a number of cooperative societies. Dominating them was the Amini Mungu Mangrove Cutters Cooperative Society, registered in 1960. It was stipulated that, "Every member must be an African of good character and a *bona fide* cutter of mangrove poles ordinarily resident in Rufiji and who cuts mangroves in the following areas: Salale, Mchinga, Kiomboni, Simba Uranga, Mchikichi, Mfisini, Nyamisati, Kikale, Bumi and Nchungu".

Table 5.2. *Export, supplier and cutter prices for mangroves, 1979* (Tsh.)

Category	Class I & II	Class III & IV	Class V & VI
Cutter price	85,-	75,-	50,-
Retained by cutter of export price (%)	41.4%	50%	67.6%
Price paid by Tan Timber to supplier	120,-	120,-	58,-
Estimated export price	205,-	150,-	74,-
No. of score exported	15,000	5,000	10,000

Note: The prices quoted are per score, i.e. 20 poles. The export price is derived from an exchange rate of US $ 1 equal to Tsh. 8.20.
Source: Data provided by Tan Timber, Dar es Salaam, and author's survey, 1979

In 1972 the following societies merged: Amini Mungu, Kiasi and Mbwera Mangrove Cutters Coop Society Ltd., and Mtunda Agriculture Product Coop Society Ltd. The new society was named, The Rufiji Delta Mangrove Cutters Coop. It was later replaced by the Vimwaruco Mangrove Cutters Society (*Vijiji vya Mwambao* Rufiji Company). It did not, however, get off the ground until 1978, when it was given a credit of Tsh. 150,000 from the National Bank of Commerce.

The intention was for Vimwaruco to supply Tan Timber, a subsidiary of the Tanzania Wood Industry Company, the sole legal exporter of forest produce from Tanzania. Due to poor organisation Vimwaruco was not able to provide mangroves. Instead private middlemen operating from Kiasi village and Mafia Island off the Rufiji coast supplied Tan Timber.

Mangrove exports and local use

After independence, mangrove exploitation for export was negligible. The cooperatives had problems organising cutting and irregularities were detected in the trade. From around 1972 the export of mangroves was suspended altogether, but by the mid-1970s exports resumed. In 1977 Tan Timber exported 20,000 score of mangrove poles (each score has 20 poles) supplied by the Rufiji Delta Mangrove Cutters. Shortly after, this company was liquidated, but the new cooperative did not function well. Thus the total of 30,000 score exported by Tan Timber in 1979 was delivered by private middlemen (Table 5.2). The Forest Ordinance of 1957 (with the Forest Amendment Rules of 1975) identifies six classes of poles classified according to physical features such as length and circumference. The largest are in class I and

Table 5.3.   *The uses of mangroves growing in the Rufiji delta*

Categories	Mkoko	Mkandaa	Mshinzi	Mchu	Mlilana	Msikundazi	Mkomafi
External Use:							
1. Boriti	x	x	-	-	-	-	-
2. Bark	x	x	x	-	-	-	x
3. Timber	-	-	-	-	-	x	x
Local Use:							
4. Houses	x	x	x	-	-	-	-
5. Fuel	-	x	-	x	-	-	-
6. Goat/cattle fodder	-	x	-	-	-	-	-
7. Canoes	-	-	-	x	x	-	x
8. Ship masts	-	-	-	-	x	x	-
9. Oars	-	-	-	-	x	-	x
10. Fish traps	-	x	-	x	-	-	-
11. Bee hives	-	-	-	x	-	-	-
12. Local beds	-	-	-	x	-	-	-
13. Medicine	-	-	-	-	-	-	x

Source: Havnevik, Survey, 1980

in 1979 the royalty rates per score were Tsh. 132 (I), Tsh. 53.50 (II), Tsh. 16 (III), Tsh. 12 (IV), Tsh. 8 (V) and Tsh. 2.40 (VI).

Only modest quantities of mangroves are used locally compared to the number of poles going to markets outside the district. The different qualities of mangrove species are reflected in the variety of local uses. In Table 5.3 both local and major external uses are illustrated. The use of the bark of the *mshinzi, mkandaa* and *mkoko* for tanning, due to its high tanning content, declined drastically since the 1950s. The large species, *msikundazi* and *mkomafi*, are utilized as timber, *msikundazi* was earlier also used for railway sleepers. *Mkoko* and *mshinzi* may also be utilized as fuel, but because of the generation of heavy smoke the species are not preferred. *Mkomafi* is the most durable for canoes. Its fruit is sometimes used to cure stomach pains and scabs on the skin. Mangroves also produce excellent charcoal, but were rarely utilized for that purpose in the late 1970s (see also von Mitzlaff, 1989).

Mangrove cutting

The survey of the Delta and Inner Delta zones registered a total of 3,098 cutters, of whom 52.3 per cent were in Delta South. There were 892 cutters in Delta North and 581 in Inner Delta North. They cut mangroves throughout the year to supplement fishing and agriculture. No special skills are involved.

Cutters work individually or in small groups. They cut, strip the bark and transport the poles in canoes to storage points close to the channels at various places in the delta. At these points larger *mashua* and *dhows* collect large quantities of mangroves.

The total input of labour for cutting, barking and transport to a storage point for three score class III poles is estimated to three ten hour days. Labour input is evenly divided between the three processes. The price obtained by cutters varies. For poles collected in the Delta North and Delta South, destined for export, the price per score for class III poles was Tsh. 75 (Mchinga). In Inner Delta North (Mtunda and Kikale) the price per score for the same class was Tsh. 45. In this case the poles were destined for the domestic market, and were collected by lorries from Dar es Salaam. Accordingly, the return on labour seems to depend on the market for which the poles are destined. The export-oriented activity gives an hourly return on labour of Tsh. 2.50, the domestic-oriented of Tsh. 1.50 (Havnevik, 1980).

Logging

A variety of species of timber are found in Rufiji District. The major part of forest royalties from the exploitation of timber comes from three species: *mninga*, *mtondoro* and *mpingo*. In 1979 *mpingo* had the highest royalty rate, Tsh. 423.60 per cubic metre. This wood is mainly used for Makonde carvings. *Mninga* and *mtondoro* timber are important in terms of both royalty revenue and volume. A tendency towards a rapid increase in exploitation from 1974 to 1978 was arrested in 1979, when felling especially of *mninga* dropped considerably (Table 5.4). The main reason was the large 1979 flood and the heavy rains that badly affected transport lines and the exhaustion of valuable species of trees was beginning to be strongly felt. *Mninga* and *mtondoro* wood are used for high quality furniture and some building purposes. The royalty per cubic metre for *mninga* was Tsh. 84.70, and for *mtondoro* Tsh. 17.65 (1979). Other species, of less importance in terms of revenue rather than volume, are: *msufi pori, mkenge, muuya, mdadarika, mvule and mtanga*. Some of these species are important in charcoal pro-

Table 5.4. *Forest royalties related to exploitation in Rufiji District* (in Tsh.)

Forest product	1976	1977	1978	1979
Mangroves	21,724	36,227	46,059	64,359
Logs	302,370	464,740	589,749	319,624

Source: Cast Region Forestry Office, Kibaha, and Office of the Ministry of Natural Resources, Kibiti, Rufiji

duction and the major part of revenue derived from them would accordingly be indirectly reflected under that item.

No major forestry inventory has been carried out for Rufiji District. Only a small portion, Utete ward (Flood Plain South), was surveyed in 1973. In this area 165 hectares were assessed as productive and 144 hectares as non-productive forest. Another limited survey has been carried out by a Finnish firm for the Rufiji Basin Development Authority. It concentrated on areas of potential exploitation along a possible southern link road from Stiegler's Gorge to Nyamwage on the south side of the Rufiji river and a parallel stretch on the northern side of the river.

In 1979 there were 262 loggers active throughout Rufiji District. The major logging areas were North Hill and Flood Plain South with 201 loggers, 77 per cent of the total. Logging activities by local carpenters and saw mill units for personal consumption are excluded. Logging was carried out by individuals or small groups. These independently operating units log partly on order. Another category of loggers is hired on a daily wage basis, and are picked up by lorries entering the forest through Kibiti and Ikwiriri.

A logger operating independently interviewed in Nyamwage (Flood Plain South) said he required six hours to walk to the areas where trees were to be felled. Logging stopped for some time on the south side of the river during the large 1979 flood, whereas on the north side it could go on unhindered as long as the forest roads were passable.

FISHERIES

Fishing in Rufiji District consist of two major categories, fresh- and saltwater fishery. Freshwater fishing takes place mainly in the 21 sizable lakes in the Rufiji flood plain area along the river and in hundreds of small ponds and creeks (Sandberg, 1974b). These lakes and creeks, which fill up during the annual floods, yield excellent catches of fish for local fishermen. Limited freshwater fishing takes place in a few lakes in the North Hill zone, but is unrelated to the major flood plain fishery. The fish is consumed locally as fresh, dried or smoked, but a substantial portion of the smoked and dried fish is transferred to major markets outside the district, notably Dar es Salaam.

Some salt water fishery takes place near the Rufiji coast. In particular, good conditions for prawn fishing exist on the sandbanks immediately off the Rufiji delta. Prawns are smoked or dried for local consumption, but a large number of prawns are sold on overseas markets. The local fishermen, utilising fish nets or barriers (wando), play an important role in prawn fishing.

Various categories of fishermen with different fishing gear participate in both fresh- and saltwater fishing. In the delta areas a small number of women participate in fishing for domestic consumption, otherwise the work is dominated by men. In the following I will look into the major characteristics of fisheries in Rufiji District both in terms of participation, organisation and income generation. I will concentrate on river plain fishery as it is of major importance to the population of Rufiji and will attempt to assess its importance in providing protein for the population's diet.

Rufiji flood plain fisheries

The freshwater fisheries of the Rufiji river flood plain attract fishermen from its three agro-economic zones, West Valley (upstream), Flood Plain North and Flood Plain South (downstream). Important research was carried out in the 1970s on various aspects of these fisheries (Yoshida, 1974; Sandberg, 1974b and Hopson, 1979). Yoshida included fishing as a separate occupation in his agricultural survey of the Lower Rufiji Plain. He divided the areas into upstream and downstream, which are roughly comparable to the agro-economic zones mentioned above. The survey included 80 households, 0.5 per cent of the total 15,697 households in the survey areas (1967). Yoshida showed fishing to be second only to rice in terms of gross farm return. Volume, value and marketed value of fish in the two areas are shown in Table 5.5.

Another finding of Yoshida's survey, which is supported by my own information and observations in the area, is that fishing has become specialised. Of the farmers in the sample, 35.5 per cent of those living upstream did not fish; the corresponding figure for farmers living downstream was 64.3 per cent. The suggestion has been made that fishing is more specialised in the downstream than in the upstream

Table 5.5.   *Volume, value and marketed value of fish per household in the upstream and downstream area, 1970–1971*

Areas	Average volume of fish obtained by households (numbers)	Average gross return per household from fishing (Ths.)	Average value of fish marketed yearly per household and % of gross catch value
Upstream	900.46	225.12	167.36 (74.3%)
Downstream	779.77	194.94	162.67 (83.4%)
Whole area	833.76	208.44	164.78 (79.1%)

Source: Yoshida, 1974, tables IX -1 and IX -2

areas. My assessment is, however, that the high participation upstream is due to fishing being more important relative to agriculture in this area. The specialisation in fishing is a consequence of the villagisation campaign, "Operation Rufiji" in 1968, in which villages were moved out of the flood plain, some at a distance of 5 to 8 miles from the escarpment. Hence, due to the long distances involved, fishing could no longer be undertaken as an integral part of farming activities (communication with Reverand R.P.G. Lambourn, Kindwitwi village).

A further observation that confirms that fishing is becoming a specialised occupation is the high percentage of fish marketed, valued at 74 per cent in the upstream and 83 per cent in the downstream area (cf. Table 5.5). This finding indicates that many people obtain fish at local markets or through casual sales in the villages. It is confirmed by a survey of Rufiji markets undertaken during 1979 which showed that of more than 50 commodities traded locally, fish, coconuts and salt were the most important (McKim, 1981:17). Further strengthening the hypothesis of specialisation in fishing is Yoshida's finding that 19 per cent of the households surveyed possessed fishing nets, one third having three or four nets and two thirds owning one or two nets. Of the households 17.5 per cent possessed canoes. However, canoes may be exclusively used to transport crops and people, so the number is not directly related to fishing activities.

In assessing the importance of fishing for employment and income generation, it is appropriate to use the following categories: professional-, part-time- and occasional fishermen (Hopson, 1979). In my survey of 26 villages in the three agro-economic zones roughly corresponding to Yoshida's and Hopson's survey area, 770 professional fishermen were recorded, i.e. those who derive the major part of their income and direct a major part of their labour time to fishing activities. In his 1971 survey Yoshida found that 2,982 households possessed nets, of which 47 per cent had one net, 20 per cent two nets, 27 per cent three nets and 6 per cent four nets. Hence 984 households possessed three or four nets, which may indicate the number of nets owned by households of professional fishermen.

In estimating the total catch for professional fishermen an average labour input of eight months per year was assumed. It was further assumed that two fishermen operate from one canoe and that the average catch per canoe was 22 kilos. Both these assumptions are based on Hopson's investigation of professional fishermen who were operating 10 canoes on five different lakes (Hopson, 1979, Table 5.4). In addition it was assumed that on average there were 24 catches a month. The total catch for professional fishermen accordingly came to 1,626 tonnes during 1979.

Due to spoilage, it was assumed that only 10 per cent of the catch was sold fresh locally at Tsh. 3.20 per kilo and that 90 per cent was dried or smoked and sold at Tsh. 1.70 per kilo wet weight equivalent. Hence the gross earnings of professional fishermen amounted to about Tsh. 3 m during 1979. This resulted in an average monthly return for each professional fisherman of Tsh. 487 and gross annual earnings of about Tsh. 3,900 (8 months of operation).

In calculating hourly return on labour it was assumed there was a labour input of eight hours per fisherman in the preparation, fishing and processing of each catch, i.e. a total monthly input of 192 hours. Hourly returns on labour came to about Tsh. 2.50, which was roughly a trebling compared to 1970/71 when fishermen earned Tsh. 0.73 per hour (Yoshida, 1974). This finding corresponded with information obtained in interviews that fish prices had doubled or trebled over the decade.

Part-time fishermen are defined as fishermen who consume part of their catch directly and market the rest. On the basis of my 1979/80 survey it was estimated that the number of fishermen in this category was 3,253 (Havnevik, 1980). The grounds for this estimate are vague as the definition of the category is particularly difficult. Yoshida's findings indicate that part-time fishermen are members of households possessing one or two nets, a total of 2,594 nets. This gives an average of 0.8 nets for each of the part-time fishermen. The majority of the part-time fishermen were found to be in the Flood Plain North, especially in the Ikwiriri area. This estimate for part-time fishermen is only slightly higher than Hopson's 3,000 part-time fishermen (Hopson, 1979).

In estimating the catch of this category it was assumed that the part-time fishermen operated for a yearly period of four months, that they operated individually from land or canoes and on average obtained 24 catches a month of five kilos each. In addition to nets their fishing gears consisted of plunge baskets, hooks and the fish barrier or *wando* net which they used to a limited extent (Hopson, 1979). The total catch based on the above assumption came to 1,560 tonnes. Its potential marketed value in 1979, assumed to be 20 per cent fresh and 80 per cent smoked or dried fish, was Tsh. 3,120,600. For each fisherman the average value of the fish caught in 1979 was Tsh. 960 (four months of operation). Assuming an eight hour input of labour per catch returns amounted to Tsh. 1.25 per hour.

Large parts of the farming community fall in the third category of occasional fishermen. Hopson describes some of the methods used: "During the early flood season it is reported that fish migrating onto the flood plain are easy to catch and the farmers improvise simple catching methods whenever the chance arises. Scooping by means of a khanga cloth or killing by the blows from a panga [matchet] are commonly practiced" (Hopson, 1979). Likewise, when the flood recedes and pools of water are drying, the trapped fish are caught by a large number of peasants. Hopson observed catches of up to 10 kilos of Clarias (Cambale) per person, well in excess of subsistence needs. Part of the catch accordingly had to be marketed. Hopson says that, "Such activity on the part of the occasional fisherman must be regarded as typical for all cultivated sections of the flood plain and the catch undoubtedly makes a significant contribution to the total catch in the area" (Hopson, 1979).

The topography and concentration of the population entail that the major part of the catch of the occasional fishermen is landed in Flood Plain North. Here the plain extends over large areas. Statistics showing the origin of transfers out of the district support this. In the months of receding floods, a period of peak activity for the occasional fishermen, exports from the district increased from of 87 tonnes in May to 227 tonnes in June and 180 tonnes in July 1979. Claria fish constituted a major portion of the increase. Transfers of Claria from Ikwiriri village doubled from May to June 1979, from 44 to 80 tonnes, and stayed at a high level for another two months. Transfers of other species from Ikwiriri also increased dramatically, especially Distichodus (*Tungu*). Observations and statistics thus show that in certain periods occasional fishermen catch far in excess of their domestic requirements. The good conditions for fishing and the large number participating lend support to the conclusion that occasional fishermen contribute significantly to the total catch of the area. My estimate for the catch contributed by this category is one third of the total catch, i.e.

1,593 tonnes. The estimate for the total catch in the flood plain is 4,779 tonnes in 1979.

The total value of the freshwater catch if applying the local price quoted by Hopson of Tsh. 3.20 per kilo fresh fish weight, comes to Tsh. 15,292,800. The figures for particpation and income generation clearly indicate that fishery is important not only for the population in the district itself, but also for other areas, like Dar es Salaam, which receives the major part of out-of-district transfers.

Marketing and Consumption of the catch

Consumption and marketing of the catches of fish in the Rufiji river plain take place at various levels. The first is consumption and marketing in the flood plain itself. The fish is either consumed directly by the fisherman and his household or it is casually sold in the villages or marketed in fresh, smoked or dried form (dry weight is 30 per cent of wet weight) by the fishermen or licenced traders. Given the restricted transport and marketing facilities the flood plain is the only area where fresh fish can be consumed and marketed.

The second level consists of marketing dried and smoked fish outside the flood plain. There are 32 daily markets in the district identified as permanent locations where buyers and sellers meet on a regular basis (McKim, 1981:10). Fish is sold at nearly all markets in Rufiji District. It is the most important commodity in terms of volume of sales. Of the sellers interviewed in McKim's survey 42 per cent "were selling at least one kind out of more than ten major varieties of fish and shellfish (prawns) sold in the district" (McKim, 1981:18). This survey also confirmed that "very few of the fish reach the market-places as fresh fish". Fish sellers said that they bought the fish directly from fishermen or from fish wholesalers in the largest market-places. Of 41 fish sellers 19 transported their fish by foot, ten by bicycle and nine by boat or canoe.

A large number of the fish marketed in the district are sold in major market-places in the North Hill zone, notably in Kibiti and Bungu villages. These markets are supplied with smoked and dried fish from the flood plain. The trade is mainly organised by licenced traders. In Kibiti a wholesaler operating behind the main market distributed fish to retailers from various North Hill markets. The fish is transported to Kibiti and Bungu mainly by bus or lorry, and from there to more remote markets by bicycle or on foot.

The estimate for dried and smoked fish from the flood plain marketed in the district, in particular North Hill, is equal to half the amount transferred out of the district, i.e. 577 tonnes (see below). This implies the average daily sales in each of the 32 local markets the equivalent to about 50 kilos wet weight, i.e. between 15 and 20 kilos dry weight. Due to the concentration of sales at major markets in North Hill, transport is less of a problem than the above figures might indicate.

The third level of marketing of flood plain fish is transfer to markets outside the district, notably Dar es Salaam. This trade is organised by a small group of highly specialised traders, in addition to the 134 licenced traders in Rufiji District in 1979 (Hopson, 1979). Only dried and smoked fish are transferred to these markets. Based on a mean fish weight for 1,000 fishes of each species (Hopson, 1979) and statistics for the amount of fish transferred north of Kibiti village, an estimate of out-of-district transfers amount to 1,005 tonnes. Statistics were collected for a 12 month period, from October 1978 to September 1979 at the Office of the Ministry of Natural Resources, Kibiti. To estimate the total out-of-district transfers, 150 tonnes were added to account for transfers by road to the south and by boat from the delta area. Total transfers out of the district of freshwater fish originating mainly in the flood plain area accordingly come to 1,155 tonnes.

By subtracting transfers out of the flood plain from the estimated total catch, the subsistence catch for the flood plain, that portion of the fish consumed directly by the fishermen and their households and by others via trade, came to 3,047 tonnes in 1979. With a total population in the Flood Plain North and South and West Valley of 54.298 (1978 Census) consumption per person comes to the equivalent of 56 kilos wet fish weight for that year. This figure is about three and a half times above the national average of 16 kilos a year, and about 18 kilos above the estimate by Hopson. An intake of fish of this magnitude in 1979 is not unreasonably high because of the large flood and the specific agricultural conditions prevailing (see below). The figures underscore the extremely important role of fish as a staple food. It is further emphasised by the limited numbers of cattle in the district (only on some of the delta islands) and the predominantly Muslim population.

The intake of fish probably varies both during the year and between years. In the course of an average "flood year", fish intake is high during and at the end of the flood, when conditions for fishing are best. A labour constraint may occur, especially for occasional fishermen, at the time of the rice harvest. In years when large floods destroy crops, like in 1979 when the flood reportedly damaged 17,000 hectares (*Mzalendo*, May 27, 1979), there are strong incentives to engage in fishing. Then there will be no labour constraint, as rice will not be harvested, and fishing compensates for the loss of crops in the food intake. This was the situation in 1979.

In years of small floods, lack of water will also destroy crops. There will be a similar urge to increase fishing; conditions will, however, not be favourable, due to the very small area being inundated by flood water.

As described earlier, the situation in Rufiji is constantly changing, as to the level and timing of floods. 1979 has considerable value in terms of investigation as it represents a year of extreme floods. Understanding the changes in ecological conditions and the peasants' shifts in labour allocation in such a year provide insights into how the economic and ecological systems adapt in the face of extreme conditions.

The role of fish as protein

The central role of fish as a staple food and particularly in the provision of protein in the flood plain has been documented in several investigations (Angwazi and Ndulu, 1973; Yoshida, 1974; Sandberg, 1974b and Hopson, 1979). The intake estimated for 1979 of 56 kilos per person or 153 grams daily, meets about half the total protein and 15 per cent of the total energy requirements of an adult. It takes 0.55 kilo of the other major staple food rice, to equal 153 grams of fish in terms of protein (King et al., 1972). With beans or peas in the diet, the staple items can be progressively reduced to obtain the same level of protein.

In assessing the flood plain as a whole in terms of the proteins acquired through eating fish, the population has to be converted into adult equivalents. A child of 5 years and one of 10 years require half and the same amount of protein as an adult. With the present age distribution, the population of the flood plain in terms of adult protein equivalents is 41,000. The 3,047 tonnes of fish consumed, i.e. about 200 grams per adult equivalent, is, if evenly distributed, sufficient to meet about 65 per cent of the total protein requirement in the flood plain.

The high estimated value of protein acquired by the population of the flood plain through fish, calls for further investigation. Particularly so as the effects of the Stiegler's Gorge project on ecological conditions and for fishing were disregarded and hence not fully understood by those responsible for its planning. It will be discussed further in Chapter 8.

Actual and potential catches

The inundated area of the Rufiji flood plain between Mloka village in West Valley and the agro-economic zones of the Inner Delta, amounted to about 1,450 square kilometers in 1979 (VHL, 1979). My estimate of the total catch for this area is 4,779 tonnes, equivalent to a catch of 33 kilos per hectare (kg/ha). It is slightly below the mean value of 37.5 kg/ha for 13 other flood plains in Africa, ranging from 0.5 to 67 kg/ha (Hopson, 1979). Sandberg has estimated that the *potential* catch for the inundated areas could be 50 kg/ha (Sandberg, 1974b). This corresponds to a total catch of 7,250 tonnes. If Sandberg's estimate is correct, my estimate of the actual catch in 1979, which is considered to be high given favourable conditions, is only about 66 per cent of the potential catch of the area.

Salt water fisheries

Salt water fishing takes place immediately off the Rufiji Delta and northwards. Fishing in the river outlets and tidal channels of the delta is included in this category. Local fishermen are drawn from Inner Delta North (678) and South (212), and Delta North (494) and South (1,401). Fishing is directed towards both home consumption and the market. Prawn fishery, mainly in the shallow waters of the Rufiji delta, predominates commercially. Most prawn fishermen come from Inner Delta North, Delta North and South, which have direct access to the shallow water fishing grounds. Fishermen from the more remote Inner Delta South take their canoes down the Mohoro river and participate in the coastal fishery for a week at a time.

Fishermen who had fishing as a major source of income were reported to be 2,785. They are exclusively male and a number of them are involved in commercial prawn fishing. 300 women were reported to take part in fishing for domestic consumption, but for a very limited time (and they are, therefore, not recorded in the figures in Table 5.12).

The *wando* is the most important net used by local fishermen in prawn fisheries. It consists of mangrove poles which are placed on the beach to form a V and attached to the poles is a barrier or net woven of coarse reeds and parts of the leaves of coconut palms. Some may cover an area of about 0.10 ha (Dorsey, 1979:9). Minor gear used by local fishermen include seine nets, gill nets, handlines and basket traps.

In marketing the prawns in the late 1970s the fishermen relied on private middlemen, Dar Ocean Products Ltd. (a private company) and the state owned Tanzania Fisheries Company (TAFICO). They distributed ice boxes to the villages from where they purchased the prawns that fishermen had deposited in them. When they collected the prawns they replaced the ice. Dar Ocean Products has been in this business since 1956, but the collection system had significant weaknesses which

Table 5.6.   *TAFICO procurement of prawns originating from Rufiji fisher-men, July 1978 to June 1979*

Purchase from	Quantity (kgs)
Mahege village	2,063
Kiomboni village	12,339
Nyamisati village	1,178
Private middlemen	11,332
Private companies	22,487
Total	49,399

Note: The figure for private companies is based on the estimate that 80 per cent of the procurement from private companies was originally bought in Rufiji.
Source: Data provided by TAFICO, Dar es Salaam

were reflected in comments made by many of the local fishermen. They claimed that the companies did not collect the prawns regularly. The ice melted and the prawns went bad, resulting in losses for the fishermen as the companies refused to pay in these cases. The companies had to strugggle with poor roads to get access to most of the delta villages. Often roads were impassable and no collection could be carried out. Irregular collection was also reported outside the rainy season. Because fishermen could not rely upon the existing marketing channels, they dried or smoked some prawns for direct consumption or sale.

Until the mid-1980s TAFICO was the sole exporter of prawns from Tanzania and procured them directly from villages or from middlemen and companies. TAFICO's procurement of prawns originating from Rufiji District in 1978/79 is shown in Table 5.6.

The average price per kg paid to fishermen was Tsh. 10. The price increased through the period of July 1978 to June 1979 from Tsh. 7.50 to Tsh. 12. Fishermen's gross earnings from the sale of prawns came to Tsh. 493,990. Total purchases of prawns by TAFICO, including other areas and from own trawlers, during this period amounted to 81,521 kgs of which 76,658 kgs were exported at an average price of Tsh. 40.25 earning Tsh. 3,085,487 in foreign exchange. The share of the export price retained by local fishermen hence comes to 25 per cent. It should be added, however, that there is a small additional cost involved in rinsing, sorting and packing of the prawns.

TAFICO undertook its own fishing operations with six large and

three smaller trawlers (1979). The fishing operations were running at
a heavy loss, due to poor administration, poor maintenance of boats
and low productivity. The operation of the boats was also hampered by
lack of fuel and other necessities. It is reported that rarely are more
than three out, but the actual peiod of fishing was not available (Dorsey, 1979:12).

TAFICO's efforts to improve collection from the Rufiji prawn
fisheries and raise profits entered a new phase in 1979 when TAFICO
and a Swiss company formed a joint venture, starting operations in
June 1979. The company placed a small mother ship outside the delta
with refrigeration and freezer capacity and some processing tables. It
could produce 10 tonnes of ice in 10 hours. The distribution of ice to
the ice boxes in the delta villages and the collection of prawns were to
be done by several speed boats with 40 hp engines. It was thought that
this costly scheme would be profitable as it was based on an estimate of
a potential catch by artisanal fishermen of 600 tonnes a year. Through
regular provision of ice and prompt collection the company hoped
that the fishermen would stop drying part of their catch and fish more
regularly so that it would be possible to attain the estimated potential
catch (Dorsey, 1979:11).

Poor planning and implementation and unrealistic goals led to the
termination of this expensive scheme after a few months. The project
must have proved a disaster economically, to TAFICO in particular. It
had chartered the mother ship for an extended period, and had to
honour this contract in spite of the premature end of the scheme.

Other efforts to increase the extraction rate in prawn fishery included a plan put forward in 1975 for a few village-centred, motorised trawlers fishing at certain points along the Tanzanian coast. Two centres
were started, one in Mbegani and the other in Kisiju. The Mbegani
Fisheries Development Centre (MFDC) has been turned into a major
fishery related aid project in Tanzania. Up to the mid-1980s MFDC was
assisted by Norwegian development aid to the tune of 250 million
Norwegian kroner. The Centre has, however, only to a limited extent
catered for the training and development needs of artisanal fishermen
(MDC, 1986). Centres in Pangani and Bagamoyo followed. In 1976
Nyamisati in Rufiji was added. It was planned to operate small wooden
trawlers built by the TAFICO boat yard from the Nyamisati Centre. An
ice plant, cold storage facilities, generators and processing buildings
would be established at each centre. During 1976–78 World Bank/IDA
funds were solicited and approved to cover about 60 per cent of the initial investment of Tsh. 23 million. The installations were built by the
Fisheries Division and were to be turned over to TAFICO and the Rufiji
District Development Company. Later information shows that most in-

stallations remained incomplete, and that the construction of the project's 46 boats did not materialise. In the early 1990s, Norway also terminated its support to the Mbegani project (MFDC).

CRAFT PRODUCTION

Blacksmiths

Nine blacksmith workshops were surveyed, seven in Flood Plain North, one in North Hill and one in Flood Plain South. The year of establishment and organisational form of each workshop varied considerably. Nearly every blacksmith had an assistant operating the bellows for him. Two of the smithys were started in the 1930s, one of which supports a single blacksmith, while a group of three work together in the other. Two workshops with individual blacksmiths started in the 1940s. A blacksmith started working alone in 1952, another in 1960 and two smithys started in the 1970s. One of these, initiated in 1972, had two blacksmiths working together. The most recent establishment tried to register as a cooperative in 1977, when an attempt was made to unite twelve blacksmiths in the district centre, Utete. At the time of the survey (1979) only three were cooperating actively. One unit of three blacksmiths did not mention the year their workshop started. The nine units in the survey accordingly comprised 16 blacksmiths, 7.8 per cent of the total registered (Havnevik, 1980). The largest number of blacksmiths work in North Hill (74), then come Flood Plain North (30) and Delta South (28).

In spite of craftsmen working in groups or cooperatives, this has little impact on specialisation or the division of labour — each blacksmith continues to operate as if he works alone. In one unit some rationalisation seems to have taken place, as three blacksmiths shared two assistants. All the blacksmiths said that they had learnt the craft from their father or grandfather. The high average age, 55 years, of 10 blacksmiths indicates that the transfer of this skill is problematic. Five craftsmen were over 60 and only one was below 40 years. The issue of recruitment to the craft is of importance if it is to be sustained (Müller, 1979).

The critical role of the craft in the rural economy becomes clear from a list of the products and services smiths provide. Major items are hoes, knives, axes and spears. Of lesser importance are hammers, needles, coconut graters (kibao cha mbuzi), arrows, tezo (small axes) and matchets. More than one model of many of the items are produced to suit specific jobs or local conditions.

Blacksmiths play an important role in repairs and in the production of a limited range of spares and special products, including fixing of broken pieces of metal, spares for bicycles and making large nails for bridge construction. In spite of variable quality, the range of products and services underlines the importance of the craft both in relation to agriculture and in providing inputs and linkages to other crafts. The majority of customers were local peasants utilising the products in cultivation. Only one blacksmith had had access to a market beyond the division, while three sold on markets at divisional level. The rest were selling in their respective wards and villages. The form of sales varied. Products were produced mainly on order; yet a few major lines were generally produced without prior sales agreement. Most customers called on the blacksmith at the workshop to collect or buy products. There were a few cases of blacksmiths taking products to village markets or other potential sales spots. All the blacksmiths in the survey participated in agriculture. Their wives did most of the work in the fields, while the men only performed a limited number of tasks.

Labour input in the smithy was limited and varied according to season and in terms of work intensity. Two units responded that they worked 16 days each month when operating, others stated they worked 12, 8, 4 and 2 days a month respectively. Daily working time varied from 8 to 12 hours. The information obtained indicated there were less labour input in the agricultural season compared to the dry. A few blacksmiths said their workshop functioned only about 3 months a year.

The blacksmiths had obtained their tools and equipment through inheritance, by producing their own and through buying. Money outlay on tools varied considerably. The cost of a well-equipped workshop in 1975 was estimated to have been about Tsh. 700 to 800. The difficulty in obtaining tools spurred blacksmiths into making their own, often simple, practical tools, which included hammers, spades, tindos, tezoes and calipers. The craftsmen owned their tools and equipment and controlled their use. Depreciation of the value of the tools was the only fixed production cost, though in itself it was negligible.

The major variable costs of production were for charcoal and scrap iron. Charcoal was either bought or produced by the craftsmen themselves. The price per bag of charcoal was between Tsh. 12 and 14 in 1979. One bag lasted 3 to 4 days depending on the amount of work. Scrap iron was bought mainly in the villages of Mkongo, Kilimani, Kibiti, Ikwiriri and in Dar es Salaam. A few blacksmiths said that they collected metal pieces from broken-down cars and lorries. Procuring scrap, due to its scarcity and the high price, was a general problem for the blacksmiths, which was exacerbated by the scrap collection campaigns of large scale iron foundries (Müller, 1979).

The cost of the scrap iron needed to produce one hoe was in the range of Tsh. 2 to 6, on average Tsh. 4. The price of the small weeding hoes produced by the nine workshops varied from less than Tsh. 10 to 20. The potential daily return on labour can be calculated from an example in which the blacksmith produces five hoes a day at an average price of Tsh. 10. Half the input of labour was spent on making modern handles of pieces of wood bought for Tsh. 1 each. The average cost of charcoal per day was estimated at Tsh. 3 and the cost of scrap iron at Tsh. 20. Net earnings of the craftsmen accordingly came to Tsh. 22 daily. This income also had to support the apprentice, who was likely to be a family member who received little payment directly. The payment in kind was estimated at Tsh. 1 per hour. If a working day was seven hours, the blacksmith's hourly return on labour came to Tsh. 2.14 in 1979.

Since 1985 a non-governmental Norwegian organisation and the Small Industries Development Organisation (SIDO) in Tanzania have together supported the establishment of four blacksmith/tinsmith co-operatives in Rufiji District. The units in Ikwiriri and Kibiti became operational in early 1987. Training and product development are led by a professional blacksmith from Norway who is funded by the Norwegian aid agency (NORAD). Both units buy scrap or rejects from the Ubungo Farm Implements Factory (UFI) in Dar es Salaam at prices ranging from Tsh. 6 to 9. The round-eyed rejects are made into tanged hoes that are sold for Tsh. 80 to 90. At the same time UFI hoes cost around Tsh. 105 in the shops. While the latter are treated and hardened, the rejects are not. In the long run the peasant may be better off buying the treated UFI hoe at the higher price. Small weeding hoes were sold by the blacksmiths at Tsh. 50 in 1987, a five-fold price increase in 8 years.

When the Ikwiriri unit was inspected in August 1987 it was operating industriously. The eight active members were cooperating well while the product range, including hoes, knives, buckets, charcoal stoves, poultry feeders, simple locks, etc., seemed to match both domestic household needs and the requirements of agricultural production. In late 1987 the Kibiti unit was, however, reported to have almost fallen apart.

Carpentry

Throughout Rufiji District 482 carpenters and 276 apprentices were recorded by the 1979 survey (Havnevik, 1980). Of this total, 348 craftsmen worked alone or with one or more of 153 apprentices. The remaining 134 carpenters and 123 apprentices worked in groups or cooperatives. The survey interviewed ten carpentry units five of which were organised as cooperatives, one was a private group and four were individual craftsmen. These units employed 37 craftsmen and 46 apprentices, 7.7 per cent and 16.7 per cent respectively of the totals recorded in the district. Carpentry was mainly based in North Hill, Flood Plain North and Delta South.

Of the five privately organised units, two were located in Flood Plain North and three in North Hill. Two individuals started work in the 1950s and two in the early 1960s. The carpenters in the latter two units worked in the craft in Kisarawe District and Dar es Salaam from 1934 and 1955 respectively before moving to Rufiji. The fifth unit consisting of two craftsmen and one apprentice was started in 1971. Occupational statistics for 1977–79 show that these units have a high degree of stability: there were six craftsmen and five apprentices in 1977, five craftsmen and five apprentices in 1978 and six craftsmen and nine apprentices in 1979. One of the craftsmen left the district in late 1978 and another was privately registered only in 1979, previously he worked in a cooperative. None of the privately organised units received any assistance from outside. One carpenter said that he would like to join a cooperative to get access to credit.

The five cooperatives were of more recent origin, all being established in the 1970s: 1971, 1976 and three in 1979. Employment in the cooperatives was declining. Between 1978 and 1979 the number of craftsmen increased from 30 to 31 while the number of apprentices declined from 56 to 37. The membership in the units started in 1971 and 1976, was initially 33 and 21, but was reduced to twelve each in 1979. At the beginning the 33 member unit in Umwe worked together with 33 masons. This high level of activity in the early 1970s was closely related to rapid in-migration due to the villagisation campaign and the increased need for houses. A cooperative established in 1978 consisting of one craftsman and 19 apprentices at the time of the survey closed down between March and August 1979. Thus employment in the units surveyed fell to 30 craftsmen and 18 apprentices, a reduction in the number of apprentices in cooperatives to about one third of that of a year previously.

In contrast to the private units, the cooperatives received considerable external assistance. Three had received funds, tools or raw materials from the Office of Adult Education (Elimu Ufundi) in 1977/78. One unit received Tsh. 8,000, another Tsh. 7,000 and the third a limited amount of tools and raw materials. Two had also received iron sheets, tools and hire/purchase credit from SIDO (Mkongo and Ikwiriri). One of the Adult Education supported units was the one that went out of business, while the other two earned Tsh. 16,020 and Tsh 38,843 respectively in 1978/79. Some of the earnings of the last unit were derived from saw milling and not from carpentry. These units were located in large villages in Flood Plain North, two in the Ikwiriri area and one in Mkongo. The fourth cooperative, which was established in Kilimani in 1978 and did not receive assistance, reported earnings of Tsh. 10,000 in 1978/79. The fifth unit in the survey had not yet registered as a cooperative, but was said to function according to cooperative principles.

Thirteen carpentry cooperatives were reported to have received assistance from the Office of Adult Education, totalling about Tsh. 50,000 in 1977/78. A year later (1978/79) it was reported that:

— three were not working
— two had no earnings
— one had not yet started operations
— three had negligible earnings of less than Tsh. 400 a year
— four had earnings ranging from Tsh. 6,000 to 39,000 a year, with an average of Tsh. 18,216.

Two of the units with high earnings were located in Flood Plain North, one in Inner Delta South and one in Delta South. A fifth high earning, non assisted unit was also located in Flood Plain North (Tsh. 10,000 in 1978/79). The financial solidity of the four high earning, Adult Education assisted units was underlined by their reported bank deposits that ranged from Tsh. 6,000 to 10,000. (Figures reported by the coordinator of the Technical Office of Adult Education [*Elimu Ufundi*].)

The major initiative to support carpentry in Rufiji District occurred in 1980 when SIDO decided to provide the cooperative unit that was functioning best (located in Ikwiriri) with machinery on a hire-purchase basis. The machines were delivered in 1980 and a large shed was built. The cooperative made the 10 per cent down payment of Tsh. 22,000 on October 1st 1981, which indicated that the total cost of the machinery was Tsh. 220,000. My information indicates that this sum was equivalent to the original estimate. The final cost of the machinery was far above Tsh. 300,000.

The cooperative ran into problems shortly after having received assistance from SIDO. A major cause was the irregular supply of electricity from the local Tanzania Electrical Supply Company (TANESCO) generator. The extremely rapid growth of the Ikwiriri area made it necessary to ration electricity strictly. In addition there was the problem of supply of diesel. During the whole 1980–87 period the problem of the supply of electricity has haunted the cooperative and made it incapable of repaying more than the 10 per cent down payment. This is a telling example of assistance which kills: too elaborate plans are founded on a weak basis.

Table 5.7. *Carpentry: Labour input in cooperatives and private groups*

Category	Months per year	Days per week	Hours per day
Cooperatives			
1.	12	6	12
2.	9-12	6	8
3.	12	2	8
4.	12	6	n.a.
5.	12	6	7.
Private groups			
6.	3	6	6
7.	12	6	1
8.	11	6	n.a.
9.	6	6	7
10.	10	6	10

Source: Havnevik, 1980

Overall labour input and work intensity vary between the two categories of organisations (see Table 5.7).

The cooperatives surveyed were characterised by a stable and relatively high labour input throughout the year. Only one of the cooperatives worked strictly on part time basis (No. 3). One of the cooperatives said that year around operations were difficult due to problems of obtaining logs in the rainy season (No. 2). The daily intensity of work was high, reaching an average of almost 9 hours. Labour inputs in the private units showed both stronger seasonal variation and a lower intensity of work compared to the cooperatives. Operating time varied from three to twelve months per year. Daily inputs of labour varied from one to ten hours, with an average of six hours.

A considerable number of the carpenters fell and saw their own logs. Apart from labour, production costs consisted of depreciation of tools, procurement of logs, either bought from saw mills or produced by the carpenters themselves, and glue, nails, paper, polish, etc. The value of tools has been computed for eight units. Two of the cooperatives received tools as grants and for these cost data was not available. In the remaining three cooperatives the value of tools per craftsman ranged from Tsh. 750 to Tsh. 1,176, an average of Tsh. 967. In the small private units the range was from Tsh. 512 to Tsh. 909, with an average per craftsman of Tsh. 672. As the ratios of craftsmen to apprentices are similar, cooperatives are generally better equipped than private units in terms of tools and equipment. This finding was not surprising as cooperatives have much easier access to assistance and credit. Most of the tools were bought in Dar es Salaam and repairs were carried out in Dar es Salaam, by local blacksmiths or by the carpenters themselves.

Mninga was the most important wood used by the units. Other species used were *mvule, mtanga* and *mkenge*. The valuable species were becoming increasingly scarce. Many of the units which felled trees and sawed wood themselves, transported it either on foot or by hiring a lorry to bring it to their workshops. Deforestation meant that distances to trees were increasing which resulted in longer walking time and higher transport costs. When trees are chopped down royalties that vary from species to species have to be paid to the district office of the Ministry of Natural Resources. The rates were fixed from 1975 to 1982, then they increased considerably. Nearly all the units produce doors, window frames, cupboards, chairs, tables and some produce beds, desks and boxes of various types. The products were seldom standardised, except when larger orders of, for instance, school desks were placed with the larger units. Accordingly the price of even the same type of product varied considerably depending on size, wood and the quality of the work.

Figures for the consumption and cost of wood were difficult to obtain due to variations in the ways wood was procured and problems in establishing conversion factors between raw material input and the final product. The calculation of the return on labour had to be based on an example of production of school desks (a standardised product) in the most efficient cooperative unit. Production of one desk required 2 days, each with a labour input of 12 hours. In 1979 the sales price was Tsh. 300 and the cost of raw materials Tsh. 250. The hourly return on labour accordingly came to Tsh. 2.50. Carpenters in general ought to get a labour return of Tsh. 2 per hour. The reduction by Tsh. 0.50 is done to obtain a representative estimate as our example was taken from a very efficient unit that was producing a standardised product.

One cooperative and a private unit had markets beyond Rufiji District, notably in Dar es Salaam and Kilwa. All the cooperatives had markets at district level, which was the case for only one private unit. Three of the private groups sold their products at divisional level and four at ward level. All the private groups claimed to have markets at the village level, which meant that only one unit served the village market exclusively. Two of the cooperatives were producing desks for the district Office of Education. Otherwise the nature of the market was not specified. A considerable amount of the production was to fill orders. There was no transport problem from the workshop to the market as most buyers came to collect the finished products. Eight of the ten units, however, said that the transport of raw materials to the workshop was a major problem. Only three of the units, all in the small or private category, mentioned that limited markets and too much competition were problematic.

Despite the creation of collective production organisations in which craftsmen and apprentices worked together, little specialisation and division of labour were found. Even in the most well-equipped cooperative, the craftsmen did not specialise, "unless they have to do something quickly". As a rule each craftsman finished the whole product. The findings revealed that there was a latent potential increase in productivity, but it was constrained by low demand.

Nine of the ten units mentioned that they had problems regarding access to credit, and three said that they lacked information on credit procedures. Of the seven units that specified what their credit needs were, all wanted credit for tools, three for building purposes and two for the procurement of raw materials.

Saw mills

Saw mills and carpentry are closely integrated. Most of the carpentry units cut and saw their own timber; many of the private groups and cooperatives do likewise. Accordingly, saw milling has greater economic significance than is indicated by the number of people having this as the major occupation. There were 179 craftsmen and 85 apprentices in individual units, comprising one craftsman and a variable number of apprentices. Private groups and cooperatives employed 121 craftsmen and 23 apprentices. There were 13 private groups with less than ten members. The survey included the four cooperative saw mills in the district; three were in Flood Plain North (two in Mkongo and one in Umwe) and one in North Hill (Kibiti B), and they employed a total of 64 craftsmen. This constituted 21.3 per cent of the total of 300 craftsmen working in saw milling.

The saw mill in Umwe formed part of the Coast Region Development Corporation (COREDECO) established in May 1976 after the liquidation of the Coast Region Cooperative Union. COREDECO became responsible for a transport fleet of 20 lorries, a boat (which sank in 1977) and the saw mill in Umwe. It took over what was left after other government organisations, the Tanzania Cotton Authority (Kilimani ginnery) and National Milling Corporation (the grain mill in Kibiti), had taken their share. For practical reasons COREDECO was established on a weak foundation. Weak planning, lack of funds and the poor state of the assets taken over had an adverse impact on future developments.

The Umwe saw mill started operations under COREDECO in 1977 with 14 employees, a number that remained constant throughout 1979. The saw mills in Mkongo, established in 1975 and 1977, employed 12 and 18 craftsmen respectively. The mill that started in 1975 was supported by the Office of Adult Education, which granted six pit saws. The saw mill and carpentry unit in Kibiti B was also supported at the beginning in 1978 by Adult Education (Tsh. 5,100 on the 1977/78 budget). If all units are taken together the number of employees was stable from 1978 to 1979.

Three of the saw mills carried on operating throughout the year. In one, however, activity declined during the rainy season due to the problem of procuring logs. The fourth unit operated seven months a year, ceasing operations in December to April and in the month of July. The three non-powered units possessed from six to nine felling and/or pit saws each. The Umwe saw mill was power driven by running a tractor engine, transferred to the saw mill from a defunct ploughing scheme. Procuring diesel for fuel was a condition for operations. The mill had three saws, two large and one small. The assets taken over by the saw mill were valued at Tsh. 240,720. The value of the workshed in 1979 was Tsh. 18,000. In spite of utilising power-driven saws, the production processes turned out to be more labour intensive than expected. This was mainly due to deficient machinery, that required constant manual cooling of the blade of the saw. Another task was that to control the accelerator of the tractor. In 1978 the mill was out of operation for four or five months due to a shortage of blades.

While the Umwe saw mill transported the tree trunks from the forests to the mill, the other units did some of the sawing operations in the field using pit saws. In the forest the division of labour was that two people did the felling while four were sawing. The trees felled were mainly *mninga, mpodo, msufipori, mvule, mtondoro* and *muuya*. *Mninga* was collected largely in the southern hills of Rufiji District, far from the the existing mills. For the units located in Flood Plain North, felling *mninga* usually involved two to five days trips. During the rainy season, floods in the Rufiji river make it impossible to procure *mninga* due to transport problems. More common species of trees were felled on daily trips from the respective saw mills. Deforestation led to an increase in the length of the transport lines.

Three of the cooperatives said that the major problem in operation was the transport of logs from the forest to the workshed. These units all had to hire lorries at an increasing cost. The Umwe saw mill was in a better position due to its access to COREDECO's lorries.

Two of the cooperatives had markets in Dar es Salaam and all supplied various district government offices, like Education, Natural

Table 5.8. *Cost estimates for the COREDECO saw mill in Umwe, 1978 and 1979* (in Tsh.)

Cost category	1978	1979
Labour	60,000	72,000
Fuel	25,000	42,000
Repair	17,000	20,000
Transport	10,000	15,000
Other	-	15,000
Total	112,000	164,000

Note: While the data for 1978 was acquired from the management of the Umwe saw mill, the 1979 data has been adjusted in various ways. The 1978 data is based on seven months of operations, the 1979 data on ten. Labour costs are as given, fuel costs are raised by Tsh. 12,000 due to lengthening of operations and higher diesel prices. Cost of repairs is as given by management, while transport costs are increased by Tsh. 5,000 for the same reasons as for fuel. Other costs are as provided by management, of which Tsh. 12,000 are labour-related costs, probably due to the hiring of casual labour in peak periods.
Sources: Data provided by the management of COREDECO saw mill and Havnevik, 1980

Resources and *Ujamaa na Ushirika* (Ujamaa and Cooperatives). In addition, three of the units sold at village markets.

Production costs consisted of depreciation of tools and machinery, forest royalties, transport and labour costs. Cost figures were sketchy and difficult to evaluate. Gross income figures were somewhat more easily obtainable. The 1978 and 1979 accounts for Umwe saw mill were constructed on the basis of estimates and the data collected (see Table 5.8).

Monthly income figures were estimated at Tsh. 20,000 which was Tsh. 4,000 below the average of sales in July and August 1979. Assuming forest royalties to be 20 per cent of sales figures and the lifetime of the assets to be five years at take over, the total costs for 1978 and 1979 added up to Tsh. 188,000 and Tsh. 252,000 respectively. If these assumptions are correct, the Umwe saw mill showed a net loss of Tsh. 48,000 in 1978 and Tsh. 52,000 in 1979.

One of the Mkongo cooperatives reported gross earnings ranging from Tsh. 23,984 in 1976, to Tsh. 9,427 in 1977 and Tsh. 28,612 in 1978, an average of Tsh. 20,672 a year (based on seven months of operation). This entailed an average monthly sale per member of Tsh.

246. When royalty costs of 20 per cent of sales and transport costs of 10 per cent were deducted, the return on labour per craftsman came to Tsh. 172 per month. Depreciation costs were assumed to be negligible. The large amount of work linked to trips to the forests to fell trees, indicated that the timber sawing operations had problems of continuity. The average monthly labour input in the period of operation was estimated to be 18 days due to problems related to access to timber. With working days of eight hours, the hourly return on labour came to Tsh. 1.19. The conditions described for this cooperative were regarded as representative for most of the units.

Boat building

Several types of boats are built in the delta area; the larger types are *jahazi* and *mashua*, the medium sized *dhow*, the smaller *ngalawa* and canoes. The boats are utilised for fishing and transport of goods and people. Most of the cash crops of Delta North and South, copra, cashew nuts and pulses are shipped to Mafia Island because of transport problems to the mainland. 52 craftsmen building larger boats were recorded, 32 were registered in Delta North, 19 in Delta South and 1 in Inner Delta North. The 1979 survey included one craftsman in Delta North (Mchinga) (Havnevik, 1980).

Among some clans along the coast, craftsmanship is hereditary (Chole and Jibondo Islands). Apprenticeship requires at least to assist in the completion of one *mashua*. On becoming a craftsman the apprentice is given about one fourth of the tools needed by the master craftsman.

Construction usually takes place along a sandy beach, so that when the boat is completed it may easily be launched on a spring tide. A shelter is built over the site of construction by the future owner of the *mashua*.

The team building the *mashua* in Mchinga village consisted of a craftsman, one apprentice and four assistants or helpers. The apprentice was chosen by the craftsman and the assistants hired by the future owner. The apprentice and assistants were paid by the owner at a rate of Tsh. 14.60 a day. In addition the owner provided food; rice, beans, maize porridge and tea twice daily. What the master craftsman charges depends on the size of the boat and his proven skills as a craftsman. In this case the amount of Tsh. 6,000 was agreed upon in 1977. There was no written contract. When the boat is completed the craftsman might ask for a raise and the owner then has to agree to renegotiate the payment. The craftsman may be paid the full amount at either the beginning or the end of the construction period. The others are paid

Table 5.9. *Cost components in boat construction (mashua)*

		Tsh.
1.	Planks: *Mninga*, 4 koreja @ Tsh. 700,-	2,800
	Teak, 2 koreja @ Tsh. 800,-	1,600
	Transport from Mohoro to Mchinga	1,600
		6,000
2.	Ribs (taruma): *Mlilana* and *mkomafi* 8 pieces @ Tsh. 17,50	1,400
3.	Keel (kitako); *Msinsi* and *mikolwe*	120
4.	Stem (fashini): 2 pieces	250
5.	Deck (mafundo): Mkomafi, 12 @ Tsh. 20,-	240
6.	Deck supporters (miamba): Msikundazi, 4 pieces	400
7.	Magogo ya juu: 7 pieces @ Tsh. 20,-	140
		8,550
8.	Nails: 14 farasila of 16 kg @ Tsh. 20,-	4,480
9.	Mast	2,000
10.	Spar carrying the sail (foromali)	2,000
11.	Sail	4,000
12.	Anchors, 3 pieces	2,700
13.	Pump	3,000
14.	Paint	3,000
		29,730
15.	Labour costs:	
	5 assistants @ Tsh. 14,60 daily 312 days	22,776
	Craftsman	6,000
	Food: Tsh. 18,- a day for 312 days	5,616
	Total cost of the *mashua* Tsh.	64,122

Source: Havnevik, 1980

daily. If the owner is unable to pay, construction stops. It was difficult to work without a break because the craftsman and the assistants had other productive activities to attend to. On average construction was limited to four months a year, and everybody worked nine hours daily. It was estimated that the construction time for this *mashua* would stretch over three years, with an effective period of work of 12 months, i.e. 312 working days. The various cost components are spelled out in Table 5.9.

On the basis of the information put forward in Table 5.9 the return on labour for the craftsman and his assistant can be calculated. With food equalling Tsh. 0.33 an hour, an hourly return on labour for the craftsman comes to Tsh. 2.47, while that for the apprentice and the assistant comes to Tsh. 1.95.

During the survey conducted during 1979, construction of three other *mashua* were observed in the delta area, in Kiechuru, Kiasi and Kiomboni. Two were also seen on the adjacent Mafia Island.

The future owner of the *mashua* was engaged in copra production and fisheries and it was money accumulated from these activities which was spent on constructing the *mashua*.

Mat-making

Mat-making is by far the most important craft in terms of number of participants. Throughout the district a total of 12,966 people were engaged in the craft, 789 of whom were males. Male participation was particularly strong in West Valley (676). Men make mats from one type of grass while women utilise a different type (*ukindu*) which results in a finer type of mat. Flood Plain North is the most important area for mat production, with 5,224 participants.

Mat production is mainly for domestic use, only a small proportion is marketed. Market-oriented production is taken up by some of the UWT (Umoja wa Wanawake, i.e. in women cooperatives) units and coupled with other production activities. Three of these units were included in the survey, two in Delta South (Kiongoroni and Mbwera West) and one in Flood Plain North (Umwe). These three cooperatives were also surveyed in respect of other production activities: pottery and coconut oil production (Mbwera West), pottery (Kiongoroni) and embroidery and making clothes and pottery (Umwe). Two were established in 1978 and one in 1979. Two of the cooperatives had 30 members engaged in mat production, the third had 36 members, a total of 96 members. In addition, two craftswomen working individually in North Hill were included in the survey.

The inputs needed for mat production are rather modest, and generally easily accessible. Needles and knives can be obtained from the local blacksmith, while *ukindu* is in abundant supply. Procurement of colours is more difficult. Some are made locally and some are bought in the stores. Local production requires access to a certain type of root (black), bark (yellow) and a certain flower (red). In addition, firewood and water are needed to cook the colours and to transfer them to the *ukindu*. The grass mats produced by men are mainly made in natural colours.

Three units collected *ukindu* themselves (two cooperatives and one individual unit), while the two craftswomen made some of the colours themselves. The cost of colours for an average size multi-coloured *ukindu* mat was Tsh. 20. The local production of two colours required two days of labour and would reduce colour costs to Tsh. 15. One average sized mat requires 15 bundles of *ukindu* Tsh. 1 each. The cost of the tools was negligible, the needle was Tsh. 1 and the knife Tsh. 5. Needles are sometimes made from bicycle wheel spokes.

Production of an *ukindu* mat starts with preparing narrow lengths of leaf that are plaited to form strips (*ukili*). The length of each *ukili* equals that of the mat and the width is about 4–5 cm. The ends of each *ukili* are joined and then they are sewn together to form a large cylindrical piece. It is cut lengthwise and the rectangular mat piece appears. The input of labour for an average sized mat was 12 days, and the price obtained locally ranged from Tsh. 30 to 85, averaging Tsh. 53 for the five units. Calculation of the daily return on labour for mat production in the case in which two colours were produced locally and the *ukindu* was bought came to Tsh. 1.50.

The average length of the working day for mat production was estimated to be five hours at the most, giving an hourly return on labour of Tsh. 0.30.

The low level of labour input observed in the UWT cooperatives could not lead to any substantial production. In 1979 the three cooperatives estimated their annual production of mats to 24, 30 and 60 respectively. One of the units also produced covers for food. One of the individual craftswomen said that her yearly production was three mats, equivalent to a continuous labour input of one and a half month. The market was mainly in the villages, but most individual craftswomen, who are the bulk of the producers, limit production to what is needed for domestic use.

Pottery production

Pottery production is exclusively done by women. Of the seven units included in the survey four were individual pottery craftswomen without apprentices and three were UWT cooperatives. Four of the units were located in Flood Plain North (three individuals in Mkongo and one cooperative in Umwe), one individual in North Hill (Hanga) and two cooperatives in Delta South (Kiongoroni and Mbwera West). The individual craftswomen started operations in 1939, 1966 and 1974 respectively (one unknown). The cooperatives were all initiated in the late 1970s, two in 1978 and one in 1979. Participants in cooperative pottery production ranged from eight craftswomen in Umwe, two craftswomen and 28 apprentices in Kiongoroni and 30 craftswomen in Mbwera.

In total, 910 potters and 311 apprentices were recorded. Three-

Table 5.10. *Average input of labour for pottery production* (20 small pots)

Process	Time (hours)
Collection of clay	6.0
Shaping	20.0
Collection of firewood	5.5
Organisation, arranging and inspection of drying and burning process	8.5
Total	40.0

Average input of labour per pot: two hours

Note: The processes of drying and burning require little input of labour in themselves. Inspection is required during burning while labour is required to arrange the pots outside to dry in the sun every day and take them inside at night.
Source: Havnevik, 1980

quarters of the potters in the district work in North Hill, Flood Plain North and Delta South.

Pottery production consists of various processes: collection of clay, shaping and designing the pot, drying, burning, polishing and some times decorating it. All the units surveyed collected clay themselves. Due to the long distances involved collection time ranged from 3.5 to 9 hours. One load was sufficient to produce 20 small pots. The labour input of shaping and designing pots ranged from one to four hours depending on the size and decoration (none of the units had a pottery wheel). A piece of iron is used to shape the pot, while a maize cob, a special piece of wood or a mango husk are used for decorating it.

The pots are then dried in the sun. The average drying time is five days depending on the size and thickness of the clay. Fire wood is collected by the craftswomen themselves for burning and the average input of labour was 5.5 hours. Average burning time was computed at 3.5 hours ranging from one to six hours. Other inputs are a piece of cloth to wet the pot and some gum from trees to make the clay more cohesive if necessary. For polishing, a minor labour process, the bark of the mango tree is pounded and mixed with water, then washed over the pots which are then polished with a sea shell or a special stone. Input of labour for the production of 20 small pots is shown in Table 5.10.

The sales price for the small pots was Tsh. 3. My calculation shows that continuous production under average conditions gives an hourly return on labour of Tsh. 1.50, Tsh. 12 a day and Tsh. 312 a month (eight hours a day for 26 days).

The actual monthly incomes quoted for the individual craftswomen when they were working were Tsh. 280, Tsh. 300, Tsh. 150 to 750, and Tsh. 1,000. The analysis shows that the highest incomes were difficult to obtain even with very long working hours and high productivity. They could only be obtained if special decorations or artistic elements were introduced, including paints and colours of various kinds. The data indicate, however, that the input of labour during the period of production is high.

The input of labour in the cooperatives was, on the contrary, low. Members normally met twice a week for 2–4 hours. In addition, pottery production also had a seasonal character. The individual craftswomen made pots for a period of three to nine months annually. The cooperatives were in operation for three, four and nine months respectively, with very low weekly inputs of labour.

Raw materials were collected by the women themselves and the tools represented no investment due to their simple character. The only items bought were various paints and colours, mainly red and black. If available, tar was used for black.

The major products are various cooking pots and pans, lids, large pots for storing water and food, and cups. All the units said their respective villages were important markets; people either come to the site of production or the craftswomen bring their pots to the village market. One individual unit sold at markets at the divisional level and one cooperative had markets in the district and beyond. In this case the members used buses to reach the market or a UWT vehicle came to collect the products.

General problems were lack of markets, transport especially when moving clay to the work site and lack of proper working sheds. One cooperative built a special working shed for pottery. Another cooperative said specifically that the low input of labour was partly caused by the attitudes of men, who prevented them from participating in the cooperative. This issue is related to the more general one of relieving women of some of their numerous duties in the household, with child rearing and in agricultural production.

Since 1985 the Norwegian non-governmental organisation supporting blacksmiths and tinsmiths has also assisted a UWT pottery cooperative in Ikwiriri together with SIDO (Small Industries Development Organisation). Initially eight to ten women were actively engaged in production which started in a newly erected shed early in 1987. Training was provided by a potter financed by Norwegian aid. An attempt was made to improve the technique by introducing simple pottery wheels. It turned out that the women used to shaping pots by hand could not get used to the wheel, hence they continued to use their traditional skills. Young girls with no prior experience of pottery have, however, been successfully trained to operate the pottery wheels.

In August 1987 the women, most of them single, came nearly every day for four to six hours. In between pottery production they plaited mats. Some produced high quality products. A new product introduced onto a readily available market was the clay charcoal stove which considerably reduces the energy used in cooking compared to the present open fire method. In addition, cooking pots, flower pots and water jars were produced. A charcoal stove was selling for around Tsh. 100 in 1987. With greater work discipline and somewhat longer working hours a woman could produce two such stoves per day, which meant that this production line was economically viable if a market was secured. The most recent information obtained about this unit (September 1992) indicate that its' production has ceased and that the premises are used as a hostel.

Coconut oil production

A total of 4,715 producers of coconut oil were recorded in the 1979 survey, 4,295 were females and 420 males. The major areas coincide with the areas abundant in coconut groves. Delta South had 53.6 per cent of coconut oil producers, Delta North 19.1 per cent and North Hill 11.9 per cent.

Except for a UWT cooperative in Mbwera West, all production was undertaken on an individual basis. Male producers were mainly oriented towards the market, while women produced mainly for domestic consumption. The UWT group started in 1978 and had 31 members involved in coconut oil production. Production of coconut oil was usually limited to the period of July to September. The rest of the year producers worked on agriculture. During the period of production work was carried out for 6.5 hours, two days a week. The group was divided into two units of 15 members, each working one day a week. A coordinator worked full time, i.e. two days a week. Some of the work was carried out in the members' homes. All the instruments belonged to individuals.

Coconuts were purchased from various coconut grove owners in the area at Tsh. 0.50 apiece in 1979. The outer shell of the coconut is split open by a wooden stick planted in the ground and sharpened at the upper end (mfuo wa kufulia). The shell is broken by using a matchet. The coconut meat is removed with a special grater (*kibao cha mbuzi*), which is produced either by a carpenter or a blacksmith. The ground

meat is soaked in water and liquid is extracted by squeezing it by hand.
Up to this point production takes one day. The liquid is then put aside
for two days after which the oil floats to the top. It is separated from
the water and boiled. After boiling, the bottom (*kashata ya mafuta*)
settles and remains in the pan while the finished oil is bottled. The
kashata is boiled with water and more oil is extracted.

Firewood and water have to be collected for two boiling processes.
Ten coconuts provide 3/4 litre of oil (one bottle). 30 bottles amount to
one debe. The average weekly production was four debes, which required 1,200 coconuts at Tsh. 0.50 each and four debes costing Tsh. 8
each. The weekly input of labour for the two sub-groups of 15 members and the full-time coordinator was 208 hours.

The market was mainly outside the coconut growing areas. Two
representatives of the UWT group travelled to other areas to sell, in
villages like Mohoro, Chumbi, Utete, Mkongo and Ikwiriri. The input
of labour in marketing was estimated to be 32 hours, for two persons
for two days of eight hours and the costs were Tsh. 60. Information
from other groups showed that men often acted as marketing agents
for women producers.

The total input of labour for the UWT group came to 265 hours a
week and the total costs amounted to Tsh. 766. The gross income from
sales equivalent to four debes was Tsh. 1,320. Bottling costs were based
on the assumption that weekly sales were two debes or 60 bottles. With
net weekly earnings of Tsh. 554, the hourly return on labour was Tsh.
2.09.

Half the net income at any time was spent on buying coconuts to
keep production going. At the end of every season of up to three
months the money remaining after deduction of expenditures was
shared equally among the members. In 1978 this amounted to Tsh.
3,600, the equivalent of an effective production period of six to seven
weeks. At the end of each season no money was left with the cashier.
To start the project each year, each member contributed Tsh. 10 to 15
for buying coconuts.

In 1979 the UWT tried to launch a soap project using coconut oil as
the raw material. SIDO had prepared a feasibility study and provided
Tsh. 55,200 in the form of a hire-purchase loan in 1978. From village
funds Tsh. 5,000 were given to enable the UWT group to make the
necessary 10 per cent down payment on the loan. Six youngsters were
sent to learn to operate the pressing machine and stayed for three
months at the SIDO training school in Kilosa. Part of the machinery
was supplied in August 1979. A SIDO report on Hire-Purchase projects in Coast Region (March 20, 1982) said that action should be taken
to identify which machinery parts were missing and what could be

done to procure them. This initiative proved fruitless. Information obtained in subsequent years indicated that soap production in Mbwera village never took off.

Jaggery production

Jaggery or brown sugar (*sukari guru*) is a poorly purified sugar product produced from sugar cane grown on the banks of the Rufiji river. Jaggery production has long traditions in the Rufiji delta area, being initiated in the last century when manually operated sugar cane presses were imported. One press arrived in 1873. Another press which was inspected during the survey was manufactured in 1916 in Ohio, USA.

A total of nine jaggery producing units, eight in Inner Delta South (Mohoro) and one in Delta South (Ndundutawa) were recorded. Each unit consisted of one craftsman who was in charge of the boiling, a process requiring specific skills, one assistant and ten workers. The owner of the sugar cane field hired the production team and provided the cane and necessary means of production, a cane press and boiling pan. One production cycle consisted of filling a drum with cane juice, which took four hours, and the subsequent boiling, five hours. The data and information presented below are based on interviews with a craftsman, a worker and a cane field owner.

The craftsman entered the craft of jaggery boiling in Mohoro in 1939. His father taught him the skills in the course of one year. The craftsman and his assistant were responsible for the boiling process, in which lime was used for purification, and cleaning the pan. Two workers fed the cane press and the other eight workers, organised in two groups, provided continuous manual labour to run the press. It was done by turning a horizontal wooden bar, two workers at each end, which was connected to the grinder by a perpendicular axle. In the heat this work is physically extremely demanding.

Under average conditions one acre of processed sugar cane fills twelwe drums with juice. The input of labour in clearing, hoeing, planting and weeding was estimated to be 50 working days. Cutting and transporting the cane from the field to the processing site were estimated to require ten working days. The labour needed for transport obviously depended on the location of the field in relation to the press. This distance was reduced by moving the presses, though they had to be placed under a big tree to provide shade for the team of workers. Total labour input for cane growing was 60 days for one acre, which meant five days of labour to provide raw material for one drum of cane

Table 5.11. *Production costs and hourly return on labour in jaggery production (pressing and boiling one drum of cane juice)*

	Individual input of labour	Cost per production unit (Tsh.)	Hourly return on labour (Tsh.)
Labour costs			
1. Two press feeders @ 2,-	4 hrs.	4,-	0.50
2. Manual labour to run press, 8 workers @ 3,50	2 hrs.	28,-	1.75
3. Craftsman: Tsh. 10 per boiling plus equivalent in naturalia	5 hrs.	20,-	4,-
4. Craftsman's assistant: Tsh. 5,- worth of naturalia	5 hrs.	5,-	1,-
5. Food for workers per unit produced	-	6,-	-
Total labour related costs		63,-	
Input costs			
6. Lime for purification	Tsh. 2.50		
7. Firewood, 6 logs @ 2,-	Tsh. 12,-	14.50	
Rent			
8. To owner of press per filling	Tsh. 10,-		
9. To owner of pan per boiling	Tsh. 10,-	20,-	
Total cost per production unit		97.50	

Source: Havnevik, 1980

juice. Assuming a working day of six hours, labour input amounted to 30 hours.

The remuneration on labour and the cost of hiring tools for processing and boiling are quoted for a drum of cane juice. The craftsman and his assistant were paid partly in kind (jaggery) which is converted into shillings. The cost of pressing and boiling one drum of cane juice is shown in Table 5.11.

The final equivalent of one drum of cane juice is 2,75 *farasila* (one *farasila* equals 16 kg) of jaggery. The selling price of a *farasila* at the production site was Tsh. 100 in 1979, implying gross earnings of Tsh. 275 per drum. The owner of the sugar cane field usually arranges for the labour for cane growing and processing. His gross earnings per drum were Tsh. 177,50. In addition to the labour input for growing cane, two nine hour days are added for organisation and one for inspection, bringing the total labour required to 57 hours. The hourly return on labour for the cane field owner thus came to Tsh. 3.11. My calculations of returns on labour show a range of Tsh. 0.50 to Tsh. 4 per hour for the various categories of labour involved.

The owner of the means of production, namely the press and the pan, appropriated a rent equalling 32 per cent of the total labour related costs. These implements are passed from father to son and provide a basis for accumulation. There are seven such presses in the Mohoro area.

There was no problem of marketing the jaggery. Middlemen bought it wholesale at the site of production. The retail prices recorded indicated that large profits accrued to middlemen. Jaggery was marketed throughout the district during the production season, which lasted three to four months in the dry season. Buyers also came from Dar es Salaam and Lindi.

The craftsman interviewed was engaged in jaggery boiling for six months of the year. In the rainy season he cultivated six acres of various crops.

SUMMARY OF FEATURES OF NON-AGRICULTURAL PRODUCTION

In this summary the complete results from the investigation of 27 individual crafts, forestry and fishing activities are included. This will make in possible to better understand the overall role of these activities in the district economy.

Participation and type of production

A major finding of my survey of non-agricultural production in Rufiji District was that large numbers of the rural population participated. The total number of nominal participants in this sector was 50,727 (see Table 5.12), which is 38.7 per cent of the total (131,055) and 76.9 per cent of the active working population (65,991) in the age range of 15–64 years (South Hill excluded) in 1979 (see Table 5.13). Crafts were of major importance, where a total of 34,408 nominal participants were recorded, including 1,433 apprentices. This total figure can be compared to 16,319 for fishing and forestry. While there were 27 different crafts there were only five other non-agricultural activities, mainly forest exploitation and fishing. Participation in these activities was more evenly distributed. The major activities of fishing, mangrove cutting and charcoal production attracted between 3,000 and 7,000 nominal participants.

The number of real producers was somewhat lower than the nomi-

Table 5.12. *Distribution of skilled labour, apprentices and producers in non-agricultural activities, Rufiji District*

Type of craft	North Hill	West Valley	Flood Plain North	Flood Plain South	Inner Delta North	Inner Delta South	Delta North	Delta South	Males	Females	Total
Forestry based											
Carpentry and saw milling (M)	221	26	206	124	84	109	39	357	1166	-	1166
Wooden beds (M)	187	94	471	38	65	115	33	154	1157	-	1157
Mortar making (M)	59	32	75	14	14	2	2	36	234	-	234
Canoe making (M)	12	127	330	48	65	32	107	160	881	-	881
Masonry (M)	81	51	94	24	36	34	8	74	402	-	402
Mat making (M)	84	676	14	15	-	-	-	-	789		
(F)	1280	122	5210	466	1287	1261	892	1659	-	12177	12966
Agriculturally based											
Jaggery prod. (M)	-	-	-	-	-	8	-	1	9	-	9
-unskilled ass. (M)	-	-	-	-	-	96	-	14	110	-	110
Coconut oil (M)	145	-	-	-	55	-	-	220	420		
(F)	420	-	-	-	669	-	899	2307	-	4295	4715
Grain milling (M)	3	-	3	-	-	-	-	-	6	-	6
-assistants (M)	10	-	-	-	-	-	-	-	10	-	10
Thatching (M)	500	-	-	548	100	65	18	1413	2644	-	
(F)	-	-	-	-	-	-	107	55	-	162	2806
Agriculturally related											
Basketry (M)	299	115	416	56	54	20	13	5	978	-	
(F)	52	35	118	-	16	15	48	453	-	737	1715
Pottery (F)	254	84	172	3	90	26	61	531	-	1221	1221
Skill based											
Blacksmith (M)	74	20	30	14	21	16	3	28	206	-	206
Carving (M)	137	-	5	-	3	1	-	6	152	-	152
Mashua (M)	-	-	-	-	-	1	32	19	52	-	52
Embroidery (F)	113	11	697	62	40	53	-	105	-	1081	1081
Tailoring (M)	94	39	93	29	46	40	36	139	516	-	516
Shoe repair (M)	12	5	18	2	2	1	-	7	47	-	47
Bicycle repair (M)	58	20	109	21	30	20	2	32	292	-	292
Radio repair (M)	8	3	12	4	7	4	3	21	62	-	62
Watch repair (M)	3	1	5	3	7	3	1	28	51	-	51
Mechanic (M)	3	-	7	1	-	9	1	-	21		21
Kofia (M)	-	-	63	13	-	18	61	421	576	-	
(F)	-	-	10	-	-	-	-	-	-	10	586
Kibao cha mbuzi (M)	-	-	-	11	-	7	2	27	47	-	47
Others											
Brick making (M)	131	42	213	2	70	20	15	49	542	-	542
Salt produce (M)	55	-	10	-	208	-	27	596	896	-	
(F)	82	10	10	-	380	-	369	1379	-	2230	3126
Fish net (wando) (M)	-	-	-	-	-	-	72	20	92	-	92
Others (M)	62	6	10	25	17	6	-	11	137	-	137
Sub-total crafts	4,439	1,519	8,401	1,523	3,366	1,982	2,851	10,327	12,495	21,913	34,408

Type of craft	North Hill	West Valley	Flood Plain North	Flood Plain South	Inner Delta North	Inner Delta South	Delta North	Delta South	Males	Females	Total
Forestry based											
Honey collection (M)	12	112	81	32	46	10	10	147	450	-	450
Mangrove cutting (M)	-	-	-	-	581	37	892	1588	3098	-	3098
Logging (M)	101	-	51	100	-	10	-	-	262	-	262
Charcoal (M)	3514	13	1199	35	182	67	-	1	5011	-	
(F)	183	-	413	-	-	-	-	-	-	596	5607
Others											
Fishing (M)	94	244	320!	578	678	212	494	1401	6902	-	6902
Subtotal	3,904	369	4,945	745	1,487	366	1,396	3,137	15,723	596	16,319
Totals	8,343	1,888	13,346	2,268	4,853	2,318	4,247	13,464	28,218	22,509	50,727

Notes: The category mechanic includes car mechanic, gun craftsman, welder and boat engine. Others include crafts like animal trap making, chokaa, drums, lorry boards, kanzu, bakers, vibatari, and other special craftsmen.
  Abbreviations used: M (male), F (female), ass. (assistants)
  The following numbers of apprentices are included: Carpentry and saw milling (384), Canoe making (72), Masonry (2), Pottery (311), Embroidery and clothes (520), Tailoring (110), Mechanic (4) and Brick making (30).
Source: Author's survey 1979

nal, because some people took part in more than one type of production in the course of the year. This was particularly true of the agro-economic zones of Inner Delta North, Delta North and Delta South. If we assume that 20 per cent of the active population participate on average in two kinds of production, a reasonable assumption based on the features of the agro-economic zones, the total number of real participants in non-agricultural activities comes to 42,273. This means that 64 per cent of the active population, about six out of every ten people, channel labour to these activities (South Hill excluded). Conditions for multiple participation were mainly found in the agro-economic zones of Inner Delta North, Delta North and Delta South where 23.7 per cent of the active working population of the district live. ·

The rate of nominal participation, the percentage of nominal participants of the active working population, is related to several factors: conditions of agricultural production, availability of or access to resources and tools, conditions for transport, access to markets and the availability of basic household commodities. In the light of the variations between agro-economic zones, it is to be expected that the rates of nominal participants vary, particularly in the different ecological zones, the delta in the east and the flood plain and the hill zones in the west.

Table 5.13. *Nominal participant rates according to agro-economić zones in non-agricultural production*

Agro-economic zone	Total number of nominal participants	Total population	Population in age group 15-64 (active)	% age of nominal participants to total population	Nominal participant rates
North Hill					
- totals	8,343	36,821	18,543	22.7%	44.9%
- male	5,959	17,774	8,372	33.5%	71.2%
- female	2,384	19,047	10,171	12.5%	23.4%
West Valley					
- totals	1,888	11,891	5,985	15.9%	31.5%
- male	1,626	5,623	2,648	28.9%	61.4%
- female	262	6,268	3,337	4.2%	7.9%
Flood Plain North					
- totals	13,346	31,971	16,140	41.7%	82.7%
- males	6,716	14,796	6,969	45.4%	96.4%
- females	6,630	17,175	9,171	38.6%	72.3%
Flood Plain South					
- totals	2,268	10,428	5,232	21.7%	43.3%
- male	1,737	5,085	2,517	34.2%	69.0%
- female	531	5,343	2,715	9.9%	19.6%
Inner Delta North					
- totals	4,853	10,708	5,400	45.3%	89.9%
- male	2,371	5,049	2,378	47.0%	99.7%
- female	2,482	5,659	3,022	43.9%	82.1%
Inner Delta South					
- totals	2,318	8,884	4,482	26.1%	51.7%
- male	963	4,155	1,957	23.2%	49.2%
- female	1,355	4,729	2,525	28.7%	53.7%
Delta North					
- totals	4,247	3,620	1,821	117.3%	233.2%
- male	1,871	1,769	833	105.8%	224.6%
- female	2,376	1,851	988	128.4%	240.5%
Delta South					
- totals	13,464	16,732	8,450	80.5%	159.3%
- male	6,975	7,706	3,630	90.5%	192.1%
- female	6,489	9,026	4,820	71.9%	134.6%
TOTALS	50,727	131,055	66,053		

Note: Nominal participant rate is the percentage of nominal participants to active population, defined as those in age range 15-64 years. Nominal participant figures are not taking into account that some producers participate in more than one line of production throughout the year, when correcting for this multi-participation the number of real participants during the year is arrived at.

Sources: Figures are derived from Table 5.12 and the *1978 Population Census*

The nominal participant rates (see Table 5.13) showed the highest values in Delta North and Delta South, a reflection of the particularly good conditions for multiple participation. Inner Delta South recorded low rates, similar to those of Flood Plain South, which is due to difficult access to the sea and the location of major markets in the north. The only zone outside the delta with a relatively high participant rate was Flood Plain North, which is related to the area's access to the flood plain fishing grounds and to the markets in the north, notably Dar es Salaam. The relatively low rate for Flood Plain South is mainly explained by difficult access to major markets, due to the river, and not because of access to resources. The agro-economic zone with the lowest rate of multiple participation was West Valley, reflecting its difficult position in terms of access to resources, transport problems and climatic conditions (low rainfall). The nominal participant rates revealed another tendency, namely high female participation in the delta zones, both in absolute and relative (to male) terms. There are probably several reasons for the distinction between the delta and the other areas: the delta is richer in resources and has relatively easy access to markets; it experienced relatively little disruption during the villagisation campaigns; and women's right of inheritance (matrilineal people) has secured them some assets, for instance coconut groves. The explanation for women's differing participant rates is complicated and requires further research into the social and economic structures in the area.

Gender-specific distribution of participation

Another major finding of the 1979 survey (Havnevik, 1980 and 1983) was the gender-specific distribution of participation in types of non-agricultural production. In crafts female participation was high in a few activities, particularly mat-making (12,177), coconut oil (4,295) and salt production (2,230). Women were represented in only eight out of the 27 crafts investigated; mat-making, basketry, pottery, embroidery and making clothes, coconut oil, salt production, thatching and making kofias (embroidered Muslim hat). Pottery, embroidery and making clothes were exclusively women's crafts (see Table 5.14). The women's participation in crafts amounted to 63.7 per cent of the total number of nominal participants.

Men participated in 25 of 27 crafts. They were exclusive in 19 crafts while there was mixed gender participation in six. There were differences in men's and women's production in these crafts in terms of raw materials used (mat-making), organisation (women worked cooperatively to a larger extent) and market orientation (men were more market oriented).

Table 5.14.   *Womens' participation in non-agricultural production*

Crafts	Nominal participants*	% of total**
Mat-making	12,177	87.2%
Coconut oil production	4,295	91.1%
Salt production	2,230	71.3%
Pottery	1,221	100.0%
Embroidery and clothes production	1,081	100.0%
Basketry	737	43.0%
Thatching	162	5.8%
Kofia (hat)	10	1.7%
Sub-total	21,913	63.7%
Other		
Charcoal	596	10.6%
Total	22,509	44.4%

*For an explanation of nominal participants, see note on Table 5.13.
**The number of women in relation to the total number of nominal participants in that activity.
Source: Havnevik, 1980

The major crafts with only male participation were making wooden beds, carpentry, running saw mills and building canoes. The highest male participation was in thatching. Characteristic of male participation was its relatively even distribution over the 25 crafts. Apart from thatching and making wooden beds, not more than 1,000 craftsmen participated in any craft.

Other non-agricultural activities, mainly forestry and fishing, were almost exclusively dominated by men. Charcoal production was an exception with 596 women, 10.6 per cent of the total, participating. Women faced the same conditions of production and had the same market orientation as men who produced charcoal.

Skills, gender and return on labour

The number of participants in non-agricultural activities provides no measure of that sector's economic importance in terms of *income generation* for producers, and the local and national economy. This section focuses on *return on labour* in cash terms for the various types of production and assessment of the corresponding potential cash income for producers. The latter is the income which accrues to producers if they continuously allocate their daily labour to a single type of production and manage to sell everything they produce. The large discrepancy between potential and actual incomes indicates that the producer does as part-time or seasonal work or that part of the production is directly consumed by the household. The total income generated, including cash income, is accordingly related to the amount of work done.

Due to data constraints, returns on labour were calculated for only 20 of the 27 crafts investigated. For the purpose of analysis the returns on labour were divided into four categories (Category I, hourly return on labour up to Tsh. 1; Category II, from Tsh. 1 to Tsh. 2; Category III, from Tsh. 2 to Tsh. 3; and Category IV, above Tsh. 3) (see Table 5.15).

Most crafts fall in categories II and III. The seven crafts of category II (saw milling, canoe building, masonry, pottery, salt production, shoe repairs and fishnet production) had an average return on labour of Tsh. 1.51 per hour. In the seven crafts of category III (blacksmith, carpentry, carving, boat construction (*mashua*), tailoring, coconut oil production and bicycle repairs), the average return on labour was Tsh. 2.45 an hour. The potential monthly income of craftsmen and women of Category II, i.e. if they were to produce continuously throughout the month, was only slightly higher than the official minimum wage for rural areas at the time of the survey. The potential monthly income of category III producers reached Tsh. 510. The rural minimum wage at the time of the survey was Tsh. 280 a month, while the urban minimum wage was Tsh. 380.

A characteristic feature of underdevelopment of the rural economy is the difficulty of earning such potential incomes, another that the bulk of producers belongs to the lowest category of income. 56.8 per cent of the nominal participants were engaged in the four crafts in Category I (wooden beds, mortar-making, mat-making and basketry) for which the average hourly return on labour was Tsh. 0.48 and the potential monthly income about Tsh. 100, only 30 per cent of the official rural minimum wage.

The bulk of the craftswomen, 63.5%, belongs to two of the lowest categories of crafts (mat-making and basketry)[1]. Two other women's

---

[1] Of the eight crafts in which women participated the rate of return on labour was calculated for five. In these calculations only craftswomen were included.

Table 5.15.   *Distribution of crafts on labour return categories*

| | Labour return categories | | | |
	I Up to Tsh. 1	II Tsh. 1–2	III Tsh. 2–3	IV Above and inclusive Tsh. 3
Number of Crafts	4	7	7	2
% of total crafts (20)	20%	35%	35%	10%
Average hourly return	Tsh. 0.48	Tsh. 1.51	Tsh. 2.45	Tsh. 5.91
Crafts included:	Wooden beds Mortar-making Mat-making Basketry	Saw milling Canoe building Masonry Pottery Salt prod. Shoe repairs Fishnet prod.	Blacksmith Carpentry Carving Boat construction Tailoring Coconut oil production Bicycle repairs	Jaggery Watch repairs
Potential monthly income; 8 hrs a day 26 days a month (208 hrs)	Tsh. 100,-	Tsh. 314,-	Tsh. 510,-	Tsh. 1.229,-
No. of nominal participants	16,072	5,866	6,305	60
% of total nominal participants	56.8%	20.7%	22.3%	0.2%

Source: Havnevik, 1980

activities are in Category II (pottery and salt production) and one in category III (coconut oil production). Even though nearly two thirds of the craftswomen were in the lowest income category, women's extensive participation in crafts with higher cash income earnings, showed that their work was not limited to low returns on labour. In crafts with mixed gender participation, the tendency was for men to produce for the market while women produced for domestic consumption (salt and coconut oil). The establishment of several women's cooperatives during the latter half of the 1970s was expected to direct women's production increasingly to the market. The Tanzanian national women's organization, UWT, had 23 branches in Rufiji District

(April 1979) and most were engaged in cooperative production. Some branches had initiated more than one cooperative. The total membership was 1,360. The UWT was assisted by the office of Adult Education, Elimu Ufundi, Rufiji District.

The return on labour tended to be better remunerated the higher the level of skill required by the craft. Most of the crafts of Category III involved longer training and more skills than those of Category II. In many areas the skills of jaggery boiling (Category IV) and boat construction (mashua) (Category III) are exclusively passed on from father to son, thereby limiting the scope for the dissemination of these skills.

This tendency is modified by several factors, some reinforcing, others counteracting it. On the one hand, most crafts of Category I seems to require a similar level of skill as those of Category II. The different returns accordingly do not reflect different levels of skill, but the large number of participants in Category I who produce for domestic consumption or a limited market cause returns to be lower than in Category II. On the other hand, the limited number of craftsmen producing for markets with a high purchasing power like repairing bicycles and watches commands a relatively higher return than can be accounted for by the skill level alone.

In other non-agricultural production returns on labour were much more evenly distributed than in the crafts. This was to be expected as they required a more uniform level of skill. Except for the collection of honey which had a return on labour of Tsh. 4.62 per hour, returns were within the range of Tsh. 1 to Tsh. 2.50. Returns were calculated for charcoal production, Tsh 1.09, cutting mangroves, Tsh. 2.50 for export and Tsh. 1,50 for the domestic market, and fishing, Tsh. 2.50 for the professional and Tsh. 1.25 for the part-time fishing (related only to river plain fishing). The average hourly return on non-agricultural activities, excluding crafts and honey collection, came to Tsh. 1.71, about 13 per cent higher than the average returns of Tsh. 1.51 for crafts in Category II.

This relatively high remuneration on activities related to fishery and forestry as compared to crafts can be largely explained by the demand created by an outside market, whether national or international. They command a purchasing power far greater than that of the local economy. Charcoal, timber, mangroves and fish have major markets in Dar es Salaam, while mangroves and fish, especially prawns, are in demand even on international markets. One should not be left with the impression that the higher level of purchasing power of these outside markets is directly transferred to the local economy. The data show that although local producers benefit to some extent, middlemen and intermediary bodies (transporters and state bodies) appropriate the major share of the final selling price. The share of the final selling price retained by producers was about 25 per cent in fishing (prawns), 30 per cent in charcoal production and about 50 per cent in mangrove cutting. An important finding is that the level of cash incomes in fishery and forestry has improved relative to agricultural exports, causing a shift in peasant production priorities. This issue will be further analysed in Chapter 7.

Organisation of non-agricultural production

The dominant mode of organisation of non-agricultural production in Rufiji District is private operations of individuals, in some cases the craftsman or craftswoman work together with one or more apprentices.

In the survey only 80 organised cooperatives and private groups were registered, on average one per surveyed village. The organised units had 1,633 producers, amounting to 3.9 per cent of the estimated total number, 42,273 participating in non-agricultural activities. In a study of crafts in Rukwa Region, Perkins found 5.4 per cent of the participants were cooperative members. This finding is not directly comparable to Rufiji District as it excludes all privately organised units, both individuals and groups (Perkins, 1978). In a study of 70 small industries in the rural areas of 13 districts, Wangwe found collective ownership, either by village or cooperative, to exist in 76 per cent of the units (Wangwe, 1979). A considerable number of units in Wangwe's study are small scale industries employing machines, while Perkin's and the present study include mainly non-industrial units.

Of the 80 organised groups in Rufiji District, 59 were cooperatives and 21 were privately organised, usually smaller than the cooperatives. Of the total, 757 participants were male and 876 female. The average per group was about 20. Most women were members of UWT cooperatives engaged in embroidery and making clothes, pottery, mat-making and coconut oil production, while organised male producers were found mainly in carpentry and saw mills, carving, blacksmithing, fishing and charcoal production (See Table 5.16).

The Technical Office of Adult Education (Elimu Ufundi) most actively assists cooperatives throughout the district. In 1977/78 the office assisted 49 cooperatives; 37 home economic cooperatives with 896 women members and 12 carpentry cooperatives with 224 men. It should be noted that the 49 cooperatives assisted by the Office of Adult Education in 1977/78 are not directly comparable to the 59 cooperatives recorded during the survey in 1979. This is due to cooperatives

Table 5.16. *The distribution of organised groups in agro-economic zones, organisational forms and gender*

Agro-economic zone	Total no. of groups	Organisational form		Employment			Line of activities
		Coop.	Private	M	F	Tot.	
1. North Hill	20	16	4	338	118	456	Carpentry and saw mills, carving, UWT-groups, charcoal, milling
2. West Valley	1	-	1	5	-	5	Blacksmiths
3. Flood Plain North	23	16	7	168	165	333	Carpentry and saw mills, blacksmiths, making bricks, milling grain, UWT group
4. Flood Plain South	8	5	3	40	54	94	Blacksmiths, carpentry, fishing and making clothes
5. Inner Delta North	7	7	-	56	238	294	Carpentry and saw milling, fishing, pottery and UWT-groups
6. Inner Delta South	8	4.	4	46	53	99	Carpentry and saw mills, embroidery and UWT groups
7. Delta North	2	2	-	16	5	21	Salt production and thatching
8. Delta South	11	9	2	88	243	331	Carpentry, saw mills and a UWT group
Total	80	59	21	757	876	1,663	

Source: Havnevik, 1980

closing down and starting up in the intervening period and because some existing cooperatives supported by Adult Education were not included in the survey as they were dormant or out of operation.

Organised groups were largely concentrated in North Hill and

Flood Plain North, 32 were cooperatives and 11 private groups. Organised groups hardly existed in West Valley (one private group with five members) and Delta North (two cooperatives with 21 members). The number of producers organised in groups was highest in North Hill (456), Flood Plain North (333), Delta South (331) and Inner Delta North (294). While men predominated in North Hill and Flood Plain North, women dominated organised activities in Inner Delta North and Delta South.

Major problems and preliminary conclusions

A limited sub-survey focussing on major constraints, revealed that 30 craft units faced the following problems: (Havnevik, 1980.)

	Character of problem	No. of units
1.	Unavailability of tools	83%
2.	Transport to workshop	80%
3.	Unreliable supply of raw materials	70%
4.	Credit for tools	67%
5.	Lack of markets	43%
6.	No repair facilities	40%

A breakdown of the major problems shows that the character of 1, 4 and 6 represents the overall problem of *access to tools*, 2 and 3 that of *access to raw materials* and 5 *access to markets*. The relatively low ranking of the problem of lack of markets is related to the fact that 26 of the 30 units investigated were located in the agro-economic zones North Hill and Flood Plain North, both with easy access to the markets of Dar es Salaam.

The problems are similar to those found among crafts in Rukwa Region, with a slightly different emphasis on categories of problems: "From surveys of the current state of small scale industry and crafts within the region (Rukwa), it became apparent that the major factors inhibiting short run production increases were shortages of and difficulty in obtaining *raw materials* (76%) and *tools* (61%), *lack of credit* (85%) to enable purchase of those, or to build workshops, difficulty in *transporting finished products to markets* (57%) outside the village and finding established *outlets* (79%) for them there" (Perkins, 1978, emphasis added). In his survey of 13 districts Wangwe found that 36 per cent of the sampled units faced major transport problems for inputs to workshop and 24 per cent had problems of transporting products to markets. Wangwe defined a major problem as one leading to curtailment of production (Wangwe, 1979).

The nature and number of constraints facing crafts indicate that there is a set of general problems linked to the workings of the total Tanzanian economy, rather than a set of individual problems related to a specific type of production in a certain locality. If this is correct, there may be limited scope for solving "local problems" through intervention from above. Any attempt to improve the situation requires an intimate knowledge of the conditions facing each activity and of the potential for linkages between them. Such an analysis will provide guidance for the sequencing of efforts to solve problems both in terms of type of product and for the focus within that particular line. For instance, improvement of access to tools or raw materials for one craft may ease production-related problems and increase productivity. If no additional purchasing power exists, however, the overall problem remains unsolved. "Problem solving" at the local level must include an analysis of inter-relating local conditions with the wider economy. However, most importantly, the actual producers must be genuinely mobilised through perceiving the projects as promoting their own interests and welfare. In Tanzania, including Rufiji District, too many state supported and external aid-based, small industrial projects have already failed due to the omission of one or more of these elements at the initiation, planning or implementation stages. (see Chapters 2 and 9 for more comprehensive national and sectoral analyses.)

Production related to fishery and forestry faces no lack of demand in the market. Fish, charcoal, mangroves and logs are in high demand in external markets, particularly Dar es Salaam. Forestry requires fewer tools than most crafts, while some fishing would benefit from greater selection of gear. The major problem faced by forestry is the serious threat to the reproduction of resources because of the intensification of charcoal production, logging and collection of fuel wood by nucleated settlements. Increase of forest royalties, better control of exploitation and more seriousness in work related to afforestation are important elements in the fight against deforestation. The threats confronting fishing and mangrove cutting are related more to the fragility of the ecological system. A drastic change to the regime of the Rufiji river, as envisaged in the Stiegler's Gorge project, would, however, affect the ecology of the flood plain and delta systems drastically (Sandberg 1974b; Kjekshus,1977b; Havnevik, 1978; Hopson, 1979; Hafslund, 1980 and VHL, 1979). I will return to the implications of the Stiegler's Gorge project in Chapter 8. The more recent threat to overexploitation of natural resources stemming from liberalisation of the economy will be taken up in Chapter 9.

The survey of non-agricultural production clearly shows the large and increasing role of major lines of these activities during the latter part of the 1970s and early 1980s. This most often implied diversification of peasant labour away from state controlled marketing channels and a further informalisation of the rural economy. These issues will be further analysed in Chapter 7.

6. Major Forms of State Intervention in Rural Production

State intervention in production activities in the rural areas occurs at the level of both production and circulation. It is important to distinguish between these two levels, because the effects of intervention at either level may differ. My hypothesis is that intervention at the level of circulation will mainly have an impact on the control and composition of the agricultural surplus, while intervention in the sphere of production will be more directly related to the size of the surplus. It is, however, impossible to clearly distinguish between the effects, as marketing arrangements and price policies may also have indirect effects on productivity and the volume of production.

The object of this chapter is to describe and analyse the four major mechanisms of state intervention related to rural production. Two are located in the sphere of circulation: agricultural marketing and price policies, including the terms of trade; and two are related to the sphere of production: villagisation and the imposition of bye-laws. These four mechanisms are central to the intervention of the state in rural production. It is important to understand their origins and intentions as well as the way they are implemented, singly or to complement each other.

HISTORICAL OVERVIEW OF EXPERIENCES AT NATIONAL LEVEL

Agricultural marketing

One hypothesis of this part is that agricultural marketing in the post-colonial period was aimed at improving state control of the agricultural surplus that originated in peasant production. An additional reason for changing the marketing structures in the post-colonial period was the intention of doing away with exploitative relations in the rural areas, which meant displacing the non-African traders.

In order to support the above hypothesis, the analysis of market arrangements will have to show that the objective of the post-colonial government's control of agricultural marketing was not just to promote a policy of expansion of government activities. Rather, the increasing control, first through intervention and later through abolition of the cooperative unions, had to be connected with the motive to gain control of the agricultural surplus. Support for the above hypothesis will also require the questioning of the official motives for state intervention: the defense of the ordinary peasants against an increasingly corrupt and inefficient leadership within the marketing organisations.

In principle there are three ways a government can organise collection of agricultural crops from the peasants: by giving the task to private agents, by persuading or forcing peasants to sell through cooperative marketing organisations or by the state creating its own institutions for handling these tasks. In much of the literature on arrangements for agricultural marketing, there has been a tendency to focus mainly on economic efficiency in handling crops and to disregard the fact that the role of cooperatives often goes far beyond crop collection. Cooperatives may supply credit and inputs, process agricultural produce and in addition they represent a network of relations that are of importance to the peasants and their communities. In a sense, they could be likened to a social movement that plays a mediating role between the state and the peasantry (Hedlund, 1986). It is, however, important to note that the character of cooperatives may differ widely, as was also the case in Tanzania (Migot-Adholla, 1972: 81–83 and Cliffe, 1985: 1–5).

During the 1950s a great stride forward in the establishment of African cooperatives took place. They were also to become instruments in the struggle for national independence. The most important cooperative union, the Victoria Federation of Cooperative Unions (VFCU) was registered in Mwanza in 1952 under the leadership of Paul Bomani, who had previously been the secretary of the Mwanza African Traders Cooperative Society, a group of traders in Mwanza town (Coulson, 1982:67). The influence of African trading interests on the leadership of the cooperative unions emerged as a major issue when the government of independent Tanzania was to decide on the future role of cooperatives in the country.

The colonial state on its side regarded cooperatives as a rational way of extending cash crop production and controlling the agricultural surplus. Incidents during the colonial period indicated, however, that in crisis situations the state did not exercise complete control over the cooperatives. Therefore its own organisations, the marketing boards, were activated to tighten control, but during the 1950s the pressure from African traders and growers to establish cooperatives could not be held back.

Generally in struggles for national independence the existence of one major enemy has a unifying effect on the broad coalition struggling for change. Tanganyika was no exception. Hence it was not until after independence that the focus shifted to an analysis of whose interests the cooperatives really served and what their functions should be. This discussion could not be limited to the cooperatives themselves, but had necessarily to include relations between the cooperatives, as major rural organisations, and the newly formed state.

Post-colonial marketing (1961–1967)

The newly born state saw the cooperatives as a useful vehicle for national development,

> When Tanganyika achieved independence in 1961 some important decisions were taken by the Government vitally affecting the movement. It was decided to embark on a crash programme for the organisation of cooperatives in vast sections of the country which until then were largely untouched by the movement: the central and coastal parts. It was decided that the cooperative form was well suited to the African setting and to the achievement of independence in the economic sense: control of the economy by the indigenous people rather than by expatriates and others non-African in origin (United Republic of Tanzania, 1966:5).

This clearly indicated that one major objective of the expansion of the movement was seen as a political move to undermine the dominance of the Asian traders in marketing of agricultural produce (Bienen, 1967:277 and Hyden, 1976). Further, the cooperative movement due to its role in the liberation of Tanganyika was seen as "one of the principal pillars in the future of our nation..." (Bomani, 1961).

Another objective of national policies was that the growth of the cooperative movement should be a means of expanding the agricultural output marketed. The three tier marketing system, constituted of primary societies, regional cooperative unions and marketing boards were looked upon as suitable organisations to facilitate this. Already in 1963 the National Agricultural Products Board (NAPB) was established and by the end of 1966 twelve national boards existed with functions that were either regulatory or advisory (Wagao, 1982:5). Marketing boards appointed cooperative unions as purchasing agents and this marketing system by law was to be the only channel for agricultural marketing, i.e. a single channel system was introduced. Cooperative unions and primary cooperative societies could be used to channel credit and inputs to the agricultural sector, thereby improving the quality of the produce, necessary to strengthen the country's position on the export market.

From 1961 to 1966 the number of registered cooperative societies increased rapidly. At least some of the more established unions accumulated large surpluses over a number of years, and central government personnel were becoming concerned about the use of these surpluses. It was argued that, "surpluses were being wasted on excessive salaries and perquisites for committee men and employees on the one hand or, when invested, directed too one-sidedly to undertakings in the processing field" (Cliffe and Saul, 1972:86). A number of observers provided illustrations of inefficiencies, corruption and undemocratic practices in the well to do cooperative unions (Dumont, 1969:49–51; Migot-Adholla, 1976:39–58; Mwase, 1976:81–86; United Republic of Tanzania, 1966:9–12; Coulson, 1982:148–152; Resnick, 1981:61–64). Discontent with both cooperatives and marketing boards was widespread, in particular among central government personnel, and also among the peasants. The government acted to try to deal with the discontent by appointing a "Special Committee of Enquiry into Cooperative Movement and Marketing Boards" in January 1966.

Investigation of the documentation "proving" the bad state of the cooperative movement, does not reveal it to be as conclusive as many observers indicated. Many of the examples of luxury spending seem to be highly repetitive (for instance the luxury of cars and buildings of the VFCU in Mwanza). A few investigations conducted on a wider sample of cooperatives do document deficiencies and that the causes were more complicated than most observers were willing to admit. What is lacking in much of the writing on the cooperative movement during the 1960s is that government intervention had already had an important impact on the movement. The most important of the thorough studies of the cooperative movement in the 1960s are the Special Committee of Enquiry (1966), Kriesel et al. (1970) and Westergaard (1972).

The Special Committee of Enquiry studied 226 cotton societies in the East Lake areas. Of these, 53 societies showed losses of one per cent of the stock handled the previous year, which amounted to 0.2 per cent of the total product handled by all 226 societies. The Committee was informed that due to moisture absorption and "broken weights", deliveries to the ginneries should have been 2 per cent more seed cotton. Thefts were also indicated as "a great many of the 226 societies showed stock gains of less than half a per cent". The Committee concluded that "it is a fair inference that 25 per cent of the East Lake cotton farmers suffer an income reduction averaging 3 per cent as a result of these factors, and that the remaining 75 per cent suffer reductions averaging one and a half per cent" (United Republic of Tanzania, 1966:10).

Further evidence by the Committee is a study of 89 cashew nut societies in southern Tanzania, where the inference is that farmers suffered income reductions averaging close to 2 per cent of the crop handled. In a study in Kahama stock losses came to 1 per cent of the crop handled (21 societies), while 15 out of 26 societies investigated in Tabora Region incurred stock losses of nearly 4 per cent of the quantities handled (United Republic of Tanzania, 1966:10). The study also reported farmers' grievances relating to producer prices, corrupt employees, wrong deduction and faulty weighing, undemocratic practices, etc.

As to the causes of these observations, the Committee emphasised four basic defects; uninformed membership, shortage of qualified manpower, absence of democracy at union level and political interference (Ibid., 9–10).

Kriesel et al. (1970) conducted maybe the most comprehensive study of the cooperative societies and unions in Tanzania. The report emphasises that rapid expansion of cooperatives in the early 1960s was undertaken in spite of the lack of educated personnel. Societies and unions were compelled to undertake various activities for which they were not prepared, like distribution of fertilisers and insecticides, loan programmes, block farms, tractor schemes and processing enterprises (Kriesel et al., 1970:65). The findings showed that these activities were badly run and only in a few cases were they successfully operated. The study showed that the cooperatives were aware of these problems, but had encountered opposition when they tried to halt these loss making ventures. "Even when members have voted to abandon some losing propositions, as the tractor program in Mtwara Region, local politicians have overruled them" (Ibid., 65). Losses on tractor schemes in particular represented a serious drain on financial resources even in large established unions such as VFCU (lost over Tsh. 3 m. in 1966 alone). In Iringa Region, union losses on tractor programmes were Tsh. 480,000 in 1966–67 and in Mtwara about Tsh. 1 m. (Ibid., 66).

However, Kriesel et al. pointed out that the major financial losses of most societies were due to produce losses. In Coast Region crop losses amounted to 31 per cent for copra and about 6 per cent for cashew nuts while crop losses in Mtwara Region reached as much as Tsh. 50 per tonne (Ibid., 66).

The second largest source of losses was from the extension of credits. According to Kriesel et al. most of the credit programmes were thrown upon societies and unions before they were ready to handle them. In Coast and Morogoro Regions cotton handling societies had bad debts of about Tsh. 10,000 each, while those in the Lake Region had bad debts and provisions for such debts of almost Tsh. 3,000 each. In Mara the bad debts amounted to Tsh. 50 per tonne among the societies studied (Ibid., 66). Cash losses seem to rank third. In 1967 in the West Lake Region 2 per cent of the societies had losses exceeding

Tsh. 5,000 each, while in Mtwara Region 9 per cent recorded losses of more than Tsh. 2,000 (Ibid., 66). In societies and unions handling mainly maize, losses of product and cash losses amounted to Tsh. 24 per tonne for 1967–68 (Ibid., 28).

Kriesel et al. also conducted an extensive survey of operating costs, which included 447 societies throughout Tanzania. They were selected to provide information on the major crops, like cashew nuts, coffee, cotton, maize, paddy, pyrethrum and tobacco. One third of all marketing societies in the country were included. One hundred cotton societies in the Lake zone area were randomly selected, hence they represent all the 540 cotton societies in this area. On this basis the study includes two thirds of all marketing societies in Tanzania and almost 425,000 tonnes of agricultural crops (Ibid., 66). This study revealed that an important relationship between the volume handled and the unit cost had been established. There was a dramatic reduction in unit cost as the volume handled increased; a volume increase from 200–400 tonnes per society showed that unit costs declined by 35–40 per cent, a further volume increase to 600 tonnes saw unit costs drop another 25–30 per cent, and an increase from 600–800 tonnes gave an additional 15 per cent reduction of unit costs. Once the average volume per society exceeded 1,000 tonnes annually, unit costs declined very slowly. The major costs, salary and wages, and travel and allowances were those which declined most rapidly as volume increased (Ibid., 70). Since most cooperatives handled rather small tonnages, an obvious recommendation of the Kriesel report was to increase the scale of most cooperatives in order to reduce unit costs for handling produce.

Kriesel et al. identified five basic problems facing the cooperative movement: duplication of functions between cooperative unions and societies and the state trading institutions; the granting of privileges to "certain chosen people" through the single channel marketing policy; the alienation of farmers; the high level of illiteracy combined with workloads associated with political directives were overtaxing the resources and personnel of cooperatives (Ibid., 76–78).

It is interesting to note that the Special Committee of Enquiry and the Kriesel report identify more or less the same causes as creating problems for the cooperative movement. Unlike the Committee, the Kriesel report, however, points to the problems inherent in a single channel marketing policy. Both emphasised outside intervention or interference as well as the lack of educated personnel. The investigations also indicated alienation or lack of democracy within the movement itself.

The two reports, however, made contradictory recommendations when it came to dealing with alienation and democracy within the movement. Kriesel et al. recommended that societies that performed well should have greater independence. For those operating unsatisfactorily, government assistance would be most effective "if gently channeled through the union committee or through the regional committee", which the report suggested should be established (Ibid., 78). The Special Committee recommended a different option for improving the performance of the cooperatives which would "diminish local responsibility and local accountability", since, "given the local circumstances at the present time, there is a greater need for central responsibility and central accountability". It recommended that a Unified Cooperative Service be created to be responsible for the engagement, discipline, terms of service, and dismissal of all secretaries of societies, managers of unions and of federations of unions, and all other employees of registered cooperatives. The subsequent acceptance of this proposition by the government led to the removal of legal control of its employees by the cooperative. The Special Committee further recommended that the Cooperative Development Division (a government organ) should be given power to take temporary emergency steps with respect to any primary society which did not function properly. Hence the recommendations adopted by the government legitimised a growing state penetration of the cooperative movement. Instead of taking initiatives to strengthen the role of the producers and democratic practices in the cooperative movement, the government took major steps towards centralising control of its critical activities.

In 1967 the Ministry of Agriculture and Cooperatives temporarily took over 16 cooperative unions, including that of Coast Region, encompassing hundreds of cooperative societies. In addition, the government intervened in the Victoria Federation of Cooperative Unions, which culminated in the creation of a transformed "Nyanza Cooperative Union" (Cliffe and Saul, 1972:86–87).

The Cooperative Union of Tanzania protested against these take overs arguing that their members would be alienated from the cooperative movement, "The government should now realise that cooperative societies or unions cannot be created the way boards are made. Societies must start from the members. Once such a simple natural law is understood the pain of having to suspend management of unions or societies will be spared on both the Ministry and the cooperators themselves" (The Nationalist, 29/8 1967). The Cooperative Union of Tanzania further claimed that the persons given the responsibility of improving the movement, government cooperative officials and agricultural officers, had "not had any cooperative training nor do they have the necessary experience" (Ibid. and Manyiki and Lumbanga, 1971:3).

It emerges from the discussion of the development of the cooperative movement in the 1960s that there were two categories of cooperatives: those which, through levies and sound economic management, had accumulated wealth for reinvestment, and those which had incurred losses for various reasons. In his analysis of the data collected for 1966/67–1968/69 on the operation of cooperatives, Westergaard showed that approximately 40 per cent of all societies had annual net deficits and 20 per cent were insolvent (Westergaard, 1973:33). Government intervention in the first category was an urge to restore accountability and efficiency. The schemes and activities which followed from this intervention were often such that the cooperatives were not in a position to handle them. Hence, for the most part they had to be imposed on the cooperative unions and societies. The cooperatives themselves, the Special Committee and the Kriesel report called much of the intervention by the state and local political bodies interference, as it was imposed from outside and had a negative effect on the performance of the movement, both in terms of financial results and alienation within it.

A spokesman for a cooperative union, which had been criticised for not using its surplus for development purposes, argued "that the activities of government agencies operating at the local level in stimulating and implementing these very development programmes had sometimes been misguided and indeed certain mistakes were made by the government" (Cliffe and Saul, 1972:86–87). As mentioned above, numerous so-called tractor schemes were thrust upon various cooperative unions causing heavy losses. The question arises of how much of the poor performance of initially well run cooperatives could be assigned to causes lying outside their control. The Special Committee elevated the issue of political interference to one of the five basic defects affecting cooperative unions. Kriesel et al. also emphasised that the continuous political pressures compelled cooperatives to undertake many tasks related to cultivation, distribution and marketing for which they were not prepared, which created unbearable burdens for the unions (Kriesel et al., 1970:65 and 78).

For the cooperatives established in the early period of independence, the Special Committee of Enquiry (1966), the Kriesel et al. report (1970) and the Westergaard study (1972) all point to problems of crop- and cash losses etc. The magnitude of such losses varies, and the combined effect does not seem to jeopardise the existence of the whole movement. As indicated by Kriesel et al. there was a strong and direct relation between volume handled and unit cost of handling, which indicated that problems like the small size of primary societies rather than poor efficiency represented the major problem for the cooperative movement.

Post-Arusha agricultural marketing policies

By the late 1960s, the cooperative movement seemed to have attained one major goal aimed at reducing exploitation: primary cooperative societies, linked to regional unions and crop marketing boards, had effectively shut out Asian traders from crop purchasing and processing. In the Arusha Declaration of February 1967 and the subsequent paper outlining the policies on rural development (Socialism and Rural Development), President Nyerere focused on another aspect of primary importance to the role of cooperatives, "For the farmers' a cooperative marketing society is an institution serving the farmers; if they are capitalist farmers, then the existence of a cooperative marketing society will mean that one group of capitalists—the farmers—are safeguarding their own interests, as against another group of capitalists—the middlemen. It is only if the agricultural production itself is organised on a socialist pattern that cooperative marketing societies are serving socialism" (Nyerere, 1967).

The post-Arusha policies focused not so much on exploitation based on ethnic characteristics, but on exploitation due to the existence of a stratified society and penetration and exploitation linked to capitalism. Numerous studies of cooperatives in East Africa, some of them mentioned above, indicated that cooperatives established in response to "Asian middlemen", were not controlled by the ordinary peasants, but by African entrepreneurs who in their turn exploited their fellow country-men. The conclusion was that cooperatives tended to reemphasise and strengthen social stratification, hence the aim of promoting an egalitarian society was frustrated. According to Tanzanian policies, a safeguard against further stratification and development of capitalism would be to transform the non-socialist marketing cooperatives into production based multi-purpose cooperatives along socialist lines. It was against this background that Tanzanian officials drew up the plan for the socialist transformation of the rural areas which aimed at collective production in so-called ujamaa villages, where each village in itself was to constitute a multi-purpose cooperative society. Already in 1971, the late Derek Bryceson, then Minister of Agriculture and Cooperatives, predicted what the fate of the cooperative movement would be: "the structure of cooperative societies and unions was similar to middlemen, the present unions are just the people's creation of middlemen. Through discussion with the peasants it has been found out that even the peasants know that. These unions are therefore bound to face the fate of other middlemen" (*Daily News*, Oct. 31 1971).

The creation of crop authorities under direct government control started in the early 1970s. The strategy was to establish one crop authority for each of the major export crops, while one authority, the National Milling Corporation, was given the task of dealing with the domestic food crops. There was a transitional period before all the authorities were established. In this period geographically specific crop purchasing continued, i.e. one authority had the responsibility for purchases of all the crops in a region or district. As crop authorities were more firmly established by 1979, all crop purchases were made crop specific, i.e. each authority had the responsibility for its designated crop or crops.

Agricultural Price Policies

Introduction

The issue of agricultural producer prices is important because the level of agricultural producer prices is a major determinant of the rural-urban terms of trade, (Ellis, 1982:264 and Svendsen, 1986). As discussed in Appendix 1 producer prices and terms of trade are important elements in the analysis of the generation of agricultural surplus.

Experience from Tanzania shows that the form of state intervention in agricultural price formation is closely connected with which type of agricultural marketing organisation that exists. In this section I will focus on experiences with state intervention through the agricultural producer price systems and trace their impact on the composition of crops marketed and rural–urban terms of trade. For a discussion of statistical and methodological problems encountered in the analysis of real producer price trends and rural-urban terms of trade in Tanzania, see Havnevik, 1988: 53–55. (The interventions in producer price formation during the 1980s are discussed in Chapter 9.)

Agricultural price systems 1965–1973

From the mid-1960s, after the establishment of a series of marketing boards including the National Agricultural Products Board (NAPB), until 1973 the three-tier single-channel marketing system functioned. Connected to the boards were 20 regional cooperative unions which as their basis in 1973 had around 2,300 primary societies (McHenry, 1979:20).

The main characteristic of this marketing system was the large number of primary societies and their geographic, rather than crop specific, basis. Further, members of these societies were individual peasant producers and the single channel was stipulated by law. Thereby all private traders were excluded from agricultural marketing of the main cash crops, and at least officially, of the main food crops outside the districts where they were produced.

Government intervention in price formation in this marketing system was to set the price at which marketing boards procured crops from the cooperative unions. This was termed the into-store marketing board price and was fixed by the Economic Committee of the Cabinet in advance of each season after consultation with the Ministry of Agriculture. The unit marketing costs of cooperative unions and primary societies were deducted from the into-store price to arrive at the producer price obtained by the peasants. The costs of both the unions and societies had to be approved in advance by the Commissioner for Cooperatives in Dar es Salaam. Since there were significant regional variations in the marketing costs of the cooperative bodies, the average producer prices varied correspondingly (Kriesel et al., 1970 and Ellis, 1982). This price mechanism operated for all crops handled by NAPB, i.e. maize, paddy, wheat, oilseeds and cashew nuts, and for cotton which was handled by the Lint and Seed Marketing Board. For other crops for which marketing boards existed, like tobacco, coffee, pyrethrum, sisal and tea, the government did not intervene in price determination, but the prices paid by the marketing boards depended on the actual export price obtained.

The investigation by Kriesel et al. of producer prices of crops marketed by NABP revealed features of relevance both to crops produced in Rufiji District and to the subsequent development of prices during the 1970s. Kriesel found that for cashew nuts, the gross difference between the return to peasants and the f.o.b. price in Tanzania had increased from Tsh. 250 per tonne in the late 1950s to more than Tsh. 450 ten years later. In percentage terms, the gross marketing margin had increased by 78 per cent (compared to the 1958–62 average), while the f.o.b. price went up by 44 per cent and the producer price by 25 per cent respectively (Kriesel et al., 1970:89). Part of the reason was because primary societies and unions debited marketing costs to cashew nuts which instead should have been allocated to other crops, in particular maize and cassava. For maize the producer price at the end of the 1960s was well above import parity and only about half the domestic costs were recovered on export sales of this crop. Twice Tanzanian maize was exported prematurely, prior to the development of serious droughts (by NAPB in 1968/69 and by NMC in 1973). Tanzania was forced to pay dearly for the necessary imports due to a grain scarcity on the world market, especially in 1973.

In the 1960s there were already tendencies for producer prices to favour domestic food crops at the expense of some export crops. For most export crops, however, the producer prices paid were linked to the actual prices obtained through exports on the world market.

Agricultural price systems 1973–1981

When crop authorities or parastatals started replacing marketing boards, a new price system was introduced. Such authorities were created for domestic crops like maize, paddy, and wheat (NMC), oilseeds (GAPEX), cashew nuts (CATA), coffee (TCA), cotton, pyrethrum, sisal, sugar, tea and tobacco. Crop authorities were delegated substantial powers, far in excess of those of marketing boards. Crop authorities were to carry out and control all aspects of marketing, including crop procurement from the villages, transport, storage, processing and final sales including exports. The only task not undertaken by the authorities was the initial purchase of crops from peasant producers, which was to be undertaken by the villages themselves as multi-purpose cooperative societies. This meant that crop authorities were designated to carry out all the former functions of marketing boards, the cooperative unions and some of those of the primary societies.

The main feature of this marketing system and what distinguished it from its predecessor, was the tightening of centralised control not only of marketing, but also to some extent of production activities. Control at the level of production was, however, mainly effected through other means, to which I will return later, in the discussion of villagisation and the government's use of legal devices. The new price system, unlike the old one, had a crop specific basis. Each crop authority was entitled to expand its services to obtain complete coverage for its designated crop or crops. The weakness observed in the three-tier marketing system of the duplication of functions between the marketing boards and cooperative unions, became even more pronounced as each crop authority expanded on a broad level, with little or no cooperation and coordination with other authorities operating in the same geographical areas.

Government intervention in price determination in the new system took the form of deciding on the uniform producer price on a national level (so-called pan-territorial price), rather than the into-store mar-

keting board price which entailed geographical variations in the producer price for the same crop. This price system was to be in effect
from 1974 to 1981.

According to Ellis (1982) there were several steps in determining the
producer price level. The procedure started about a year before the
crop season. The initial set of proposed producer prices for regulated
crops originated in the Marketing Development Bureau within the
Ministry of Agriculture. These prices were then discussed with the
crop authorities concerned before being submitted to the Economic
Committee of the Cabinet for final approval. This procedure did not
allow any representatives from the primary societies in the villages to
participate and the peasants' views on the prices were not solicited.
Joint action from peasants or villages to oppose this price fixing procedure was preempted by the atomisation of the cooperative movement into nucleated villages with little or no contact between one
another. Only for coffee and sisal did price determination differ. Here
producer price levels were set on the basis of the sales prices realised
minus marketing costs and export taxes. This system operated with an
advance and a final corrective payment (Ellis and Hanak, 1981).

As Ellis pointed out, crucial to the normal price level decision procedure was "the weight which tended to be attached to the financial position of the crop parastatals both in deriving the initial set of price recommendations and in their subsequent modification. The underlying approach, observed particularly clearly in the case of export crops,
was that the marketing margin should be sufficient to cover the projected marketing costs of the crop authority" (Ellis, 1982:266). It was
evident that the projected costs were far from minimum marketing
costs, but "were typically based on past accounts which in themselves
represented a severely sub-optimal level of efficiency" (Ibid.). Such a
system of residual producer price determination was in principle similar to that of the export parity pricing that determined the into-store
price in the three-tier marketing system. For such a system to operate
on a just basis for all participants, marketing should be undertaken at
minimum cost. Since this was not the case and there was no way to control the spiralling costs of crop authorities, the peasants had to carry
the burden of the inefficient system. Crop authorities' audited accounts were years in arrears and no other internal or external corrective mechanism existed.

Now, let me look more closely at the empirical substantiation of
some of the above arguments. I will focus on the effect of the above
policies on real agricultural producer trends, on the volume of officially marketed agricultural crops and on rural-urban terms of trade.

Agricultural producer price trends and officially marketed crops during the 1970s

In the analysis I distinguish between three crop categories: export crops, staple grains and drought resistant crops (together, the last two will be termed domestic crops). At the onset of the 1970s, officially marketed output consisted mainly of export crops and staple grains. From 1970/71 to 1972/73 imports of staple grains were kept at a low level, averaging about 57,000 tonnes per year. Then, during 1973/74 and 1974/75, an agricultural crisis occurred. Severe drought and the short-term effects of the villagisation campaign coincided, and domestic production was substantially reduced. The ensuing food shortages necessitated massive imports of grain, as surplus stocks had been exported immediately prior to the food supply crisis. The value of grain imports increased from US $ 3.5 m. in 1972/73 to US $ 101 m. in 1973/74, then fell to US $ 51.5 m. in 1974/75. The food crisis was immediately transformed into a balance of payments crisis. Total food imports (including non-grain) increased from 8.1 per cent of total imports in 1973 to 20 per cent in 1974, then went down to 17.7 per cent in 1975 (World Bank, 1981b).

The government's response to the food supply crisis was to encourage food production by increasing producer prices of domestic crops in relation to export crops. Official purchases of drought resistant crops such as millet, sorghum, cassava and beans were initiated at the time the first crop authority was established in the early 1970s. Many of these crops were traditionally consumed directly or stored in households as a buffer against production setbacks and famine. The evolution of producer prices in nominal and real terms from the crisis year 1973/74 to 1979/80 is shown in Table 6.1.

From 1973/74 to the end of the decade producer prices of domestic crops increased substantially in real terms while those of export crops declined. These changes in relative prices coupled with a purchase guarantee for drought-resistant crops had a profound impact on the composition of agricultural marketed output (cf. Table 6.1).

Development of rural-urban terms of trade

Governments commonly use price policies as a mechanism to change the inter-sectoral balance of the economy (see Appendix 1). The motives behind such changes may vary. It is clear, however, that the alteration of the terms of trade through active use of price policies is a powerful instrument, albeit not easily detectable, through which class forces can operate (Mitra, 1977).

Table 6.1.   *Weighted average producer price indices of major crop categories (1969/70 = 100)*

Crop category	Money prices 1973/74	Money prices 1979/80	Real prices [1] 1973/74	Real prices [1] 1979/80
Export crops[2]	106.8	234.5	65.8	57.5
Domestic Crops	115.8	344.7	71.4	84.4
Staple grains	109.9	323.0	67.7	79.1
Drought resistant crops	207.5	426.2	127.9	104.4
All crops				
Export crop prices as per cent of domestic crop prices	92.2%	68%	92.2%	68%

Notes: The prices are weighted by the share of each crop in the total producer value, calculated for each year separately.
[1] Money prices deflated by a modified National Consumer Price Index.
[2] Export crops include cotton, tobacco, pyrethrum, coffee, sisal, cashew nuts and tea. Staple grains include maize, wheat and rice. Drought-resistant crops include sorghum, cassava and beans.
Source: Ellis, 1982, p. 269 and 283

In this sub-section I shall illustrate the effect of the agricultural price policy on rural-urban terms of trade. Two measurements are involved, the *price terms of trade* which show how agricultural producer prices move in relation to the general price level facing the peasants, and the *income terms of trade* which, in addition to comparing price levels, includes the impact of changes in the volume of marketed output. My presentation here will be based on the methods and results of Ellis (1982) as they seem to be most solidly founded, given the limitations of the available data (cf. Havnevik, 1988:53–55).

This analysis is limited as it relates to the operation of the terms of trade through price policies. For a complete analysis of the rural-urban terms of trade more data would be required on the total set of transactions between the two sectors. Incomes generated in non-agricultural production and further taxes and subsidies between the two sectors should be included. To obtain an exact picture, price levels should ideally also be adjusted to incorporate the effects of sales and purchases on illegal and parallel markets. Needless to say, it would be impossible to undertake this venture. The results obtained from available statistics should, however, be weighed in relation to the irregular or non-recordable factors.

Ellis shows that the overall price terms of trade for the period 1969/

70 to 1979/80 fell by 35.9 per cent, export crops declined by 42.5 per cent and domestic crops by 15.6 per cent (Ellis, 1982:272). Only drought resistant crops like sorghum, cassava and beans registered a gain in real prices (4.4 per cent) over the decade.

During the first half of the decade a massive decline in the price terms of trade of the investigated crops was recorded. An improvement in the second half of the decade could not compensate for it. The increase for all crops during the latter period was 7.2 per cent, but export crops declined by a further 2 per cent (Ellis, 1982:273).

The income terms of trade based on an analysis of crops marketed officially also evidenced a drastic decline, 33.4 per cent for all crops through the decade (based on two year averages at the start and end of the decade to avoid the impact of erratic fluctuations). Export crops, as shown above, deteriorated far more in income terms of trade, by 42.5 per cent, while domestic crops declined by only 10.2 per cent. While export crops declined in both the first and second part of the decade, the income terms of trade for domestic crops improved tremendously in the second half due to the 1973 changes in the price policy which led to a substantial increase in the officially marketed output of domestic crops (Ellis, 1982: 273).

Sales on parallel markets did increase during the last years of the 1970s due to food shortages and subsequent price differences on the official and parallel markets. Maize and rice are the major crops sold at parallel markets, in addition to export crops like coffee which is smuggled for sale to neighbouring countries (coffee from Kilimanjaro/Arusha to Kenya and from Kigoma Region to Burundi). The prices obtained by peasants for these crops were higher than official ones, and as well increases in non-agricultural production which could be sold on markets not controlled by the state (fish, forestry products, especially charcoal) may have compensated to varying degrees in different locations for the harsh decline calculated on the basis of official prices. Much of this compensation was likely to have been lost because peasants had to compete on parallel markets to purchase basic commodities. Secondly, during the 1970s there were increasingly fewer benefits for peasant agriculture from the development budget. Thus the income terms of trade based on official market prices and volumes may represent a rough indication of the decline in the agricultural sector. In addition comes the reduction in government expenditure on social services and education affecting the whole of the rural population.

Peasants in Rufiji District were hurt by the extremely negative development of the price of cashew nuts, a major cash crop in the area. The peasants could compensate by selling maize and rice on parallel markets as well as by engaging in non-agricultural production because of the varied resource in the area. These aspects are studied more in detail in Chapters 5 and 7.

The active use of agricultural price policies by the government had the effect of transferring huge financial resources out of the agricultural sector during the 1970s, thus making possible the rapid expansion of the state bureaucracy. However, at the same time these transfers led to impoverishment of the rural areas and blocked the potential for increasing the agricultural surplus. This provides one explanation for the increased reliance and dependency of the Tanzanian state on external aid (cf. Chapters 2 and 9).

Villagisation

Introduction

During the pre-colonial and colonial periods the tendency was for peasant households to be part of a pattern of dispersed settlement. Growing population density would usually cause the average productivity of labour to fall, and migration and dispersed settlement tended to counteract this trend.

During the colonial period so-called villagisation campaigns were initiated. The purpose of the first attempts of the 1930s was to fight sleeping disease which had spread in some areas of Tanganyika. During the colonial period more production oriented settlement campaigns did not start until the 1950s. Cliffe and Cunningham (1973) claim that two types of settlement schemes were initiated or encouraged by the British: supervised settlement schemes and co-operative farming settlements. The first were set up by the government exercising direct control over the producers. Control was exercised through the granting and withdrawal of licences to produce.

In 1953 the Tanganyika Agricultural Corporation (TAC) was set up to handle three development areas previously occupied by the Groundnut Scheme. TAC was discontinued in 1964 after having started nine schemes for cattle, tobacco and groundnut production. The commercial ranches were handed over to the National Development Corporation (NDC) and the remaining settlements to the Village Settlement Agency (VSA) which had been set up in 1963. Cooperative farming settlements were initiated by the Ministry of Agriculture in 1959 in Coast Region. A total of 45 cattle and coconut schemes with support from local political leaders were started (Cliffe and Cunningham 1973:132).

Policies and village settlements 1961–1967

The post-colonial Tanganyikan state continued to urge people to form settlements. The character of settlements and the ideology underpinning them was, however, in the period up to 1967 of different strands.

As early as April 1962 Nyerere published "Ujamaa—The Basis of African Socialism" (A TANU pamphlet). Here Nyerere examines socialism as an attitude of mind. "The foundation, and objective, of African socialism is the extended family." "Ujamaa, then, or Family-hood, describes our socialism." Thus Nyerere tried to concretise the attitude of mind which was to be a feature of the type of socialism Tanzania should pursue. It was a socialism based on African tradition and it was centrally placed within the framework of "African Socialism", a concept which had developed among different African leaders. Nyerere did not, at that time, attempt to define the institutions which would embody this type of socialism in a modern society.

In his inaugural address as president in the same year, Nyerere introduced the idea of villagisation. First he emphasised that only 200,000–300,000 of the country's population of about ten million lived in towns. Tanganyika was a land of agriculture and the government had decided to place the greatest importance on outlining the first three year plan in that sector. He continued,

> But it is ridiculous to concentrate on agriculture if we are not going to make any change in our old methods of cultivation and our old ways of living ... The hand-hoe will not bring us the things we need today ... We have got to begin using the plough and the tractor instead. But our people do not have enough money, and nor has the Government, to provide each family with a tractor. The first and absolutely essential thing to do, therefore, if we want to be able to start using tractors for cultivation, is to begin living in villages ... Unless we do so we shall not be able to use the tractor: we shall not be able to provide schools for our children: we shall not be able to build hospitals, or have clean drinking water, it will be quite impossible to start small village industries, and instead we shall have to go on depending on the towns for all our requirements: and even if we had a plentiful supply of electric power we should never be able to connect it up to each isolated homestead (Nyerere 1966: 183–184).

In the immediate post-independence period, Nyerere's policy formulations on the need to live in villages led to the establishment of a series of spontaneous co-operative settlements alongside the government supported and supervised schemes.

Government supported and supervised schemes

A Ministry of Lands, Settlement and Water Development was set up in 1961. This Ministry controlled the Village Settlement Agency (VSA) and took over the villagisation programme which had been launched in 1962 (Cliffe and Cunningham 1973:132). VSA was set up to initiate the pilot settlements of the First Five Year Plan (FFYP 1964–9). In this plan the government concluded that the long-term prospects of Tanzanian agriculture lay in transforming it by changing the spatial, organisational and technical conditions. The "transformation approach" consists of two major aspects:

1. In the semi-arid zones of the country, the policy would aim at re-grouping and resettling farmers on the most favourable soil under a system of private or collective ownership, and introducing supervised crop rotation and mixed farming to permit the maintenance of soil fertility.
2. In the more densely populated areas the aim of the policy would be to reduce agricultural underdevelopment. In this regard Government policy aimed at river basin development since these seemed to offer a large potential for resettlement with their vast stretches of fertile land.

By 1980 the objective in terms of resettlement was to create viable villages for about 1/2 million people in the first category of area and to settle the same number of people in the Pangani, Wami and the Kilombero River basins (Ibid.).

The agricultural assumptions of this policy reveal a complete unawareness of the historical reasons for dispersed settlements and the achievements of traditional pastoralism and agriculture in maintaining and increasing production without long-run deterioration of the soil. The plans for the river basins might have been spurred on by the recently submitted FAO study on the Rufiji Basin, which rightly pointed to a vast potential for agricultural production. It should be pointed out, however, that it would be difficult to tap (FAO, 1961).

In Chapter 8 I will return to the more detailed plans and attempts to tap the potential of the Rufiji river valley, the lower part of the Kilombero system. In the Wami and Pangani valleys discovery of widespread salinity soon led to a virtual stop in the plans for their development (Coulson, 1977:89).

The actual projects launched within the FFYP turned out to be less ambitious than announced. Most of the river basin planning was to be investigative (Coulson, 1977:89). In terms of settlement, it was planned that nearly half a million people would be affected on 74 schemes supported by GB£ 12 million (or 14.5 per cent of the total agricultural development budget). Yet, the Village Settlement Agency was given funds to establish only 49 village settlement schemes (Newiger,

1968:254). On the ground the VSA did not control more than 23 schemes, including seven schemes taken over on former land of the defunct Groundnut Scheme (Coulson, 1977:89). In April 1966 these VSA activities were stopped, when Vice-President Rashidi Kawawa announced the end of the policy. The major reasons for the failure were said to be poor planning, weak organisational structure and heavy over-capitalisation of most schemes (Newiger, 1968:271; Groeneveld, 1968:242–7; Cliffe and Cunningham, 1973:132, and Coulson, 1977:89).

Kawawa's alternative suggestion to improve agriculture was to step up support to the traditional agriculturalist through the cooperative movement. In this he was supported by Paul Bomani, but Nyerere was convinced that it would entail a return to the policy of supporting progressive farmers, which would increase differentiation in the rural areas (Pratt, 1976: 227–37). The experiences gained from the various forms of settlement schemes and the development within the cooperative movement as portrayed in the 1966 Report of the Special Committee, made Nyerere choose a different option.

Autonomous settlements

After Independence cooperative farming settlements were initiated, many spontaneously, throughout the country. Some were started by unemployed youths from the towns, others by groups of workers on estates. About half of the settlements were initiated by TANU Youth League members and a few were started by exceptional leaders who had been dismayed by the approach to agricultural policy of the colonial government. One of the latter groups were the so-called Ruvuma Development Association (RDA), in south-west Tanzania. There is no accurate account of the number of such settlements, but Cliffe and Cunningham have made a rough guess that around 1,000 existed by the end of 1963. Most settlements of this type did not last for more than a year or two. Probably, the best organised autonomous group was that of the RDA (for a detailed analysis of its development see Musti, 1979; Coulson, 1982).

The RDA was formed in early 1961 by TANU Youth League members from Songea after a first unsuccessful attempt. In 1963 there were 3 member settlements involving 70 families and in 1967 they had increased to 17 with over 400 families. Most of the villages were thus very small and were far apart, one was 200 miles east of Songea, another 100 miles to the west and another 100 miles to the north. The consciousness of the members was enhanced by assistance from the "Social and Economic Revolutionary Army", a group of people from within the RDA settlements who took it upon themselves to visit settlements and projects in order to assist in solving problems and enhancing development.

The first objectives of the RDA were to become self-sufficient in food, to improve health through more nutritious food, to build a school and improve the water supply and later to start up village industries. A constitution which in principle was approved by Nyerere, made the RDA a cooperative body, owned and controlled by the villagers themselves. On most counts the RDA was successful, but during its development several severe conflicts with the Tanzanian government emerged.

By July 1969 the undercurrent of misgivings about autonomous settlements had grown so strong that the Central Committee of the Party decided to investigate them. Groups were sent of three members of the Committee to such villages. Their visit to the RDA confirmed their worst fears. It was autonomous, receiving funds directly from abroad and was promoting socialism outside the control of the Party. In an interview in 1979 with a former trusted RDA member, I was told that the three committee men visiting the RDA had reported that attempts had been made on their lives. "Nyerere must have cried when he read their report", was the comment by this former RDA member.

On September 24 1969 the Central Committee met again in Dar es Salaam and 21 of its 24 members voted in favour of disbanding the RDA (Coulson, 1982:271). This was shortly after a three day tour by Nyerere and the TANU National Executive Committee of Rufiji District during which the state supported establishment of ujamaa villages during "Operation Rufiji" of 1968/69 was praised (*The Nationalist*, September 24, 1969). On September 25 the major headline on the front page of *the Nationalist* read, "TANU to run all Ujamaa Villages". The article continued:

> The TANU Central Committee resolved yesterday that the time has now come for the Party to take charge of all Ujamaa villages with the aim of creating uniformity in their development. The Committee felt that because socialism in villages is TANU's policy the Party should be fully involved with the development of all Ujamaa villages.
>
> ... the Central Committee discussed at length the involvement of various organisations in the establishment and organisation of Ujamaa villages.
>
> The Central Committee paid tribute for their efforts and involvement in propagating TANU's policy of Ujamaa in villages. But because TANU has taken the trouble to ensure that the policy of Ujamaa is well understood all over the country, it is better for the Party to take charge of all Ujamaa villages.

"The Party should also involve itself in all development programmes instead of leaving other ujamaa villages to private organisations", was the agreement. The Central Committee concluded that the development of most villages left much to be desired.

The RDA was not mentioned. The decision to close it down was announced by the government in Songea the next day and immediately all the assets of the RDA were confiscated: the sawmill, the grain mill, vehicles, equipment and a mechanical workshop. The police were sent into villages to remove all the RDA's property and the expatriates involved left the country within a few days.

This forcible disbanding of RDA by TANU hence represents the first major contradiction between the policies and implementation of the ujamaa village policies. The RDA was actually an association which had grown and developed according to the principles spelled out by Nyerere, first in 1962 and later in 1967.

Let me return to 1967 and look at the formulation of the ujamaa policies and their implementation in the period 1967 to 1972. My hypothesis, which I will try to substantiate in the following, is that there were two distinct phases of ujamaa and villagisation. The first between 1967 and 1972 in which ideology was the driving force, and the second, between 1972 and 1976 in which the emphasis had shifted to economic forces.

The ideological phase 1967–72: ujamaa and voluntarism

In September 1967 Nyerere published the paper "Socialism and Rural Development". Here he formulated a strategy for rural development which brought together his previous ideas on ujamaa and villagisation. This policy was accepted by the Party. Towards the end it states:

> Any model which is drawn up should just be a guide which draws the attention of the people to the decisions which have to be made by them; each village community must be able to make its own decisions. Nonetheless, the experience of existing ujamaa villages, such as those now operating within the Ruvuma Development Association, could be helpful, and the Ministry of Local Government and Rural Development should try to make this experience available to people from different parts (Nyerere, 1968:143).

Hence, less than two years before being disbanded by the government, the RDA was held up officially by the President as an example of how ujamaa villages could be organised in a fruitful way by and for their members.

Nyerere further noted that the present trend was

> away from the extended family production and social unity, and towards the development of a class system in the rural areas. It is this kind of development which would be inconsistent with the growth of a socialist Tanzania in which all citizens

could be assured of human dignity and equality and in which all were able to have a decent and constantly improving life for themselves and their children (Ibid.).

Then Nyerere went on to spell out the content of ujamaa agriculture and organisation. The emphasis was to be on equality and non-exploitation, collective farming practices and other activities. The communities should be big enough to take account of modern farming methods and the twentieth century needs of man. Land would be denoted "our land" and crops "our crops". According to Nyerere such groups already existed in Tanzania, and he stressed that there was no need to wait for the government to organise them and give all the instructions. "What is required is sensible organisation which can be shown to be to the benefit of all members" (Ibid., 125).

Ujamaa villages would according to Nyerere reestablish "all the advantages of traditional African democracy, social security and human dignity ...". Ujamaa villages were to grow through self-reliant activities and would be created by the people themselves and maintained by them. The government's role would only be to help people "make a success of their work and their decisions". Government institutions should provide the necessary agricultural advice. The Ministry of Local Government and Rural Development should assist in drawing up a model village constitution for villages at different stages, "although it must be stressed that no one model should be imposed on any village" (Ibid., 143).

"Socialism and Rural Development" expressed a dream of an ideal world and did not give directions as to how to deal with the most problematic issues related to the transition, like how to solve land conflicts caused by villagisation, how central and local government agencies ought to act during the transition and how the government should more concretely support agriculture in terms of the supply of inputs and extension services. Support for productive activities is talked about in very general terms; the notion underlying it is the need to organise, so that modern methods of cultivation could be introduced, either on state farms or in peasant agriculture. The "Arusha Declaration" and "Socialism and Rural Development" both have an air of ideological and political features. Neither economic necessity nor crisis seemed to exist in Tanzania at that time which would warrant drastic state intervention. Rather, the policy formulated and measures taken were primarily aimed at arresting a tendency towards differentiation caused by the penetration of capitalist production relations.

Three categories of villages

Three types of villages can be identified in the first phase of villagisation, 1967–72. First there were those that remained of the spontaneously created early villages; highly politicised, rather small and having a large amount of communal cultivation, like the RDA and Mbambara in Tanga. In Rufiji District there were two villages in this category, Tawi in the South Hill and Nyambili in the North Hill agro-economic zones.

The second type were those that were founded in order to obtain some kind of concession from the government like access to previously owned settler land, to parcels of land which had belonged to forest reserves, or in order to get state support for capital investment or famine relief. Both Sender, in his study of villages in the Lushoto mountains (1973) and von Freyhold (1971) when examining the establishment of villages in Tanga Region found such concessionary issues to be at the root of the creation of the villages. It is interesting to note Sender's finding that, "The incentive for collective cultivation stopped altogether when villagers realised that once plans for water supply, dispensary or a school had been approved by the government, the project continued even if collective work or cultivation was reduced or stopped" (Sender, 1974:33). Communal production is likely not to have amounted to more than 1 or 2 per cent of the cultivation in the established "ujamaa" villages (Coulson, 1982:246).

The third category of villages were started through so-called operations or campaigns. The very first was the resettlement in the Rufiji river valley, "Operation Rufiji", that began in 1968. Its background and implementation will be taken up later in this chapter about the Ujamaa village scheme and villagisation in Rufiji District (p. 218-224). Let me just mention at this point that President Nyerere during a three day visit to the newly created villages in Rufiji District (September 20–24, 1969) spoke at a rally at Mkongo village. Once again he emphasised that, "people must ensure that no one exploits them ... It is a necessary condition that whenever people work together, exploitation must cease or else the work done will not yield fruits". Nyerere said that by a complete removal of all sorts of exploitation the work and sweat of the people would be repaid by the outcome of their labour because, "all the rice, maize, cashew nuts and cotton are yours" (*The Nationalist*, September 24, 1969).

In 1970 Dodoma Region was to experience a villagisation campaign. Here for the first time the so-called "Presidential planning teams" were employed, though the embryo for the creation of such teams can be identified in "Operation Rufiji". These teams identified sites for villages and prepared plans for them. Subsequently teams were sent to Kigoma, Tabora, Rukwa and West Lake Regions to prepare for and assist in the settlement activities. There is no indication that there was any qualitative shift in policies like more emphasis on aspects of production nor of the use of more coercive methods in 1970 and 1971. In her investigation of "Operation Dodoma" Frances Hill found that, "There was no attempt to introduce improved agricultural methods or even to adopt methods to the changed human-resource relationship caused by population concentration" (Hill, 1979:111). Hence, the more active involvement of the Party, in particular in the Dodoma campaign, must be interpreted as a wish to speed up the exercise. It must be remembered that the first two major campaigns in Rufiji District and Dodoma Region were initiated after serious floods and droughts in the respective areas.

Even though the speed of the establishment of villages increased during 1971, still it was far slower than expected, and quite uneven throughout the country. By the end of 1969, 1970 and 1971 respectively, 809, 1,956 and 4,484 villages had been created. The total population living in these villages were about 1.5 million (Economic Survey 1973–74, tables 33 and 35). A further element that emerged was that opposition to the villagisation policy had been growing among larger land owners. It climaxed with the killing of the Regional Commissioner for Iringa Region who was shot by an African kulak maize farmer when propagating for the creation of villages in Ismani on Christmas Day 1971.

In the campaigns and operations of the 1967–1972 period, there is little evidence to show that force or coercion was used by government agencies, at least not in any systematic sense. Turok (1971:402) mentions that during the Rufiji campaign, the Regional Police Commander wanted to "resort to force to drive the reluctant villagers from the valley and destroy their houses". The Regional Commissioner, however, "let it be known that the President was totally opposed to the use of force and this particular lobby was silenced" (Ibid.). A few persons were arrested, but mainly for obstructing progress or for discouraging people from moving. According to Turok it was, nevertheless, clear that large scale force was not used. In the campaign in West Lake there is mention that Party officials were punished because of their use of force to start ujamaa villages (Coulson, 1982:242). In Handeni District, during 1969, several families who refused to join a particular village and instead established their own were more than once jailed for up to two weeks (von Freyhold, 1979:75).

The first phase of resettlement was primarily based on ideology and politics. The policy formulated was general in character and did not offer concrete directions for implementation. Even though there was much verbal emphasis on the need for communal production, it only materialised to a limited extent. Villagers looking for concessions from the government, realised that collective farming was not a prerequisite to get access to government support. There seemed to be little preoccupation with the economics of village creation or how to enhance the productivity of labour in cultivation. The government relied mainly on persuasion and the promise of supplying social infrastructure to the village, and made little use of force or coercion in order to establish villages, even though there is evidence that some sections of the bureaucracy would have liked to do so. During the early part of 1972 new aspects seem to have entered the process of implementation. I will first briefly look at the reasons behind this and then deal with the main elements of policy implementation during the second stage, from 1972–76.

The production and enforcement phase 1972–76

By early 1972 it was clear that the creation of ujamaa villages was proceeding much more slowly than expected, the extent of communal production was marginal, opposition from kulak farmers had become more pronounced and there was even disagreement within the Party as to what the ujamaa concept contained, examplified by the banning of the RDA in 1969. Problems of leadership in the government had also emerged and were dealt with in the TANU Guidelines (1971). The ideological and political framework employed for the mobilisation of ujamaa had not given substantial results, either in terms of changing the social relations of production or in increasing agricultural production and productivity. Concern for the latter became increasingly more pronounced as macro-economic indicators started to show declining growth trends and, from the early 1970s, Tanzania had to import food grains.

The above are some of the elements which constitute the background for the shift from an ideological to a production oriented focus in the implementation of ujamaa. This shift was first manifested in the document, "*Siasa ni Kilimo*" ("Politics is Agriculture" or the "Iringa Declaration" of May, 1972). Here the old call for the need to transform agricultural techniques is re-emphasised, but in a different way. Earlier transformation had meant a shift to the use of tractors for cultivation (refer, for instance, Nyerere's inaugural presidential speech in 1962) and the establishment of capital-intensive settlement schemes. The rather general ideological statements about agricultural development, never focussed on the constraints and prospects of switches in agricultural techniques. There was an ideal perception of the need to re-establish traditional relations of production, but there seemed to be no realistic framework nor assessment of the costs of an agricultural transition.

The "Iringa Declaration" represents a break with the above tradition in certain important aspects. For the first time the ideological framework is dropped as there is no emphasis on the need to move towards communal production. Another important change is the focus on technical and practical means of increasing productivity in agriculture and related activities. The emphasis is on the need for increased used of oxen in cultivation, on the need to plant early, on spacing, the use of manure and fertiliser. Tractors, it is stated, should only be used when there exists an apparatus which can properly maintain them and when there is a need to carry out cultivation on large farms. But the objective of increased agricultural production and productivity, even at the level of intermediate technology can, according to the document, not be obtained unless the sizes of farms are expanded. Hence, it is argued, the creation of "Ujamaa villages" has to be speeded up. There is, however, no mention of communal production.

In July 1972 another important policy initiative aimed at speeding up the creation of new villages, the "decentralisation" policy, was adopted. This meant that the local government in each region and district was replaced by an extension of the central civil service under the umbrella of the Prime Minister's Office (PMO): The move was not one of decentralisation of control, but rather one of decomposition, i.e. of physical decentralisation of staff from the technical ministries to the various departments of the PMO that were set up to administer the regions and the districts. Rather the policy led to an enlargement of the control span of the ministries and government, which means that "centralisation" is a more appropriate characteristic of this policy initiative (Coulson, 1982:254). After a year of streamlining the organisational set-up, the staff in the regions and districts were ready to move.

In September 1973 the TANU Biennial Conference decided that the whole of the rural population should live in villages by the end of 1976. Already in November 1973 the President himself was quoted in *The Daily News* saying that, "To live in villages is an order". *The Daily News* further reported that, "Addressing a public rally at Endabashi, Mbulu District, Mwalimu said there was a need for every Tanzanian to change his mode of life if rapid progress was to be achieved. People who refused to to accept development changes were stupid, if not ignorant or stubborn" (*The Daily News*, November 7, 1973). Thus the voluntary character of resettlement had ceased and during 1974 and 1975 nearly all those remaining outside villages were moved into villages, mainly through a series of operations. The term ujamaa village was dropped, instead the term villagisation was used, implying that communal production was no longer a central feature of new villages. These changes were in accordance with the intent of the "Iringa Declaration".

This fundamental change in the approach to major aspects of rural development had been felt, not only by peasants, but also by most observers. In the analysis of the underlying factors for the change, there is, however, a wide range of interpretations. The President himself explained it in this way in a speech made in 1973 when touring Kigoma Region to familiarise himself with "Operation Kigoma": "He urged for a rapid villagisation of the rural population as an absolute precondition for the development, and in which he expressed the need to use force to villagise people and speed up the production. The country had no time to wait for the voluntary villagisation based on the education of the people" (Boesen et al., 1977:170).

In summing up in "The Arusha Declaration 10 years after" in January 1977, Nyerere in this report to the TANU Executive Committee, stated that,

> Consider, for example, the question of villagisation. In my Report to the 1973 TANU Conference I was able to say that 2,028,164 people were living in villages. Two years later, in June 1975, I reported to the next TANU Conference that approximately 9,100,000 people were living in village communities. Now, there are about 13,065,000 people living together in 7,684 villages. This is a tremendous achievement. It is an achievement of TANU and Government leaders in cooperation with the people of Tanzania. It means that something like 70 per cent of our people moved their homes in the space of about three years (Nyerere, 1977).

It is correct that this was a tremendous achievement in terms of a massive physical movement of people. All the more so, when one takes account of the state of the economy in Tanzania. It clearly shows an extremely strong determination on the part of the Party and the government to ensure that villagisation was carried out. This further shows that the Tanzanian state commanded an administrative machinery which was highly efficient in moving people. It seems evident that this dramatic increase in the speed of resettlement could not have been carried out without the above-mentioned fundamental changes in the policy related to villagisation. It cannot be denied, however, that recourse to force, directly or indirectly, came to constitute an element in the various campaigns. Reports from Morogoro Region (Lwoga, 1978:12 and 13), from Mara (Matango, 1975:17), from Maasailand (Parkipuny, 1976:154–55), from Mwanza and Shinyanga (Mwapachu, 1976:119) and from Iringa (deVries and Fortmann, 1979:130–31) show this. It is likely that the use of force or, maybe more importantly, the threat of using it backed by reports of force being used in other districts or villages, made people comply. They either moved by themselves or were moved with the help of the government and local authorities to the planned sites.

The existence of nucleated villages throughout the country thus paved the way for major initiatives. For instance, according to Nyerere: "Universal Primary Education by the end of 1977, for example, would have been out of the question had the people not been living in village communities by now." In fact most of the bureaucrats claimed that villagisation would make it easier to provide social infrastructure, like education, dispensaries, famine relief, clean water and agricultural extension services to the villagers. But this Nyerere had argued all along, since before Independence. The promised level of social infrastructure and services to the villages was completely unrealistic, and could only have been furnished through dramatic increases in production. Further, even in some areas with a dense population, where social and other services could easily have been supplied without moving people, people were still ordered to move. The provision of services could thus not have been the only consideration underlying the massive movement of people (Coulson, 1982).

The experience of the Ruvuma Development Association clearly shows that an additional unspecified objective linked to ujamaa villages or villagisation was political control of the rural areas by the Party. There was, however, no urgent reason for rapid expansion of political control of the countryside during the years from 1973 to 1976. Thus the urge for political control cannot alone explain the enforced and rapid move.

Boesen, Moody and Storgaard argue that the difficult economic situation emerging in Tanzania during 1973 and 1974 made it clear that the country had to struggle more consciously to obtain a higher degree of self-reliance and that this could only be done through increased agricultural production in particular of food crops. This, however, required firmer plans and measures and more control over the use of resources. They see the two major initiatives taken during 1974, the nationwide campaign for increased food production and the nationwide "Operation Villages" (Operation Vijiji) and the decision to implement these at the expense of other rural development efforts, as evidence supporting this claim (Boesen et al., 1977:170). After the rapid escalation of food imports during 1974 and 1975 the argument related to the need to increase agricultural production was taken up by other observers. This argument is also used by Nyerere after 1975 (Coulson, 1982:256).

The massive resettlement of 1973–76 must, however, have required planning prior to the onset of the economic problems that hit Tanzania in 1973 and 1974. It is true that the decentralisation of 1972 was a necessary condition for the initiation of the massive movements of 1973–76, but decentralisation in itself cannot explain nor be the cause for the determination of the Party and government to undertake these massive movements. Rather, the decision to go for a speedy conclusion of resettlement must have emerged at the latest during the second half of 1971 or early 1972.

Frances Hill has claimed that the objective of increasing production was there as early as 1971 (Hill, 1979). Her argument is that until 1970 "ujamaa villages were nationally approved local experiments". But, "during 1970–71 ujamaa became a top priority effort by the central organisations of the party-state to mobilise the rural populations". And further that, "these efforts centred on Dodoma Region as a potential showcase for the benefits of socialist transformation". She argues that Nyerere had hoped to show that rural socialist transformation would increase local production and consolidate a peasant constituency for Tanzanian socialism (Hill, 1979:106).

My argument is, however, that the emphasis on production becomes important only in the second phase of villagisation, from 1973 onwards, when the ideological requirement of communal production was dropped. In my view the Dodoma campaign was not significantly different from the Rufiji Operation. They both aimed at changing the social relations of production and were both initiated because of widespread famine, due to flood and drought.

The production argument has, however, to be linked to other and equally important policies, not only related to villagisation and resettlement but also to changes in agricultural marketing and the use of legal and coercive mechanisms.

Legal and Coercive Mechanisms

Introduction

The use of legal and coercive instruments in relation to agricultural development has a long history in Tanzania. The British colonial government was, as its German predecessor, quite clear about its objectives and priorities. Maybe the governor of the territory put it most simply:

The first objective of the government is to induce the native to become a producer directly or indirectly, that is to produce or assist in producing something more than the crop of local food stuffs that he requires for the sustenance of himself and his family (quoted in Nindi, 1979).

The importance of an agricultural surplus runs all through the history of the government of the colonial powers. In fact the history of colonial rule is to some extent about the mechanisms of extracting an agricultural surplus for the benefit of the metropolitan countries. Here the focus is on legal instruments including bye-laws, rules, orders and directives used to effect this extraction.

In Tanganyika, the Native Authorities were established by the governor under the provisions of the Native Authority Ordinance of 1926. The Authorities were empowered with the task of maintaining order and good government among the natives and to make rules aimed at securing peace and welfare for the natives. The Ordinance gave the Native Authorities power to make orders for a number of purposes, including cultivation practices (Fimbo, 1977:5).

Sir Donald Cameron, the governor instituting this legislation, thought it was more in line with the advocacy of Indirect Rule. Cameron indicated in his writings that the provisions in the new Ordinance for giving of orders by the chiefs implied a new approach towards native administration: the colonial administrative officer was no longer the executive authority for native affairs, as under the former Ordinance, now his role was to advise, guide and supervise. He would give direct orders only if a Native Authority neglected or refused to issue an order if directed so by the administrative officer (Morris and Read, 1972). Through Indirect Rule the administrative set-up for generating and enforcing bye-laws, orders and directives were issued by the administrative officers and government appointed local chiefs. However, it should be kept in mind that most of these regulations, even though imposed by the Native Authorities, had been initiated by the central colonial administration. This is evidenced by so many individual orders and bye-laws having identical contents (Cliffe, 1972:17). According to Cliffe:

The various regulations related to every conceivable aspect of farming practice and land use. There were Orders on everything from 'improving bees wax and honey production in Central Province' to 'the control and eradication of banana weevil' around Lake Victoria. Basically, however, they could be grouped together into three categories: those dealing with anti-erosion measures (compulsory tie-ridging and terracing, destocking, control of grazing, etc.); those aiming at improved methods of cultivation (destruction of old cotton plants, mulching of coffee, etc.); and those designed to prevent famine (compulsory production of some famine crops such as cassava or groundnuts) (Cliffe, 1972:18).

To enforce the laws the Native Authorities could resort to sanctions including fines and imprisonment:

> A peasant who contravened or failed to obey any order was liable to a fine not exceeding two hundred shillings or to imprisonment not exceeding two months or to both imprisonment and fine (Fimbo, 1977:5).

The rationality behind using legal, coercive instruments to force peasants to adopt what was thought to be proper farming habits was reflected in the statement of a senior agricultural officer in the Lake Province in 1945, "the consensus of opinion still seems to be that the African cultivator must be compelled to help himself" (quoted in Fimbo, 1977:6). In going through the District Annual Report for Rufiji District this attitude of the colonial administrators towards his subjects are reinforced. Statements about the natives included the following:

- "The native do not care for manual labour" (DAR).
- "The Rufiji native being extremely indolent and apathetic to all hard physical labour" (DAR 1943).
- "Native conservatism and laziness" (DAR).
- "It is too much to hope for that the Rufiji should abandon all intrigue" (DAR, 1941).
- "As usual Mohoro is never happy unless it wants something. This month it was the market" (DAR, 1940).

The number of convictions for breaches of bye-laws and orders indicate that they were not popular with the peasants. For instance in 1944 the Native Authorities in the Lake Province made orders demanding tie-ridging. According to Fimbo (1977:6) the Provincial Commissioner reported in 1945 that there were 12,096 convictions against this rule in 1943 and 14,408 in 1944. Peasant resistance to the colonial directives for land conservation in the 1950s was strong and took on various responses, but there are no concrete numbers giving the extent of convictions. To indicate the detailed character of such rules, let me mention the Native Authority Land Usage Rules for Morogoro Region issued in 1951. They prohibited the planting and cultivation of crops, the felling of trees, the lighting of fires and the grazing of cattle, goats or sheep in areas which (a) bordered on a stream spring or dry river bed, (b) were severely eroded, (c) were land from which water run off courses threaten to cause soil erosion on land below it and (d) on the advice of an agricultural or veterinary officer were stated to be unsuitable for cultivation or grazing purposes (Fimbo, 1977:6).

Bye-laws to enforce cultivation of certain crops had a long history in

Rufiji District. Already in 1902 the German colonial administration forced peasants to supply labour for cotton fields (Iliffe, 1969). In 1936 bananas were introduced as famine relief crop and in 1940 cassava, in both instances backed by bye-laws. In 1951 a regulation was instituted that each household should grow one acre of cassava or 100–150 banana trees. A considerable amount of the district agricultural staff's time was taken up by enforcing this regulation. The fine for not complying was Shs. 20,- (DAR, 1951). The enforcement seems to have been strict and the practice established so that it helped lessen or counteract famines in some years of poor harvest during the 1950s. Sandberg retells a story that the District Commissioner Young, who served in Rufiji District for close to 20 years, "forced the people to plant bananas at gun-point, as a famine relief crop" (Sandberg, 1974a:15).

Another set of legal regulations representing a powerful mechanism on the part of the colonial government was taxation. It had already been instituted by the German Colonial Administration and the British administration saw to its continuity by issuing the Hut and Poll Tax Ordinance of 1923. The official motive for such taxes emphasised the need to recover the costs of government administration. It is, however, quite clear that the real motives were different. Already in 1913 the governor of the East African Protectorate stated:

We consider taxation as the only possible method of compelling the native to leave his reserve for the purpose of seeking work. Only in this way can the cost of living be increased for the native.... and it is on this that the supply of labour and the price of labour depends (Shivji, 1979).

In Tanganyika the tax instrument seems to have been used quite actively in creating regions of "labour reserves". For instance in Kigoma Region, one of the least developed, the colonial government used bye-laws to obstruct peasants from growing cash crops which could have provided an alternative way of enabling tax payment without engaging in migrant labour (Nindi 1979:22). Shivji (1979:4) indicates that in many districts tax drives were planned "to flush out" labour when most needed by employers.

In Rufiji District the emphasis on tax collection was also pronounced. In the Annual Report for the District of 1935 it is stated that, "Tax has been mentioned in almost every paragraph of this report. It remains a regrettable fact that the Native Administration is entirely dominated by this question. The time of Administrative officers which should be devoted to better causes, is largely monopolised by the necessity of re-enforcing the effort of the native Collectors." In 1945 the tax rate in Rufiji District was the highest for any coastal district and the district report for that year estimated that the tax levy was 25 per cent of gross income per tax payer. Tax defaulters were employed by the district administration in various types of work, grass clearing along roads, as porters for safaris, etc. In 1941, 432 persons were forced to supply labour because of default on taxes which represented a total of 12,620 man days (DAR, 1941). As Rufiji District in a sense constituted a labour reserve for a growing capital, Dar es Salaam, many of the taxes were alien taxes paid in Dar es Salaam township. This was particularly so for the western part of the district with low rainfall which was more prone to flooding. In 1943, 500 of 2,333 taxes paid in the west, in Mtanza and Kwangwazi, were alien taxes of this kind (DAR, 1943).

Post-colonial legal mechanisms

Native Authorities were replaced in 1953 by District Councils under the Local Government Ordinance. At Independence six such councils were in operation and by July 1962 councils were established in other districts. Under the Local Government Ordinance, the District Councils were given permission to carry out a range of activities related to agricultural production and marketing. Some of them included:

- to provide services for improving agriculture;
- to control and prescribe the methods of husbandry in respect of any agricultural land;
- to take all necessary measures for the prevention of soil erosion and the protection of crops;
- to prohibit, regulate or control the use of agricultural land whether for agriculture, grazing, forestry or any other purpose whether of a like nature to the aforegoing or not;
- to prescribe steps to be taken by the occupier of agricultural land to maintain and improve its productivity and preserve the fertility of the soil;
- to require adult persons who occupy agricultural land in accordance with customary law to sow or plant such land or a specified proportion or acreage of such land with a specified crop or crops and to tend such crop or crops;
- to promote, regulate or control the disposal or marketing of any agricultural or animal produce in the area (Fimbo, 1977:7).

To facilitate administration at lower level, each district was divided into divisions, wards and villages, each level with its own executive officer. One of the objectives of these officials was to ensure that peasants complied with the bye-laws, which had to be approved by the Minister for Local Government and to be published in the Gazette. At village level, Village Development Committees (VDC) were established whose main function was to organise self-help projects. In July 1969, Ward Development Committees (WDC) replaced the VDCs. The WDCs were granted the power to issue orders demanding that all adult ward residents take part in the implementation of development projects. The District Councils were given the power to pass bye-laws which had to be approved by higher authorities, as explained above.

When the Government administration was decentralised in 1972, the District Councils were replaced by District Development Councils. The Decentralisation of Government Act of 1972 did not provide the District Development Councils with bye-law making powers. This was conferred on the councils by the Prime Minister who has to approve all bye-laws (Fimbo, 1977:12).

Investigation of the functioning of the WDCs has shown that middle and poor peasants generally did not participate in the discussion and initiation of development schemes (Finucane, 1974:98). And further, although there was local initiative in the planning and design of development schemes, there was rigid control from above (Fimbo, 1977:8). Finucane claims that the WDCs did not differ much from the former VDCs. In his study in Mwanza he found that common features of WDCs were low participation of officials in meetings, a localised nature of most of the activities, poor attendance of TANU cell leaders, and the tendency for the better off cell leaders to attend. The District Development Councils created after decentralisation were too large to perform all their functions efficiently. The Council was controlled by the centre through the Office of the Prime Minister.

The administrative structure became increasingly complex with decentralisation (1972) and on village level with the introduction of the Ujamaa and Ujamaa Villages Act of 1975. Thus the state established prior to and under the massive phase of the resettlement campaign an administrative structure which could help to generate and enforce the legal mechanisms enacted.

Bye-laws, orders and directives did exist during the 1960s, but their usage had declined compared to the colonial period. For instance, there was a strong reaction against all measures instituted to fight soil erosion and land degradation. Bye-laws in these areas were hardly ever enforced during the 1960s.

Many observers find that bye-laws were revived mainly in 1974 and 1975 (Coulson, 1982:256 and Fimbo, 1977:13). On the 13th August, 1974 *the Daily News*, a government organ, explained the significance of the revival of bye-laws in the following way:

Bye-laws requiring people to cultivate the land and care for their farms have been operating in the country for many years. After independence their enforcement was somehow neglected. They are now being revived in many parts of the country to combat laziness and drunkenness.

In some districts the District Development Councils seized the opportunity and enacted new bye-laws (Bagamoyo, Singida and Mbinga, 1976), in other districts enforcement of bye-laws led to numerous prosecutions, like in Mafia (*The Daily News*, August 13, 1974), in Rufiji (*The Daily News*, September 8, 1974), in Rungwe (*The Daily News*, September 2, 1974) and in Pare (*The Daily News*, August 19 ,1974). The conviction of people for contravening bye-laws, the majority related to agricultural practices, continued throughout the 1970s. Williams (1979) cites examples published in *The Daily News* column "Regional round up" from the following regions and districts during 1979; Sengerema (Catholic leader jailed six months for inciting villagers not to use fertilisers on their farms) (March 3, 1979), Tabora (three people fined for ignoring directive to cultivate farms in a village. The directive required every villager to cultivate at least one hectare of cash crops) (May 5, 1979), Masasi (six peasants fined for having burned their cashew nut trees. The fine was Tsh. 300 each or six months imprisonment) (undated), Nachingwea (two residents fined for having put fire to their cashew nut trees instead of weeding them) (July 2, 1979), Maswa (District Party Secretary warns that drastic steps will be taken against people who go back to their pre-villagisation villages. The government had information that some "irresponsible" people were instigating others to desert the new villages) (November 27, 1979), Kyela (launching of cassava growing campaign. Peasants required to grow at least one acre of cassava by April, otherwise legal steps would be taken against them) (February 27, 1979).

AGRICULTURAL MARKETING IN RUFIJI DISTRICT

There existed no cooperatives in Rufiji District before 1958. Until then traders, mainly of Asian origin, had been given licenses to purchase the produce from peasants. In 1958 the colonial administration made a determined effort to establish cooperatives in the district. About ten societies were started and in 1960 these societies formed a union known as the Rufiji Cooperative Union (Plumbe, 1974:6 and Manyiki and Lumbanga, 1971:3). This was the first of three periods of the establishment of cooperatives in Coast Region. The second followed independence, from 1962–66, but affected mainly Kiserawe District and Mafia. Only two societies were created in Rufiji District during this period. After the Arusha Declaration there was another upsurge in the organisation of cooperatives, which emerged as an integral part of the Ujamaa Programme, "Operation Rufiji". This was the first attempt by the government to establish ujamaa villages, where each village should function as a multi-purpose cooperative society. Another trend was for cooperatives to be established at old trading centres to replace the Asian traders still operating (Plumbe, 1974:7). In the initial phase of the programme in 1969 the establishment of ujamaa villages was limited to the middle and the upper part of the Rufiji valley flood plain, i.e. to those villages which were moved after the severe 1968 flood and re-established at a new location on the high ground either north or south of the Rufiji river valley (Flood Plain North and South and West Valley zones).

In those areas where a cooperative society extended over large areas, buying posts were established in order to lessen the burden for the peasants of transporting their produce to the selling point. The spread of multi-purpose ujamaa cooperatives and buying posts linked to the Coast Region Cooperative Union and the National Agricultural Products Board (NAPB) gave the single channel market organisation good coverage of each district. Private and Asian based marketing channels became obsolete. Earlier, farmers sold crops directly to traders or to Asian shops in the trading centres which were linked to private trading houses, and arranged transport to the capital or nearest point of processing.

The Coast Region Cooperative Union was established in 1965. By 1967/68 it had 66 active primary societies which increased to 84 by 1969/70. In its first year of operation, the aim was to consolidate operations and settle financial claims. In 1966/67, the year after its establishment, the union had a financial crisis and the government intervened. The entire personnel, of both the primary societies and the union, was suspended and Cooperative and Agricultural Officers were appointed by the government to run the cooperatives. This change did, however, not put an end to the crisis, and in the subsequent year the government decided that the cooperative personnel should resume their duties (Manyiki and Lumbanga, 1971:3). This particular case in Coast Region showed clearly that government intervention could not ensure that cooperatives would operate as desired. It implied that marketing cooperatives could not be used as vehicles for government policies.

In Rufiji District 33 primary societies had been established by January 1st 1971. The variation in the major activity of these societies indicates the differing resources in the district: 23 societies were based on farming, three on mangrove cutting, three were store societies, two timber and two fishing societies (Ibid., 6).

Investigations indicate that produce losses for Coast Region were greater than the average for the unions as a whole. For instance, for the period 1966/67–1968/69, on average 78 societies recorded produce losses of over 4 per cent. A major cause for part of this high crop loss was the great shrinkage of an important Coast Region crop, copra. The cooperative inspector who investigated the crop losses, suggested that the farmers sold their copra when it was not yet completely dry, and consequently net weight loss took place in the hands of the unions or the buying institutions. Other causes suggested were double weighing, thefts, destruction of crops by rodents due to poor godowns, writing of fictious receipts and problems associated with grading, which was introduced in 1967/68 (Ibid., 10–11).

Manyiki and Lumbanga reported that "a number of solutions to the above problems have been worked out by the union" (Ibid., 11). During 1969–70, 24 stores were built and a five year plan for the construction of additional stores at a cost of Tsh. 1.8 million had been drawn up. In order to curb thefts, a system was designed where a person responsible for buying cash crops would not be given additional money until he had returned written documents of crop values equalling the initial sum of money given to him (Ibid., 11 and Plumbe, 1974:21). This procedure functioned in a number of unions in the country. Unions managed to reduce thefts related to transport by establishing their own transport unit. Thereby transport delays were also curbed (Manyiki and Lumbanga, 1971:11).

A study conducted by A. Sandberg (1974a) showed that agricultural marketing services were not uniformly available throughout Rufiji District. His investigation took place in the Inner Delta and Delta zones of the district, areas in which the peasants refused to comply with the government directive to move to ujamaa villages both in 1968 (Operation Rufiji) and during the second campaign in 1973 (Operation Pwani). Prior to 1968 all agricultural marketing in Inner Delta South was carried out by the Msomeni and Usimbe Farmers' cooperative societies, which according to Sandberg, were closely controlled by the members themselves. The societies lost almost all their powers to the Coast Region Cooperative Union when they were disbanded in 1968–69. Sandberg reported a growing resentment among delta farmers against the cooperative union, because the union refused to provide services to those who rejected the move into ujamaa villages, and partly because peasants who brought their crops to the primary society in Mohoro ujamaa village were served last. Often they had to wait 2–3 days before they could sell, because the union had run out of money (Sandberg, 1974a: 39–40). This might, however, be due to the union's increased control of cash handling. Another study reported that an effect of the tighter control of cash could be that, "societies are closed for up to two weeks at a stretch, even in the peak harvesting season" (Plumbe, 1974:21). Hence lack of money for purchases in Mohoro, rather than poor service at the buying point, could be an effect of the control scheme. Another effect was that many farmers hired transport to take their crops to the nearest buying post that had cash for purchases which implied that agricultural produce was not necessarily marketed in the society closest to the location of production (Ibid.).

The delta peasants complained that although three-quarters of the produce marketed at Mohoro ujamaa village originated from their fields, they were excluded from all decision making. Resentment against the union led many peasants to try marketing their crops themselves, in spite of it being illegal. It could be done on trading trips to Mafia, Kilwa and Songo-Songo, using canoes to get to the ocean and from there transport continued on a larger boat. Sandberg shows that marketing rice through such illegal channels would only be profitable for dehusked rice, which in turn was based on the harsh exploitation of female labour during dehusking. For this work of pounding the rice the women were paid only one eighth of its' increased value. The hourly pay corresponded to 20 cents an hour, which can be compared to the national minimum wage of Tsh. 1.60 per hour. Thus if women were paid the legal wage, the illegal marketing of rice would have been uneconomic. According to local estimates, as much as two-thirds of the rice harvest from this area might be marketed through illegal channels (Sandberg, 1974a:41).

Another effect of the negative relations between farmers and the co-operative union, was observed through a change in the composition of production and particularly in the river valley further west. For cotton, which had to be sold to the union, farmers were substituting *kunde* (cow-peas) which had a remunerable alternative marketing channel. *Kunde* was easily cultivated, it could be consumed directly or legally marketed at a fair price (Ibid.).

Some interesting observations were made about the expansion of crop sales through non-union channels. Those trading in *kunde* were local well-to-do people, with good positions in the political and cooperative machinery dominating these villages. They thus used their influence to get access to village lorries to transport the crop for their own benefit. So as not to jeopardize their position of trust, they hired kin to help do the crop purchasing and transport work. The trade in fish, according to Sandberg, was carried out along the same lines as the *kunde* trade, while the illegal trade in rice was conducted by the growers themselves (Ibid., 42). Thus a new type of middle-men seemed to emerge alongside the official system, yet, integrated with it and exploiting its resources.

The abolition of cooperative unions in 1976 and the establishment of crop authorities did not seem to improve marketing conditions for Rufiji peasants. By 1979 most of the crop authorities were established in the district, but my survey of Rufiji villages during the same year showed that a large number of villages were faced with problems of late or no payment and delayed collection of crops. These villages included Utunge, Umwe, Nyaminywili, Mchukwi, Nyamatanga, Ruaruke/Maunga, Kiechuru, Mbuchi, Kiasi, Mbwera, Chumbi A and Kiomboni. In Utunge village (Flood Plain South) it was reported in October 1979 that crop authorities had collected neither cotton nor cashew nuts from the previous crop season for which they were still awaiting payment (own survey 1979).

UJAMAA VILLAGE SCHEME AND VILLAGISATION IN RUFIJI DISTRICT

In Chapter 4 the characteristics of the Rufiji agricultural system, the impact and role of floods, the occurrence of famine etc. were analysed. During the past century about 20 major famines occurred. Right after Independence in 1962 a serious famine was caused by a large flood in the Rufiji river valley. It was embarrassing to the newly formed Tanganyikan government that food had to be requested from external sources. This was the first time prior to 1974 that the inner delta area, around Msomeni and Usimbe, had to accept food relief (Sandberg, 1974a:9).

When the large flood in 1968 caused tremendous destruction of crops and houses in the flood plain, the government decided to launch an ujamaa village campaign to move the population of the flood plain on to the higher flood plain banks. On the one hand it was an emergency programme, and on the other it was a resettlement campaign, the first in Tanzania in which the principles of creating ujamaa villages were to be transformed into a concrete scheme. Both these factors are important when evaluating its successes and failures. At that time the peasants were destitute, their crops had been washed away and their houses had been destroyed. Just as before when flood and famine struck they were looking for government assistance. For the first time the government decided to implement the general ideas and policies of rural development and living along ujamaa principles.

The destruction caused by the flood was not much felt in the inner delta areas, and not at all in the delta itself. The upper and lower parts of the flood plain were the most affected. Hence it was in these areas that the main thrust of the "Operation Rufiji" was directed. In the first phase the aim was to establish 25 ujamaa villages on higher ground.

The following account of some of the major principles, the organisation and the implementation of "Operation Rufiji" is based on an article by Ben Turok, "The Problem of Agency in Tanzania's Rural Development: Rufiji Ujamaa Scheme" (1971) and a detailed interview with Turok in June 1986. In 1968 Turok was a regional surveyor and town planner in Coast Region (*Idara ya Upimaji*). He supervised the whole of the demarcation of land during "Operation Rufiji". Thus the picture given is from a person participating in the standing committee of the scheme and in most of the meetings of officials and between officials and peasants. Since it is the view of one person, it is subjective, and cannot fully represent and reflect the attitudes and positions of the peasants, for instance. Nevertheless, the view of an implementor can provide information about the decisions and thinking that prevailed in the bureaucracy while implementing the campaign. Some of the issues related to principles of policy, the role of force in implementation and the focus on production in the new villages are of major relevance to the questions discussed in this chapter.

The initiative of starting "Operation Rufiji" was taken soon after the flood, and the message was that the issue was relocation in an organised way. It was quite clear that there was strong pressure from above for quick results. These signals were communicated by the Regional Commissioner who was in close contact with the President.

Early it was realised that the general principles of ujamaa villages and self reliance would not be easily operationalised in a concrete setting. Thus the implementors had to ask for directives and policies, which were delayed for several weeks. Only vague notions existed about the role of the government in providing social infrastructure and there was no principle dealing with how productive activities in the villages should be organised. After some time the message to villagers looked like this in terms of priorities: Firstly, living in the new ujamaa villages would enable the peasants to survive the next flood, secondly, it would be easier for the government to supply them with food and seeds; thirdly, villages would be able to enjoy access to roads and social infrastructure, like health and education; and only as a last priority did considerations about production and its organisation enter. Turok argues that the motive of political control was not important in this operation. Instead it was the conjuncture of a natural calamity with the ideology of ujamaa.

To persuade the peasants to agree to move from the river valley to the higher and infertile escarpment was extremely difficult. The fertile land of their ancestors was in the valley, where it had been cultivated for generations. Yet they were well aware of the dangers of excessive floods. To increase pressure on the peasants the government made it clear that it would not again support an orderly movement. Reluctantly the peasants took part in the move to villages, but at the same time kept their option open to cultivate in the flood plain. Wisely, the government did not insist that they should stop cultivating in the flood plain, only that the houses were to be moved and that some kind of complementary production was to start on the higher ground. Promises were made to locate the villages as closely as possible to the river valley edge to minimise walking times to the fields in the valley. The peasants had no faith in communal farming on the high ground, however, even though some cultivation was initiated. In Ikwiriri, for instance, tractors were brought in to clear a large area. It is of interest to note that the idea using river water to irrigate the higher ground existed. The surveyors were told to take account of the fall of the land in order to identify where water could be run. Nyerere said that they should do the same as the North Koreans.

A standing committee consisting of regional heads of departments and high level district officials, under the guidance of the then Second-Vice-President, Rashid Kawawa, was set up to provide leadership for the operation. According to Turok, "the regional officials had obviously never given the ujamaa policy serious consideration" (Turok, 1971:399). The Regional Commissioner presided over most meetings of the commission and undertook to discuss policy issues directly with the President, since he was in regular contact with him. This was gladly accepted by the local officials who were thereby relieved of responsibility for the scheme and of the necessity to think politically about its implementation and objectives (Ibid.).

In clarifying the concrete issues related to the scheme, the President ruled out both the expensive settlement schemes of the early Independence period and collective farms. He said that the villages should be "small enough to maintain a sense of close neighbourhood, but containing sufficient people for the rational provision of elementary services. The community should also be large enough for communal work and new farming methods when these were introduced" (Ibid.). It was further clear that the scheme should run along principles of self-reliance and that dependence on the government was to be discouraged.

The first 20 villages were surveyed during a period of two months, indicating the emergency character of the operation. There was no time to investigate the quality of the soil round the new villages and very poor investigation of the availability of water was made—the water engineer was neither a good engineer, nor interested in the operation. As a result, the planners neglected both the soil and the water aspects. Ecological issues like deforestation were hardly considered.

When some of the areas were cleared of big trees they were uprooted by tractors. Peasants had warned that this would lead to destruction of the soil. It seems that to the extent that planners asked for and took note of advice from the peasants, the implementation of the operation improved. The following describes the design, location and establishment of villages.

First the surveying team made an abstract model design of a village which was approved by the standing committee. The surveyors together with the Area Commissioner then went to the villagers to ask their advice about the location of a village. A local official would say, "We think this is a good spot". Villagers would agree or reject the suggestion and have a meeting of their own, come back and guide the officials to a nearby spot where they thought it should be. They argued that the land there was more fertile, there were more trees, etc. Once a location was selected, often after taking the advice of the peasants, the model village was transferred to the ground. 10–20 peasants would assist in clearing, using their own matchets and axes, so that survey lines could be established. Peasants went on to clear their own plots and very soon temporary shelters were set up. The National Service came to assist in uprooting or cutting down the big trees, and poles and wood were given to the villagers for building houses. For every day of work the peasants would get a ration of maize to take to their families.

The TANU Youth League set up a camp at Ikwiriri. They were to assist by making blocks for houses. They did not, however, seem to understand the objectives of the operation, nor did they seem to believe in it. In a way this attitude was reflected in the whole scheme. A major cause of the failure of the scheme was a lack of political inputs from the centre which could have given shape to the whole project. There was no clear idea of what socialism was, only a certain utopianism and idealism about villagisation.

In the first period there was a certain mobilisation for the operation among the peasants. But after two or three months, as difficulties arose and resistance to the operation grew, the standing committee for the operation began to lose self-confidence and faith. There was no proper planning to show the way forward when difficulties occurred. The original enthusiasm for the operation could not carry it through. Technocratic government employees increasingly took over the implementation.

The problems of implementation had the effect of shifting much of the responsibility for the efforts on to the peasants. "Some people were so thin, working so hard. It was terrible to see". That things nevertheless happened was, according to Turok, due not so much to persuasion, but to the desperate need of the peasants.

On reflection in 1986, Turok said the following about the campaign: "There was a strange ambiguity about the whole thing. There was the Party and several layers of structures, the Area Commissioner, departments etc. They were all interlocking institutions, meshed together when things were going well. There was a lot of good will, even enthusiasm for this project. On the other hand, there was some essential glue missing and different people were giving different kind of glue. My own understanding was that the glue should have been a clear ideological and policy understanding of what this operation was going to be. That was what I found frustrating. It was not there and not even in my own Ministry. We had marvelous young fellows, bright and competent (technicians, not graduates). They really believed in Nyerere and the whole thing, but they did not understand it. The Rufiji project was penetrated with the lack of understanding. The conception of 'what are we really doing' was lacking" (personal communication with Turok, June 1986).

Even though the 1968 flood did not destroy any houses in the villages of the inner delta area, they were also told to move to the higher banks of the flood plain. Mohoro, a strategically located village, resisted the move and in the end was allowed to remain,with the new name of Mohoro ujamaa village. Villages like Msomeni, Ngoaro and Usimbe officially ceased to exist and the people there were told to move to the newly established village Chumbi (Sandberg, 1974a:16). Villages in the delta proper, like Mbwera, Kiechuru and Jaja were not issued with a directive to move and were not affected by the operation other than by a deterioration in communications (Ibid.). Many of the people who did officially move to newly created villages, moved back, at least for parts of the year, to their stilthuts in the valley to cultivate the land. Sandberg claims that some kind of "nomadic" adaptation took place. Even though a lot of villages were erased from official maps, some people still lived there. Without political recognition, they faced increasing problems of communication with the official villages. Roads and bridges to the resistant villages were not maintained. As these villages were prohibited from obtaining trading licenses they could not continue to trade legally, presenting further obstacles to the people.

In 1973, 75 per cent of the population of the district were living in ujamaa villages (Angwazi and Ndulu, 1973). During "Operation Pwani" in 1973 the remaining 25 per cent were urged to move to villages. Most of those who refused to move in 1968 again refused to move. One important reason for this persistent resistance to moving, was that the alternative village sites were situated far from the delta where the rich and varied resources of agriculture, fishing and forestry (mangroves) were located. In the North Hill area of Rufiji District, also affected by "Operation Pwani", houses were burnt down to force people to move (communication with missionary working at that time at the Mchukwi mission hospital). People were moved to nearby villages, but six years later, even in 1979, villagers refused to use the official name of the village, preferring the name of their destroyed village.

In the delta area, communications were difficult because of swamps and variations in the tidal water, decaying bridges and poor roads. In addition, the alternative sites were simply not acceptable to the population. The village of Kiechuru agreed to provide self-help to a large salt project initiated by district officials in 1973, hoping that then the authorities would agree to leave the village in its original location. The need for village labour to support the project was grossly underestimated and it dragged on. In 1975 the necessary machinery was brought to the village. Three years later, work on the project stopped, but was resumed in 1979. Later it was reported that the village chairman and secretary were suspended for embezzlement of the project's funds. According to a lower rank district official who had supported the project, the village chairman was illiterate and had been signing papers without knowing their contents. In 1982 the district planning officer said that the project had come to a stand-still because villagers refused to provide labour unless they were paid. The District was ready to withdraw its support at that time. Probably the project will never reach the production stage, but resistance to the move from Kiechuru was successful. Most other villages in the delta were also left intact, the most pronounced change being the insertion of "ujamaa" in their names. The influential village of Mohoro once again fought off the demand to move and remained in its strategic position where the road to southern Tanzania touches a Rufiji river tributary. During the 1979 flood, most likely the worst of this century, Mohoro was badly hit. Even houses on the high ground were affected and many seemed about to fall down. The district officials once again demanded that Mohoro should be moved on to higher ground. An alternative location was surveyed in 1980 and the district officials put pressure on the village, but it still refused. When the top officials finally went to Mohoro to execute the move in early 1981, several were locked up in the village prison. The government sent the special Field Force Unit from Dar es Salaam to resolve the conflict and several of the villagers were taken to court for their action. Yet Mohoro remains in the same location.

None of the official newspapers reported these incidents. But they were confirmed by direct questioning of officials from Mafia District, during a conversation in Dar es Salaam in April 1981.

In Rufiji District in 1979 in the North Hill area houses were built in or near the older homesteads. The ward secretary in Kibiti informed us that people taking such steps would be forced to move back to the official villages. During visits in 1981, 1982, 1983, 1985 and 1987 a clear tendency could, however, be observed in the establishment of peripheral single houses or small clusters of houses. This implies that during the economic crisis, the Party had given up its strict policy of containing people in the official villages. Similar tendencies of establishing satellite houses or clusters of houses took place without government interference in other areas, like the Rukwa and Kigoma Regions (see also Chapter 9).

LEGAL COERCION IN RUFIJI DISTRICT

There were numerous prosecutions in Rufiji District for the contravention of bye-laws at the time of their revival in 1974 (*The Daily News*, September 8, 1974). The spread and enforcement of bye-laws and other legal instruments continued unabated. In this section I will focus on bye-laws and their enforcement in Rufiji District at the onset of the economic crisis in 1978/79.

As shown in Chapter 4 the drop in cashew nut production had been dramatic since 1973. National production went down from 145,000 tons in 1973/74 to about 40,000 tonnes in 1978/79 and the corresponding Rufiji figures were 6,500 and 1,800 tonnes. There were several reasons for this decline which will be discussed in more detail in Chapter 7. The most prominent ones were the dislocation of trees after villagisation, a rapid drop in the real value of producer prices for cashew nuts, both in relation to food crops and other export crops, the existence of alternative opportunities for earning a non-agricultural cash income, in particular charcoal production and fishing.

In February 1979 the government initiated a cashew weeding campaign in the cashew growing areas along the coast. The slogan was, "Avoid burning, weed your cashew nut trees" (*Epuka moto, palilia mikrosho yako*). Posters were hung on Party offices and official buildings all over the district. In Rufiji District the major cashew nut growing area coincided with the area in which charcoal production was increasing rapidly, the North Hill area. About 75 per cent of the cashew nuts of the 1978/79 crop season originated from the charcoal producing villages. Thus the labour input required to weed vast cashew nut fields was bound to conflict with charcoal production.

On an economic level the motivation for the cashew nut campaign was revealed by the government official who said, "Cashew nuts bring foreign exchange, charcoal does not". Bye-laws were issued compelling peasants to weed the cashew nut fields, some of which were far from the villages.

Throughout 1979 I travelled extensively in Rufiji District, visiting nearly all of the 90 villages, some of them several times. This gave me a good opportunity to follow the cashew weeding campaign. The deadline for weeding cashew trees was June 30, after which non-compliance would be punishable by law, according to the statement by the District Party Secretary in *The Daily News* (June 15, 1979). By the end of May it was clear that the campaign had not produced significant results. Consequently during the last month, June, the campaign was intensified.

On 9th June we drove from Kilimani village in the Flood Plain North through the cashew nut/charcoal belt to Kibiti Village in North Hill. The divisional secretary of Kibiti travelled with us and we stopped in the villages of Ngulakula, Miwaga and Kimbuga to interview craftsmen of various types, including charcoal producers. The divisional secretary did not show much interest in the problems and prospects of craftsmen and craftswomen, but was preoccupied by the cashew weeding campaign. He campaigned for it strongly in all the villages we visited and every time we passed a weeded cashew field he would exclaim, "Umeona, umeona", (you have seen, you have seen). Once he added, "Kama estate" (Just like an estate).

The district officials became increasingly worried about the effect of charcoal production on the cashew weeding campaign. There was a need to divert some of this labour to weeding round the trees. Thus, not surprisingly on June 15, *The Daily News* could report that,

> Rufiji District has banned petty businesses which make it difficult for peasants to concentrate on working on cashew nut farms. The ban prohibits burning and selling of charcoal, fishing and transporting of fish outside the district. The District Party Secretary, Ndugu N. Millinga, has said the ban will remain in force until weeding and clearing of cashew nut farms was completed.

Markets were closed down to divert people from trading. Peasants were not allowed to leave their home areas before the cashew nut fields had been weeded. This restriction was similar to that applied to cotton in Rufiji in 1979, when a minimum acreage of cotton had to be planted before peasants could obtain permission to leave their home villages. To enforce the weeding of cashew trees peasants, who were travelling out of the district during the campaign in February–June, had to obtain a permit from the relevant authority. During June, when the campaign was most intense, nearly all buses leaving the district were stopped at the northern gate of Kibiti village and people had to show their papers.

Information provided by the divisional secretary of Kibiti in late August 1979 showed that 60 persons had been fined between Tsh. 100 and 200 for not tending to their cashew nut trees. At the same time the divisional secretary in Ikwiriri stated that two people had been fined, Tsh. 75 and Tsh. 150 respectively. In Muyuyu village in Flood Plain North it was claimed that fields had been weeded, hence no one was fined. When we drove between the villages of Muyuyu and Njianne, we saw cashew nut fields which had recently been burnt with most trees being severely damaged. Burning was also observed in other areas, like the far North Hill area, but it was not on a large scale. On November 2 1979, the divisional secretary of Kibiti stated that an additional 30 persons, i.e. 90 in all, had been brought to court for neglecting their cashew fields. 15 people who could not pay their fines were imprisoned, most for three months.

The other side of the enforcement of the cashew nut campaign was the ban on charcoal production. The response of the peasants to the charcoal ban will be presented and analysed in Chapter 7. In January 1985 the authorities issued a second directive to stop charcoal production and people were instead ordered to engage in afforestation programmes by preparing fields for planting trees. Posters were displayed in various regional and district offices and in the villages. The posters claimed that the rapid rate of deforestation was due to charcoal production.

7. Effects of State Intervention on Rural Production

INTRODUCTION

In this chapter I will focus on the effects of state intervention in the post-independence period. The time series data for rice and cotton sales depicted in Table 4.6 and additional data for specific crops, like cashew nuts, show that from the end of the 1960s there is a decline in the official purchases of agricultural produce. It cannot be explained by corresponding physical changes such as rainfall and floods and the decline increases further from around the mid-1970s onwards. The negative correlation between rice sales and duration of floods and the positive correlation between cotton sales and peak floods, characteristic features of the agricultural system, are broken. Another significant trend in the mid-1970s is the rapid decline of officially purchased food crops, like paddy and maize and the marketing of cashew nuts.

An important question is whether the indicated tendencies for official purchases of agricultural crops, represent real trends in the production of these crops. Has state intervention in Rufiji upset the labour balance of the agricultural system, or are production levels maintained, but disguised by increasing marketing through parallel channels, made possible by a change in the composition of the agricultural crops?

The answers to the above questions are not easy to determine as there are no readily available and reliable statistics for agricultural produce. Hence, answers have to be sought by analysing the entire rural production system in the district, in order to identify trends which can tell us something about changes in the labour allocation of the peasantry. As has been shown in the previous chapters, the peasant is not only an agriculturalist, but also engages in non-agricultural production like forestry, crafts and fishing.

Other elements which can throw light on the development of agricultural production and the responses of the peasantry, are data and information related to changes in the level of famine relief and the degree and changes in the monetisation of the local economy.

Data related to the nutritional status of the local population may provide some insight in checking the real levels of agricultural production.

In Rufiji District one cannot overlook fishing, which plays an important role in both the provision of food and the maintenance of nutritional levels.

My contention is that data and information of this nature will help support or weaken the hypothesis that state intervention in rural production and society, as explained in Chapter 6, has led to stagnation or decline in agricultural production, and to clarify the position of the peasantry with regard to withdrawal versus market integration. Two further issues will be taken up which relate to the latter, namely the relations between the peasant, the state and the commercial class, and the issue of peasant's supply response to relative producer price changes. The final sections of this chapter will focus on the effects of state intervention on the balance of labour in agriculture and issues related to equalisation, differentiation and accumulation.

Before going into the specific issues, let me mention that state intervention in agricultural production and the responses of peasants have been vigorously discussed in the Tanzania and Sub-Saharan context during the 1980s. Goran Hyden set this discussion in motion by publishing *Beyond Ujamaa in Tanzania — Underdevelopment and an Uncaptured Peasantry* and *No Shortcuts to Progress* (Hyden, 1980 and 1983). In the former he claimed that the peasantry in most Sub-Saharan regions is yet to be "captured" by other social classes. Hyden's analysis says that the character of the social and economic relations of the peasantry can be seen as affective ties which give rise to an economy of affection. Because of the existence and endurance of this affective mode, the peasants have the freedom to stay outside the state system. They have the "exit" option as they can withdraw from, or ignore demands put upon them by state officials (Hyden, 1980:25–26). But Hyden not only emphasises the power of the peasants in terms of avoiding the state, his notions of withdrawal relate to the exit option in subsistence production. To illustrate this in the Tanzanian case, Hyden quotes Ruthenberg and provides statistics showing the role and increase in subsistence production as a share of the total agricultural production (Hyden, 1980:80–81). The tendency is for subsistence crops to get priority over cash crop production and Hyden cites Bukoba, Usambara Mountains and Sukumaland as examples. He is aware of the problems related to statistics for subsistence production, but that does not prevent him from presenting such statistics, implying that they show that peasant producers have a real orientation towards subsistence production. Though Hyden's arguments and analysis, at least superficially, seem most relevant to the developments of the 1970s, which was a decade of massive state intervention, he presents statistics only for the period 1960–68 (Hyden, 1980:81). Hyden wrongly implies that a decline in officially

purchased crops means that the peasants are using the force of their affective ties to avoid the state marketing agents and to retreat into subsistence production. (For a critical view of Hyden, 1983, see also Mamdani, 1985.)

DIVERSIFICATION, WITHDRAWAL AND MARKET
INTEGRATION OF PEASANT PRODUCTION

Production trends and observations related to non-agricultural production

In forestry related production, charcoal, mangrove cutting and logging, the available data show the following: For charcoal there has
been a dramatic rise in production, measured by the number of bags,
from 1,260 in 1976 to 493,244 in 1982. This rapid rise was accompanied by a parallel increase in nominal producer prices which trebled
from Tsh. 10 per bag in 1976 to Tsh. 30 in 1982. In real terms this represented a decline due to the high level of inflation. From 1983 onwards charcoal production, however, dropped rapidly, in spite of
further increases in producer prices (Table 5.1). In 1985 producers
got Tsh. 50 per bag of charcoal. The main reasons for the decline were
exhaustion of trees suitable for charcoal production and the general
deterioration of transport due to lack of spare parts and fuel caused by
Tanzania's balance of payment problems.

The data available on the collection of forest royalties for mangroves
and logs for the period 1976 to 1979, show that royalties paid for mangroves rose steadily, from Tsh. 21,724 in 1976 to Tsh. 64,359 in 1979.

There was a rapid increase in the rate of felling of logs from 1976 to
1978 and royalties increased from Tsh. 392,370 to Tsh. 589,749. A
large reduction in royalties for logs occurred as early as 1979, which
reflected the exhaustion of suitable trees, the most valuable being
mininga and *mtondoro*. Due to heavy exploitation these species had disappeared from accessible areas in the North Hill. Exploitation of these
species increased south of the river. The heavy flood in 1979
obstructed the collection of logs, during the long flood. The dramatic
decline in royalties from Tsh. 589,749 in 1978 to Tsh. 319,624 may
thus exaggerate the decrease in logging (see Table 5.4). Data showing
royalties for logs from 1980 and onwards were not available. They
would have helped to assess the rate of decline in this activity. With the
introduction of structural adjustment exploitation of timber for export has increased rapidly during the late 1980s and early 1990s
(Tibaijuka, 1991b).

Combined, the three lines show a rapid increase in the volume of production. The most important, charcoal, increases dramatically. Information obtained in villages about the growing number of people producing charcoal confirms the rapid production increase emerging from royalty figures. The labour input needed to produce charcoal clearly indicates that a major shift in the allocation of peasant labour to charcoal production must have taken place during the second half of the 1970s and into the 1980s.

For flood plain and salt water fishery activities in Rufiji District, data were not available on trends in the catch of fish and prawns marketed. Data for 1979, show that flood plain fisheries are extremely important in terms of part-time employment, in provision of food and protein for most of the flood plain dwellers and for people in the hill areas of the district (Chapter 5). Conditions of production for flood plain fisheries are closely related to the flood regime, as most fishing takes place in lakes inundated by the river floods. In years of medium to large floods, fishing is an important complementary food and protein source for inhabitants of the river valley. In years of badly timed large and excessive floods, fishing represents a crucial alternative source of food as most valley crops will be washed away. This diachronic relation of agriculture and fishing to floods is extremely important in understanding the capacity of reproduction and survival of these ecological and agro-economic systems.

One particular observation related to flood plain fisheries during the 1970s seems significant. After the relocation of villages from the flood plain onto the elevated escarpments, fishing was no longer an integral part of farming, as it had been before. Hence increased specialisation ocurred in fishing. In West Valley a considerable number of people may have given up agriculture as their main activity and turned to fishing. The data collected by Yoshida 1970/71 showed that as many as 65 per cent of the farmers in the sample survey participated in fishing. Given the long distances to the flood plain fields, the data may indicate that fishing was becoming much more important relative to agriculture than in other areas of the flood plain. In the Flood Plain zones Yoshida found that only about 35 per cent of the farmers in the sample engaged in fishing (Yoshida, 1974: Tables IX-1 and IX-2).

The data available does not allow a conclusion to be drawn about the tendency of market orientation and actual trends for the total catches over time. The findings from the flood year of 1979 do, however, indicate that fishing is an extremely important activity in terms of employment, income, food, protein and is also an important source of food in out of district areas, notably Dar es Salaam.

In salt water fisheries the survey conducted in 1979 indicated that about 2,800 people living in the Inner Delta and Delta zones have fishing as a major source of income. Prawn fishing immediately off the Rufiji delta is the most important. Data for the year 1978/79 show that the artisanal fishermen of the Rufiji delta areas supplied about 49,500 tonnes of Tanzania Fishing Company's (TAFICO) total prawn purchases of about 81,500 tonnes, including all sources, even TAFICO's own trawling activities. Since data for these fisheries were limited to one year, it is impossible to state anything about the development over time of catches by Rufiji fishermen. What is undisputable is that Rufiji fishermen account for the major share of all the prawns that are purchased by TAFICO and exported to external markets. On international markets the demand for prawns has been increasing and so have prices, even those received by the fishermen. Information obtained in the villages during 1979/80 indicates that there has been an increasing rather than a decreasing engagement in fishing. The major problem, however, has been low efficiency in the marketing channels. Rufiji fishermen use traditional simple fishing gear, mainly the *wando*, which seems well suited to local conditions. There are indications that the existing prawn resources could allow a higher rate of exploitation off the Rufiji delta. Plans for trawling in shallow waters by TAFICO and private international companies, may create disturbances for the local fishermen, who would also be affected by a possible future implementation of the Stiegler's Gorge project. It would mean that a large dam would be built at the Gorge which would trap much of the silt and nutrients carried by the river water. I will return to this when discussing the consequences of the Stiegler's Gorge project in Chapter 8.

Despite the weak data available, it can be concluded that fisheries in the district are unlikely to have experienced a decreasing trend either in total catch or in the per capita catch marketed.

The data on crafts production in Rufiji District collected during 1979/80 showed a wide variety of production in four major sectors, forestry based, agriculturally based, agriculturally related and skill based. About 34,000 nominal participants were engaged in crafts during 1979 (see Table 5.12). The survey data cannot show how participation developed over time, but information indicates that use and exchange values in crafts were increasing slightly. It was a response to the diminishing supply of most of the basic commodities provided by national industries. Local raw materials were utilised as ingeniously as possible to supply commodities which to some extent at least could substitute for the reduction in external supplies. There was an intense search for all types of scrap, for example rubber and scrap iron were sold to craftsmen. We saw in Chapter 5 that in Rufiji District a large number of blacksmiths have the skills to do repairs and make farm implements which are specific for the area.

The data and analysis presented above and the discussion of non-agricultural production in Chapter 5 indicate an increase both in the
number of people producing and in the total labour time allocated annually by the peasants to non-agricultural production. The data indicates a rapid rise in marketed forestry products from the mid-1970s
onwards, which levels off and from 1982 onwards turns into a decrease, for instance for charcoal. The major role of charcoal in the
whole of non-agricultural production, implies that total production as
well as its marketed share increased so long as accessible raw materials
were available and transport to the Dar es Salaam market was without
major constraints. Thus there is no indication of withdrawal of non-
agricultural production lines from the market. On the contrary, a
range of important activities seem to be more deeply integrated in the
market, in particular those external to the district. This include charcoal production, logging, mangroves and possibly also fishing. Observations made and information obtained during a visit to Rufiji District
in 1987, indicated that charcoal production again was on the increase.
Likewise, small-scale trawling for prawns off the Rufiji coast has accelerated during the period of structural adjustment, i.e. after 1986 (see
Chapter 9).

Monetisation of the local economy

The degree of monetisation of the local economy and its development
over time indicate the degree of integration of peasant production into
the market. Historical records (Guillain, 1856 and Loarer, 1848) show
that peasants exchanged commodities through the market during the
nineteenth century. The colonial regime in the annual district reports
recorded information about marketing of crops and levels of taxation.
The historical records do not indicate that the peasants of Rufiji District belonged to an economy based solely on production for own consumption. The priority on producing food crops, like rice, does not
imply, as many claim, that the economy is subsistence oriented. Rufiji
District has a long history of exports of rice to Zanzibar and other areas
(see Table 4.6).

Nor does a high or increasing degree of market orientation of local
producers necessarily imply that the relations of production are of a
capitalist nature. There is a need to investigate the relations of production concretely, as in Chapters 4 and 5, to assess their character and
content.

In this section I will focus on the degree of and trends in the monetisation of the local economy in the 1970s. My hypothesis is that if an increasing degree of monetisation of the local economy is detected, it

runs counter to the notion that peasant producers are withdrawing from the market into subsistence relations. The data and observations already presented in relation to non-agricultural production, indicate that peasants increasingly divert their labour to the production of commodities which can be marketed through non-state controlled channels. At the same time the official marketing of major food crops and cashew nuts declined from the mid-1970s onwards. As no firm data exists for the real and marketed levels of most sectors, it is necessary to approach the issue of market integration or withdrawal via areas which provide more indirect information, like trade through the Regional Trading Company, trade in local markets, occupational groups' expenditure on food, and conditions related to health and nutrition.

Trade through the Regional Trading Company

In the rural areas of Tanzania in the 1970s, the volume of sales of basic commodities imported into the district can be traced, as the monopoly on wholesale trade is in the hands of the so-called Regional Trading Companies (RTC), one for each region. The sale of basic commodities through the Coast Region Trading Company to Rufiji District can be divided into three categories: food products (sembe flour), general merchandise and textiles. The composition of sales from the three different RTC branches in Rufiji District (Kibiti, Utete and Mohoro) for the 12 month period starting in October 1978 is shown in Figure 7.1.

The graph in Figure 7.1 shows that by far the largest RTC sales in Rufiji District are through the Kibiti branch. For the investigated year they amounted to Tsh. 10.5 m, compared to Tsh. 6 m for Utete and Tsh. 3.4 m for Mohoro. The reason for this diversity of sales seems partly to be the relatively dense population in the North Hill zone and partly its strategic location. There is easy access to Dar es Salaam and it is within easy reach of most of the population living north of the Rufiji river. Kibiti village stands out as the major trading centre for the district. The sales per inhabitant through the Utete branch of RTC are higher than those of the Kibiti branch, due to the concentration of wage earners, particularly government officials, at the district headquarters.

The total RTC sales in Rufiji District 1978/79 amounted to about Tsh. 20 m. If 40 per cent is added as gross profits on retail outlets, the total value of purchases by consumers reached Tsh. 28 m for that year.

There is a large variation in the respective sales of RTC branches over the year investigated (see Figure 7.1). The sales for the Kibiti and Utete RTCs are high during the rainy seasons (October to May). They

Figure 7.1.   *Regional Trading Company (RTC) Sales: Rufiji District, Oct. 1978–Sept. 1979 (one units equals Tsh. 100,000)*

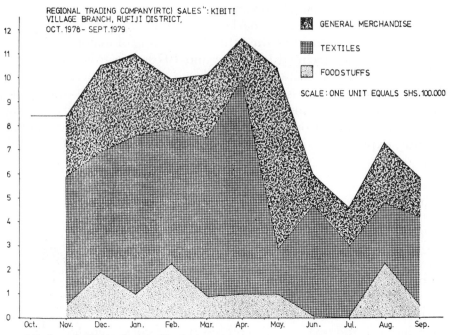

1. For the month of October, the composition of sales is unknown

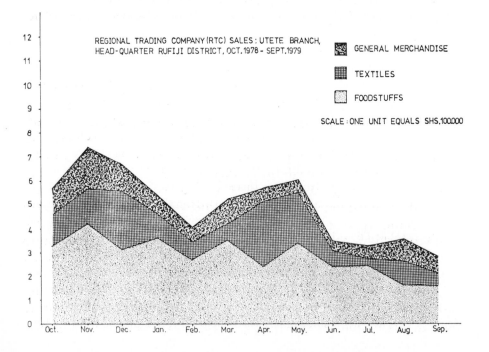

Figure 7.1 continued

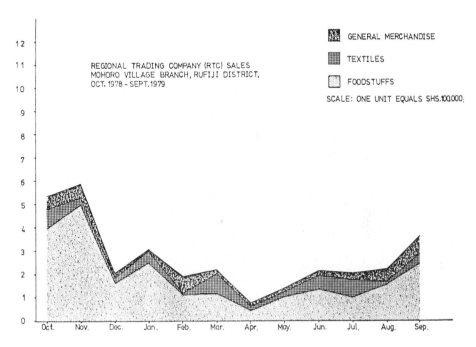

Source: RTC branches Kibiti, Utete and Mohoro.
Note: For the month of October, data on the composition of sales were not available for Kibiti branch.

fall dramatically during the rest of the year mainly due to the decline in the sales of textiles and food. The reduction in food sales is connected with the harvest of rainy season crops, which makes households with direct producers more self reliant. The extremely low food sales by the Kibiti RTC during June and July can also be explained by favourable rainfall for the hill agriculture in 1979. The high proportion of food sales through the Utete RTC throughout the year is not only due to the above-mentioned concentration of wage earners, but also to the extremely poor harvest of rainy season crops due to the excessive flood of 1979. Salaried district officials also engage in cultivation to some extent, partly through employing family members, and partly through hiring labour.

The excessive flood in 1979 caused severe problems for Utete and Mohoro which are both located on the south side of the river. During high floods, Utete may still be supplied by diverting a small ferry to an alternative up-river crossing at Kipo. The problems of supplying Mohoro were compounded by the closure of the road along the southern bank between Utete and Mohoro for several months. The figures for sales through the Mohoro RTC branch show that its total sales are closely connected with the variation in food sales which account for the major share. They are high in October and November, fall drastically from December to July and increase again in August and September. This trend may indicate a relatively good harvest of early rainy season crops and poor yields of long rainy season crops due to the large flood, which for the first time in decades also affected severely Mohoro and the inner delta areas.

The decline in total RTC sales in Kibiti from June to September is mainly attributed to a reduction in the sales of textiles. This trend is probably related to constraints of supplies. This interpretation is supported by the information that peasant producers, if regularly paid by the crop authorities, receive their pay for the upland rainy season crops a this time. Textile and total sales also decline during the same period.

The seasonality of agricultural production and the variability of cash income that follows, has increasingly lost relevance for explaining the variation in the sales of non-foods. Non-agricultural cash incomes from charcoal, mangroves, logging and fishing have come to dominate payments on the demand side.

Data available for the volume of total imports of the main food items, *sembe* (maize flour), rice, beans, sugar, and cassava to Rufiji District through the RTC for 1979 and 1980 show large increases for all items. *Sembe* imports increased from 1,237.8 tonnes to 1,515.7 tonnes, rice imports from 165.8 tonnes to 1,170.2 tonnes, bean imports from 55.7 tonnes to 166.1 tonnes, sugar imports from 436.3 tonnes to 1,219.0 tonnes and cassava from 146 tonnes to 720.4 tonnes. The monthly break-down of the total imports for each item show no clear correspondence with the pattern of the agricultural season. This may indicate that the total imports of food items are dependent mainly on national availability (Bantje, 1982:47–48).

The foregoing analysis of sales of food-stuffs (mainly sembe), textiles and general merchandise, however, does indicate that there is some correspondence with seasonal patterns. This implies that some imported items are stored in RTC godowns, but does not necessarily mean that imports are sufficient to meet local needs. Actual sales depend on demand and demand, in turn, on cash incomes. Even though the variation in sales for 1978/79 (Figure 7.1) reflects seasonal patterns to some extent the level may be much lower than real needs require.

Another problem detected of RTC trade in Rufiji was caused by the government confinement policy of certain basic commodities at intervals during the early 1980s. By confining large hoes they could only be sold through village cooperative shops. Peasants in many villages wanted to buy such hoes, but were unable to do so because these shops did not have sufficient money to purchase them from the RTC branch in Kibiti. This was the prevailing situation in the district at the end of 1983 (Mothander et al., 1989). (For a discussion of rationing and its impact on peasants' supply responses, see Chapter 9.)

Most RTC commodities are channeled to the public through small shops, *dukas*, which account for most of the sales of textiles, general merchandise and part of the food sold in the villages. Most of the 251 *dukas* in a survey of 77 villages in Rufiji District in 1978 were privately owned (McKim, 1981). Some traders of Asian or Arab origin still remain and played an important role in the retail trade in the major villages of Kibiti and Mohoro, despite their loss of control of crop purchases due to the reorganisation of trade and cooperatives during the 1960s (see Chapter 6). During the latter part of the 1970s, the government largely in vain, tried to encourage villages to establish efficient communal or cooperative *dukas*. The cooperative department of the local administration assists such *dukas* to become established and operational. Their records were found to be poor and the confinement policies only made their problems more apparent.

The RTC/*duka* trading system is the major supply channel for basic commodities produced externally. In particular in the trading centres such *dukas* were found to carry a limited supply of products of local craftsmen, like the small weeding hoe and the coconut grater. Many craftsmen and women only produce on order. The major channels for locally produced commodities and foodstuffs are at the numerous daily market places of the district.

Trade on the local market places

In the traditional market places of Rufiji District virtually all the sellers are male. Men also predominate when it comes to purchasing. The market place is hence a male-dominated sphere both economically and socially. In a survey of Rufiji markets, McKim found more than 50 different commodities for sale. The most important items traded were fish, coconuts and salt. Fish was the number one product in terms of the volume of sales and 42 per cent of the sellers interviewed sold at least one of more than ten varieties of fish and prawns caught in the district. Most of the fish reached the market in dried or smoked form. Other commodities McKim found in several market places were bananas, cassava, spinach, tomatoes, sugar, sugar cane, tobacco, spices, fruits and vegetables. Onions and cigarettes were brought in from Dar es Salaam and citrus fruits from Kilwa District in the south. Locally produced craft items like hoes, rope and sandals were also marketed, but not regularly. In larger markets various local sweets and ready-to-eat foods were also found (McKim, 1981:17–18).

According to McKim the sellers at the markets consisted of two categories: the marketeers who were selling the surplus production of a household and the professional traders who made the major share of their earnings through selling commodities they themselves had purchased from various sources. In Rufiji District three markets existed with 1 to 4 sellers, ten markets with 5 to 9, nine markets with 10 to 19, eight markets with 20 to 39 and two markets with 40 to 60 sellers (McKim, 1981:11). The concentration of sellers was highest in the North Hill, Inner Delta and Flood Plain agro-economic zones which had 4.8 sellers per 1,000 people compared to 1.3 in the Delta zones and 1.4 in West Valley.

In terms of the density of markets, the Delta North and South agro-economic zones contained the fewest, only two market places each. These zones had a population of around 20,000. Relocation of villages in this area did not succeed because of resistance and in the end the original villages were simply renamed ujamaa villages. In areas of relocation it seems that local markets have acquired a more important place in the lives of the people, which may imply that the newly created nucleated villages have a less versatile economic basis than the delta villages. This subsequently led to a certain degree of specialisation and a need to intensify market exchange. If this observation is correct, it corresponds with the development of specialisation in fishing. Thus the villagisation programme itself has contributed to increasing the market orientation of production.

This development meant that use values tended to be replaced by exchange values, i.e. a process of commoditisation took place. In Rufiji District peasants tended to engage increasingly in new production lines which was reflected in increased marketing of agriculturally related and non-agricultural commodities, like local sugar, salt, coconut oil, rubber sandals, rope and hoes.

McKim is more concerned about emphasising the limited extent of trade in local markets. He notes that less than one thousand people, or below 1 per cent of the population of the district derive an income as traders from market places or shops. McKim suggests there are three principal causes for the low level of market place activity: a high proportion of the people in the district are primarily subsistence farmers; three of the four major crop income earners (cotton, rice and cashew nuts) have been declining, hence the potential demand for local trade is low; and thirdly, problems of transport represent a major obstacle to the movement of commodities to and from markets. In my opinion McKim's arguments are far from convincing. He does not have a clear concept of what a subsistence farmer is, nor can he substantiate that most people are primarily subsistence farmers. He grossly underestimates the earning potential of non-agricultural production, like forestry and fishing, and underrates the existing transport network. The river is a major obstacle for heavy transport, but during floods canoes can easily move on the water. There are many more regular bus routes than McKim registers. For instance from Ikwiriri to Dar es Salaam there are regular services twice a day (McKim, 1981:22–23).

Expenditure on food and occupational categories

The expenditure on food of occupational groups adds another perspective on the degree of dependence upon the market. During the 1979 survey 53 craftsmen engaged in carpentry, carving and saw mill cooperatives were interviewed about their involvement in agriculture and expenditure on food. 87 per cent of the households of these craftsmen cultivated their own fields. 31 per cent had fields of less than 2 acres, 59 per cent had fields of between 2 and 5 acres and 20 per cent had fields larger than 5 acres. In spite of this nine of 52 craftsmen (information missing for one of them) spent between zero and 25 per cent of their cash income on food, 17 spent between 25 and 50 per cent, 11 between 50 and 75 per cent and 15 said that they spent between 75 and 100 per cent of their cash income on purchasing food (Havnevik, 1980, Tables 6 and 7).

Han Bantje investigated food flows and dietary patterns in the largest village in Rufiji District, Ikwiriri, during 1979–81 (Bantje, 1982). During this period crop harvests were poor. Nationally there were also problems of food shortages. One effect was a rapid price rise of most food items, most of which fall outside the regime of government regulated prices. Even the regulated prices of some foods doubled during 1981. Maize flour increased from Tsh. 1.25 to Tsh. 2.50 and sugar from Tsh. 5 to 10. Bantje reports that food prices were soaring in Ikwiriri in the latter part of 1981; a kilo of maize flour sold for Tsh. 5 to Tsh. 7 on the black market while it was unobtainable in shops. The official price for a kg of rice was Tsh. 5.50 in 1981, but in June it sold for Tsh. 8.50 right after the harvest, for Tsh. 12.50 in September and for Tsh. 17 in January 1982. The price of a bottle of locally produced coconut oil (3/4 litre), increased from Tsh. 20 to Tsh. 50 in the course of 1981 (Bantje, 1982: 12–13).

Table 7.1. *Mean per capita expenditure on food by occupational group* (Tsh.)

Group	Mean per capita	Mean Household	Number of households
Employed	4.85	35.66	71
Petty trade	4.41	26.08	53
Fishing	5.06*	25.88	39
Farming	3.16	19.68	74
Total	4.26	26.91	237

* High because this group included many single men.
Source: Bantje, 1982, p. 14

Between November 1981 and January 1982, when nearly all households had to purchase their food, Bantje was able to record the actual expenditure on food for 237 meals of households from four different occupational groups: employed, petty traders, fishermen and farmers. His results are presented in Table 7.1.

The mean per capita expenditure of Tsh. 4.26 was, according to Bantje, "Just enough for one full meal". It was clear that many households could not even afford one good meal per day. It appears that there is a small difference in expenditure between occupational categories and that the registered level of expenditure on food is extremely high, amounting to a mean of Tsh. 27 per household per day. On a monthly basis this amounts to Tsh. 810, well above the regulated urban minimum wage of Tsh. 600 at that time. This contrasts with McKim's claim of the low potential demand. It further underlines that the degree of market orientation must be significant and that there is a need for both peasants and other occupational groups to secure their basic food supply, at least at intervals, through the market. But, more than anything this finding indicates that the situation of minimum and non-wage earners in the major cities was most precarious during the severe crisis which emerged in the late 1970s and intensified into the 1980s.

It must be stated that the findings from Ikwiriri village are unlikely to be representative for Rufiji District as a whole. The Ikwiriri/Umwe/Mgomba area has nearly 20,000 inhabitants and it is an important agricultural centre. Cash incomes and cash expenditures are likely to be relatively high in this area even in the context of Rufiji District.

Development in health and nutritional status

The health and nutritional status of people in the district may indicate something about the conditions of agricultural cultivation. There are, however, only a few historical sources which provide information on these issues.

One of the first indicators of the health situation in the district appears in the District Annual Report for 1943. Of 1,558 military recruits, despatched in 1941, 1942 and 1943 from Utete, 526 were rejected at the central civil depot. The main reasons for rejections were underweight, anaemia, hydrocele, teeth, yaws and gonorrhea (DAR, 1943).

R. Moore and A. Roberts (1957) in the course of dispensary treatment, examined people in the villages of Utete, Mtanza, Ndundu and Kikale. They found that the average weight of all the people examined was 10 per cent below the normal standard. Malaria, anemia, hookworm, scabies and gonorrhea were quite common leading the examiners to conclude that health conditions in Rufiji District were worse than anywhere else. They may, however, not have taken into account that their sample was not representative, since it only included people who had come for dispensary treatment (Bantje et al., 1979:8).

In 1960 J.M. Liston did a medical appraisal as part of a major FAO study of the Rufiji river basin. For the lower Rufiji he found that the incidence of diseases (all ages) was hookworm (78 per cent), bilharzia (3 per cent) and filariasis (13 per cent and 9 per cent for males and females respectively). The low incidence of bilharzia for the population of the river valley has been subsequently confirmed again. The water of the Rufiji river is constantly running so conditions for the development and spread of the disease are bad. Liston found high incidences of malaria in the form of spleen enlargement and parasites, particularly in the three to ten year age group (Liston, 1961).

M.C. Latham examined 173 people in the villages of Kibiti, Kikale, Utete, Mtanza and Msomeni after the 1962 flood, of whom about 30 per cent were children. He found anemia to be widespread as well as protein and vitamin A and B deficiencies. (The results of Latham's investigation are taken from Bantje et al., 1979:9).

Bantje, Mrisho and Ljungqvist examined 533 children between six months and five years of age in the villages of Mohoro, Ikwiriri, Ngorongo and Mtanza in 1979. I will summarise the conclusions related to anthropometric indicators, which are the most reliable indicators of nutritional status for large numbers of children. It involves measuring height, weight and arm circumference and relating this to the age of the children. Although the weight for age (per cent SWA) indicator has some limitations, it is the most commonly used indicator of nutritional status. In all four villages the team found that a high percentage of children were underweight (below 80 per cent SWA). In three of the villages this situation did not improve with age, which indicates that the main problem is chronic rather than acute undernutrition. It was further found that the percentage of severely malnourished children (below 60 per cent SWA) was low when compared to the high percentage of underweight cases, but that it was high in relation to national standards. An additional important finding from the survey was that environmental and socio-economic factors not only had an impact directly on the nutritional status of the children, i.e. through food intake, but also indirectly through low birth weight, which stems from poor nutritional status as well as the health of the mother (Bantje et al., 1979:55; see also Bantje, 1980b). The findings related to nutritional status varied little between the four villages located in different parts of the river valley. They indicate that the nutritional situation is precarious, and that there is no sign of improvement in the nutritional conditions over time. That the survey was undertaken in January 1979, before the harvest of the short rain crops when food supplies were low, does not alter the significance of these findings.

Developments in famine relief operations

Increases in famine relief indicate problems or stagnation in agricultural production. Investigation of famine relief operations also represents a way to check the real trends in cultivation. A picture of famine and food relief in Rufiji District during the previous century has been given in Chapter 4. Some general conclusions can be drawn from this material. In Rufiji District food shortages have developed into famines, in particular in the West Valley zone. They might be caused by adverse floods or drought. The colonial government was able to check these famines by restricting exports of foodstuffs and by enforcing the cultivation of famine crops.

From 1940 onwards, as famines increased, they could no longer be checked in this way. The famines which developed during the 1950s were less serious than in the previous decade, but in the 1960s, in particular in 1962 and 1968, the post-colonial government had to make a determined intervention to fight severe famines caused by excessive floods. In addition, because of the flood of 1968 the government decided to implement "Operation Rufiji", which required all the peasants living in the flood plain to be moved to the elevated banks to the north and south of the valley. The main objective was to avoid the repetition of the effects of destructive floods. An additional goal was to create the first ujamaa settlements along the principles set out in the Arusha Declaration and "Socialism and Rural Development". The frequency and severity of food shortages and famines were, however, not reduced during the 1970s. On the contrary, the government had to provide famine relief during localised famines in West Valley (1971– 72, 1973–74 and 1976–78) and in the middle sections of the flood plain (1974 and 1978–79). In 1971–72 about 10,000 people were to be affected, in 1974 they were about 50,000.

The data available on food shortages, famines and famine relief indicate increased state intervention during the 1970s compared to the 1960s. The famines in 1973–74 and 1978–79 were caused by excessive floods, but in the remaining cases resettlement is one of the major causes of agricultural problems.

Conclusions

The above summaries of the findings of Chapters 4–6 and the presentation and analysis of additional data related to non-agricultural production, trends in famine relief, level and direction in the monetisation of the local economy as well as nutritional conditions seem to lead to the following conclusions:

During the 1970s there has been a strong tendency for diversification of activities, in particular non-agricultural production. These products can be legally marketed outside government controlled channels, for instance, charcoal, mangroves, logs and fish and, to some extent, crafts. The indicators discussed underline that there is no tendency for a retreat into a subsistence economy, in which the peasants produce primarily for their own consumption. The increase in famine relief operations, the high level of expenditure on food-stuffs, and the lack of improvement of nutritional conditions show that there is no large fund of subsistence production that can be directly consumed by the producers.

This means that from 1972/73 onwards state intervention in the forms of villagisation, price policies, market organisation and the application of bye-laws did not succeed in its objectives of increasing either the marketed agricultural surplus or the appropriation of that surplus. The peasants countered by diversifying their production. In agriculture peasants responded to changes in producer prices and intensified production of drought resistant crops, like cassava, cow peas and pigeon peas (see below). The most pronounced diversification was into activities related to forestry, in particular charcoal production. The data available show that the peasants are responsive to prices if the remuneration offered is seen as reasonable for the labour expended and *if* there is no major physical or infrastructural constraint on production and marketing. For instance, charcoal production dropped dramatically from 1982 onwards (relative to other production lines/crops) although the producer price increased rapidly because of the exhaustion of trees and declining transport capacity. This means that price policies, i.e. changes in relative prices and real increases in producer prices, are not guaranteed to provide the expected economic text-book results. In economies like the Rufiji, and Tanzania as a whole, it is of crucial importance to take account of the physical and infrastructural limitations operating and as well the issue of diversification of peasant labour (see also Chapter 9).

THE PEASANT/STATE/COMMERCIAL CLASS RELATIONSHIP

In Rufiji District the diverging interests of the state and the peasants emerged most clearly on the issue of cashew nut versus charcoal production. In this section I will analyse the means and effects of state intervention to increase the production of cashew nuts, while most peasants gave priority to the production of charcoal. The divergence of state/peasant interests was a major issue during the latter half of the 1970s and helps shed light on peasant withdrawal from the state sphere and the development of their relations with a growing commercial class.

Production of cashew nuts in Rufiji District showed a dramatic and continuous decline from 1973/74 to 1977/78, from 6,500 tonnes to 1,276 (see Table 4.7). Nationally, production declined from about 145,000 tonnes in 1973/74 to around 40,000 tonnes at the end of the decade. This drop is consistent in all producer areas, which are mainly the coastal areas of the country. Cashew nuts were a major foreign exchange earner during the 1960s, ranking fourth after sisal, cotton and coffee. The fact that the percentage drop of cashew nut production in Rufiji District exceeded that recorded at national level, considerably weakens the often employed government explanation for this decline. This says that the major cause for the decline was the withdrawal of cashew nuts originating in northern Mozambique from the Tanzanian market after 1975.

The major share of cashew nut production originated in 34 of the district's 90 or so villages, which were located in North Hill and Flood Plain North. Between 70 to 80 per cent of Rufiji District's cashew nut production during 1976/77 to 1978/79 came from the same 34 villages where about 5,550 peasants had taken up charcoal production.

There seemed to be two major causes for the decline of cashew nut production. The villagisation drive in 1974, "Operation Pwani", directly affected the Flood Plain North and North Hill zones, as people were moved to villages far away from their cashew nut fields. Proper tree husbandry was difficult due to the long distances involved. Weeding by burning further destroyed the trees. "Operation Rufiji" in 1968/69 did not have a negative effect on cashew nut production as people were moved from the flood plain onto the elevated northern and southern banks, where they were encouraged to start growing cashew nuts as an additional cash crop. Many of the communally cultivated fields of the first period were planted with cashew nuts. Labour constraints were, however, created for individual peasants due to increased walking distances to fields still located in the river valley.

Other major reasons for the fall in cashew nut production are the stagnant producer price and the tendency of relative prices to favour other products, like food crops, cotton and charcoal. Over the period 1973/74 to 1978/79 the nominal producer prices for cashew nuts increased by 42 per cent, for cotton by 109 per cent and charcoal by 400 per cent.

Other causes for the decline in cashew nut production can be found in the lack of replanting of trees and the diseases that affected the trees by the end of the 1970s. The lack of proper husbandry of trees, like poor weeding, evidently also affected the yields.

Another important reason for the shift from cashew nut to charcoal production was the peasants' experience of a completely new marketing structure which offered immediate returns, efficient collection, little coercion and rapidly rising prices. Subordination to the crop authorities (especially the Cashewnut Authority), which involved irregular payment and delayed collection of crops made the peasants frustrated by this marketing relationship. During my survey of production in 1979, peasants made statements such as the following: "Charcoal means easy cash at any time", "Returns are immediate", "Consistent price increases", "Easy marketing". To the peasants the marketing of charcoal seemed to be free of all the problems associated with the crops handled by the government agencies.

For the government the decline in cashew nut production also entailed dramatic economic losses. By the end of the 1970s processing capacity for 103,000 tonnes of cashew nuts had been developed, yet purchases had dropped to only about forty per cent of that capacity. The government decided to launch a cashew nut campaign in February 1979. It had already raised the producer price of cashew nuts for the 1979/80 season from Tsh. 1.35 to Tsh. 1.70. This increase of 35 cents compared favourably with the preceding year's 20 cent rise, but not with the rise in producer prices for charcoal nor with the official annual inflation rate of about 30 per cent. Inflation was, however, much higher in real terms due to the calculation of official inflation rates on the basis of officially regulated prices, which were not effective in times of shortages and crises. The rationale for the campaign was basically technical, i.e. the declining collection of cashew nuts was seen by the government to be mainly related to poor weeding or to the burning of the undergrowth, which damaged the trees. The instructions given to the peasants was, "Avoid burning — weed your cashew nut trees". Such posters were hung on all official buildings throughout the district.

The government's economic motivation for the cashew nut campaign was perhaps most clearly revealed by the official who pointed out that, "Cashew nuts bring foreign exchange, charcoal does not". This statement clarifies the conflict between the objectives of cashew nut and charcoal production. The direct link between cashew nut production and foreign exchange earnings stood out clearly for the government official. But the idea that charcoal production is not related to foreign exchange does not take into account the indirect effects of the use of charcoal. In urban areas charcoal and kerosene are interchangeable cooking fuels. To the extent that charcoal replaces kerosene, the import bill for kerosene will go down and foreign exchange is saved.

The situation related to charcoal production was such that the producers and middlemen shared an increasing profit margin at the expense of deforestation and the final consumer. The trend of charcoal prices during the cashew nut campaign, i.e. from February to June 1979, is indicative. The producer price per bag of charcoal increased from Tsh. 12 to Tsh. 15 (25 per cent), the price from transporter to wholesaler increased from Tsh. 27 to Tsh. 40 (48 per cent) while the retail price in Dar es Salaam went up from Tsh. 35 to Tsh. 43 (23 per cent). When taking the cost structure into account, it is apparent that the transporters improved their position relative to those of producers and retailers. Households that could afford to buy one bag of charcoal at a time saw the cost for their cooking fuel increase by 43 per cent over three months. For those who could only afford to buy small quantities, i.e. the poorest, the fuel costs increased by 50–75 per cent. The price of charcoal accelerated during June because of reduced supplies caused by the cashew nut campaign, non-availability of kerosene and higher petrol prices.

In the short run the growing pressure on the peasant economy was compensated for by increasing charcoal production and thus their cash incomes. In the medium- and long-term, however, the result was bound to be the disappearance of the forest cover. For some years this tendency had been observed around nucleated villages, but through the intensification of logging and charcoal production it accelerated. Efforts at afforestation were far from able to cope with the situation. In 1978/79 the plan was to plant 80,000 eucalyptus trees in the district. Due to problems of procuring seedlings only 25,000 trees were planted. In 1979 the government made no changes in the forest royalties which had remained constant at a low level for several years in spite of the increase in exploitation. No directive for the limitation of forestry licenses had been given at the onset of the cashew nut campaign in February 1979.

By May the cashew nut campaign had still not led to the desired results. Many cashew nut fields had not yet been weeded, and an intensification of the campaign took place. A bye-law was activated which entailed that:

> Rufiji District has banned petty business which makes it difficult for peasants to concentrate on working on cashew nut farms. The ban prohibits burning and selling of charcoal, fishing and transporting of fish outside the district (*Daily News*, June 15, 1979).

Market places were closed down to divert people from trading and movement became restricted. Peasants could not leave their home areas before their cashew fields were weeded. The approach was similar to that of 1974, when the government attempted to control the content of peasant production and minimum acreages by the revival of colonial bye-laws. In the period of most intense enforcement of the cashew nut campaign, all party and government agencies at district level were directed to support the campaign and any official vehicle could be used to enforce it. This led to results. Observations from extensive trips through the Flood Plain North and North Hill zones during June showed that most cashew fields had been weeded. In November 1979 the party divisional secretary for Kibiti reported that 90 peasants had been taken to court for not tending their cashew fields and 15, who were not able to pay their fines, were imprisoned, most of them for three months (see Chapter 6).

The immediate results of the weeding campaign was not matched by increased yields of cashew nuts. For the crop year 1979/80 production of cashew declined further to 1,252 tonnes compared to 1,987 tonnes for 1978/79. In the ensuing years up to 1984/85 cashew nut collection by the Cashewnut Authority (CATA) in Rufiji District varied from 1,000 to 2,000 tonnes. A representative of CATA claimed that the cashew harvest would have increased had it not been for the spread of disease in the cashew trees.

What were the effects of the cashew nut campaign on charcoal pro-

Table 7.2.   *Monthly marketing of charcoal in Rufiji District, 1979* '

Month	Number of bags
January	16,549
February	16,790
March	21,692
April	24,609
May	24,054
June	3,521
July	39,663
August	39,106
September	29,411
October	26,313
November	23,749
December	18,145
Total	283,602

Source: Data provided by the Coast Region Forestry Office in 1979 and 1980

duction? The data for charcoal production on a monthly basis for the year 1979 reveals the trend shown in Table 7.2.

Only 381 of the 283,602 bags marketed during 1979 were produced on the southern side of the river, which demonstrates the predominance of the northern part of Rufiji District in charcoal production. The monthly figures reveal some interesting findings. The most important is that the bye-law banning charcoal production in June 1979 did not affect production levels. Its effect was limited to a marked drop in the marketing of charcoal from 24,054 bags in May to only 3,521 in June. During June, peasants simply produced charcoal for storage until the cashew nut campaign ended and the ban on production was lifted.

I witnessed people producing charcoal for storage when I visited one of the major charcoal producing villages, Mkupuka, on June 19 1979. This procedure is also manifested in the dramatic increase in the marketing of charcoal for the months of July and August. During these months the charcoal stored in June was released onto the market, raising marketing figures to more than 39,000 bags. They dropped to about 29,000 bags in September, a figure more likely to represent real production. This development implies that the peasants managed to circumvent the government directives. On the surface they aquiesced, but in reality they maintained their own production priorities. This finding supports Hyden's claim that peasants have the possibility, at least in some areas, to counteract state intervention. The economic effect of the charcoal ban was of direct benefit to the peasants and transporters as it created an artificial shortage of charcoal which caused prices to rise rapidly within a short time.

The maintaining of production levels for charcoal further indicates that the labour provided to weed the cashew nut fields was diverted from other types of production, possibly agriculture. In 1979 such labour may have been available, particularly in the flood plain. As the rice crop had been destroyed by the excessive flood, labour freed from harvesting could be channeled to cashew nut weeding. Labour could also have been diverted from other less remunerative types of production.

The data on the monthly marketing of charcoal, when adjusted for the delayed marketing of what was produced in June, indicate that by 1979 charcoal had become a fairly stable year round production activity. Production is hardly affected by rain or bad weather, making stable production technically possible. This means that charcoal production is not subject to the seasonal labour requirements of agriculture.

These observations from Rufiji show that the state was not able to stop the stagnation of cashew nut production and control the composition of the agricultural surplus. The imperative of increasing export crops followed from the unfolding national economic crisis. The peasants managed to circumvent state enacted bye-laws by seemingly paying heed to the regulations, but in reality pursuing their own priorities.

PRICES AND SUPPLY RESPONSES OF PEASANT PRODUCERS

This issue has been touched upon previously. Here I shall examine a shorter period, from 1976/77 to 1978/79 for which data for most variables, prices, production volumes and flood profiles are available. I shall widen the analysis to include maize and drought resistant crops, such as cassava and cow peas, in addition to the major non-agricultural commodity, charcoal. Such an analysis, however, has several limitations apart from the general problem of reliability of official statistics. The analysis covers only three crop years, although central to the period under investigation. This means that only short-term supply responses to price changes can be accommodated. For cashew nuts, a perennial tree crop with long gestation period, supply responses can only reflect actual changes in collection or harvesting from existing trees. The discussion as well only revolves around individual crop or product supply responses. The inclusion of charcoal in the analysis, however, gives the advantage of capturing supply responses in non-agricultural production and comparing these with individual agricul-

Table 7.3. *Development of producer prices 1973/74–1978/79* (current prices in Tsh. pr kg for crops, for charcoal Tsh. pr bag)

| Year | Export Crops | | Food Crops | | Drought resistant | | Non-agri-cultural |
	Cashew I	Cotton AR	Maize	Paddy	Cassava	Cow peas	Charcoal
1973/74	0.95	1.15	0.35	0.60	0.30	n.a.	6,-
1974/75	1.05	1.50	0.50	0.65	0.35	n.a.	8,-
1975/76	1.05	2.00	0.80	1.00	0.40	n.a.	8,-
1976/77	1.10	2.30	0.80	1.00	0.50	n.a.	10,-
1977/78	1.15	2.30	0.85	1.20	0.60	3.25	10,-
i978/79	1.70	2.40	0.85	1.20	0.65	3.25	15,-
% Increase 76/77–78/79	54.5	4.3	6.3	20	30	-	50
% Increase 73/74–78/79	79	117.4	142.9	100	117	-	150

Note: The price per bag for charcoal is from the village of Jaribu Mpakani on the northern edge of the district.
Sources: CATA, Ministry of Agriculture, Marketing Development Bureau, and Havnevik, 1980

tural crop supply responses. Thereby the issue of diversification of peasant labour out of agriculture is introduced. (For a discussion of prices and supply response elasticities of African and Tanzanian producers, see Gibbon et al., 1993 and Eriksson, 1993). To provide a background for this short period, producer prices are presented from the 1973/74 season onwards.

The significant long-term trends, 1973/74 to 1978/79, are high nominal producer price increases for charcoal and maize and relatively low for cashew nuts. The short-term trends, 1976/77 to 1978/79, show that cashew (due to the price increase in 1978/79) and charcoal registered the highest price increases while those for cotton and maize were the lowest. Paddy and cassava are in the medium range both for long- and short-term trends. Prices for cow peas were introduced and quoted at a high level in 1977/78. (The same holds for pigeon peas.) Charcoal is the only commodity where producer prices increased rapidly throughout, and is the only commodity which is legally traded outside government control.

The analysis of trends of the volume of major crops and commodities in Rufiji District is organised around five themes: conditions

Table 7.4. *Volume changes for crops officially marketed and charcoal, Rufiji District 1976/77–1978/79* (in tonnes, except charcoal)

Category	Total Volume 1976/77	Absolute Volume Changes 1977/78	1978/79	Total Volume 1978/79	%-age Change 78/79-76/77
Food Crops					
Paddy	561	-434	-77	50	-91.1
Maize	20	-13	-12	1	-95.0
Drought resistant					
Cassava	25	+16	-37	4	-84.0
Cowpeas	n.a.	+145	+163	308	112.4
Pigeon peas	15	+122	+136	273	1,720.0
Export Crops					
Copra	369	+731	-660	440	19.2
Cashew nuts	3,282	-2,006	+711	1,987	-39.5
Cotton	121	-10	+873	984	713.0
Non-agricultural commodities					
Charcoal (bags)	8,840	+83,214	+200,388	+283,602	3,108

Sources: Tanzania Cotton Authority, Rufiji Branch; National Milling Corporation, Rufiji Branch; GAPEX, Rufiji and Mafia branches, Havnevik, 1983

for physical production, agronomic conditions (including disease), the role of parallel markets, production for subsistence, and finally, the role of changes in relative producer prices. By sequencing the analysis in this way, the impact of changes in relative producer prices on crop/product supply responses may to some extent be isolated from the complex set of factors influencing overall supply. Such a sequential analysis, however, does not correspond well with the complexity of "real life". But it may provide indications and explanations which go beyond the mere calculations of price supply elasticities. Table 7.4 shows changes in the volume of major crops and commodities marketed during the period 1976/77–1978/79.

The *conditions for physical production* relate to flood profiles and rainfall. In Chapter 4 it was shown that the floods during the first three relevant years, 1976, 1977 and 1978, were moderate. The 1978 flood had, however, a larger peak and volume compared to the two preceding ones. In 1979 the flood was excessive, and is possibly unparalleled in this century. Cotton is dependent upon the previous year's flood, while most other crops depend on the flood occurring within the same crop year (from July to June the following year). Consequently four flood profiles are necessary to analyse the effects on three consecutive crop years. Graphs of these floods are shown in Figure 4.2. Rainfall was extremely low in 1976/77 (542 mm), about the average in 1977/78 (851 mm) and very high in 1978/79 (1,246 mm).

The cotton harvests of 1976/77 and 1977/78 were extremely small and almost identical in size, 121 and 111 tonnes. Yet the flood affecting the 1976/77 harvest reached a maximum height of 19.6 feet, five feet above the subsequent flood. The increase in the harvest of 1978/79 correlates well with the increase in height of the 1978 flood. Copra is the only crop for which production is related mainly to rainfall since dry years provide the best conditions for drying coconuts. The output marketed does not correlate directly as the output of the wet year of 1978/79 is higher than that of the extremely dry year 1976/77. Rice and maize harvests are related mainly to the duration of floods. The duration of floods in the two first years examined should have led to a larger harvest than that portrayed in Table 7.4. The extremely small rice and maize harvests of 1978/79 are due to the excessive flood of 1979 that destroyed all the crops in the flood plain. Thus this analysis of a wider range of crops during three consecutive years reinforces the situation depicted in the analysis of the physical conditions and the development of harvests in Chapter 4. It indicates that the balance of labour in the flood plain agricultural system has been upset by the relocation of villages during "Operation Rufiji" and "Operation Pwani". In addition, the changes in relative prices seem to have fuelled the tendencies towards diversification.

Agronomic conditions mainly affect production in the longer run. A disease of coconut trees has been identified; but has not had any major differential impact during the short period in question. Cashew nut trees are believed to be plagued by an unidentified disease which, together with low replanting rates and lack of weeding, may have reinforced the declining production trend. The simultaneous drop in collection throughout the cashew nut growing area (along the coast of the Indian Ocean) up to 1977/78 indicates that non-agronomic considerations have a major explanatory value.

The option of selling on the *black market* is mainly relevant for paddy and maize, as they are in high demand. The trends of these crops on the official markets run counter to changes in physical conditions for production and to observations about the acreage planted. My conclusion is that the declining trend emerging in Table 7.4 is partly caused by an increase in the channeling of these crops to parallel markets and partly by the imbalances created by the resettlement programmes. They include longer walking distances to fields, lack of access to fertile agricultural areas, increased intrusion of vermin and lack of proper government support for agricultural production.

An increase in *production for subsistence* is mainly related to cassava. The large area planted in 1978 (see Table 4.9) and the declining rate of the officially marketed output, indicate that direct consumption by peasant households is increasing. Maize and paddy also have a direct consumption component. My assessment is that peasants only retain a minor share of the increase in total production. It is supported by information from the district authorities on the provision of famine relief to the West Valley in 1978, a year of relatively good conditions for production. Several other famine relief operations indicate that no large fund exists for subsistence (see Chapter 4).

The remaining, unexplained, changes in volume may be attributed to *changes in relative producer prices*. In terms of changes in volume, with the exception of cassava, the drought resistant crops show rapid increases in the officially marketed output. This is closely related to increased producer prices relative to other crops. Cashew nuts, the major crop of the district, show a declining trend, which corresponds to the relative decline in producer prices for this crop up to 1977/78. The major non-agricultural commodity, charcoal, shows large and uninterrupted increases in production, which reflect producer price increases in both absolute and relative terms. The strong signals of higher prices on the unofficial markets and the rapid decline in the official marketing of rice and maize indicate that, as regards individual crops, peasants are responsive to changes in prices.

EFFECTS ON THE BALANCE OF LABOUR IN AGRICULTURE

As outlined in Chapter 4 the harvests of the flood-season crop, rice, and the dry season crop, cotton, represent the main indicators of performance during these two seasons. The production figures for these crops capture the variation and contradictory impact of floods during both flood- and dry season cultivation.

On the basis of historical observations the data presented in Chapter 4 were used to test two major hypotheses about the agricultural system. The first hypothesis tested was that floods of long duration, which normally are voluminous floods which occur early in the year, usually lead to the drowning of young plants leading to poor harvests. Hence a negative correlation between the duration of floods and rice sales should be expected. For the decades 1928–37 and 1938–47 there was no systematic trend in the correlation coefficients (0.2 and 0.5 respectively). The correlation coefficients for the decades 1948–57 and 1958–67 turned out to be high and negative, -0.8 for both decades. These values correspond well to the hypothesis. The following decade has a correlation coefficient of 0.3, which runs counter to the hypothesis.

As for cotton, historical observations led to the hypothesis that the size of the cotton harvest was conditioned by the size of the inundated area. Two variables could be identified that were linked with the size of the inundated area; the peak of the flood and its duration. The hypothesis is that there should be a positive correlation between cotton harvests and each of these variables. The correlation coefficients calculated in decades from 1928 to 1977 for cotton harvests and peak floods gave a correlation coefficient ranging from 0.4 to 0.7 until 1967. The coefficient for the following decade, 1968–1977, represented a complete break, as it was negative, -0.2. There were recorded lower correlation coefficients for relations of cotton sales to duration of floods, indicating that the peak flood is more important than its duration for cotton cultivation. The findings indicate that the decade from 1967 onwards represents a break in the functioning of the agricultural system. Historical observations and calculated correlations between the characteristics of floods and the harvests of the two main flood plain crops, rice and cotton, no longer hold.

The reason for this break cannot be traced to physical factors. For instance, the rainfall data for the 1970s (see Table 4.2) corresponds fairly well with rainfall data covering 52 years. Only the 1968 and 1974 floods stood out because of their high peaks (1968 and 1974) and long duration (1968) (see Figure 4.2).

The major cause for the changes in the functioning of the agricultural system may be the effects of state intervention. My assessment is that these effects upset the precarious balance of labour in the agricultural system. Resettlement outside the flood plain disrupted flood plain cultivation due to greater distances to fields and increased infestation by vermin. The protection against vermin infestation created by the flood plain settlement was underrated by everyone except the peasants.

This disruption of the balance of labour in the agricultural system is further exacerbated during the following decade, leading up to the economic crisis. During 1973–1983 the use of price policies as a mechanism for appropriation of the agricultural surplus gave the peasants further incentives to move out of the agricultural sector and take up fishing and forestry production, in particular charcoal. The introduction of bye-laws to force peasants to produce the composition of crops desired by the state only had the effect of further straining the relations between the state and the peasantry (see Chapter 6). Hence the political legitimacy of the state and its organ was gradually eroded during this decade (see Chapter 2).

EFFECTS ON EQUALISATION, DIFFERENTIATION AND ACCUMULATION

The effects of state intervention on equalisation, differentiation and accumulation have direct components working through the level and changes in producer prices and the terms of trade, and indirect ones which are related to the impact of resettlement, changes in market organisation and the use of legal instruments. State intervention may, through its impact on relations of production, on religious practices and migration, also have more medium- and long-term effects on equalisation, differentiation and accumulation. In which direction the effects of state intervention will work, favouring more equalisation or greater differentiation, and to what extent it will obstruct or promote accumulation, will depend upon the relations of production, the social structure and the availability of land and additional resources in a given locality.

It is evident that the effects of the price policy pursued during the 1970s combined with a general inflationary situation turned the terms of trade against the rural sector. On a general level this obstructed the potential for capital accumulation, reinvestment and improved techniques among the Tanzanian peasantry. The peasants responded in various ways to counteract the negative effects of the overall price policies and inflation on their standard of living.

During the 1970s and into the 1980s it is possible to distinguish between two major periods in which the price policies functioned in combination with different mechanisms of state intervention. During roughly the first half of the decade, price policies worked together with villagisation policies the major impact of which, at least in the short-term, ended in 1975/76. This period was characterised by a major reorganisation of government administration and the campaigns of physical resettlement. It was not a crisis period, but a severe periodic crisis occurred in 1973 and 1974 due to the combined effect of resettlement and drought.

During the second period, price policies worked in conjunction with a number of factors: state intervention in the sphere of agricultural marketing; the application of legal instruments (from 1974 onwards); increasing macroeconomic and structural imbalances; unfavourable regional development (war with Uganda, break-up of the East African Community); and international factors (second oil price boom, falling world market prices for agricultural exports, etc.). This period developed into a serious social, political and economic crisis which manifested itself from 1978 onwards.

During the period of villagisation the majority of people living in the most prosperous agricultural area, the Inner Delta and other parts of the delta, refused to move. People with moveable wealth shifted to the larger "ujamaa" villages and provided their services from that base; i.e. tractor ploughing, lorry transport, bus services, trade and logging. The areas in which people refused to move were no longer recognised by the government, which meant that official crop purchases stopped and the infrastructure was not maintained. This led to the ujamaa based well-to-do acquiring a better position to exploit the non-recognised peasants (Sandberg, 1974a:49). Influential people were also able to use village property for their own benefit. There was no land shortage in Rufiji District, but villagisation did upset the balance of labour of the existing agricultural system as analysed previously. The increased demand for transport services linked to the introduction of this labour imbalance, coupled with the large sections of non-recognised peasants, opened the way for increased differentiation between the peasantry as a result of villagisation. Some sections of the more well-to-do peasantry reportedly invested in houses in both larger ujamaa villages and in Dar es Salaam. Parts of such houses are rented out, and parts utilised by the extended family, providing it with a rural and urban base. Historically migration from Rufiji District to Dar es Salaam has always been high. Thus already existing linkages between the town and rural areas could be better exploited by many Rufiji families. Transporters and traders originating from Rufiji established an additional base in Dar es Salaam, ferrying resources and commodities between urban and rural areas to exploit differences in prices. The majority of the Rufiji population, however, irrespective of whether they were in recognised or unrecognised villages, could never afford this type of double settlement. For them double settlement meant erecting a hut in the fields to decrease distances to the homestead after villagisation. In this process, as shown by Sandberg (1974a), more of the agriculturally related work fell upon the women.

The impact of villagisation depended on the specific local situation. In an area of land shortage, like the Hanang District in Arusha Region, Kjærby reports that the effects of villagisation tended towards equalisation. Between 1973 and 1978 in the two villages investigated there was a decline in the number of capitalist farmers and tractors operating, and a reduction in the acreage of private farm land and borrowed and shared or rented land. Villagisation gradually but significantly undermined the degree of concentration of land ownership. The overall effect of villagisation in this area was "to strengthen the landed position of the middle and rich peasantry at the expense of the capitalist farmers, but not to the effect of eliminating them as capitalists, since they were allowed to remain with their main capital assets, their tractors, machinery and livestock (Kjærby, 1987:41–43).

In the second part of the 1970s and into the 1980s, peasants in Rufiji District, particularly those who could not exploit the opportunities created by villagisation, had to identify ways of defending their standard of living. The balance of labour of the existing agricultural system had been upset and the agricultural producer price policy, the general inflation and subsequent commodity shortages, demanded new responses. The escape route for the Rufiji peasant was to exploit the non-agricultural resources of the district, like fish, mangroves and charcoal that could be sold through non-government controlled channels. Peasants thus increased their exposure to the commercial class, i.e. transporters and traders, and benefited economically by this reorientation of their labour to these activities. The transporters and traders appropriated the lion's share of the profits, but the peasants also improved their incomes (Havnevik, 1983:85). Sales of maize and rice on parallel markets helped peasants to counter the effects of the crisis, which was manifested through frequent shortages and high prices of basic commodities. The decline in supplies from national industries and regional trading companies was to some extent compensated for by increased local production of basic commodities like sugar (ghur) and salt and an intensification of repairs of, for instance, farm implements and bicycles. Craftsmen and women also seem to have become more active, shifting some of the labour they previously allocated to agriculture, into crafts.

The varied resource base of the area and the availability of relevant skills are likely to have worked as a brake on tendencies towards excessive differentiation during this period of the crisis. Certainly transporters, traders and businessmen did take the opportunity to exploit the shortages, but the peasantry was able to compensate by diversifying their production.

In areas of Tanzania which commanded a smaller range of resources, the option for peasants included migration to small towns or urban areas to seek wage labour or to increase cultivation of crops for sale on the parallel markets. Rasmussen documented the latter tendency in the Southern Highlands where the cultivation of maize with biochemical inputs spread (Rasmussen, 1986). In Hanang villages, peasants responded to the crisis in the early 1980s by actually increasing the cultivated acreage through greater use of ox-ploughs. Thus the crisis led to the using of more marginal land and set in motion processes of technical change in agriculture (Kjærby, 1986 and 1987:71). (See also the discussion of technical changes in agriculture under structural adjustment in Chapter 9.)

In the Hanang villages access to unofficial trading, sales on parallel markets, expansion of ox-drawn technology, together with more embezzlement of public funds, from the official marketing system and village shops, led to "a new process of growing social differentiation" (Kjærby, 1987:59). As in Rufiji District there is no evidence to support the thesis that peasants in Hanang District villages withdrew from the market into a subsistence economy because of lack of purchasable commodities and inputs (cf. Hyden, 1980).

As for accumulation, constraints are not posited simply at the level of producer prices and developments of the terms of trade. Studies show that the allocation of resources is also conditioned by social and cultural values. The Islamic religion represents an integral part of Rufiji culture; it guides both the religious and the social system. As indicated in Chapter 3, in Africa Islam has adapted to local conditions and outlooks, and the Sunni variant in Rufiji District may be an African synthesis of Islam.

Religious and social practices in Rufiji, particularly towards the delta, have the function of promoting prestige. These practices require considerable outlay of money for religious fees, gifts and costly ngomas (drum parties). The expenses are used on non-material items which administrators and outsiders view as wasteful. Such practices also had a redistributive function (Sandberg, 1974a:43). So-called *utani* or joking relationships had much the same function between neighbouring tribes (Lucas, 1975). Through the *utani* relationship a person could demand food or clothes from a neighbouring *utani*-brother who could not refuse. In societies with such redistributive mechanisms it appears that accumulation and investment will be constrained. The owner of wealth faces continuous demands to participate in redistributive practices. Sandberg points out that before villagisation, wealth was visible, as there was few exit options and "social obligations could play their full role to produce some kind of equality" (Sandberg, 1974a).

"Under the new order in Rufiji there are more escapes; people can to some extent hide their wealth by having a double settlement, or they can invest in a house in Dar es Salaam" (Ibid.). The new social pattern and reorganisation emerging as a consequence of resettlement may have weakened some of the religious and social constraints on accumulation. No information or observation indicates that people give up the traditional social and religious practices (see Swantz, 1985).

State intervention has thus led to processes of both equalisation and differentiation. In Rufiji District such a tendency continued throughout the 1970s. In other areas with a different social structure and availability of resources other trends were identified, for example in Hanang. Villagisation and the ensuing economic crises have opened up possibilities for accumulation by a small social group. The relations of production remained static up to the early 1980s and there was no indication of a rapid increase in hired labour or changes in agricultural techniques. (For developments in Tanzanian agriculture during the 1980s under the regime of structural adjustment, see Chapter 9.)

PART III

Hydropower versus People: The Stiegler's Gorge Project

8. State Intervention and Development Assistance; Evidence from the Stiegler's Gorge Project

INTRODUCTION

The Stiegler's Gorge Project is the name given to a large dam and hydropower project located at Stiegler's Gorge on the western edge of Rufiji District. Upstream three major rivers, the Great Ruaha, the Kilombero and the Luwego converge to form the Rufiji river, which then flows through Stiegler's Gorge before entering the Rufiji river valley and the cultivated Rufiji flood plain (see Maps 3 and 5).

Throughout this century a number of investigations of the Rufiji river Basin have been conducted. Already in 1904, 1907, 1909 and 1911 the Germans undertook technical expeditions of the Basin. Their main purpose was to assess the advantages of navigable transport on the rivers in comparison with that of transport by rail. As secondary objectives they examined possibilities for irrigated agriculture and hydropower production. The leader of the 1907 expedition, Stiegler, was killed by an elephant at the gorge which came to bear his name.

These investigations found that transport by rail was most advantageous. Navigation was possible only on the lower reaches of the Rufiji river, to a limited extent on the Kilombero and for short distances on some of their tributaries.

The next major investigation of the Rufiji Basin was carried out by A.M. Telford in 1928/29. He took cross-sections of the river at various points, but they were not related to sea level. He estimated the potential for agriculture without irrigation in the Kilombero and the Lower Rufiji valley to be about 146,000 hectares for the growing of rice, cotton and maize (Telford, 1929).

In 1940 a water consultant to the Tanganyikan government, C. Gillman, said that nothing was known of the flows of the main rivers, including the Rufiji. Nevertheless he provided the advice that "these rivers did not lend themselves to major schemes of irrigation or navigation which might justify the costs of gauging their flows" (FAO 1961:5). Gillman (1945) does not appear to have consulted the important article written by Marshland on *mlau* cultivation in the Rufiji valley published in Tanganyikan Notes and Record in 1938, nor the Telford study, nor the data and knowledge about Rufiji floods collected and accumulated by Rufiji District colonial agricultural officers. According to FAO Gillman's mistaken advice had the effect of postponing systematic observations of river flows throughout Tanganyika (Ibid.).

In 1952 Sir Edward Twining, then Governor of Tanganyika, discussed several proposals for investigations in Tanganyika with the Director-General of FAO. Among them was a reconnaissance survey of the development possibilities of the Rufiji Basin. From October to December a small team visited the Basin and a first interim report was published in 1954. It recommended undertaking a reconnaissance survey including an investigation of soils, geology, topography and water control (FAO, 1961:6). In 1955 Tanganyika formally requested assistance from FAO to carry out a major survey of the Rufiji Basin.

The early German investigations and most subsequent reports recognised the multipurpose nature of a dam and power project at Stiegler's Gorge. The investigation of the major forms of production in the downstream area of the Rufiji Basin, including agriculture, fishing and forestry, and their relation to floods have been outlined in Chapters 4 and 5. A dam at Stiegler's Gorge would have an impact on all these activities and on transport, health and the ecology of the area. Let me identify some of the possible effects upstream and downstream that must be fully accounted to plan such a project soundly (cf. Chapters 4 and 5).

Upstream in the catchment area, information about rainfall and river flows as well as agricultural development and forest exploitation is needed to assess water flows and surface run-off conditions relevant to the flow of the river. A thorough understanding of these conditions and how they developed over time must be at the core of statistical models for the calculation of water inflows to the reservoir and the analysis of flood probability. Investigations are also needed of how a future reservoir will function, the behaviour of silt in the reservoir and the quality of water which leaves it. The climatic effects of the creation of a large reservoir and its impact on wildlife in the surrounding Selous Game Reserve are required. It is necessary that the technical design of the dam and power stations and the capacity of the dam outlets meet the requirements of the non-power purposes of the project, like downstream agriculture and fishing. The new potential for fishing in the reservoir and ways of harvesting the catch must also be examined.

In the downstream area the most significant challenge is the transformation of the agricultural system that is naturally adapted to floods into one that is artificially irrigated. The change in the quantity and quality of the flow of water will also have an impact on fisheries in the flood plain, in the delta and in the Mafia channel. With regard to forestry, most directly affected by the project will be the mangroves of the Rufiji delta. There is a need to investigate the impact of changes in water salinity on the mangroves and as well the role of the mangroves for the rich prawn fisheries of the delta. Transport will also be directly affected downstream. A lower and more stable flow of the river will improve conditions for transport both on and across the flood plain. Health is likely to be influenced by the introduction of irrigated agriculture, in particular in the form of bilharzia, that hardly exists in the area at present. The changes in the flow of the river and the quality of the water are bound to have ecological consequences downstream, which in turn will change the conditions for important production activities. Hence there is a need to trace the ecological and productive impact in both the immediate and more long-term perspective.

These are some of the major issues that have to be investigated for the planning to correspond to the project's multipurpose character. Such investigations, carefully designed, executed and integrated, are vital for assessing the viability of the project as well as for protecting the interests of the people residing in and generating their income from the area affected by the project.

Major issues exist outside the Stiegler's Gorge Project area. It is bound to loom large in the national economy. Its implementation will require resources of such magnitude that investments and support to most other developmental projects will have to be restricted for a long time. Another extremely important issue is related to its power generating capacity, which is so large that the economics of the project require identification of new users of power in the foreseeable future. These may be either power consuming domestic industries or the export of power to neighbouring countries. Thus the mere size of the project in the national economy and the creation of a new demand for electricity are crucial issues which must be assessed and investigated carefully at the stage of preparation of the project.

Now let me turn to the major planning studies presented from 1961 to 1980 and assess their handling of the multipurpose character of the project.

SINGLE PURPOSE PLANNING OF A MULTIPURPOSE PROJECT

In the post-independence period numerous studies have been presented about hydropower production in Stiegler's Gorge and agricultural development on the Rufiji flood plain. From 1961 to 1980 three major studies were published, the FAO study (1961), the Norconsult study (1972) and the Hafslund report (1980). In between, other studies were undertaken. My method of assessing the relevance of these studies to the multipurpose character of the project will be to focus on their terms of reference. The underlying hypothesis is that the inability of the studies to grasp the multipurpose character is likely to be related more to limitations in the terms of reference than to the quality of work performed.

The FAO Report on the Preliminary Reconnaissance Survey of the Rufiji Basin of June 5, 1961

In 1955 the Government of Tanganyika formally requested the FAO to carry out a survey of the Rufiji Basin with the following objectives: ".... to assess the irrigation potential which exists in the Basin, as well as the probable cost of exploitation of that potential. To this end the irrigable areas are to be defined reasonably closely, and their relative merits ascertained. The extent to which storage is required, and the sites of dams to achieve that storage, along with an estimate of probable construction costs for each dam, are to be investigated. The soil and topography of the irrigable areas are to be recorded" (FAO, 1961:4).

The terms of reference are concerned with the control of water for improving land utilisation; the question of hydropower is not raised. The request from the Tanganyikan government is not for an overall plan for the Basin as a whole. In spite of this, the FAO survey raises the question of power production: "it will be technically feasible to generate hydro-electric power on a considerable scale by the construction of dams at the following points: Lower Rufiji/Stiegler's Gorge (tentative forecast for firm power 150 to 400 Megawatts, according to height of dam) and Great Ruaha/Mtera (forecast of firm power 21 Megawatts)" (Ibid. 17). The FAO survey then notes that whether such developments are likely to be justifiable can only be determined by consideration of the future power requirements of Tanganyika as a whole. In addition, the survey mentions that: "minor and varying amounts of power can be generated at a number of the dams proposed for control of rivers" (Ibid.).

The FAO study commented on the trade-off between agriculture and the production of hydropower as follows: "a dam to provide 6.4 million acre-feet (at Stiegler's Gorge) of capacity is estimated to cost about £10 million, equivalent to £50 pr acre of the net irrigable area expected to be available. This is a high figure, and if the full cost has to be so charged, the project appears to be quite uneconomic: but such a reservoir could also be used to generate a large parcel of "firm" or reliable power. If, in consideration of this, only half or perhaps less, of the total cost of the dam had to be charged to flood control and irrigation, the position would be very different" (Ibid., 41).

USAID: Rufiji Basin; Land and Water Resource Development Plan and Potential, 1967

This study was prepared for USAID by the Bureau of Reclamation, the US Department of the Interior and was presented to the Tanzanian government in March 1967. The terms of reference of the study were "to undertake a physical examination of the Basin, a review of existing data and studies completed or underway in the basin and to suggest guidelines for the possible formation of a Rufiji Basin Development Authority" (USAID, 1967:1). This study seems to have shifted the focus of the subsequent studies to the hydropower aspect of basin development: "Before proceeding on a large-scale development of hydroelectric energy, Stiegler's Gorge should be fully evaluated. This evaluation should include determination of the optimum amount of storage at the site, and upstream storage which would provide regulation. Location and arrangements of generating plants to develop the maximum available head at Stiegler's Gorge should be studied" (Ibid. 160).

JETRO (Japanese) pre-feasibility of the Stiegler's Gorge hydropower project, 1968

During 1967/68 the Overseas Technical Cooperation Agency of the Japanese Government (JETRO) carried out a pre-feasibility study of the Stiegler's Gorge hydroelectricity project. Its primary concern was development of hydropower for industrial expansion. It concluded that the Stiegler's Gorge hydropower project was viable including transmission lines, at an estimated cost of US $ 121 m. (1968). 600 MW could be installed in the project, but the use of the energy required an industrialisation programme based on power consuming industries. An aluminum refining industry was regarded as a necessary precondition for the implementation of the Stiegler's Gorge Project. According to Nkonoki (1983) no formal document exists showing the Tanzanian government's acceptance of the JETRO conclusions. However, an almost immediate request by the government to UNDP for assistance to undertake a feasibility study of the Stiegler's Gorge hydropower project, a study proposed by the JETRO report, indicates that in principle the JETRO study had been accepted (Ibid. and Legum and Drysdale, 1970). Nothing materialised from the request to UNDP. A few years later the Norwegian aid agency, NORAD, was requested to assist in the planning of the Stiegler's Gorge project.

Norconsult: Stiegler's Gorge Hydropower Utilisation. Power Production. Preliminary Report, 1972

Like the FAO survey, the Norconsult report acknowledges the multipurpose character of the Lower Rufiji Basin development. The report says that even though the Stiegler's Gorge Project has a multipurpose nature, it will deal primarily with the hydropower aspect. The other aspects will be regarded as secondary and will be discussed in that context. This approach seems to correspond to the terms of reference, which simply ask Norconsult to prepare a preliminary project for a dam and a power station, and to come up with realistic costs for the electric energy produced (Norconsult, 1972:2).

Norconsult's study rests on the assumption that flood control and irrigation will not entail a net income for the project in the near future. Therefore, the sale of energy to power consuming industries will be the financial base of the project (Ibid., 63). As a result Norconsult concludes that the optimal size of the total project — and thus of its various components — is determined solely by the economics of power production. The height of the dam and the highest regulated water level, elements closely related to the multipurpose character of the project, are chosen with the aim of optimising one single purpose: power production. The highest regulated water level set is equal to the level that gives the lowest variable unit cost for the electric power, 178 m above sea level (Ibid., 63).

Norconsult concludes that a hydropower project at Stiegler's Gorge can be developed with a power unit cost which makes power consuming industries economic. No local market exists for full consumption of Stiegler's Gorge power as projected, nor is there any prospect of such a market developing in the near future. Norconsult calculated the firm power production capacity to be 620 MW. Accordingly Norconsult states, as did JETRO, that the establishment of power consuming industries is essential in order to create a demand for electricity at a level justifying the construction of the dam. Norconsult bases its analysis on the assumption that only firm power is of value to the power consuming industries.

Hafslund A/S: Stiegler's Gorge Power Project, 1980

The terms of reference state that the Norconsult report shall be used as a basis for the Hafslund study (Terms of Reference (TOR), August 1976:2), indicating that the planning perspective is still limited. The terms of reference identify the preliminary aims of the project, including:

- supply of electrical energy at competitive prices for bulk delivery to TANESCO for power consuming industries and for other purposes;
- establishment of an effective flood control in order to improve the conditions for the agriculture in the Lower Rufiji Basin and communications as the river crossing will be simplified. Improvement of communications is seen as one of the factors necessary in order to promote tourism;
- further improvement of the agriculture downstream can be achieved by introducing irrigation schemes;
- improvement of the fishing in the artificial lake created by the establishment of the water reservoir, and in the regulated river. (TOR, 1976:para.1.4)

Accordingly some consideration is given to the multiple purposes of the project. The specific instructions for the planning of hydropower are formulated like this: "the Hydropower Development shall be planned with the main object of maximum power production. Consideration shall however also be paid to the demands for flood control and irrigation in the Lower Rufiji Basin. To this effect the Government will prepare a general programme for the agricultural development in this area by means of flood control and irrigation" (TOR, 1976:para.5).

The call for maximum power production coupled with consideration to be given to the demands for flood control and irrigation introduce a contradiction into the terms of reference: maximum power production requires maximum water storage which implies a greater probability of floods than lower levels of water storage.

How this contradiction is resolved during the planning process will indicate what the real priorities are: maximum power production, or flood control and agricultural development. It is clear from the terms of reference of 1976 that the requirements of flood control and irrigation are not known. According to para. 3.3 and para. 5, the Tanzanian Government's executing agency, Rujiji Basin Development Authority (RUBADA), ought to have provided a general programme for agricultural development so that the related requirements could be made more concrete. RUBADA did not provide this important input in the alloted time. Hafslund was thus forced to hire its own consultant to verifiy the preliminary design criteria. A crucial parameter in the design of the dam was the capacity of its low level outlets. As it was realised that the transformation from flood adapted agriculture to an artificial irrigation system would require time, the dam outlets had to be designed so that sufficient water could be released to create floods downstream. Hafslund's preliminary design of a minimum capacity of 2,500 m^3/s for the low level outlets was found to be satisfactory by the consultant, who stated that a flood discharge of 2,500 m^3/s would create extensive flooding throughout the river plain.

It was already known at that time that because of the degradation of the river bed after closure of the dam, it would require more than 2,500 m^3/s for floods to occur downstream. When Hafslund presented the preliminary project report in Dar es Salaam on January 11 1979, it was claimed that Stiegler's Gorge could not stand the release of more than 2,500 m^3/s through low level outlets due to problems of erosion in the gorge. Consequently, if more water was needed for flooding, it would have to be taken from the spillways of saddledams. Given this limitation, the capacity of 2,500 m^3/s for the low level outlets must be seen as a maximum rather than a minimum

When Hafslund carried out their study, mainly during 1978 and 1979, no adequate studies had been done of the agricultural potential of the downstream area, of flood control benefits and of alternative ways of obtaining flood control. When further studies were undertaken and more information was available, it was found that the net benefits of building a dam for flood control were marginal (Norplan, 1983, vol. 1:9). But in 1978/79 the Hafslund study could not reflect the multipurpose nature of the project, as the data for incorporating such a perspective in the planning was simply not available.

UNEVEN DEVELOPMENT OF MAJOR AREAS OF THE PROJECT

Already in 1977 a growing anxiety had developed among concerned parties because of the uneven development of major areas of the project. It was realised that the progress in the planning of the project and the demands of the schedule for implementation would lead to the finalisation of the technical design of the dam and power stations before adequate analyses were conducted on the critical issues of the use of hydropower and the downstream effects in Rufiji District. A frenetic process was initiated to provide the necessary reports and analyses on the demand for electricity, to make the project appear bankable and to make aspects of downstream planning match the project's multipurpose objectives.

The Norwegian Agency for International Development (NORAD), the major funder of the planning process, as well became increasingly concerned with the important financing element of the project. By 1979 the project coordinator in NORAD tried to stop the project design development at a stage where, according to his judgement, it was possible to provide a reliable cost estimate. Such an estimate could be used for initiating the process of securing project financing which so far had not appeared as an item for discussion between NORAD and the Tanzanian government. The Tanzanian minister responsible for the project, however, referred to strong political pressure from the government and argued that there would be no problems of financing the project when he urged NORAD for continued support to complete the project design. NORAD obliged (personal communication with the former NORAD project coordinator, 1992).

The demand for electricity

Uncertainty about the demand for power in Tanzania had all along plagued the large Stiegler's Gorge Project. It was feared that even from a narrow hydropower perspective the project would not appear feasible. TANESCO gave the Canadian firm of consultants, Acres International Ltd., the task of preparing a power generation development master plan up to the year 1995. This plan was also to be used as a basis for the planning the Stiegler's Gorge Project.

Acres used two methods in their report. The grid system forecast was based on a model which related the Gross Domestic Product to total energy generation and sales. The forecast for an additional 17 isolated branches was based on a time trend analysis of both industrial and non-industrial demand and a survey of new demand that was planned at each load centre.

The preliminary version of Acres' report was published in 1978, but the promoters of the Stiegler's Gorge Project were not happy with its recommendations. Acres estimated that by 1995 only 225 MW additional capacity was needed. This was partly based on one of their recommendations that, in the intermediate period, the building of coal thermal units to produce 450 MW would ensure an adequate supply of electrical power. In 1978, the capacity of the Stiegler's Gorge Hydropower project was estimated to be between 600 and 1,000 MW which should come on stream towards the end of the 1980s. Acres' analysis of different options to expand power production concluded that the Stiegler's Gorge Project should be given very low priority. Commissioning of the Stiegler's Gorge Project would only be feasible if major non-power benefits were linked to the project. Acres' 1978 recommendations were rejected by the Tanzanian authorities and more immediate advice was sought from other sources.

In 1978 two forecast studies of demand for electricity were initiated, one by RUBADA conducted by George Joseph of the Department of Statistics at the University of Dar es Salaam and one by the Ministry of Industries and the Ministry of Water, Energy and Minerals, which was executed by M.D. Segal of the Ministry of Industries and S.L. Mosha of TANESCO. The objective of the latter study was to evaluate the options available to TANESCO for the generation of electricity to meet an increased demand in all local centres. The load forecast of the Segal/Mosha study was based on an analysis of newly planned industrial loads at each centre and a background growth rate. For the period 1978 to 1985 the electricity demand was expected to increase by 11.5 per cent annually and beyond 1985 the growth rate of demand was set at 6.5 per cent per year. Acres' forecast was of a compound growth rate of 7.2 per cent per annum for the period 1976 to 1995. The Acres and Segal/Mosha basic forecasts did not differ much in terms of demand and capacity build-up. The major difference in relation to the Stiegler's Gorge Project was that Acres advised against it, while Segal/Mosha did not. Hafslund was instructed to use the Segal/Mosha report as a basis for planning the Stiegler's Gorge Project.

Joseph encountered problems when he was about to finalise his forecasts of demand. The Segal/Mosha study was completed by the time he reached the last stage of his work. Joseph found it quite surprising that RUBADA withdrew their support for his work and took back the equipment they had lent him to conduct the necessary statistical calculations. The Bureau of Resource Assessment and Land Use Planning (BRALUP), the research institution at the University of Dar es Salaam which was involved in discussions about the environmental impact studies in 1977 and 1978, decided to assist Joseph to finish his work. This is reflected in a note on page 1 in Joseph's study, which was published by BRALUP in 1979; "This project was initially funded by RUBADA, with assistance from BRALUP at the finishing stages" (Joseph, 1979:1). Maybe unexpectedly Joseph, like Segal/Mosha, concluded that the estimates of demand required the commissioning of the Stiegler's Gorge Project before the turn of the century (Joseph, 1979).

In his report Joseph made several attacks on the Acres (1978) study. He claims that, "at the level of specification, the GDP model applied at the aggregate level subsumes significant differences in the determinants of electricity sales for domestic, commercial or industrial categories and therefore increasing the likelihood of serious specification errors which could lead to biased forecasts". And further that, "...point predictions based on a single future growth rate of GDP are unsatisfactory. Interval predictions based on, say, assumptions of 'high', 'medium' and 'low' growth scenarios would be more realistic" (Joseph, 1979:14).

Guiding Joseph's choice of method for demand estimation seems to be giving proper weight to the expected increase in industrial demand for electricity. Joseph maintains that the Acres' study treatment of this demand, "which constitutes and is likely to constitute in the future about three quarters of the total demand, is fairly inadequate in that differences between various industries in their electricity requirements are ignored" (Joseph, 1979:15). Joseph expected a dramatic increase in the demand for industrial electricity, based on NDC estimates that in ten years time the iron/steel complex would require 75 MW, the paper and pulp complex another 21 MW which would be tripled over time and, further, that sugar projects, textiles, ginneries, foundries and machinery and electronics would take another 60 to 75 MW. In ten years time industries along the TAZARA railway would require 200 MW (Joseph, 1979:16).

Joseph concluded that during the four consecutive five year periods from 1980–85 to 1995–2000 the Tanzanian power sector would need to provide electricity to meet additional maximum demand for 91MW, 110 MW, 166 MW and 299 MW. Given the capacity installed (1979, only TANESCO capacity included) an additional 670 MW of electrical power would be required by the year 2000. Assuming that the Stiegler's Gorge Project would have the capacity of producing electricity in the range of 600 to 1000 MW Joseph concluded that it did not appear as though TANESCO would have difficulties in utilising this capacity in the perspective of a long-term projection horizon (Joseph, 1979:41–42).

When Joseph's conclusions were published, RUBADA became very interested in obtaining a copy of his report. The then BRALUP director would, however, provide it only on the condition that his institution received a copy of the preliminary Hafslund report on the Stiegler's Gorge Project which had already been submitted to the government. The above is an example of the problems of dissemination of information between national institutions that are involved in the research and planning of a major development projects in Tanzania. These conflicts originated from differences in the interests of the two institutions in terms of priority and emphasis in the planning of the Stiegler's Gorge Project.

The Downstream issues

The multipurpose character of the Stiegler's Gorge Project required that flood control and irrigation were integrated into the planning of the project. In addition, its overall impact on fisheries, forestry (mangroves), transport, health and various ecological impacts came to be included in the downstream issues. Upstream from the Stiegler's Gorge issues were raised and discussed as for instance regarding the need for rescue of animals from creation of the artificial lake and the impact of a construction camp with some 25,000 persons and a possible permanent settlement on the Selous Game Reserve.

As stated previously, the investigation and analyses of the downstream issues had not been taken seriously in the formulation of the terms of reference for the Hafslund study in 1976. Hafslund was instructed to plan for maximum power production while the responsibility for providing inputs for non-power issues rested with RUBADA. RUBADA was created by the Rufiji Basin Development Authority Act of 1975. In outlining the functions of RUBADA, the Act covers all the multipurpose aspects related to the implementation of the Stiegler's Project (The RUBADA Act, 1975, para. 6). The organisation was, however, weak in terms of both manpower and other resources. In the early stages there was neither the capacity nor interest in dealing with and treating the non-power aspects of the Stiegler's Gorge Project seriously.

In the University of Dar es Salaam, the Bureau of Resource Assessment and Land Use Planning, (BRALUP) had been concerned about the development constraints and prospects of Rufiji District since the late 1960s. Field studies had been conducted on soils (Cook, 1974), on the socio-economic system of the inner delta areas (Sandberg, 1974a), on the impact of villagisation for the environment and for productive activities (Sandberg, 1973; and Angwazi and Ndulu, 1973). Another major study of the productive system of the Rufiji valley was commissioned by the Ministry of Water Development and Power and led by Yoshida during the 1970/71 agricultural season (Yoshida, 1974).

Due to his extensive travels and investigations in the district Sandberg, in particular, became concerned about the impact of the Stiegler's Gorge Project on the downstream area. Norconsult's single purpose pre-feasibility study was already circulating. In 1974 Sandberg outlined his critique of the Norconsult approach and provided arguments and data based on extensive field studies in the potentially affected area (Sandberg, 1974a and 1974b). Other assessments of the Norconsult study also pointed to weaknesses and the need for adjustments in order for the planning to be carried forward in a multipurpose context (Havnevik, 1975). These criticisms had been communicated to the Norwegian Agency for International Development (NORAD) in good time before the preparation of the terms of reference for the Hafslund study. Criticism of the planning of the project had also developed inside NORAD. The impact of this criticism on the direction of planning was, however, marginal. Whether this was due to the attitudes of NORAD or RUBADA or both is only known to those who were centrally placed at that time. Further critiques of the planning of the project appeared in 1977 and 1978. At the request of NORAD the World Bank let it be known that a single purpose project would not be endorsed for financing by the World Bank. At a stroke it became apparent to promoters of the project that multiple purpose planning was essential to its successful financing. In 1978, the agricultural consultant to Hafslund made the important point that a full perspective of the irrigation potential of the Rufiji flood plain also required consideration of irrigation development without the dam at Stiegler's Gorge. Let me now summarise some of the major criticisms related to the downstream issues:

The first phase of the criticism, directed at the Norconsult study (1972) pointed out that by directing planning at a single purpose, i.e. hydropower, the multipurpose nature of the project was completely ignored. To the extent that explanations of the agricultural system were advanced, they were erroneous (Sandberg, 1974b). There was a complete lack of understanding of the problems of the transformation of agriculture from the system that was naturally adapted to flooding to artificial irrigatation.

It was argued that any change of system would have to be transitory, which required the flood adapted agricultural system to be modified over a period of years after the closing of the dam. Norconsult completely glossed over the importance of fishing in the flood plain and the delta areas and there was no discussion of the ecological impact of the dam. This was in line with the terms of reference which stressed the technical and economic aspects of the project. But even on technical and economic aspects the study seemed to err, as it proposed that the capacity of power production and the highest regulated water level should be fixed according to the lowest variable average cost per unit of energy produced, rather than the long-term alternative cost (Havnevik, 1975:35–36).

The second phase of critique was directed mainly at the Hafslund study. It is important to note that the project design had been changed in an attempt to accommodate a transitory change of the agricultural system. Outlets were to be designed to allow downstream flooding even after dam construction. The critics claimed that the potential for releasing floods had to be based on an intimate knowledge of the differential requirements and impact of flooding in the various sub-sections of the flood plain and delta. As such studies had not been carried out, even modified designs only paid lip service to the real needs and effects on agriculture, fishing and the ecology. It was also pointed out that the hydraulic studies undertaken (VHL, 1979) showed erosion of the river bed which would soon require the release of additional water which could not be accommodated by the low level outlets in the gorge. Thus the flood adapted agricultural system could not be sustained. It was further indicated that the most important area for wildlife and tourism, Tagalala Lake, was most likely to be silted up and destroyed as a tourist attraction. Another important criticism related to agriculture was the finding that the dam would trap nutritious silt, thus robbing the flood plain of its natural fertilizer. Fishing in the flood plain would suffer dramatically, as floods would not be large enough, even in the early phases, to fill the lakes which comprise the major fishing grounds.

The World Bank's position made the promoters of the project, in particular NORAD, see that impact studies had to be designed and implemented.

ATTEMPTS TO RECTIFY THE PROJECT PLANNING

NORAD became increasingly concerned about the direction of planning in the course of 1977, having supported the process since the beginning of the decade, The knowledge of the World Bank misgivings and an increasing uneasiness about the quality of planning and the follow up on the Tanzanian side, forced NORAD to act. Towards the end of 1977 a high powered Norwegian delegation from NORAD and the Norwegian Ministry of Foreign Affairs visited Tanzania. The delegation was extremely concerned to persuade the Tanzanian authorities to accept the seriousness of the multipurpose issues, which would require giving much higher priority to RUBADA as coordinator of the impact studies and the major agency of implementation. NORAD repeatedly stressed that its involvement in the project was limited to the planning phase and did not provide any assurances of support for financing the project.

The most critical step of restoring the multipurpose character of the project was the design and implementation of impact studies in the downstream area. Within NORAD there were two positions about how to implement such studies. One faction wanted foreign consultants, while the other argued strongly that such studies mainly should be undertaken by Tanzanian institutions, especially the University of Dar es

Salaam, in order to utilise, enhance and widen Tanzanian competence. The model envisaged by the latter was to bolster RUBADA as the coordinator cooperating closely with university institutes. NORAD enhanced its own capacity to deal with the multifaceted issues of the Stiegler's Gorge Project. It employed a high powered project coordinator and, on the research side, able and committed people actively promoted the build-up of local competence model.

In January 1978 a NORAD delegation went to Tanzania to promote the Environmental Impact Assessment (EIA) programme in conjunction with RUBADA and the University of Dar es Salaam. In this phase some progress was made. RUBADA and the university were able to work together and formulate large sections of an EIA document. The organisational issues were left to be dealt with at a later stage. NORAD took on the role of mediator between the Tanzanian institutions, and also played the role of catalyst by assuring that funds for the EIA programme were available and by providing ideas about the content of the programme. Sandberg, member of the NORAD team at this time, was well informed about the personalities and priorities of various Tanzanian institutions.

When it later came to more concrete formulation of the studies, priorities, organisational issues, etc., things started to go wrong. In the meantime NORAD financed and recruited a well qualified assistant to the director-general of RUBADA and a coordinator of studies. At the same time university people involved realised that there was conflict about the focus of the impact studies and whose interests they should serve. It also added to the problems that personal affection had never characterised relations between the key people in the various Tanzanian institutions involved.

The bureaucratic promoters of the project in Tanzania, in RUBADA and a group within NORAD as well, were irritated by the dispositions and arguments at the university. The promoters blamed the university for not having a unified leadership that could take the lead and build up momentum in the execution of impact studies. In this they were partly right. But real conflicts about perspectives and interests also played an important part in causing the breakdown of cooperation. One of the NORAD factions began to get a firmer grip, arguing alongside RUBADA that the university would never be able to deliver the impact studies on time and that it would be necessary with a heavy involvement of international consultants. The supporters of the local model had by then become frustrated and some had left NORAD.

Three different sets of impact studies subsequently appeared. The major part of NORAD's money was diverted to international consultant companies. RUBADA used university researchers to a limited extent to carry out impact or identification studies. University personnel with a critical attitude to the Stiegler's Gorge Project found it, however, extremely difficult to be hired for such studies. A third line was the continuation of the Rufiji studies that had been undertaken by BRALUP since the early 1970s. Their orientation was much wider than he impact of the Stiegler's Gorge Project. But most of them were relevant to the impact studies in one way or another.

What was originally intended as a major programme of environmental studies that would enhance the capacity and competence of Tanzanian institutions, had in the end emerged as a more or less closed circuit comprising external consultants who did the impact studies, the national agency of project implementation, RUBADA, and the supporting aid agency, NORAD. The university's competence on Rufiji was marginalised.

In November 1979 when Hafslund presented its draft report, representatives from concerned university departments and research institutes requested and were allowed to participate in the discussions between RUBADA, Hafslund and NORAD. Their participation was marginal and when more sensitive issues were discussed, the university representatives were asked to leave. It became clear that the assistant to the director-general of RUBADA who was financed by NORAD had developed a negative attitude to the planning of the Stiegler's Gorge Project. His comments during the open sessions were kept to a minimum by the director-general. (A new prominent director-general had been appointed by the Tanzanian government after NORAD emphasised that the organisation needed political muscle.) The person who stood out as the substitute right hand of the director-general was an expatriate expert with the Ministry of Industries and the co-author of the electricity demand forecasts, Mr Mark Segal.

After some adjustments and updating Hafslund in cooperation with Norplan presented the final, "Stiegler's Gorge Power and Flood Control Development, Project Planning Report" in July 1980. In Appendix 3 (Studies of the Impact of the Projected Dam at Stiegler's Gorge on the Lower Rufiji) 27 reports are listed including Hafslund's final report. These reports have been presented by the official apparatus of project planning. Let me relate some interesting features of these reports to my previous discussion (cf. Appendix 3).

Eighteen of the reports, including the most strategic and demanding of resources were conducted by international consulting companies and international agencies (1, 3, 4, 5, 6, 7, 8, 9, 10, 11, 12, 13, 16, 17, 21, 25, 26, 27). Of the nine reports presented by Tanzanian institutions, two were produced by RUBADA (19 and 24), three by University of Dar es Salaam staff (14, 18 and 20, some of whom were expatriate personnel) and four by other Tanzanian institutions (2,15, 22 and 23). This clearly shows that the execution of studies related to the project, including the impact studies, was carried out mainly by external consultants which left little in terms of the build-up of competence for Tanzanian institutions. Only a few of these external studies had an effective working relationship with Tanzanian counterparts during their implementation including that of the Norwegian River and Harbour Laboratories (VHL, Report No. 25). Here the counterpart system seemed to work to support a build-up of Tanzanian competence within the field. Apart from field studies it was a more common method of many external consulting firms to appropriate the research material produced by the relevant Tanzanian institution and to reproduce it, often without either proper references or credits.

Most of the reports,for which the date of publication is available, including impact studies, came out after the major Hafslund/Norplan project planning report (No. 1, presented in July 1980). This indicates that the impact studies had little or no influence on the technical and economic aspects of the project design.

The most important and final effort to rectify the planning process of the Stiegler's Gorge Project appeared in August 1983 with the publication of the "Lower Rufiji Valley Integration Study". It was financed by NORAD for presentation to RUBADA and was executed by Norplan, in association with Mark Segal. In the preface of the main report (Volume 1) the two main objectives of the Study are outlined:

- A final overall assessment of the Stiegler's Gorge Power and Flood Control Development with a view to determining whether or not it is worth constructing the dam and associated works taking into account all related costs and benefits.
- A long-term integrated plan for the optimal development of the resources in the Lower Rufiji Basin. This plan should focus on the integrated development of the area with the view that the hydropower project will eventually be realised. However, given the long lead time and possibility of delays with a project as large as the Stiegler's Gorge power project, the plan should also identify viable projects suitable for capital financing within the next five years regardless of the dam project.

The object of the Integration Study was "to review and draw together the findings and recommendations of the various studies into one single integrated analysis" (Preface).

It is mentioned that, in agreement with RUBADA, Norplan contracted the responsibility for Part I — The Overall Assessment — to

Mark Segal, while Development Progammes and Physical Impacts were contracted to Stokes Kennedy Crowley of Dublin. Overall responsibility for the study rested with Norplan. All the major actors involved in the Integration Study had earlier participated in planning the project; Norplan cooperated with Hafslund in the main planning report of 1980 (Study 1); Segal had a prominent role in producing the electricity demand forecasts which were used as a basis for the Hafslund/Norplan 1980 report, and acted as chief adviser to the director-general of RUBADA at crucial moments; while Stokes Kennedy Crowley had prepared the feasibility study on the development of tourism in Rufiji in 1981 (Study 11).

The Integration Study was thus conducted by actors who had participated in preparing the project and who accordingly were to some degree responsible for the plans. If the objective had been to improve the project through a sound integration of sub-studies and a critical analysis of the work already done, a different approach would have been needed. For instance, an independent group might have looked with fresh eyes at the project preparation and the possible integration aspects. Instead, in my opinion, when Norplan was given responsibility for the Integration Study in 1982, vested interests were called upon to save the project without a critical analysis of its weaknesses.

Below are some important reasons why this approach did not succeed.

Flood control and low-level outlets

The Agrar- und Hydrotechnik report (Study 4) said that fully irrigated agricultural development downstream should be designed with a 1:100 year assurance against uncontrolled flooding. When this requirement was built into the flood frequency simulations of the TANZA computer programme it emerged that a controlled flood of 4,000 m^3/s would be optimal. Compared to the recommendations made by Hafslund, this would require nearly a doubling of the release capacity of the low level outlets at Stiegler's Gorge. The Integration Study (IS) is, however, content with recommending an increase in the capacity of the low level outlets to 3,000 m^3/s at 158 m elevation as this is regarded to be sufficient to secure the 1:100 year flood security. The additional 1,000 m^3/s is expected to come from discharge of the turbines and, after phase III, there will be additional controlled release facilities through the gated spillway, when reservoir levels are above 174 m (Norplan, 1983, Vol. I:11-12).

There are two major problems which may undermine the above calculations. Firstly, the simulations on the power production and flood control programme — TANZA — is based on run-off data for the 22 years from 1956-1978 (Norplan, 1983 Vol. 1, Appendix A:A6). It is understandable that the Hafslund/Norplan 1980 report did not utilise flood data beyond 1978. The Integration Study, however, had ample opportunity to do so. Then probably the largest flood of this century, the flood of 1979 which exceeded 11,000 m^3/s at Stiegler's Gorge, would have been included. Taking this flood into account would probably have cast doubt on the conclusion that 4,000 m^3/s capacity at low level outlets would be sufficient to ensure a 1:100 year security against uncontrolled flooding. (Norplan rejected this hypothesis in 1989 but has not for the present been able to substantiate this rejection.) Why did the Integration Study overlook available data which would have strengthened the reliability of the TANZA simulations? Secondly, no historical analysis of the land use of the catchment area is linked to the development of floods. This is required for an understanding of the impact of non-physical factors on flood profiles over time (see Chapter 4). Hence the TANZA simulations have not used available data and have not analysed flood data in a relevant manner. A 1:100 year security against uncontrolled flooding is likely to require in excess of the projected 4,000 m^3/s capacity at the low level outlets.

The capacity of the low level outlets and its relation to erosion of the gorge is another major problem of the approach of the Integation Study. It is pointed out earlier that Hafslund claimed that 2,500 m^3/s was a maximum low level release due to erosion problems. The Integration Study states that the technical review panel (no. 5) approved of an increase in the capacity of low level outlets because it would decrease the frequency with which the spillway structure needed to be operated and added flexibility to the operation of the reservoir (Norplan, 1983, Vol I:11). It would be interesting to know what the panel's judgement was on the impact of erosion of the increased capacity of the low level outlets. Was the panel ignorant of Hafslund's warning or had it undertaken additional studies which had added insights on this vital issue? Until a reasonable explanation of the above question is offered, I will assume that the Hafslund recommendation is the sound one. Hence the increase in the capacity of the low level outlets as recommended by the Integration Study is not advisable.

Prognosis of electricity demand

The Integration Study emphasises that the forecast of demand is of fundamental importance to the evaluation of cost-effectiveness of supply alternatives (Norplan, 1983, Vol. I:14). The Integration Study, which was carried out in 1982/83, adopted the July 1981 TANESCO forecast, "because it has been the official load forecast of Tanzania throughout the preparation of this study" (Ibid.). A few paragraphs later it says that "Since 1981/82, Tanzania has been experiencing an acute payments crisis triggered by the coincidence of numerous external and internal factors. This situation has been developing during the implementation of the Stiegler's Gorge Integration Study" (Ibid., 16). The Integration Study emphasises that the industrial load accounts for about two-thirds of electricity consumption in Tanzania, hence a major emphasis of the forecast is on the expected evolution of the industrial load (Ibid., 15). The members of the team, the Bureau of Statistics and the Ministry of Industry in Tanzania, all knew by early 1983 that industrial production had declined dramatically in 1981 and 1982 and that the decline was expected to continue during 1983. Why did the Integration Study team not attempt to adjust TANESCO's July 1981 forecast to more realistic levels? One reason given by the team is that a large amount of work is required to construct well-grounded short term forecast alternatives (Ibid., 14). This is not a good argument, as not developing such forecasts, which are badly needed to account for a changing economic situation, casts doubt on the whole exercise of demand forecasts. In the statistical appendix of the Integration Study sectorial growth rates are recorded up to 1980 and capacity utilisation for individual industries up to 1974. In 1983, the year of its publication, far more up-to-date figures were available.

In my assessment the weaknesses of the Integraton Study in relation to flood security, of the capacity of low level outlet and forecasts of electricity demand, cast serious doubt on its credibility. The attempt to present a sound and modified project has thus failed. This conclusion is reinforced by the findings of a more recent survey (1985) of suitable hydropower projects throughout Tanzania. In this survey the Stiegler's Gorge alternative is low on the list of priorities (Havnevik et al., 1988:265). In the most recent version of the energy policy of Tanzania (1992), Stiegler's Gorge is not mentioned among the six new hydroelectric projects to be developed as the next project generation (URT, 1992:11).

CONCLUSIONS

The history of Stiegler's Gorge Project is a striking example of a large-scale multipurpose project for which single purpose planning of hydropower generation was carried out. The single purpose approach led to neglect of the interests of the population in the impact area of the project. The government agencies responsible for planning it, the Ministry of Water and Natural Resources and the Rufiji Basin Development Authority (RUBADA), made little attempt to redirect the planning process to give it a multipurpose, integrated character which took account of the impact on people's productive activities and the ecological environment, be it on land or in the sea. None of the state agencies involved issued a warning that the mere size of the project would reduce expenditure in other sectors for a long time. Implementation of the project as originally planned would have required a build-up of power consuming industries which would have led to Tanzania becoming increasingly dependent on imported technology and external markets.

The donor agency most vigorously supporting the Stiegler's Gorge Project, NORAD, did not investigate its implications at the proper stage, but seems to have been guided by the sectoral interests of the Norwegian hydro-development lobby (see for instance Amland, 1993). Critical views in Norway and Tanzania were marginalised by creating a close-knit organisation for project implementation consisting of international consultants and agencies, NORAD, and RUBADA and the Ministry of Water and Natural Resources.

When finally approached, the World Bank made it clear that only a proper plan for a multipurpose project would stand a chance of Bank financing. The frenetic attempts, in particular by NORAD, to rectify the planning approach failed, because of the extremely uneven development of the technical and non-technical aspects of planning and because of internal disagreements that reflected different interests within NORAD and in Tanzania. There was neither the will nor the capacity to redirect the planning process in a constructive way. The Integration Study of 1983, the final attempt to save the project, is a good example of this.

The planning of the Stiegler's Gorge Project illustrates a case where the state and external donors intervene through a major project in a rural area without taking due consideration either of the people and ecological environment affected or of its wider economic implications. Unfortunately the Stiegler's Gorge Project is not a single "accident" as evidenced by case studies of five other man-made lakes in East Africa (Roggeri, 1985). Implementation according to the original project plan and schedule would have further aggravated the economic crisis in Tanzania. The build-up of related power-consuming industries in the 1980s would have been impossible, and the Stiegler's Gorge Project would therefore have become an economic disaster. The Tanzanian state's pursuit of this project into the 1980s reflects one aspect of the breakdown of the post-colonial model.

PART IV

Structural Adjustment and Agriculture in Tanzania

9. Structural Adjustment and Agriculture since 1980

The object of this chapter is to analyse structural adjustment policies and their impact on agriculture– the content of the conditionalities, their degree of implementation and actual outcomes with emphasis on the 1980s. As a background, developments during the early part of the 1980s are investigated and in particular Tanzania's own attempts at coming to grips with the crisis which unfolded from the late 1970s onwards.

BACKGROUND TO STRUCTURAL ADJUSTMENT

During the latter part of the 1970s a series of external shocks combined with internal imbalances set the Tanzanian crisis in motion. Up to 1977 the World Bank (WB) and bilateral donors had provided substantial support for the post-Arusha, state-led Tanzanian development strategy. As the crisis unfolded, criticism of the Tanzanian development model began to emerge. In January 1980 World Bank President McNamara went to Tanzania to initiate a new phase in the Tanzanian/World Bank relations with emphasis on structural adjustment. It took until 1986 before Tanzania signed an agreement on a structural adjustment programme which was endorsed by the International Monetary Fund (IMF) and the World Bank.

The period 1980–86 was one in which Tanzania encountered serious disagreements with the IMF and the World Bank. Tanzania's experience reflects the growing coordination of these International Financial Institutions (IFIs) in the era of structural adjustment.

In September 1980 Tanzania reached a Standby Agreement with the IMF and subsequently approached the World Bank for structural adjustment assistance. The IMF agreement broke down in December already due to Tanzania's inability to meet certain performance targets. Further discussion with the IMF during early 1981 about a possible Extended Fund Facility did not lead to any results as the Tanzanian authorities regarded the standard IMF conditionality as one that would undermine the Tanzanian development strategy. Tanzanian/IMF relations soured to the extent that the Swedish head of the IMF mission was declared *persona non grata* and given 48 hours to leave the country. Tanzanian/IMF relations were not renewed until 1986.

Though things went wrong between Tanzania and the IMF, the World Bank was somewhat sympathetic and understanding, even if the relationship was strained and difficult at times. When Tanzania requested structural adjustment assistance in 1980/81, the World Bank found the programme proposal unrealistic (25 per cent growth of exports over the previous year), and instead offered Tanzania a more limited Export Rehabilitation Credit (ERC), approved in April 1981. The lengthy negotiations leading up to this agreement clearly illustrate the diverging views of the Bank and the Tanzanian authorities (World Bank, 1990a:80).

In 1981 disagreements between the World Bank and Tanzania emerged regarding the development budget, over the relative importance of price and non-price constraints to agricultural development and over the pace of implementation of certain measures. The Tanzanian/World Bank relationship was further strained when the latter revealed reluctance to go ahead with any further loan support "before access to IMF's facilities had been restored to Tanzania or prospects for an early agreement improved" (World Bank, 1990a:80). Because of its frustrations with the international finance institutions, Tanzania launched its own National Economic Survival Programme in late 1981 (NESP, 1981). The targets of this programme were unrealistic and it did not provide a coherent plan for mobilising resources and people (Wangwe, 1987:151).

The World Bank did, in early 1982, recommend that the Tanzanian government develop a major programme of structural adjustment and it financed a technical advisory group (TAG) acceptable both to the World Bank and Tanzania. The Bank also proceeded to prepare its second agricultural sector report on Tanzania (World Bank, 1983) as a possible input to the structural adjustment programme. This report recommended three broad categories of policy changes: the need for exchange rate-, producer- and consumer price adjustments; improvement of the institutional framework for agriculture through increased pluralism and support to private initiatives; and the need to increase the share of foreign exchange going to agriculture by correcting the budgetary imbalances between industry and agriculture and between productive and social services in the rural sector (Lele and Myers, 1989:43). The most important differences between the 1974 Agricultural Sector Report and that of 1983 were the latter's views that Tanzanian developments should be agriculturally led and that the role of the public sector should be reduced.

The Tanzanian government prepared a national agricultural policy (NAP), which on important issues like institutional pluralism, marketing, agricultural prices and the need to increase transfers to agriculture, went some way towards meeting World Bank demands (URT, 1982). Some of the recommendations were, however, watered down in the officially published national agricultural policy publication of 1983 (URT, 1983).

The structural adjustment programme (SAP) put forward by the Tanzanian government on the basis of the TAG recommendations "confirmed that there was broad general agreement between the Bank and Tanzania on principles although not on exact magnitudes of public sector expenditure cuts and of price adjustments" (World Bank, 1990a:81). The SAP did protect the social profile of the development strategy and one means to attain this was to reduce military expenditure (Kiondo, 1989). The proposal did, however, not go far enough in meeting IMF conditions and the World Bank could not give Tanzania a satisfactory answer as to the minimum conditions for a structural adjustment loan. One important reason for this was the lack of consensus within the World Bank on conditionality. Another was the increasing subjugation of the World Bank to the IMF. The result was that the structural adjustment programme was not accepted by the IFIs and external assistance to Tanzania started to drop from 1982 onwards (see Table 2.2).

Tanzania then proceeded unilaterally to introduce policy changes which went beyond the structural adjustment programme of 1982. A major breakthrough came with the 1984/85 Budget. Recurrent expenditure for agriculture was more than doubled from the 1983/84 budget, agricultural producer prices were raised significantly, a large devaluation was announced as well as the removal of subsidies on maize meal (the urban staple food) and partially on agricultural inputs. The budget also considerably weakened emphasis on social services and education. The "own-funded import scheme", where residents were allowed to import freely on a no question basis if they could raise foreign exchange, was also introduced. The 1984/85 Budget represented a significant retreat by the state bourgeoisie and included major concessions to the policies promoted by the IMF and the World Bank. As such it signified the breakdown of the Tanzanian post-colonial model (Havnevik, 1991 and Chapter 2).

The tactic of the Tanzanian government was to seek increased financial support from sympathetic donors, like the Nordic countries and the Netherlands, not tied to the harsh conditions set by the IMF. In November 1984, during a joint high level Nordic/Tanzania government sponsored symposium, the head of SIDA in his introductory remarks closed the door to this option saying that, "a basic assumption on the Nordic side at the outset of these deliberations, hence our working hypothesis, is that resources from our countries would serve to supplement, and not to be a substitute for, those emanating from an agreement with the Fund" (Swedish introductory statement at Tanzania-Nordic symposium, 1984:3). Hence the Nordic countries also aligned themselves with the IMF/World Bank conditionality. In the lengthy Nordic background paper to the symposium, no attempt was made to develop an alternative understanding of the Tanzanian crisis or identify measures which could help the country to ease or to overcome it. In the area of agriculture the Nordic paper encouraged the revival of private large-scale farming, but stated that it should not be done at expense of the smallholders. The latter, the paper stated, can be said never to have been given a chance to show their capacities (Nordic background paper, 1984:24).

The new Tanzanian policies opened the way for rapprochement with the international financial institutions. After the Nordic countries had rejected an expansion of their assistance without an IMF agreement, discussions between Tanzania and the World Bank ensued which eventually would reroute Tanzania's development path towards IMF/World Bank guided structural adjustment.

THE STRUCTURAL ADJUSTMENT REGIME FROM 1986 ONWARDS

Objectives, policies and financial support

The Economic Recovery Programme (ERP) was prepared during 1985/86 in close cooperation between the World Bank and Tanzanian authorities and was thereafter used as a basis for concluding negotiations with the IMF in August 1986. The major objectives of ERP were to increase the output of exports and food crops; to rehabilitate physical infrastructure and raise industrial capacity utilisation; and to restore external and internal balances through prudent fiscal, monetary and trade policies (URT, 1986:14). The major policies announced in pursuance of the programme's objectives included raising producer prices by 5 per cent per year in real terms or to the extent of 60-70 per cent of the world market price whichever was higher; adopting an active exchange rate policy removing the overvaluation of the shilling within three years; further liberalising external and internal trade by the tightening of budget expenditure and money supply control; and improving parastatal efficiency and the foreign exchange allocation system (URT, 1986:14-16 and Wangwe, 1987:153).

Tanzania embarked on the adjustment agenda and external donors responded quickly by increasing total disbursements of aid (excluding technical assistance) from a low level of US $ 487 million in 1985 to US $ 680 in 1986. By 1989 the level of donor assistance reached US $ 850 million of which about US $ 400 million was provided in the form of import- or balance of payment support. World Bank lending under structural adjustment included a Multisector Rehabilitation Credit (MRC) for US $ 135 million approved in November 1986 and supplemented in January 1988 with US $ 56 million. An Industrial Rehabilitation and Trade Adjustment Credit (IRTAC) of US $ 135 million (approved in December 1988) supported restructuring of the industrial sector and measures aimed at trade reform, like the Open General License (OGL) facility which was introduced in February 1988. Increasingly bilateral donors switched their import support or balance of payments assistance to the OGL. A more recent fast disbursing Agricultural Adjustment Credit was established in 1990 to support measures for the reform of the agricultural marketing system. Over the fiscal years 1986–1990, total World Bank lending to Tanzania amounted to US $ 941 of which about 47 per cent was related to adjustment lending operations. The sectoral allocation of the remaining loans was 28 per cent (of total US $ 941) for transport, 8.7 per cent for agriculture, about 5 per cent for health and nutrition and about 4 per cent each for education and energy.

Devaluation and liberalisation

The cornerstone of the Economic Recovery Programme is the adjustment of the real exchange rate, which is a pre-condition for the unification of the official and unofficial markets and doing away with rationing. The international financial institutions had reason to be pleased with Tanzania as the observed real exchange rate has depreciated by more than 80 per cent from 1985 to 1990. At the same time the ratio of the parallel to the official exchange rate dropped from 9:1 to 1.5:1 (World Bank, 1991a:7).

During the first years of reform, most adjustment implementation was linked to economic liberalisation, an area in which Tanzania had already initiated changes. The liberalisation of the external trade regime was initiated with the own funds scheme in 1984. From 1985 to 1990 this scheme allowed for an average annual increase in imports of US $ 230–240 millions per year, about half the amount of the income derived from exports. The process of liberalisation of trade continued with the establishment of the OGL facility in February 1988. This facility gradually expanded and from early 1992 allowed for all kinds of imports, including luxuries. During 1990 it accounted for about 10 per cent of imports, but only 12–15 per cent of OGL funds for the years 1988 and 1989 were directed to the agricultural sector. The World Bank expected that there would be a substantial increase in OGL funds for 1992 (World Bank, 1991a:92).

During 1988 the tariff structure was simplified and the maximum rate was lowered to 100 per cent. Consumer goods tariffs were in the range of 40 to 60 per cent, while items for basic needs were subjected to lower rates (Ibid.).

The government adopted various measures to liberalise internal trade, including price decontrol (a reduction from 400 to 10 categories) and deconfinement. In 1989 legislation was approved to end confinement for all firms and products with the result that in 1990/91 only 10 manufactured items were confined and under price control.

The industrial sector

Structural change in the industrial sector, in particular of the para-statals, has been very limited. While the increase in commodity import support assistance under the Economic Recovery Programme contri-buted to raising the level of output in some industries, this recovery has not been accompanied by structural changes such as lowered im-port intensity or increased production efficiency. An examination of the industrial rehabilitation measures during the Economic Recovery Programme indicates that they have been driven by the objectives of modernisation and output maximization in a static sense, in which con-sideration of technological learning over time is secondary. The de-sign and implementation of the industrial rehabilitation programme are similar to those of new projects and tend to reinforce the same fea-tures of dependency and low technological learning observed during the earlier ill-designed industrialisation initiatives (Wangwe, 1990). Structural change has also been inhibited because the administrative allocation criteria for industries in the programme for economic re-covery were so general that they did not exclude any industrial line or sector. The improvement in manufacturing growth rates from 1987 onwards seems to be based mainly on increased availability of foreign exchange, which improved the capacity utilisation from 25 per cent in 1985 to 35 per cent in 1989 (Table 9.1).

On the basis of industrial surveys conducted in 1984 and 1989, the World Bank claims that "from the analysis of both surveys it is appa-rent that a significant restructuring in production has begun to take

Table 9.1. *Tanzanian GDP growth 1983-1990, percentage change over previous year*

	1983	1984	1985	1986	1987	1988	1989	1990
Agriculture	2.9	4.0	6.0	5.7	4.4	4.5	4.6	2.9
Manufacturing	-8.7	2.7	-3.9	-4.0	4.2	5.4	9.7	7.8
GDP	0.8	4.4	0.7	4.7	4.0	5.1	4.4	4.2

Source: World Bank, 1991b, p. 141

place" (World Bank, 1991a:93). In spite of this apparent break with the past, no inefficient enterprise surveyed in 1984 had been closed down by 1989 (Ibid.). One reason for the slow pace of restructuring of the industrial sector, was the unwillingness of government to withdraw grants and subsidies to state enterprises. During the 1980s, government transfers of funds to the parastatals actually rose from 6 per cent of total expenditures to 8.8 per cent. What emerges from an analysis of the industrial sector under the Economic Recovery Programme is that to some extent the state bureaucracy managed to protect its interests in the state enterprise sector. This was made possible primarily through an increase in development assistance, in the form of import support allocated by the Ministry of Finance. In order to break the bureaucracy's control, the World Bank urged donors to increase assistance through the Open General Licence system. As late as June 1991 at the Consultative Group Meeting for Tanzania, the World Bank argued that, "further shifts in resources from traditional import support programmes into the OGL will be essential" (World Bank, 1991d).

Supply of incentive goods and the agricultural sector

Increased utilisation of industrial capacity and liberalisation of the external trade regime have had a marked impact on the availability of consumer goods. The World Bank sees the increased growth rates in agriculture from 1984 onwards, as stemming mainly from this increased supply of consumer goods, called incentive goods. The implication, according to the World Bank, is that agricultural growth during this period had a once and for all character which is not a sustainable process resulting from structural change. Agriculture's share of GDP increased gradually from 52.8 per cent in 1983 to around 60 per cent in 1986, a level which was maintained until 1989 when it dropped to 59 per cent and further to 58.2 per cent in 1990. Manufacturing's share of GDP did not show a similar increase. It remained stable at around 7 per cent from 1983 to 1987, was 8.5 per cent for 1988 and 1989, then it decreased to 5.1 per cent in 1990 (World Bank, 1991b:140). In spite of the focus of the Economjc Recovery Programme on the productive sector, the sectoral allocation of government development resources available to agriculture and livestock declined from 30.6 per cent in 1986/87 to 20.1 per cent 1988/89, while the allocation to industry remained around 10 per cent during the same period (except for a 1987/88 allocation of 16 per cent) (Kiondo, 1989:366).

The financial sector

The financial sector had not yet been restructured by the early 1990s. Both the public financial sector (World Bank, 1991a:58) and the overall financial sector were still in severe crisis after half a decade of World Bank led structural adjustment (Ibid., 47–50). At the 1991 Consultative Group Meeting these were among the concerns that made the World Bank call for "a need to deepen the reform effort across the broad spectrum of sectors" and to suggest that "achieving sustainable growth with poverty reduction will require, wherever possible, an acceleration in the pace of implementation" (World Bank, 1991d:3). It bluntly stated that the result of World Bank led structural adjustment in Tanzania, "has been five consecutive years of positive per capita income growth and improved welfare — in sharp contrast to the previous decade" (Ibid., 1). Such unqualified statements reflect the general character of World Bank analyses which miss underlying economic and social processes, including differentiation between social groups.

Before turning to the analysis of structural adjustment and agriculture more specifically, let me present some of the available evidence on income inequalities and differentiation in urban settings.

Income inequalities, differentiation and gender issues in urban settings

The decline in real wages had been initiated around the mid-1970s. This continued during the crisis of the 1980s. In real terms minimum and average wages dropped by 53 and 70 per cent respectively from 1980 to 1986. Rapid devaluation, price increases and the abolition of consumer subsidies as a result of structural adjustment policies led to further erosion of the purchasing power of wages. Tibaijuka

(1991a:79) points out that estimations in June 1989 showed that a family of four in Dar es Salaam needed a montly minimum of Tsh. 9,000 for expenditure on food alone. The monthly minimum wage current at the time could only cover 23 per cent of such a household's food needs. In January 1991 the purchasing power of the minimum wage could only meet 16.7 per cent of the same household's food needs.

As for social differentiation under structural adjustment, limited data is available. From urban areas, like Dar es Salaam, only one recent survey (November 1990) is available. It includes 1,000 households and focuses on changes in real total household incomes from 1980 to 1990. During the decade only 10 per cent of the households reported a rise in real incomes while 20 per cent experienced stagnation. The remaining 70 per cent of the households reported that incomes declined up to 25 per cent (15 per cent of the households), 25 to 50 per cent (20 per cent of the households), above 50 per cent (35 per cent of the households). 10 per cent of the households surveyed reported negative incomes, i.e. they responded that they were depending on relatives and borrowed funds (Tibaijuka, 1991a:69-70).

One effect of real wages in urban areas declining was to push women and children into money making activities in order to reduce the income gap for the household. In terms of access to credit and resources, women are discriminated against on the basis of gender and are harassed at workplaces (Vuorela, 1988:177–187). In the informal sector only 3 per cent of the loans approved by the National Bank of Commerce went to women or women's groups in the late 1980s. Self-employed women have developed counter-strategies including the establishment in 1989 of the Business Association of Women; rotating credit arrangements, Upato; in which half of the self-employed women in Dar es Salaam are said to be involved; and in 1991, a campaign against sexual harassment of women was launched (Tripp, 1991).

STRUCTURAL ADJUSTMENT IN THE AGRICULTURAL SECTOR

Agricultural marketing

Structural adjustment led to a continuation of the liberalisation of agricultural marketing which had begun in 1984 when interregional marketing of food grains by individuals was introduced. By March 1987 all weight restrictions on such trade had been eliminated and private traders started to compete with the National Milling Corporation

(NMC). From the 1988/89 crop season, primary societies and cooperative unions were allowed to sell directly to private traders and in 1990 individual farmers were also given this option, hence competition between the parastatal/cooperative system and the private sector had become fully legalised. But implementation of the reforms was problematic at times and "characterised by contradictions, arbitrariness and uncertainties" (Kiondo, 1989:372-5).

The increased liberalisation led to the rise of a new class of indigenous traders engaged in grain collection, wholesaling and retailing. According to the World Bank 100 private traders existed on the Dar es Salaam wholesale grain market (World Bank, 1991a:61). As Rasmussen (1987:201–3) has shown, the existence of a large number of private grain traders and transporters had already occurred in the major maize producing areas in the Southern Highlands in the early 1980s. High levels of parallel trading was also observed in Hanang District, Arusha Region in 1983 and 1985. Traders came from Shinyanga and Mwanza to buy maize and beans in exchange for sugar, cooking oil and other items. Very little maize and virtually no beans were sold to NMC during these years (personal communication with F. Kjærby, who undertook field work in this area). Estimates provided by the Marketing Development Bureau indicate that during the crop season 1982/83, a year of severe food shortages, private sales and trading of maize amounted to about 250,000 tonnes, nearly 55 per cent of the estimated total sales of about 460,000 tonnes. The price differentials between the parallel and official markets during this period led to enormous profits for the traders (Ibid., 203).

The MADIA studies correctly bear out the institutional instability of agricultural marketing in Tanzania and its effects on undermining farmers' confidence (Lele and Christiansen, 1989:16). This continued with the restoration of the cooperative movement in 1982 and marketing boards as replacements for the government's crop authorities.

In the period of increased liberalisation, dramatic problems occurred within the cooperative movement in terms of both conflicting objectives between management and members and financial control. The membership structure of the new cooperative movement was 80 per cent male and 20 per cent female smallholders (Tripp, 1991). This implied that whatever direct benefits filtered down to the producers, female farmers had less access to them.

By the end of the decade the movement was characterised by undemocratic rules and was in arrears with an overdraft of about Tsh. 25 billion, which far exceeded the annual crop and input requirements of about Tsh. 15 billion. The growth of cooperative credits as well as those of the marketing boards, in particular the NMC, led to the government's failure to meet the credit benchmarks and targets of the Economic Recovery Programme.

It took the government until April 1991 to pass a new Cooperative Act which incorporated provisions for voluntary membership in democratically-controlled societies and unions and economic viability as the principle for the establishment of operating societies (World Bank, 1991a:75). According to the World Bank, donor pressure and threats to withdraw support were instrumental in bringing about the new Act. The degree of autonomy to be enjoyed by the cooperative movement on the basis of the new Act, remains to be seen. The Executive Committee of the then single legal party, Chama Cha Mapinduzi (CCM), stated in conjunction with the launching of Acts providing autonomy to mass organisations that, "The Party is satisfied that any child who is being brought up will reach the stage of being fully grown and mature.... These organisations (including the cooperative movement) have now freedom of choice as to what sort of relations they would like to have with their parent, the CCM" (*Daily News*, May 6 1991).

While the government finally bowed to pressure on the liberalisation of grain trade, the single channel marketing monopoly for export crops continued throughout the 1980s. Export crops could only be purchased by the marketing boards. It was not until July 1990 that partial liberalisation took place in this area when the cotton and cashew marketing boards ceased purchasing and sales, and ventured instead into the provision of various types of marketing services. Such changes have led to large lay-offs of personnel in the boards. Alongside this, cooperative unions also lost their monopoly on the purchase of export crops. Primary societies, farmers associations, private estates and licensed traders (cashew nuts) could sell crops directly through auction and tender systems in 1991, at the world market price. It was, however, in early 1992, not clear if and how far these policies have been implemented. During the 1990/91 crop season the government finally stopped further financing of the NMC, which effectively eliminated it from the market, except for its responsibility for the 150,000 tonnes Strategic Grain Reserve.

Terms of trade and rural welfare

A major objective of structural adjustment has been to improve the real incomes of peasants by increasing producer prices and tilt the terms of trade in favour of the agricultural sector. As late as January 1990 the World Bank reported that, "The measures being undertaken in the agricultural sector are already significantly improving the stan-

dard of living of the rural population through improved prices received for production" (World Bank, 1990b:21). However, only about
a year and half later the World Bank spelled out that the Economic Recovery Programme had not led to the anticipated overall rise in
farmers' income through an improvement of their terms of trade
(World Bank, 1991a:64).

A significant feature of agricultural terms of trade for export crops
under the structural adjustment programme, unlike that of the previous period, was that those facing official marketing agencies and actual producers differed. From the mid-1970s to 1984 the decline in the
terms of trade for producers and crop authorities or marketing boards
was about 50 per cent. With the onset of devaluation in 1984/85 there
was a reversal in the terms of trade for marketing boards which improved by more than 100 per cent between 1984 and 1988. Terms of
trade for producers increased by about 30 per cent during 1985, but
failed to improve in subsequent years. The implication was that the
marketing boards and the cooperative unions absorbed nearly all the
benefits of the improved terms of trade. The major reason was a lack
of full adjustment of agricultural producer prices to reflect movements of the exchange rate. One effect, also running counter to the objectives of the Economic Recovery Programme, was that the farmers'
share of the final value of major export crops dropped from around
80 per cent in 1986 to only 35 per cent in 1988. 1989 saw an improvement to around 50 per cent (World Bank, 1991a:64; see also EIU,
1989:4; Stein 1990:19; Maganya 1990:111; and Booth 1991:15–16).
In a report published in 1988 the Cooperative Union of Tanzania had
already signalled that depreciation of the shilling and rising input costs
far outweighed the nominal increases in producer prices. While the
average producer price for cotton increased by 70 per cent, the average prices of agrochemicals for cotton went up by 475 per cent from
1985/86 to 1988/89. Instead of the producer price increasing in real
terms, there was a decrease of 14.6 per cent (CUT, 1988:1–2).

Yet, the World Bank claims that "substantial declines in incomes and
living standards of the pre-reform period have been arrested. In fact,
on average, peasants' welfare appears to have improved significantly"
(World Bank, 1991a:25). This claim has been made in spite of the evidence that peasant cash incomes have not increased substantially during the reform period. The World Bank sees the improvement in welfare to be linked rather to greater consumption of food and to increased availability of consumer goods. The analysis is based on four
different approaches: per capita real cash balances held by peasants,
which is supposed to indicate the trend in peasant incomes; per capita
estimates of peasants' real income from crop sales; estimates of per

capita availability of consumer goods in the economy and per capita food consumption by peasants (World Bank, 1991a.:25). Such an analysis is problematic due to its treatment of peasants as a homogeneous group and the exclusion of all forms of collective consumption like social services, water supply and education from the welfare function. Further problems associated with this approach are discussed later in this chapter.

The Economic Recovery Programme focussed on improving the productive sectors and had no special programme aiming at the provision of social services. Real per capita expenditure on such services dropped by about 50 per cent, from Tsh. 50 in 1982 to about Tsh. 25 in 1986 (Tsh. in 1970/71 prices). 1987 saw no improvement, while per capita government expenditure increased to slightly above Tsh. 30 in 1988 and 1989 mainly due to a rise in expenditure on health. These figures include expenditure at local government level (World Bank, 1991a:114). In spite of this it has been argued that real levels of social service provision have declined due to the high costs in foreign exchange of some of these services and the rapid depreciation in the value of Tanzanian currency (Tibaijuka, 1991:77). But declining services at the local level cannot be entirely explained by a reduction in real expenditures. The negative effect on services of spreading resources thinly over a large number of activities is another contributory factor (Semboja and Therkildsen, 1989:24).

Both the government and the donors expressed concern about negative developments on the provison of social services under the Economic Recovery Programme. The second phase, called the "Economic and Social Action Programme" (ESAP, 1989), for 1989–92 specifically aimed to rehabilitate social service provision. No immediate results were forthcoming. In March 1991 the then Minister of Health, Sarungi, reported to the government's daily paper *Daily News*, about appalling conditions in rural hospitals after having visited twelve of the country's 20 regions (*Daily News*, March 24, 1991). As late as at the Consultative Group Meeting in June 1991, the World Bank still maintained that social expenditures as a per cent of the total available budget had not yet increased (World Bank, 1991d:9). In spite of verbal emphasis and the mobilisation of resources for the social sector through cost-recovery and community participation, the provision of social services as well as the quality of education and water supply have declined further during the first five to six years of structural adjustment. This decline probably cancelled out some of the possible gains in welfare of the rural population that emerged due to an increased availability of incentive goods.

Table 9.2.   *Officially marketed production of major export crops 1983/84–*
1990/91 ('000 tonnes per crop year)

	1983/84	84/85	85/86	86/87	87/88	88/89	89/90	90/91
Coffee	49.5	49.0	55.0	54.0	49.3	49.5	37.1	55.8
Cotton	47.0	51.9	32.5	56.0	66.3	63.3	42.1	52.0
Tea	11.9	16.8	15.5	14.1	13.8	15.6	20.1	18.0
Cashew nuts	47.0	51.9	20.5	17.6	24.2	18.9	16.5	22.0
Tobacco	11.0	13.4	12.5	14.0	7.4	10.7	11.0	11.8
Sisal	46.2	39.3	32.9	30.2	33.2	33.3	32.2	33.5
Totals	212.6	222.3	168.9	185.9	194.2	191.3	159.0	193.1
Percentage change (over previous year)		4.6%	(24%)	10.1%	4.5%	(1.5%)	(16.7%)	21.4%

Note: Figures for 1990/91 are estimates.
Sources: The Economist Intelligence Unit; Tanzania–Country Profile 1990–91, p.13
and 1991–92, p. 13 and URT (Basic Data 1981/82–1985/86, Planning and Marketing
Division, Ministry of Agriculture and Livestock Development) for sisal production in
the years 1983/84–1985/86

Output response

The growth trends in total agricultural production in Table 9.1 indicate that there has been a positive total agricultural growth per capita
since 1984. This development has been aided by a reduction in annual
growth rates of the population from about 3.3 per cent in the 1970s to
2.8 per cent during the 1980s. But estimates of total agricultural production are very uncertain due to the problems of estimating the
amount of the production that is not sold and unofficially marketed.
The official figures for export crops are probably more reliable as
there are no alternative marketing channels for most of these crops.
Statistics for production of officially marketed major export crops
from 1983/84 to 1990/91 are shown in Table 9.2.

  The statistics available show that official marketed export production increased slightly by 4.6 per cent between 1983/84 and 1984/85,
then dropped dramatically by 24 per cent in 1985/86 due mainly to a
decline in cotton and cashew nut production. In 1986/87 production
levels increased by 10.1 per cent mainly due to cotton and remained
fairly stable, at a level of between 185,000 and 195,000 tonnes for the

Table 9.3. *Production estimates for major food crops 1981/82–1988/89* (000'metric tonnes)

	1981/82	82/83	83/84	84/85	85/86	86/87	87/88	88/89
Maize								
-production	1,402	1,740	1,712	2,013	2,671	2,787	2,429	2,527
-area (000'hect.)	1,294	1,232	1,230	1,412	1,576	1,626	1,675	1,669
-yield kgs/hect.	1,080	1,410	1,340	1,420	1,620	1,710	1,450	1,520
Sorghum	233	254	301	442	384	367	424	405
Millet	155	149	168	272	301	259	198	219
Paddy	309	255	328	276	418	566	782	768
Wheat	59	59	72	67	98	72	75	81
Total prod.	2,158	2,457	2,581	3,070	3,872	4,051	3,908	4,000

Source: URT: Basic Data Agricultural & Livestock Sector 1981/82–1985/86 and 1984/85–1988/89. Planning and Marketing Division, Ministry of Agriculture & Livestock Development

rest of the decade, except during 1989/90 when production dropped to 159,000 tonnes. The variation occurring in 1989/90 and 1990/91 was linked to both cotton and coffee production. The production levels of 1983/84 and 1984/85 were never again attained later in the decade. The annual variation in figures marketed, at least for some crops, is also associated with bottle-necks and problems related to infrastructure, transport capacity, processing and credit. The great variation in cotton marketing is linked to weak infrastructure and limited ginning capacity, as well as to cooperatives not paying growers properly. The existence of such constraints makes it difficult, for instance, to calculate relevant price elasticities for crops.

Estimates of total maize and food production differ from one publication to the next. Many seem to confuse marketed production with total production. The extent of marketed production is also difficult to verify due to changes in the volume of non-official marketing, which was illegal in the pre-reform period of food shortages.

Table 9.3 shows production estimates for major food crops for 1981/82 to 1988/89. Estimates for acreages cultivated and yields of maize are also shown. It appears that the total production of food crops increased by about 500,000 tonnes between the crop season 1983/84 and 1984/85 and then remained at around 4 million tonnes for the rest of the decade. Most of the increase is attributed to a rise in maize production between 1983/84 and 1985/87 when peak production levels were attained. Paddy also increased steadily between 1984/85 and 1987/88.

Table 9.3 indicates that the increase in maize production is linked to simultaneous increases in the area planted and in yields per hectare. The marked increase in yields in 1982/83, which thereafter remained stable during the rest of the decade, cannot be explained by the growth in distribution of fertilizers (which may exceed what is actually purchased and used by farmers). Distribution rose from the low level of 88,480 tonnes in 1983 to about 190,000 tonnes on average in 1986 and 1987 (URT, undated). Unexpectedly the distribution of fertilizers dropped to about 114,000 tonnes in 1988. A major and increasing share of fertilizer has been used in the Southern Highlands in the four major maize producing regions, which are also known for a high degree of use of improved seeds. Sales of certified seeds during the 1980s fluctuated between 4,000 and 6,000 tonnes from 1980 to 1987 with no clear increasing trend. Maize comprised more than fifty per cent of such seed sales. The fluctuation of sales has been more pronounced for hybrids, while that of open-pollinated composites has been relatively constant (Friis-Hansen, 1988:27). Hence improvements in maize yields and production are probably closely related to improved weather, which was particularly marked from 1984 onwards.

The increased domestic production of food crops is also reflected in declining imports of for instance maize. It dropped from 232,000 tonnes in 1981/82 to 138,00 tonnes in 1984/85 and to the negligible level of 26,000 tonnes in 1985/86. In the later part of the decade a food surplus even permitted Tanzania to export maize, though it was at a loss.

Official purchases of maize by the National Milling Corporation (NMC) were stable at around 80,000–90,000 tonnes during the crop years 1981/82 to 1984/85. In this period parallel market prices were much higher than the official ones due to food shortages. Through increased equalisation of official and parallel prices from the mid-1980s onwards and the overall rise in grain production, National Milling Corporation purchases increased to around 170,000–180,000 tonnes for 1985/86 and 1986/87 and then to a peak of 227,000 tonnes in 1987/88. The reason for this rapid increase in NMC purchases during the liberalisation of grain marketing, was due partly to the official prices offered exceeding those paid by private traders in many areas. A survey from the late 1980s showed that in the major maize producing regions farmers received prices as low as Tsh. 3 per kg in Rukwa Region, Tsh. 5 in Ruvuma and Tsh. 6 in Iringa and Mbeya from private traders. This can be compared to the official producer price of around Tsh. 11 per kg of maize at that time (Tibaijuka, 1990:13). Little data exists on the proliferation of private traders in the rural areas in conjunction with agricultural liberalisation (World Bank, 1991a:61 and Booth, 1991:9).

During the 1987/88 crop season the government directed NMC to buy maize from the unions at an into-store price of Tsh. 12.30 per kg, which was above the official retail price. Hence there was no margin to cover NMC marketing costs (Havnevik et al., 1988:63). In April 1988 the general manager of the Rukwa Region Cooperative Union said that its total costs per kilo of maize was Tsh. 14.80, implying there was a loss of Tsh. 2.50 per kg handled. Costs were heavily influenced by a 25–27 per cent interest rate on its overdraft at the National Bank of Commerce. Political authorities directed the union to provide credit to smallholders for fertilizers, loans which could never be recovered. By 1988 this union alone, after three to four years of operation, had accumulated debts of about Tsh. 300 million (Ibid.). The severe financial difficulties emerging in the Iringa-Mufindi Cooperative Union (IMUCU) were also linked to "ill-advised and unrecoverable input credits to smallholders and villages" (Booth, 1991:17). This led the banks to refuse further credit. The increasing liberalisation of food marketing led to drastic declines in IMUCU procurement and supplies activities in 1989 and eventually they collapsed (Ibid.). The failure of the new cooperative movement was also based on gross incompetence and allegedly corrupted practices (Booth, 1991:17 referring to Cooperative College/Afro-Aid 1991).

The World Bank attempted to calculate indices of marketed crops and corresponding prices for the period 1982/83 to 1987/88. Such a venture is bound to be uncertain because different marketing channels exist, official and unofficial, where prices vary. The World Bank indices are presented to provide an idea about the relation between marketed sales and estimated real prices, i.e. what can be termed the market- rather than the production response of farmers.

Table 9.4 indicates that the output of maize marketed increased rapidly from the crop season 1984/85 to 1986/87, The trend for rice increased for the two consecutive crop years 1984/85 and 1985/86, then sales dropped in 1986/87 and picked up to regain the 1985/86 level in 1987/88. The relation which emerges is negative, i.e. a general increase in sales takes place in spite of real prices declining. For export crops a slow, but not continuous, growth of marketed production can be discerned ending in 1987/88 with an increase of about 20 per cent compared to 1982/83. The real price only increased by around 10 per cent during this period, though not steadily. Accordingly the conven-

Table 9.4.   *Indices of crops marketed and corresponding prices 1982/83–*
             1987/88

	1982/83	1983/84	1984/85	1985/86	1986/87	1987/88
Maize sales	100	87	103	149	173	180
-Prices (real) [1]	100	150	122	86	76	84
Rice sales	100	92	120	195	118	91
-Prices (real)	100	143	304	148	111	98
Export crop sales	100	101	102	90	119	121
-Prices real [2]	100	101	95	107	106	111
All crop sales	100	94	105	125	139	151
All crop prices	100	125	114	100	93	101

Notes: [1] Price indices based on weighted average of open market and official prices.
[2] All the traditional exports produced by small-scale farmers (coffee, cotton, cashew nuts, tea, tobacco, pyrethrum, cardamom).
Source: World Bank, 1991:a, p. 61

tional neo-classical price-output relationship does not hold. The explanation for the increased marketing of agricultural produce, in particular food crops, has to be found elsewhere, and a series of possible contributory factors will be discussed in turn.

IMPROVED WEATHER AND INCREASED SUPPLY OF CONSUMER GOODS

In spite of uncertainties, the statistics available indicate that agricultural production started to increase around 1984 and continued growing between 4 and 6 per cent annually at least up to 1989. One reason for agricultural growth, at least for some years, was improved weather conditions. There seems to be no controversy about this.

Another important and often mentioned reason for the expansion of agriculture is linked to the increased availability of consumer goods as a result of economic liberalisation, initiated by the Tanzanian government in 1984 and supported through the Economic Recovery Programme from 1986 onwards.

This explanation is also embraced by the World Bank, which argues that post-reform growth has to be understood in relation to pre-reform decline. The extreme shortages of consumer goods in the rural areas during the decline, fundamentally altered the relationship between prices and supplies of crops. The underlying idea is that sales of crops are linked to the expectation that the resulting cash incomes can be spent on desired purchases. With less to buy, peasant households' need of a cash income declined and fewer crops were sold. Hence during the acute shortages of the early 1980s, crop sales were determined more by the availability of consumer goods than by conventional price mechanisms. In the face of such shortages, the World Bank argues that the relationship between prices and supplies of crops appears to have been reversed. In Tanzania where peasants were faced with limited cash incomes that could be spent on rationed goods, higher prices for crops were offset by lower sales. The Bank refers to econometric tests from 17 regions for the period 1978–84 in which the volume of crop sales were positively and significantly related to the supply of consumer goods in rural areas (World Bank, 1991a:66). A major uncertainty associated with such a study seems to be the estimation of the volume of crops sold outside official channels. Such marketing increased during the crisis unfolding from 1978/78 onwards, and the problem of estimating its volume is compounded by its illegality.

A further problem is related to the fact that smallholders are not only crop producers, but channel labour to a series of non-agricultural activities, like crafts, fishing, logging, charcoal and woodfuel production and various forms of wage labour, etc. (see Chapter 5 and Havnevik, 1988). A nationwide household survey performed in 1976–77 showed that 25 per cent of smallholder earnings originated from a non-agricultural income (Sahn and Sarris, 1991:265). The amount of labour channeled to non-agricultural activities and the relation between the marketed and the directly consumed shares of such production (excluding wage labour) may change over time, depending on needs, on remuneration for labour, availability of resources, existence of markets and the nature of state–peasant relations. To understand peasant's marketing of crops as responses to changes in the supply of consumer goods one can not exclude smallholders' whole range of non-agricultural activities. It is possible that increased crop sales are not primarily a response to an improved supply of consumer goods, but could be a reflection of a declining relative remuneration for non-agricultural activities compared to agricultural production between the pre-reform and post-reform periods. The implications of this will be further discussed below.

The World Bank analysis sees the positive relationship between the availability of consumer goods and crop sales as being maintained throughout the post-reform period since peasants increased their crop sales to get access to cash for pent-up demands. Furthermore the strongest producer response was in food crops which are regarded as being linked to the steps to liberalise the grain trade. Hence, the reorganisation of marketing as a result of the economic recovery programme had the effect of providing better marketing opportunities for peasants than those which existed under government control in the pre-reform era. This argument does not hold when looking at marketing statistics because official food purchases increased rapidly even during the post-reform period (see pages 302–303 and Tibaijuka, 1990).

In spite of the lack of incentives in terms of improved prices, the peasants' response was to increase production and marketed output. As the World Bank itself acknowledges, the nature of such a response is essentially short-term. After more than half a decade of reform, the work still remains of effectively translating signals and incentives "into improved producer terms of trade, for output responses to occur in a setting where scarcity of consumer goods no longer prevails" (World Bank, 1991a:67).

AGRICULTURAL INPUTS

During the crisis years in the early 1980s agricultural production was also constrained by a critical shortage of tools. The monopoly producer/supplier of farm implements, the Ubungu Farm Implements Factory (UFI), distributed in the range of 1.1–1.6 million hand hoes annually from 1980 to 1983, compared to an estimated demand of about 3 million hoes for 1983/84 (Mothander et al., 1989:113-4). The Ministry of Agriculture estimated the national demand for hand hoes in 1987 to be around 2.5 million, while distribution the previous year had amounted to 1.9 million. Hence the gap in the supply of hand hoes had been narrowed in 1986/87 compared to the crisis years (URT:Basic Data 1984/85–1988/89:Table 9.4, p.112). As for ox-ploughs, the total average annual supply during 1979 to 1983 amounted to only 13,600 against an official figure of annual demand of 75,000 for 1983/84 (Mothander et al., 1989:115). Surveys undertaken during 1983, however, put the demand for ox-ploughs at around 50,000 per annum (Ibid., 120). Thus a shortage of more than 35,000 ploughs existed. The national demand for ploughs in 1987 was estimated to be 40,000, while distribution during 1986 amounted to around 25,000, bringing the gap in supplies down to around 15,000 units (URT Basic Data, 1984/85–1988/89:112). A general improvement in the supply of other hand implements and spares and accessories for ploughs also took place during the 1980s. Overall this must have contributed to improving conditions for production when it comes to hand tools and ox-ploughs, essential to the major techniques employed in Tanzanian agriculture.

As for other inputs, a survey conducted by the Bureau of Statistics in 1987/88 and covering about 3 million ha in 50 villages in all 20 mainland regions (Bureau of Statistics, 1990:Table 35, p.34) showed fertilizer was applied on 10 per cent of the total area cultivated and increased with the size of holdings. For various holding sizes up to 2 hectares, fertilizer application on any holding category did not exceed 10 per cent, whereas for holdings between 2 and 10 hectares, the range of application of fertilizer for various holding categories was 18 to 27 per cent. 48 per cent of the holdings above 10 hectares were reported to have benefited from fertilizer application. Similar tendencies were recorded for the use of insecticides and advice of extension officers, while a more even pattern of distribution was found for the use of compost, farm manure and improved seeds. The overall finding of the Bureau of Statistics survey was that larger holdings enjoyed a regime of more intensive input use than smaller holdings. The implication is that farmers of medium and large holdings had access to and were using a greater share of agricultural inputs. This tendency was already recorded in field studies during the pre-reform period (Kjærby, 1989). The rising price of inputs in the reform period is likely to have made this differentiation more pronounced.

The supply of fertilizers increased from a low base, in the pre-reform to the post-reform period. It was particularly high during 1986 and 1987 when it reached about 190,000 tonnes annually, about 100,000 tonnes above the average annual supply during 1981 to 1984. One major reason for this increase was the increase in commodity import support in which fertilizer and agricultural inputs were given high priority. Fertilizer application is, however, very uneven between the farming systems and agro-ecological zones in Tanzania. The Southern Highlands had the most intensive use of fertilizer throughout the decade. It is estimated that over 90 per cent of the maize farmers in Ruvuma and 60–70 per cent in Rukwa apply fertilizer. Overall the highland regions account for nearly 70 per cent of the total national consumption of fertilizer, up from about 40 per cent in the mid-1970s. Even by African standards the application of fertilizer per hectare in this region is high, estimated at 114 and 124 kilos per hectare in Mbeya and Iringa respectively during 1986 to 1988 (Rasmussen, 1987 and World Bank, 1991a:71).

In spite of the announcement that input subsidies would be cut back in 1984, fertilizer prices continued to be heavily subsidized throughout the decade. During the 1990/91 crop season the World Bank calculated that the level of subsidy was 80 per cent for the Southern Highland regions. On top of this, farmers selling to the National Milling Corporation received a considerable transport subsidy. Hence the policies related to inputs during the post-reform period not only favoured medium- and large farmers at the expense of smallholders (due to their greater access to heavily subsidised fertilizer and transport services), but the policies also had the effect of fostering regional concentration on food production, in particular to the Southern Highlands.

INCREASES IN ACREAGE, LABOUR INPUTS AND THE LAND ISSUE

The increase in food production in the post-reform period is also linked to an increase in the acreage planted. Many factors are likely to have facilitated this. In the early 1980s political circles silently acquiesced that peasants would not be forced back to the official villages, once they had moved their homesteads closer to their fields and hence reduced the walking time required for cultivation (Interview with the Director of Town and Country Planning, Ministry of Lands, May 1988). Movement out of villages has probably became more attractive as social services, education and water facilities in villages became run down. Decreases in primary school enrollment and attendance rates are not only a reflection of the declining quality of education, but also an indication of an increase of child labour in agriculture and petty trading. The primary school enrollment rate (percentage of the relevant age group) is reported to be as low as 66 per cent in 1989 (World Bank, 1991b:139). In the Bureau of Statistics survey, children of fourteen years and younger accounted for 35 and 44 per cent of the household members who occasionally worked on and off the family holdings during the 1987/88 crop season (Bureau of Statistics, 1990:22-3). These developments may have had the effect of providing a net addition to the input of household labour in planting, harvesting and herding livestock, where youth can provide effective help, and for collection of water and firewood and other domestic chores.

The National Agricultural Policies of 1983 introduced the possibility of private ownership of land and gradually interest in land titles and investment in agriculture has increased (Interview Ministry of Lands, May 1988 and Kiondo, 1989:385). Land allocation and insecurity of land tenure will become increasingly critical issues in the 1990s as population growth and pressure on the land results in more land disputes between private and village or collective interests. These problems are foreseen by the Tanzanian government, which in January 1991 established a Commission of Inquiry Into Land Matters to make recommendations on land and tenure policies and the resolution of land disputes (URT, 1991). Recent information shows, however, that laws have been enacted disfavouring customary land rights, before the report of the Commission was completed.

The land question is hampered by the lack of demarcation and registration of village titles. A process of establishing such titles was initiated in 1985, but in the early 1990s, only 20 per cent of the 8,000 registered villages had been demarcated. Problems are also encountered because of the lack of clarity of demarcations of village boundaries, for instance, whether or not these are to include public lands (World Bank, 1991b:81). The Director of Town and Country Planning claimed that boundary demarcation and village titles would not be sufficient to speed up agricultural productivity. Only after the completion of proper village land use plans, which could provide the basis for individual titles, would conditions be established for a title and tenure system which could lead to productivity gains (Interview May, 1988). The pressure on village land will overtake the long term process of land use planning and titling, though it is reported to have gained some momentum recently.

Statistics about private encroachment on village land or direct land grabbing hardly exist. Observations indicate that such processes are taking place not only around cities and towns but also in both densely and thinly populated rural areas. Information from Loliondo Division, Ngorongoro District, shows that if all recent applications for crop-land had been granted, 80 per cent of all land would have been privatised. (Personal communication with F. Kjærby, 1992.) In spite of low world market prices for most agricultural export crops and the costs associated with cultivation, the land struggle seems to be intensifying. It is also a struggle for control of land in the future.

SHIFT OF EMPHASIS IN AGRICULTURAL TECHNIQUES

The increased acreage planted may also be associated with a shift in emphasis on the techniques of cultivation. In the late 1970s the Tanzanian government estimated that 85 per cent of the acreage was tilled by hand implements, 10 per cent by ox plough and the remaining 5 per cent by tractors. It was assumed that the effect of the crisis would be a decline in the use of tractors for cultivation due to problems of procuring imported spare parts and diesel. In major tractor ploughing regions like Mwanza and Iringa this happened though it was not uniform. A field study in three villages in Hanang District in Arusha Region shows that the number of tractors operated by capitalist farmers doubled from 11 to 22, between 1978 and 1985 (Kjærby, 1989:55). Information indicates that Kilimanjaro Region and Aru-Meru District in Arusha Region maintained their fleets of tractors during the pre-reform crisis. Figures provided by the Ministry of Agriculture show a marked decline in the tractors available and operating if one compares 1985/86 (1,131) and the remaining years of the decade (on average

166 tractors operating in each of the years 1986/87–1988/89). (URT undated: Basic Data, 1984/85–1988/89:113.) The validity of such statistics is, however, questionable, though they may indicate that devaluation associated with the post-reform period have made it very difficult for individuals to import tractors and farm machinery. Interviews conducted with commercial farmers and transporters in Iringa Region in 1989 indicated that an accelerating process of de-tractorisation and de-mechanisation was under way (Booth, 1991:12, see also Maganya, 1990:112). The theoretically increased availability of tractors and lorries due to liberalisation could not be compensated for by the steep rise of their cost in local currency. The availability of credit and the price of fuel were also major concerns of the interviewees.

The likely major change in agriculture during the 1980s, is the expansion of the ox plough at a relatively faster rate than either hand-tilling or tractor ploughing. The potential for such a development is, however, limited to the livestock rearing regions in the Southern Highlands except Ruvuma; Central Tanzania; the Lake Zone except West Lake; and northern Tanzania.

Estimates show that the number of ploughs in the ox-ploughing regions almost doubled from the mid-1970s to the mid-1980s, from around 100,000 to 200,000 units. A major catalyst was the declining yields associated with villagisation. The concentration of settlements and cultivated land led to a transformation of agriculture from an extensive fallow farming system to a more permanent cultivation of the same fields. Farmers in many regions tried to compensate for the lower yields associated with this change by extending the acreage cultivated through hiring or purchasing ox-ploughs (Kjærby, 1986:183-84). This expansion of ox-ploughing up to the mid-1980s took place in spite of the shortage of implements during the crisis. In the post-reform period the supply of ox-ploughs has improved. This should have made it easier to gain access to tools for further expansion of ox-ploughing in the livestock rearing regions.

CHANGES IN DIVERSIFICATION REGIMES OF SMALLHOLDERS

A major issue linked to an analysis of Tanzanian agricultural development, which is often omitted, concerns the changes in processes and structures of diversification in the pre-reform crisis period compared to the post-reform adjustment period. Such diversification is of both intra- and inter-sectoral nature. The MADIA study, covering Kenya, Malawi, Tanzania, Cameroon, Nigeria and Senegal, found that the primary focus of economic analysis in the period 1970 to 1984 had been input and output prices. It points out that the role of non-price factors, particularly public and donor investment, formed significant, but overlooked parts of the overall picture. Such investments had affected the levels of taxes and subsidies on production and consumption as well as the relative returns on factors of production, due to their influence on technical development. The actual allocation of land, labour and capital in agriculture was influenced by the capacity of smallholders to use resources efficiently, which again was affected by both market and non-market factors. The MADIA study found that competition for these public investment resources was influenced by three types of diversification in agriculture: (i) out of agriculture and into industry and construction; (ii) within agriculture, in particular in favour of food crops; and (iii) by smallholders into activities outside the traditionally defined and often state-controlled spheres (Lele, 1989:24).

Such processes of diversification were also observed in Tanzania in the pre-reform crisis period. What we are concerned about here is that diversification of smallholder labour, which was channeled into informal activities not officially registered or inadequately registered in national accounts in the pre-reform period, compared to the post-reform period. Estimates of the magnitude of this hidden economy in Tanzania show a dramatic increase from 9.8 per cent of GDP in 1978 to 31.4 per cent in 1986 (Maliyamkono and Bagachwa, 1990:54).

The "hidden" economy's manifestations included rapid increases in parallel maize marketing and channelling of peasant labour to uncontrolled clearing of forest land — at a rate of 300,000–400,000 hectare a year — for cultivation of fuel wood. Fishing and craft activities were other major production lines into which smallholders diversified in the pre-reform period (Havnevik, 1988). Under the banner of liberalisation, a rapid increase has occurred in the newly legalised exploitation of high-value tree species like ebony and teak for the export market. The recorded export of timber and timber products increased from US $ 2.8 millions in 1986 to US $ 12.3 millions in 1989 (Tibaijuka, 1991b). By 1989 recorded exports of fish and fish products had reached about 1,400 tonnes, valued at US $ 5 millions (*The Express*, July 5, 1992). This includes trawling in very shallow waters which is already threatening the traditional prawn fishing of coast based farmers, and in the longer run, the regeneration of these resources are at stake (see Chapter 5).

An important issue related to the impact of reforms on agriculture is whether the magnitude of production in the hidden economy of smallholder labour, has changed. One macro-objective of the adjustment policies has been to use exchange rate policies to merge the hidden and official economies. This is the area in which the adjusment policies have had the greatest "success".

The next question is how this has affected the official figures for GDP and agricultural production. A recent World Bank report shows awareness of the hidden economy and special efforts have been made to estimate the magnitude of its various elements over time. These "hidden economy adjustments" are subsequently incorporated into the national accounts (World Bank, 1991b:65–100). It is questionable whether these estimates capture the real economic differences between the pre-reform and post-reform periods. Doubts appear when the value added in handicraft production is estimated to have fallen continuously through the pre-reform period from Tsh. 161 million (in 1976 Tsh.) in 1979 to Tsh. 113 million in 1986 (Ibid., 92). This is a function of the World Bank's calculations, because the handicraft value added is stipulated as a fixed percentage of the manufacturing value added. Hence, when manufacturing value added fell during the pre-reform crisis, the value added in handicrafts also went down. This implies that the World Bank has not registered the important expansion of handicrafts which emerged as a survival strategy for large numbers of the rural population, including farmers (Havnevik, 1988). The reverse occured in the post-reform period as handicraft production rose with manufacturing production. This means an underestimation of non-agricultural rural production activities is likely in the pre-reform and an overestimation in the post-reform period.

Furthermore, no "hidden economy adjustments" are made in relation to forestry and fishing, implying that official statistics indicate real trends. These activities are consequently reported to have declining trends (percentagewise) in terms of value added in relation to the total value added in agriculture. Forestry's share declined from 4 per cent in 1977 to 1 per cent in 1984 and fishing dropped from 9 per cent in 1977 to 4 per cent in 1982, after which it increased in the period 1983–86 (Ibid., 81). It should be expected that the growth of the overall "hidden economy" would be reflected in an increasing, not a declining, share of value added by forestry and fishing in relation to agriculture. Such exit options from agricultural cultivation were readily available to large numbers of Tanzanian smallholders during the crisis years.

Problems regarding quantification of the hidden or informal sector are admitted by the World Bank. Difficulties are also related to problems of definition and measurement. The importance of fully understanding this economy and its changing structure is underlined by placing it on the World Bank's future work programme agenda (World Bank, 1991b:69).

My hypothesis is that real production changes in the parallel economy particularly in the pre-reform period have not yet been adequately reflected in official statistics. It would have increased small-holder production levels (non-agricultural activities included) in the pre-reform period and the economic gains associated with the post-reform period would have been reduced.

But there are also reasons to be uneasy about the reported growth rates in agriculture during the reform period, because the real growth rates of value added by agriculture in the series of adjusted national accounts series turns out to be significantly lower for 1986, 1987 and 1988 (2.3 per cent, 3.8 per cent and 0.9 per cent respectively) than the official series (5.7 per cent, 4.4 per cent and 4.5 per cent, see Table 9.1). Differences between the official and adjusted series of accounts emerge from reviewing the performance of growth rates crop by crop. Many crops such as seed cotton, sugar cane, cashew nuts, wheat and legumes performed poorly in 1986. In 1988 declines in coffee, tobacco, cashew nuts and cereals resulted in low overall growth (World Bank, 1991b:59-60).

SOME CONCLUDING REMARKS

A major conclusion emerging from this study is that the structural adjustment programme and the conditionality associated with it have only to a limited and partial extent led to the fulfillment of its objectives. A major finding is that whatever agricultural improvement occurred, it has primarily been associated with food crops, not export crop production. The improvement in agriculture has only been recorded over a limited time span, indicating that production increases were not integrated in a sustainable process. Agricultural improvement was most closely linked to better weather conditions. There seems to be little disagreement about this. The World Bank claims that another important cause of production increases is connected with improvement in the supplies of incentive goods. This is the explanation given for increases in food crop production, in spite of declining real producer prices. Hence the characteristic features of production changes are those of an economy where there is rationing of supplies, i.e. the underlying assumptions of the neo-classical model are not present. Hence the neo-classical relationship between prices and production is not operating. This does not imply, according to the World Bank, that there is anything wrong with the model as such. The Bank hence argues that there is a need to enforce the conditionalities of the adjustment programme more strongly in order to restore the assumptions of the neo-classical model and thus the "normal" relationship between prices and production responses.

The experiences from Tanzania show that actual outcomes in terms of agricultural production, changing diversification regimes of small-holders, ecological impact and differentiation instead cast serious doubts on the claims of the World Bank that it has identified a model for African agricultural development. By narrowing the explanations for the lack of attainment of goals to concepts like rationing and problems of implementation, the World Bank is arguing that the basic model is intact, but that there is something wrong with the terrain in which it is employed. Analyses of findings of other case studies (Gibbon, Havnevik & Hermele, 1993) identify problems with the political economy assumptions of the adjustment model of the international financial institutions (IFIs). These assumptions do not reveal a genuine understanding of the ongoing economic, social and political processes in Sub-Saharan Africa. In addition, the assumptions and objectives of adjustment policies are associated with the particular interests pursued by the IFIs, which are most clearly manifested in the emphasis of adjustment programmes on debt repayment. Investigations in 12 African countries show that the external interest payment as a share of total government expenditure increased from 7.7 per cent in 1980–81 to 12.5 per cent in 1985–87 and that this increase was even higher for other Third World continents (Stewart, 1991:1852).

Bibliography

ACRES (1978): *Tanzania Power Sector Study*. Draft Final Report. Niagara Falls.

Amland, B. (1993): *Bistand eller Børs*. Næringslivets rolle i norsk u-hjelp. J.W. Cappelens Forlag, Oslo.

Angwazi, J. and B. Ndulu (1973): *Evaluation of Operation Rufiji 1968*. BRALUP Service Paper No. 73/9, University of Dar es Salaam.

Bagachwa, M.S.D., Y. Mbelle and B. van Arkadie (eds) (1992): *Market Reforms and Parastatal Restructuring in Tanzania*. Economics Department and Economic Research Bureau, University of Dar es Salaam.

Bangura, Y. (1989): "The political and social context of structural adjustment in Sub-Saharan Africa". In *Nytt från Nordiska Afrikainstitutet*, no. 24, pp. 22–34.

Bank of Tanzania (undated): *Twenty Years of Independence (1961–1981). A Review of Political and Economic Performance*. Dar es Salaam.

Bantje, H., F. Mrisho and B. Ljungqvist (1979): *A Nutrition Baseline Survey in Four Villages in the Lower Rufiji Valley*. BRALUP Research Paper No. 55, BRALUP and TFNC, Dar es Salaam.

Bantje, H. (1979): *The Rufiji Agricultural System: Impact of Rainfall, Floods and Settlement*. BRALUP Research Paper No. 62, University of Dar es Salaam.

Bantje, H. (1980a): *Floods and Famines, A Study of Food Shortages in Rufiji District*. BRALUP Research Paper No. 63, University of Dar es Salaam.

Bantje, H. (1980b): *Seasonal Variations in Birthweight Distribution in Ikwiriri Village*. BRALUP Research Report No. 43 (New series), Dar es Salaam.

Bantje, H. (1982): *Food Flows and Dietary Patterns in Ikwiriri Village*. BRALUP Research Paper No. 74, University of Dar es Salaam.

Bantje, H. and R. Niemeyer (1984): "Rainfall and Birthweight Distribution in Rural Tanzania". In *Journal of Biosocial Science*, No. 16, pp. 375-384.

Baran, P.A. (1957): *The Political Economy of Growth*. New York.

Barker, R. de la B. (1937): "The Rufiji River". In *Tanzania Notes and Records*, No. 4. Dar es Salaam.

Beardall, W. (1881): Exploration of the Rufiji under the Orders of the Sultan of Zanzibar. In *Proceedings of the Royal Geographic Society*, No. XI, Nov. 1881.

Bernstein, H. (1977): "Notes on Capital and Peasantry". In *Review of African Political Economy*, No. 10, Sept.–Dec.

Bienen, H. (1967): *Tanzania. Party Transformation and Economic Development*. Princeton University Press.

Boesen, J., B. Storgaard Madsen and T. Moody (1977): *Ujamaa—Socialism from above*. Scandinavian Institute of African Studies, Uppsala.

Boesen, J. (1979): "Tanzania: from Ujamaa to Villagization". In B. Mwansasu and C. Pratt (eds), *Towards Socialism in Tanzania*. Tanzania Publishing House, Dar es Salaam.

Boesen, J., K.J. Havnevik, J. Koponen and R. Odgaard (eds) (Boesen et al.) (1986): *Tanzania. Crisis and Struggle for Survival*. Scandinavian Institute of African Studies, Uppsala.

Bomani, P. (1961): *The Cooperative Movement in Tanganyika 1961*. Dar es Salaam.

Booth, D. (1991): *Structural Adjustment in Socio-Political Context: Some Findings from Iringa Region.* Tadreg Research Report III, August. Dar es Salaam.

Boserup, E. (1965): *The Conditions of Agricultural Growth.* George Allen & Unwin, London.

Bowles, B.D. (1980): "The political economy of colonial Tanganyika 1939-1961". In Kaniki, (ed) (1980), pp. 164–191.

Brehme, G. (1977): "State and Law in Post-Colonial Independent States". In H. Othman (ed), *The State in Tanzania*, pp. 118–141. Dar es Salaam University Press, Dar es Salaam.

Bryceson, D.F. (1981): "Colonial Famine Responses. The Bagamoyo District of Tanganyika". In *Food Policy*, May, pp. 91–104.

Bryceson, D.F. (1982): "Tanzanian Grain Supply. Peasant Production and State Policies". In *Food Policy*, May, pp. 113–124.

Bull, E. (1973):*Østafrikansk Bakgrunn. Kenya, Tanzania og Uganda i fortid og nåtid.* Gyldendal, Oslo.

Bureau of Statistics (1990): *Agricultural Sample Survey of Tanzanian Mainland 1987/88. Final Report.* October. President's Office, Planning Commission. Dar es Salaam.

Christiansson, C. (1986): "Soil Erosion and Conservation in the Drylands". In Boesen et al. (1986), pp 143–157.

Cliffe, L. and C. Cunningham, (1973): Ideology, Organisation and the Settlement Experience in Tanzania. In L. Cliffe and J. Saul (eds) (1973), *Socialism in Tanzania*, Vol. 2, pp. 131–140. East African Publishing House, Dar es Salaam.

Cliffe, L. (1972): "Nationalism and the Reaction to Enforced Agriculture Change in Tanzania during the Colonial Period". In L. Cliffe and J. Saul (eds) (1972), *Socialism in Tanzania*, Vol. 1. Dar es Salaam, East African Publishing House.

Cliffe, L. and J. Saul (1972): "The District Development Front in Tanzania". In *The African Review*, Vol. 2, No. 7.

Cliffe, L. (1985): *Experiences of Agricultural and Rural Cooperatives in Socialist Countries in Africa.* Report prepared for FAO for regional consultation on the role of rural cooperatives in the productive sectors in Africa, ECA, Addis Ababa, 7–11 October 1985.

Collier, P. (1987): *Aid and Economic Performance in Tanzania.* Institute of Economics and Statistics, University of Oxford.

Cook, A. (1974): *Land-use Recommendations for Rufiji District.* BRALUP Research Report No. 11 (New Series), University of Dar es Salaam.

Cooperative College/Afro-Aid (1991): *The Failure of Cooperative Unions on Mainland Tanzania: Final Report. Vol. 1: National Policies and Institutional Relations.* Ministry of Local Government, Social Welfare, Cooperative and Marketing. Dar es Salaam.

Coulson, A. (1977): "Agricultural Policies in Mainland Tanzania". In *Review of African Political Economy*, No. 10, pp. 74–100.

Coulson, A. (ed) (1979): *African Socialism in Practice. The Tanzanian Experience.* Spokesman, Nottingham.

Coulson, A. (1982): *Tanzania: A Political Economy.* Clarendon, Oxford.

CUT (The Cooperative Union of Tanzania) (1988): *Cotton Producer Price Recommendations 1989/90 Marketing Season.* RP/1–PMU.

Datoo, B.A. (1973): *Population Density and Agricultural Systems in the Uluguru Mountains, Morogoro District.* BRALUP Research Paper 26, University of Dar es Salaam.

D.K.B. (1893):*Deutsches Kolonial Buch.* Berlin.

Daily News, various issues.

DAR (DISTRICT ANNUAL REPORT RUFIJI DISTRICT), various years. Tanzania National Archives (TNA).

　　DAR 1931, file 3/VI/D, TNA.
　　DAR 1934, file 3/IX/D, TNA.
　　DAR 1935, file 3/X/D, TNA.
　　DAR 1936, file 3/XI/D, TNA.
　　DAR 1939, file 3/XIV/D, TNA.
　　DAR 1940, file 3/XV/D, TNA.
　　DAR 1941, file 3/XVI/D, TNA.
　　DAR 1943, file 3/XVII/D, TNA.
　　DAR 1945, file 3/XVIII/D, TNA.
　　DAR 1946, file 504, TNA.
　　DAR 1947/48, file 504 Vol. III, TNA.
　　DAR 1951, TNA.

Department of Agriculture (1956): *Annual Report of Department of Agriculture 1955.* Part I. Government Printer, Dar es Salaam.

DeVries, J. and L. Fortmann (1979): "Operation Sogeza in Iringa Region". In Coulson (ed) (1979), pp. 128–135.

Dorsey, K.T. (1979): "Report on the Prawn Fisheries of the Rufiji Delta with particular reference to possible Changes Resulting from Modifications to the Environment by the Proposed Dam at Stiegler's Gorge". Project Technical Paper No. 2, FAO/TCP/URT/8806(i), Fisheries Department, FAO, Rome.

Dumont, R. (1969): *Tanzanian Agriculture after the Arusha Declaration.* Report presented to the Government of Tanzania. Dar es Salaam.

Economic and Social Action Programme (ESAP) (1989). The Government of the United Republic of Tanzania (URT), Dar es Salaam.

Eile, Lena (1985): *History of Religion.* Seminar paper, University of Lund.

EIU (The Economist Intelligence Unit) (1989): *Country Report: Tanzania. Mozambique.* London.

EIU (The Economist Intelligence Unit): *Tanzania—Country Profile 1990–91* and *Tanzania—Country Profile 1991–92.* London.

Ellis, F. (1980): "Agricultural Pricing Policy in Tanzania 1970-79; Implications for Agricultural Output, Rural Incomes and Crop Marketing Costs". Presented at seminar on Development, Employment and Equity Issues, University of Dar es Salaam, 21–25 July.

Ellis, F. and E. Hanak (1981): *An Economic Analysis of the Coffee Industry in Tanzania 1969/70–1978/79: Towards a Higher and More Stable Producer Price.* ERB Paper 80.4, University of Dar es Salaam.

Ellis, F. (1982): "Agricultural Price Policy in Tanzania". In *World Development*, Vol. 10, No. 4, pp. 263–283.

Ellis, F. (1983): "Agricultural Marketing and Peasant–State Transfers in Tanzania". In *Journal of Peasant Studies*, Vol. 10, No. 4, pp. 214-242.

Elton, J.F. (1898):*Travels and Researchers among Lakes and Mountains of Eastern and Central Africa.*

Eriksson, G. (1993): *Peasant Response to Price Incentives in Tanzania.* Research Report No. 91, Scandinavian Institute of African Studies.

FAO (1961): *The Rufiji Basin. Tanganyika.* Report to the Government of Tanganyika on the preliminary reconnaissance survey of the Rufiji Basin. Volume I, General Report, Rome.

Fei, J.C.H. and G. Ranis, (1964): *Development of the Labour Surplus Economy.* Richard D. Irwin.

Fimbo, G. Mgongo (1977): *The State and the Peasantry in Tanzania, A Study of Agrarian Law and Administrative Instructions.* Paper presented to a Seminar in Law and Rural Development, Kisumu, Kenya, July 18–22, 1977.

Finucane, J.R. (1974): *Rural Development and Bureaucracy in Tanzania, the Case of Mwanza Region.* Scandinavian Institute of African Studies, Uppsala.

Friis-Hansen, E. (1988): *Seeds of Wealth—Seeds of Risk? The vulnerability of Hybrid Maize Production in the Southern Highlands of Tanzania.* Centre for Development Research (CDR) Project Paper 88.2, Copenhagen.

Frostin, P. (1988): *Liberation Theology in Tanzania and South Africa.* Lund University Press.

Gibbon, P. and M. Neocosmos (1985): "Some Problems in the Political Economy of 'African Socialism'". In H. Bernstein and B.K. Campbell (eds), *Contradictions of Accumulation in Africa.* Sage, California, pp. 153-206.

Gibbon, P., K.J. Havnevik and K. Hermele (1993): *A Blighted Harvest. The World Bank and African Agriculture in the 1980s.* James Currey, London.

Gillman, C. (1945): *A Reconnaissance of the Hydrology of Tanganyika Territory in its Geographical Settings.* Government Printer, Dar es Salaam.

Grant, B.K.S. (1939): "Mangrove Woods of Tanganyika Territory, their Silvi-culture and Dependent Industries". In *Tanganyika Notes and Records*, No. 5, pp. 5–16. Dar es Salaam.

Groeneveld, S. (1968): "Traditional Farming and Cattle-Coconut Schemes in Tanga Region". In H. Ruthenberg (ed) (1968), pp. 219–247.

Guillain, M. (1856): *Documents sur l'histoire, la geographie et le commerce de l'Afrique Orientale.* 3 vols. and 1 Album. Paris.

Hafslund A/S (1980): *Stiegler's Gorge Power and Flood Control Development, Project Planning Report.* Volume I. Oslo. Report presented to RUBADA.

Havnevik, K.J. (1975): *En Vurdering av Norconsult's Stiegler's Gorge Rapport.* DERAP Working Paper No. A 71, Chr. Michelsen Institute, Bergen.

Havnevik, K.J. (1978): *The Stiegler's Gorge Multipurpose Project 1961-1978.* DERAP Working Paper No. 131, Chr. Michelsen Institute, Bergen.

Havnevik, K.J. (1980): *Economy and Organization in Rufiji District: the Case of Crafts and Extractive Activities.* BRALUP Research Paper No. 65, University of Dar es Salaam.

Havnevik, K.J. (1982): "Behov for en helhetsvurdering i Tanzania". In *NORKONTAKT*, no. 6, NORAD, Oslo, pp. 9–11.

Havnevik, K.J. (1983): *Analysis of Rural Production and Incomes, Rufiji District, Tanzania.* DERAP Publication No. 152, Chr. Michelsen Institute, Bergen.

Havnevik, K.J. (1988): *State Intervention and Peasant Response in Tanzania.* Ph.D dissertation, University of Bradford.

Havnevik, K.J. (1991): *The Emergence, Development and Breakdown of the Postcolonial Model in Tanzania.* Paper presented to a Workshop on "Adjustment Models and Adjustment Politics", 24–26 April at Nordiska Afrikainstitutet (Scandinavian Institute of African Studies), Uppsala.

Havnevik, K.J. and R. Skarstein (1982): *Agricultural Backwardness and Foreign Aid in Tanzania.* Paper presented at a symposium on "Aid and Poverty", at the Chr. Michelsen Institute, Bergen, January 1982.

Havnevik, K.J., R. Skarstein and S. Wangwe (1985): *Small Scale Industrial Sector Study: Review of Experiences and Recommendations for the Future.* Report presented to the Ministry of Industries and Trade, Dar es Salaam.

Havnevik, K.J. and R. Skarstein (1987): "Agricultural Decline and Foreign Aid in Tanzania". Mimeo, Bergen/Trondheim.

Havnevik, K.J., F. Kjærby, R. Meena, R. Skarstein and U. Vourela (Havnevik et al.) (1988): *Tanzania—Country Study and Norwegian Aid Review*. Centre for Development Studies, University of Bergen.

Hedlund, H. (1986): *Kaffe, kooperation och kultur; en studie av en kooperativ kaffeförening i Kibirigwi, Kenya*. Scandinavian Institute of African Studies, Uppsala.

Hill, F. (1979): "Ujamaa: African Socialist Productionism in Tanzania". In Desfosses, H. and J. Levesque (eds): *Socialism in the Third World*. Praeger 1975, pp. 216–51. Based on extract from this article in Coulson, A. (ed) (1979), pp. 106–113.

Holmquist, F. (1983): "Tanzania's Retreat from Statism in the Country Side". In *Africa Today*, 4th Quarter, 1983, pp. 23-5.

Hopson, A.J. (1979): "Draft Report on the Freshwater Fisheries of the Lower Rufiji with Particular Reference to Possible Changes Resulting from Modifications to the Environment by the Proposed Dam at Stiegler's Gorge". Report prepared on behalf of FAO for RUBADA.

Hyden, G. (ed) (1976): *Cooperatives in Tanzania: Problems of Organisation*. University of Dar es Salaam Studies in Political Science No. 4, pp. 78-93.

Hyden, G. (1980): *Beyond Ujamaa in Tanzania. Underdevelopment and an Uncaptured Peasantry*. Heineman, London.

Hyden, G. (1983): *No Shortcuts to Progress*. Heineman, London.

Iliffe, J. (1969): *Tanganyika under German Rule*. Cambridge University Press.

Iliffe, J. (1971): Agricultural Change in Modern Tanganyika. Historical Association of Tanzania Paper No. 10. East African Publishing House.

Iliffe, J. (1979): *A Modern History of Tanganyika*. Cambridge University Press, Cambridge.

ILO (1981): *Basic Needs in Danger*. Draft Report, Addis Ababa.

Jack, D. (1957): "The Agriculture of Rufiji District". (Mimeo in *Tanzania National Archives*).

Jamal, A.H. (1965): *The Critical Phase of Emergent African States*. East African Institute Press, Nairobi.

Jedruszek, J. (1978): "Economic Efficiency and the Process of Development". *Mimeo, University of Dar es Salaam*.

Johnston, B.F. and J.W. Mellor (1961): "The Role of Agriculture in Economic Development". *In American Economic Review*, September.

Joseph, G. (1979): *An Econometric Approach to Forecasting Demand for Electricity in Tanzania to the year 2000 A.D.* BRALUP Research Report No. 38, University of Dar es Salaam.

Kaldor, N. (1967): *Strategic Factors in Economic Growth*. Itaca, New York.

Kaldor, N. (1975): "What is wrong with Economic Theory". In *Quarterly Journal of Economics*, August.

Kaldor, N. (1979): "Equilibrium Theory and Growth Theory". In M. Baskia (ed), *Economics and Human Welfare: Essays in Honour of Tibor Scitovsky*. Academic Press.

Kalecki, M. (1976): "Observations on Social and Economic Aspects of 'Intermediate Regimes'". In *Essays on Developing Economies*. The Harvester Press, Sussex, pp. 30–37.

Kaniki, M.H.Y. (ed) (1980): *Tanzania under Colonial Rule*. Longman, London.

King, M.F., L.D. Morley and L.A. Burgess (1972): *Nutrition for Developing Countries*.

Kiondo, A. (1989): *The Politics of Economic Reforms in Tanzania 1977–1988*. Ph.D Thesis, University of Toronto.

Kjekshus, H. (1977a): *Ecology Control and Economic Development in East African History: the Case of Tanganyika 1850–1895*. Heineman, London.

Kjekshus, H. (1977b): "Ecological Aspects related to the Stiegler's Gorge Project". In *Forum for Development Studies* No. 10, NUPI, Oslo.

Kjærby, F. (1980): "Agricultural Productivity and Surplus Production in Tanzania". In *UTAFITI*, Vol. 5, No. 1, Dar es Salaam.

Kjærby, F. (1986): "The Development of Agricultural Mechanisation". In Boesen et al. (1986), pp. 173–191.

Kjærby, F. (1987): *Villagisation and the Crisis. Agricultural Production in Hanang District, Northern Tanzania.* Centre for Development Research Project Papers D. 87.4, Copenhagen.

Kriesel, H.C., C.K Laurent, C. Halpern and H.E. Larzelere (1970): *Agricultural marketing in Tanzania. Background Research and Policy Proposals.* Dar es Salaam.

Legum, C. and J. Drysdale (eds) (1970): *Africa Contemporary Record: 1969–1970.* Vol. 2, African Research Limited, Exeter.

Lele, U. (1989): *Agricultural Growth, Domestic Policies, the External Environment and Assistance to Africa. Lessons of a Quarter Century.* MADIA Discussion Paper 1, World Bank, Washington D.C.

Lele, U. and L. R. Meyers (1989): *Growth and Structural Change in East Africa. Domestic Policies, Agricultural Performance and World Bank Assistance, 1963-86 Parts I and II.* MADIA Discussion Paper 3. World Bank, Washington D. C.

Lele, U. and R. E. Christiansen (1989): *Markets, Marketing Boards and Cooperatives in Africa. Issues in Adjustment Policy.* MADIA Discussion Paper 11. World Bank, Washington D. C.

Lema, A.J. (1979): *Crop Water Requirements and Beneficial Flood for the Rufiji Flood Plain Agriculture.* BRALUP Research Report No. 36, University of Dar es Salaam.

Liston, J.M (1961): *Medical Appraisal of the Rufiji Basin.* FAO Report presented to the Government of Tanzania.

Lonsdale, J. (1981): "States and Social Processes in Africa: A Historiographical Survey". In *The African Studies Review*, Vol. XXIV, Numbers 2/3, June/September, 1981, pp. 139–227.

Loarer (1849): *Ports au sud et au nord de Zanguebar.* Archives Nationales: Section Outre-Mer (A.O.M.). Paris.

Lucas, S.A. (ed) (1975): *Utani Relationships in Tanzania.* Vols. I–VII. Dar es Salaam.

Lwoga, C.M. (1978): "Bureaucrats, Peasants and Land Rights: A Tanzanian Case Study". Mimeo, Department of Sociology, University of Dar es Salaam.

MacManus, P. (1991): "Heksenes genkomst—et essay om afrikanske udviklingsperspektiver" (in Danish). In *Den Ny Verden*, 24 Årgang, nr. 3, Center for Development Research, Copenhagen, pp. 29–44.

Maganya, E. N. (1990): "The Structural Adjustment Programmes and the Agricultural Sector: The Case of Tanzania". In *Taamuli*, Vol. 1, No. 1 & 2, Department of Political Science, University of Dar es Salaam, pp. 103–115.

Maliyamkono, T. and M. Bagachwa. (1990): *The Second Economy and State Legitimacy in Tanzania.* James Currey, London.

Mamdani, M. (1985): "A Great Leap Backward: Goran Hyden's No Shortcuts to Progress". In *Social Science Research Review*, Vol. 1, No. 1.

Manyiki, A. and M. Lumbanga (1971): *An Economic Base-Line Study of the Co-operatives in the Coast Region Based on the Accounts for 1966/67–1968/69.* Economic Research Bureau, University of Dar es Salaam.

Mapolu, H. (1973): "The Workers' Movement in Tanzania". In *Maji Maji* No. 12, Dar es Salaam, pp. 31–43.

Marketing Development Bureau (1980 and 1985): *Price Policy Recommendations for the Agricultural Price Review. Summary.* Dar es Salaam.

Marshland, H. (1938): "Mlau-cultivation in the Rufiji Valley". In *Tanganyika Notes and Records*, No. 5, pp. 55–59. Dar es Salaam.

Martin, E.M. and C.P. Martin (1978): *Cargoes of the East. The ports, trade and culture of the Arabian Seas and Western Indian Ocean*. Elm Tree Books, London.

Matango, R. (1975): "Operation Mara: Paradox of Democracy". In*Maji Maji*, No. 20, Dar es Salaam, pp. 17–30.

McHenry, D.E. jr. (1979): *Tanzania's Ujamaa Villages: The Implementation of a Rural Development Strategy*. Institute of International Studies, Research Series No. 39, Berkeley, California.

McKim, W. (1981): Report on Market Place Activity in Rufiji District. Presented to Rufiji Basin Development Authority.

Meyers, K. (1985): *Agricultural Performance and Policy in Tanzania*. Revised Draft, World Bank Files (RBW/Agric/10-24- 85), Washington D.C.

MDC (Ministry of Development Cooperation/Norway) (1986): *Evaluation Report 4.86. Mbegani Fisheries Development Centre Tanzania*. Oslo.

Migot-Adholla, S.E. (1972): "The Politics of Mechanization in Sukumaland". In C. G. Widstrand (ed), *African Co-operatives and efficiency*, Scandinavian Institute of African Studies, Uppsala.

Migot-Adholla, S.E. (1976): "Power Differentiation and Resource Allocation: The Cooperative Tractor Project in Maswa District". In G. Hyden (ed) (1976), pp. 39–57.

Ministry of Foreign Affairs/DANIDA (1992): "HIMA (Njombe). Njombe District Natural Resources Conservation and Land Use Management Project (Background Material to Chapter 3)". Dar es Salaam.

Ministry of Tourism, National Resources and Environment (1991): *Management Plan for the Mangrove Ecosystem of Mainland Tanzania*. Vol. 11, Part II, Block 7: Mangrove Management Plan of Rufiji Delta. Catchment Forestry Project, Dar es Salaam.

Mitra, A. (1977): *Terms of Trade and Class Relations*. Frank Cass, London.

Moore, R. and A. Roberts (1957): "An Investigation of the Pattern of Disease Prevalence in Parts of the Rufiji District". In *East African Medical Journal*, Vol. 34, No. 11.

Morgan, P.R. (1959): "A Rufiji Experiment". In *Tanzania Notes and Records*, No. 52. Dar es Salaam.

Morris, H.F. and J.S. Reed (1972): *Indirect Rule and the Search for Justice*. Clarendon Press, Oxford.

Mothander, B., F. Kjærby and K.J. Havnevik (1989): *Farm Implements for Small Scale Farmers in Tanzania*. Scandinavian Institute of African Studies, Uppsala.

Mujwahuzi, M. (1978): A Survey of Rural Water Supply in Dodoma District. BRALUP Research Paper No. 57. University of Dar es Salaam.

Müller, J. (1979): *Liquidation or Consolidation of Indigenous Technology*. Aalborg University Press. Development Research Series No. 1. Aalborg.

Müller, S.D. (1980): "Retarded Capitalism in Tanzania". In Miliband, R. and J. Saville (eds), *The Socialist Register 1980*. Merlin Press, London.

Musti, B. de Gennaro (1979): "Ten Years After. A Comment on the Ruvuma Development Association". Seminar Paper Economic Research Bureau, University of Dar es Salaam.

Mwapachu, J.V. (1976): "Operation Planned Villages in Rural Tanzania". In *African Review*, IV, 1, pp. 1–16.

Mwase, N.R.L. (1976): "Cooperatives and Ujamaa: A Case Study of the Arusha Region Cooperative Union Limited (A.R.C.U.)". In G. Hyden (ed) (1976), pp. 78–93.

Mzalendo, 27 May 1979. (Sunday edition of Chama cha Mapinduzi (CCM) newspaper *Uhuru*.)

NESP (National Economic Survival Programme) (1981). United Republic of Tanzania. Ministry of Planning. Dar es Salaam.

Newiger, N. (1968): "Village Settlement Schemes: The Problems of Cooperative Farming". In H. Ruthenberg (ed) (1968), pp. 249–273.

Nindi, B.C. (1979): "Colonial Agricultural Policy in Tanganyika between First and Second World Wars". Mimeo, History Department, University of Dar es Salaam.

Nimtz, A.H. (1980): *Islam and Politics in East Africa: The Sufi Order in Tanzania.* University of Minnesota Press, Minneapolis.

Nkonoki, S.R. (1983): *Cooperation in Energy Development in Eastern Africa.* DERAP Publication No. 166, Chr. Michelsen Institute, Bergen.

Norconsult (1972): *Stiegler's Gorge Hydropower Utilization. Power Development.* Preliminary Report, Oslo.

Nordic Background Paper (1984): "Tanzania's Economic Crisis, Structural Adjustment Efforts and the Role of Development Cooperation". Presented to TAN-NORDIC Symposium, Dar es Salaam, November 16 and 17. Swedish Foreign Ministry, Stockholm.

Norplan A/S (1983): *Lower Rufiji Valley Integration Study.* Four Volumes. Presented to RUBADA.

Nurkse, R. (1962): *Equilibrium and Growth in the World Economy.* Harvard University Press.

Nyerere, J. (1962): *Ujamaa—The Basis for African Socialism.* TANU Pamphlet.

Nyerere, J. (1966): "President's Inaugural Address". In Nyerere (1966): *Freedom and Unity. A selection from writings and speeches 1952–65.* Oxford University Press, pp. 176–187.

Nyerere, J. (1968): "Socialism and Rural Development". In Nyerere (1968): *Ujama-Essays on Socialism.* Dar es Salaam, pp. 106–144.

Nyerere, J. (1977): *The Arusha Declaration 10 Years After.* Dar es Salaam.

Nypan, A. (1977): "Lokal medvirkning i planleggingsprosessen i Tanzanias tredje femårsplan". In Bjönnes and Butenschön (eds), *Planlegging i u-land,* pp. 88–99.

Ofstad, A. (1992): "Evaluation of import support to Tanzania. Pre-study". Chr. Michelsen Institute–ASU, Bergen.

Openshaw, K. (1976): *Woodfuel—A Time for Reassessment.* Faculty of Agriculture, University of Dar es Salaam—Morogoro.

Parkipuny, L. (1976): "Some Crucial Aspects of the Maasai Predicament". In Coulson (ed) (1979), pp. 136–157.

Perkins, F. (1978): *Small Scale Industry in Rukwa Region. Survey, Analysis and Recommendations.* BRALUP Research Paper No. 28 (New Series), University of Dar es Salaam.

Plumbe, A.J. (1974): *Marketing Cooperatives and Spatial Cross-Subsidisation in Tanzania.* Paper presented at the Institute of British Geographers Conference at the School of Oriental and African Studies, September 18, 1974.

Population Census 1978.

Pratt, C. (1976): *The Critical Phase in Tanzania 1945–1968: Nyerere and the Emergence of a Socialist Strategy.* Cambridge University Press.

Raikes, P. (1975): "Ujamaa and Rural Socialism". In *Review of African Political Economy,* No. 3, pp. 33–52.

Raikes, P. (1978): Rural Differentiation and Class Formation in Tanzania. In *Journal of Peasant Studies,* Vol. 5, No. 3.

Raikes, P. (1986): "Eating the Carrot and Wielding the Stick: The Agricultural Sector in Tanzania". In Boesen et al. (1986), pp. 105–143.

Ranger, T. (1986): "Religious Movements and Politics in Sub-Saharan Africa". In *The African Studies Review,* Vol. 29, June 1986, No.2, pp. 1–69.

Rasmussen, T. (1986): "The Green Revolution in the Southern Highlands". In Boesen et al. (1986), pp. 191–205.

Reeves, G.W. (1979): *The Development and Diffusion of Swahili Culture in Tanzania*. African Studies Working Paper No. 8 (April), African Studies Seminar, Murdoch University, Australia.

Resnick, I.N. (1981): *The Long Transition. Building Socialism in Tanzania*. Monthly Review Press, New York.

Roggeri, H. (1985): *African Dams. Impacts on the Environment. The Social and Environmental Impact of Dams at the Local Level: A Case Study of Five Man-Made Lakes in Eastern Africa*. Environment Liaison Centre, Nairobi.

RUBADA Act 1975.

Ruthenberg, H. (ed) (1968): *Smallholder Farming and Smallholder Development in Tanzania*. Weltforum Verlag, Munich.

Rweyemamu, J. (1973): *Underdevelopment and Industrialization in Tanzania*. Oxford University Press.

Sahn, D. E. and A. Sarris (1991): "Structural Adjustment and the Welfare of Rural Smallholders: A Comparative Analysis form Sub-Saharan Africa". In *The World Bank Economic Review*, Vol. 5, No. 2, World Bank, Washington D. C., pp 259–289.

Saith, A. (1985): "Primitive Accumulation, Agrarian Reform and Socialist Transitions: An Argument". In *The Journal of Development Studies*, Vol. 22, No. 1, Frank Cass, London.

Sandberg, A. (1973): *Ujamaa and Control of Environment*. Paper presented at East African Universities Social Sciences Conference, Dar es Salaam.

Sandberg, A. (1974a): *Socio-Economic Survey of Lower Rufiji Flood Plain. Rufiji Delta Agricultural System*. BRALUP Research Paper No. 34, University of Dar es Salaam.

Sandberg, A. (1974b): *The Impact of the SG Dam on Rufiji Flood Plain Agriculture*. BRALUP Service Paper No. 74/2, University of Dar es Salaam.

Savile, A.H. (1945): "A Study of Recent Alterations on the Flood Regime of Rufiji River". In *East African Agricultural and Forestry Journal of Kenya, Tanganyika, Uganda and Zanzibar*.

Schultz, J. (1971): *Agrarlandschaftliche Veränderungen in Tanzania*. Weltforum Verlag. Munich.

Schädler, K. (1968): *Crafts, Small-Scale Industries, and Industrial Education in Tanzania*. Weltforum Verlag, Munich.

Schäfer, H.B. (1983): *Landwirtschafliche Akkumulationslasten und Industrielle Entwicklung*. Springer Verlag, Berlin.

Sembajwe, I. (1979): *The 1978 Population Census of Tanzania: A Preliminary Assessment of its Implications*. BRALUP Service Paper No. 79/7, University of Dar es Salaam.

Semboja, J. and O. Therkildsen (1989): *Recurrent Cost Financing at District Level in Tanzania*. Centre for Development Research (CDR) Working Paper 89.5, Copenhagen.

Sender, J. (1974): *Some Preliminary Notes on the Political Economy of Rural Development in Tanzania*. Paper 74.5 Economic Research Bureau, University of Dar es Salaam.

Sheriff, A.M.H. (1971): *The Rise of a Commercial Empire: An Aspect of the Economic History of Zanzibar, 1770–1873*. Unpublished Ph.D thesis, University of London.

Shivji, I.G. (1976): *Class Struggles in Tanzania*. Tanzania Publishing House, Dar es Salaam.

Shivji, I.G. (1979): *Semi-proletarian labour and the use of penal sanctions in the Labour Law of colonial Tanganyika (1920–1938)*. Paper presented at a Criminology Conference at the University of Cambridge, July 1979.

Shivji, I.G. (1980): "The State in the Dominated Social Formations of Africa: Some Theoretical Issues". In *International Social Science Journal*, Vol. XXXII, No. 4, pp. 730–742.

Shivji, I.G. (1988): "Right to Life and Liberty in Tanzania: Selected Aspects". Background document for Havnevik et al. (1988).

Skarstein, R. and S. Wangwe (1986): *Industrial Development in Tanzania: Some Critical Issues*. Scandinavian Institute of African Studies, Uppsala.

Skarstein, R. (1986): "Growth and Crisis in the Manufacturing Sector". In Boesen et al. (1986), pp. 79–104.

Skarstein, R., K.J. Havnevik and W.D.S. Mmbaga (Skarstein et al.) (1988): *Norwegian Commodity Import Support to Tanzania—Background, Design and Implementation*. Trondheim.

Stein, H. (1982): *The Political Economy of Planning and the State: The Case of Tanzania*. Department of Economics, University of Riverside.

Stein, H. (1990): "The Economics of the State and the IMF in Tanzania." In *Taamuli*, Vol. 1, No. 1 & 2. Department of Political Science, University of Dar es Salaam, pp. 1–25.

Stewart, F. (1991): "The Many Faces of Adjustment". In *World Development*. Vol. 19, No. 12.

Svendsen, K.E. (1986): "The Creation of Macroeconomic Imbalances and a Structural Crisis". In Boesen et al. (1986), pp. 59–79.

Swantz, M.L. (1985): *Women in Development. A Creative Role Denied*. C. Hurst & Co., London.

Swedish Introductory Statement at TAN-NORDIC Symposium (1984), Dar es Salaam, November 16–17.

Tandon, Y. (1982): *University of Dar es Salaam: Debate on Class, State and Imperialism*. Tanzania Publishing House, Dar es Salaam.

Telford, A. (1929): *Report on the Development of the Rufiji and Kilombero Valley*. Crown Agents for the Colonies, London.

Temple, P.H. and Å. Sundborg (1973): "The Rufiji River; Tanzania—Hydrology and Sediment Transport". In *Studies of Soil Erosion and Sedimentation in Tanzania*. BRALUP, University of Dar es Salaam.

Temu, A.J. (1980): "Tanzanian Societies and Colonial Invasion 1875–1907". In Kaniki (ed) (1980), pp. 86–127.

TFNC (1980): *Data Report on Food and Nutrition Situation in Tanzania 1973/74-1977/78*. Dar es Salaam.

The Nationalist, various issues. Dar es Salaam.

The Iringa Declaration (1971).

The Economic Survey, various issues. Government Printer, Dar es Salaam.

The Forest Ordinance of 1957 (amended 1975). Dar es Salaam.

Therkildsen, O. (1986): "State, donors and villagers in rural water management". In Boesen et al. (1986), pp. 293–309.

Thirlwall, A.P. (1986): "A General Model of Growth and Development on Kaldorian Lines". In *Oxford Economic Papers*, Vol. 38, pp. 199–219.

Thomas, C. (1973): *Dependence and Transformation*. Monthly Review Press, New York.

Tibaijuka, A. (1990): "Grappling with the Urban Food Insecurity in the Midst of Plenty: Government Launches 'Operation Okoa Mazao'". In *Tanzania Economic Trends*, Vol. 2, No. 3 1989 & Vol 2, No 4 1990. Economic Research Bureau, University of Dar es Salaam and Planning Commission, Dar es Salaam, pp. 13–23.

Tibaijuka, A. (1991a): "Social Effects of Reconstruction Programmes". In Ström, G. W. (ed): *Country Analysis Tanzania. The Decade of 1980–90 and the Future*. Draft, pp. 68–85.

Tibaijuka, A. (1991b): "Issues Arising from the Non-Traditional Export Drive Policy of Economic Adjustment: The Case of Wood and Wood Products in Tanzania". In *Tanzanian Economic Trends*, Vol. 4, No.1, April, Dar es Salaam.

Trimingham, J.S. (1968): *The Influence of Islam upon Africa*. London.

Tripp, A. M. (1991): *Women and Democratization in Africa: Reflection on the Tanzanian Case*. Paper presented at 34th Annual Meeting of the African Studies Association, St. Louis, November 23–26.

Turok, B. (1971): "The Problem of Agency in Tanzania's Rural Development: Rufiji Ujamaa Scheme". In L. Cliffe, P. Lawrence, W. Luttrell, S. Migot-Adholla and J. Saul (eds) (1975): *Rural Cooperation in Tanzania*. Tanzania Publishing House, Dar es Salaam, pp. 396–417.

Udo, R.K. (1963): "Patterns of Population Distribution and Settlement in Eastern Nigeria". In *Nigerian Geographical Journal*, Vol. VI, pp. 73–88.

URT (1977): *The Threat of Desertification in Central Tanzania*. Paper prepared for a U.N. Conference on Desertification.

URT (1964): *First Five-Year Plan for Economic and Social Development*. Dar es Salaam.

URT (1966):*Report of the Presidential Special Committee into Co- operative Movement and Marketing*. Dar es Salaam.

URT (1982): *The Tanzania National Agricultural Policy (Final Report)*. Ministry of Agriculture. October, Dar es Salaam.

URT (1983): *The Agricultural Policy of Tanzania*. Ministry of Agriculture. March. Government Printer, Dar es Salaam.

URT (1986): *The Economic Recovery Programme*. Ministry of Finance and Planning. May, Dar es Salaam.

URT (1991): *Presidential Commission of Inquiry into Land Matters*. Terms of Reference of the Land Commission.

URT (1992): *The Energy Policy of Tanzania*. Ministry of Water, Energy and Minerals. April 1992.

URT (undated): *Basic Data 1981/82-1985/86*. Planning and Marketing Division, Ministry of Agriculture and Livestock, Dar es Salaam.

URT (undated): *Basic Data 1984/85-1988/89*. Planning and Marketing Division, Ministry of Agriculture and Livestock, Dar es Salaam.

USAID (1967): *Rufiji Basin; Land and Water Resource Development Plan and Potential*. Prepared for USAID by Bureau of Reclamation, US Dept. of the Interior.

VHL (Norwegian River and Harbour Laboratories) (1979): *Report on Hydraulic Studies in the Lower Rufiji River*. Trondheim.

Villiers, A. (1940): *Sons of Sinbad*. Charles Scribner's Sons, New York.

Villiers, A. (1948): "Some Aspects of the Arab Dhow Trade". In *Middle East Journal*, Vol. 2, pp. 399–416.

von Freyhold, M. (1977): "The Post-Colonial State and Its Tanzanian Version". In *Review of African Political Economy*, No. 8.

von Freyhold, M. (1979): *Ujamaa Villages in Tanzania: Analysis of a Social Experiment*. Heineman Educational Books, London.

von Mitzlaff, U. (1989): *Coastal Communities and their Mangrove Environment*. A Socio-Economic Study Prepared for Forest Division, Catchment Forestry Project, Dar es Salaam.

Vuorela, U. (1988): "Social Reproduction: Issues Related to Women in Development". In Havnevik et al. (1988), pp.177–187.

Wagao, J. (1982): *State Control of Agricultural Marketing in Tanzania 1961–1976*. Economic Research Bureau Paper 82.7, University of Dar es Salaam.

Wangwe, S.M. (1979): *Decentralisation and Rural Industrialisation*. Dar es Salaam.

Wangwe, S.M. (1987): "Impact of the IMF/World Bank Philosophy, the Case of Tanzania". In Havnevik, K.J. (ed) (1987): *The IMF and the World Bank in Tanzania*. Seminar Proceedings no. 18, Scandinavian Institute of African Studies, Uppsala.

Wangwe, S. M. (1990): *Industrial Development in Tanzania: Are Infant Industries Maturing?* Paper presented to the Sixth Economic Workshop, Dar es Salaam, January 2–4.

Westergaard, P.W. (ed) (1972): *Economic Base-Line Studies of the Co-operative Societies in Tanzania. Based on the Accounts for 1967 onwards*. Economic Research Bureau, University of Dar es Salaam/Cooperative College—Cooperative Education Centre.

Westergaard, P.W. (1973): *Analysis of the Accounts of the Co-operative Societies in Tanzania for the Years 1967–1969*. Economic Research Bureau Paper 73.2, University of Dar es Salaam.

Williams, D.V. (1979): *Authoritarian Legal Systems and the Process of Capitalist Accumulation in Africa*. Paper presented to the Southern African Social Conference, University of Dar es Salaam, 23–27 June, 1979.

Williams, D.V. (1982): "State Coercion against Peasant Farmers: The Tanzanian Case". In *Journal of Legal Pluralism and Unofficial Law*, No. 20, pp. 95–127.

World Bank (various years): *World Development Report*. World Bank, Washington D. C.

World Bank (1961): *The Economic Development of Tanganyika*. John Hopkins Press, Baltimore.

World Bank (1977): *Tanzania—Basic Economic Report: Main Report*. Washington D.C.

World Bank (1981a): *Accelerated Development in Sub-Saharan Africa: An Agenda for Action*. Washington D.C.

World Bank (1981b): *Economic Memorandum on Tanzania*. Report No. 3089 TA, Washington D.C.

World Bank (1983): *Tanzania: Agricultural Sector Report*. Report No. 4052-TA, Southern Africa Division, August, Washington D. C.

World Bank (1990a): *World Bank/Tanzania Relations, 1961- 1987*. Report No. 8329-TA. *Volume I: Overview*. Washington D. C.

World Bank (1990b): *Tanzania Policy Framework Paper for 1989/90 to 1991/92*. Washington D.C.

World Bank (1991a): *Tanzania Economic Report. Towards Sustainable Development in the 1990s. Volume I: Main Report*. Report No 9352-TA. *June. Southern Africa Department. Washington D. C.*

World Bank (1991b): Tanzania Economic Report. Towards Sustainable Development in the 1990s. Volume II: Background Papers. Report No. 9352-TA. Southern Africa Department. Washington D. C.

World Bank (1991c): *Review of External Resource Requirements*. Presentation by the World Bank to the Consultative Group Meeting for Tanzania, Paris, June 24–26. Enclosure no. 5.

World Bank (1991d): *Economic Performance and Future Policies*. Presentation to the Consultative Group Meeting for Tanzania. Enclosure no. 4. Paris, June 24–26, 1991.

Yoshida, M. (1972): *Agricultural Survey of the Lower Rufiji Plain*. Preliminary report presented to a seminar at BRALUP, University of Dar es Salaam.

Yoshida, M. (1974): *Agricultural Survey of the Lower Rufiji Plain*. Ministry of Water Development and Power, Dar es Salaam.

Ziegenhorn (1890): "Das Rufiji Delta". In *Mitteilungen aus dem Deutschen Schutzgebiet*, IX.

Appendix 1

THE CONCEPT OF THE AGRICULTURAL SURPLUS AND DEVELOPMENT

In an economy dominated by agriculture, the size and growth of the agricultural surplus are major determinants of the growth rate of the national economy. The concept "agricultural surplus" has been treated by several authors who emphasise the role of agriculture and linkages between the agricultural and the industrial sectors in development. As the content of the concept changes from one author to the other, it requires clarification.

In this study the concept of agricultural surplus does not refer to the conventional neo-classical economic terms that concern consumers' and producers' surplus. Rather it relates to the classical economic concept that defines economic surplus as the difference between aggregate output and aggregate essential consumption. To avoid ambiguity it is necessary to define the economic or agricultural surplus, when focusing solely on the agricultural sector, as only consisting of physical quantities. The agricultural surplus defined in this way constitutes two categories of physical agricultural products: the transfer of agricultural products from the agricultural sector to other domestic sectors or abroad, and agricultural taxes and excises paid in kind, in the form of physical products (Schäfer, 1983:61).

Hence, the aggregate marketed agricultural output may be used as an indicator of the agricultural surplus. As this measure also includes transfers within the agricultural sector itself, it will somewhat exaggerate the size of the surplus. Such an indicator requires that actual consumption of agricultural produce by the agricultural sector corresponds to an essential consumption aggregate which is defined as a historical minimum subsistence norm, uniformally applied to all those involved in the production process.

This definition implies that the agricultural surplus could be seen as the gross investable surplus of the current output. Another definition concerns the potentially investable surplus, i.e. the potential aggregate output if the unutilised and underutilised resources of the agricultural system were fully used (Baran, 1957). Given the conditions in African countries, where agriculture predominates, from the point of view of planning it is desirable to shift the analysis from the gross investable to the generation of a potential investable surplus.

The agricultural surplus concept defined above, in terms of physical agricultural quantities, should not be confused with the intersectoral net resource flows (ISNRF) from agriculture to other sectors of the economy. While the agricultural surplus is an absolute magnitude, ISNRF represents financial resources of relative magnitude which cannot be conceived of independently of the terms of trade between the agricultural and the non-agricultural sector. This type of transfer may be effected through voluntary or compulsory transfers of agricultural monetary savings or by the direct taxation of agriculture. It could be seen as the agricultural sector's total transfers/exports less total imports in monetary terms (Schäfer, 1983:61; and Havnevik and Skarstein, 1987). ISNRF is purely an accounting framework used to estimate net exchange flows from the agricultural to the industrial sector, to assess whether agriculture generated a "surplus" for financing industrialisation in, for instance, the Soviet Union, Taiwan or Japan. The concept denotes balances of trade or payments in the exchange between sectors. As a financial accounting framework it is, however, not likely to be very revealing for detecting real historical trends, since transfer pricing is widespread in inter-sectoral exchanges (Saith, 1985:18).

A third category of the surplus concept is related to primitive accumulation in Marxist theory. Here surplus extraction or transfer of surplus does not take place between different sectors, but between different modes of production. Hence, this concept is qualitatively different from those discussed above. If economic restructuring aimed at reaping the potential investable surplus in an economy implies a movement from a non-capitalist to a capitalist mode of production, it would be compatible with the Marxist concept. This process of change would be characterised by increased commoditisation in production and the labouring people progressively losing access to the means of production. Numerous studies of development in the Third World note that processes of this character are taking place. The empirical substantiation of these processes is often unclear or lacking in the African context. The Marxist concept of surplus value is related only to the capitalist mode of production proper, and has thus only partial relevance for this study.

Several non-Marxist economists have stressed the role of the agricultural surplus in development and the imperative of focusing on demand linkages between the agricultural and industrial sectors. Nicholas Kaldor is maybe the strongest proponent of this approach. In the early 1960s he argued, "Indeed, the ratio of agricultural production to the self-consumption in the agricultural sector, which is invariably low in countries where agriculture is backward, is perhaps the best available indicator of the 'development potential' of an economy". He maintained that "any attempts to increase non-agricultural employment at a faster rate than the agricultural surplus permits, will sooner or later be frustrated through rapid inflation and/or severe food shortages" (Kaldor, 1967:55–56). Kaldor later developed a basic model of agricultural and industrial growth which has been used by other economists (Kaldor, 1975 and 1979).

At an early stage Ragnar Nurkse also pointed to the need to focus on demand linkages between the agricultural and industrial sectors. He maintained that the relationship between the two sectors represented the clearest and simplest case of the balance needed to stimulate economic growth. In countries where the peasantry does not produce more than its own subsistence needs, there is little or no incentive for industry to establish itself, as there is not a sufficient market for manufactured goods. Improvements in agriculture may be obstructed by a lack of markets for peasant produce, if the non-agricultural sector of the economy is backward or underdeveloped. Each of the two sectors must, according to Nurkse, move forward. If one sector remains passive, the other is slowed down (Nurkse, 1962).

In an article published in 1961, Johnston and Mellor touch upon the potential conflicts inherent in the multiple roles taken by the agricultural sector. "There is clearly a conflict between emphasis on agriculture's essential contribution to capital requirement for overall development and emphasis on increased farm purchasing power as a stimulus to industrialisation" (Johnston and Mellor, 1961). In the early 1980s, Thirlwall, building on the above-mentioned contributions, developed a general model of growth and development. It aimed at identifying the equilibrium terms of trade rate, which is consistent with the supply and demand balance of the agricultural and industrial sectors (Thirlwall, 1986).

Governments which want to alter the intersectoral balance in the economy often use the mechanism of price policies to influence the terms of trade. For instance, by turning the terms of trade against agriculture and increasing industrial prices with respect to agricultural producer prices, the net transfer of savings from agriculture will be reduced (given reasonable assumptions about elasticities). If at the same time real wages in the non-agricultural sector are unchanged, profits within this sector will increase. Hence, increasing the net savings transfer from agriculture and turning terms of trade against agriculture may be considered substitute mechanisms for increasing the investable resources available to the non-agricultural sector. The former mechanism entails that non-agricultural firms will have to borrow investable funds (agricultural savings), while the latter will enable them to generate their own profit for investment (Mitra, 1977:141–165). The utilisation and size of transfers of investable funds from agriculture will depend on the economic and class structure of society and the character of the state. Mitra takes the step from the classical economic framework to Marxist theory by concerning himself with a construct of how class forces, operating through the terms of trade, affect the prospects and modes of growth in a poor country (Mitra, 1977:92).

In discussing the role of the agricultural surplus in a developing economy dominated by agricultural production, I assume that the agricultural sector embraces all "primary" production. Furthermore I assume that the potential for increasing the productivity of labour is limited, as the major part of the land is manually cultivated. Hence the size of the labour force determines how much land can be cultivated. The reproduction of agriculture is essentially "simple" or "static", and takes place in regular cycles affected mainly by droughts, floods or other natural events, or by wars, epidemics, migration, etc. Such assumptions are a simplification of the real situation. They indicate that the production system is characterised by non-capitalist relations. This does not rule out the existence of pockets of capitalist farming or large-scale mechanisation. The assumptions entail, that the impact of such production is limited, and that the overall agricultural and rural production systems lack the dynamic features of capitalist accumulation and expanded reproduction.

In such a pattern of reproduction the advance of agricultural produce for the next production cycle and the necessary consumption of produce by the agricultural population are pressed down to the minimum necessary to ensure continued simple reproduction. The agricultural surplus can, therefore, be increased mainly through the growth of the total agricultural production. A substantial long-term increase in production can only be achieved if agriculture escapes from its static state and enters a process in which the productivity of labour increases steadily.

To discuss the functions or use of the agricultural surplus, I shall divide it into three components:

— food for the non-agricultural population;
— raw materials for the industrial sector; and
— the component of the agricultural surplus which is exported, i.e. "export crops".

It is important to note that in an economy with the characteristics assumed above, it is the growth of the total agricultural surplus which is limited. Any component of the surplus may grow, at least for some time, but it will take place at the expense of other components. A substantial growth of the food surplus may, for example, be achieved by increasing the producer prices of food crops relative to those of export crops. Peasants may change their production priorities and, at least to some extent, increase production of food at the expense of export crops. The food surplus will thus increase, whereas the export surplus will decline by a similar amount.

The above does not necessarily imply that the overall level of agricultural producer prices and the intersectoral terms of trade between agriculture and non-agriculture are of no importance to the size and the growth of the agricultural surplus. One of the objectives of this book is to shed light on the relations between these variables. In Chapters 4, 5, 6 and 7 the analysis of these and other policy mechanisms of the state are investigated. Here let me expand on some of the mechanisms through which agriculture may stimulate or make possible industrial development in an agriculturally dominated, static economy:

a) Agriculture produces a food surplus for the non-agricultural population, in particular workers in the urban and non-agricultural sectors, such as industry and services. The rate at which non-agricultural employment can increase depends on the rate of growth of the food surplus. Food is the primary "wage good", and attempts to increase non-agricultural employment at a faster rate than the agricultural surplus permits, are bound to lead to rapid inflation and/or severe food shortages (cf. Kaldor, 1967).

b) Agriculture supplies the industrial sector with raw materials. Expansion of industrial production capacity at a faster rate than the growth of the agricultural surplus permits, will result in shortages of industrial raw materials and underutilisation of the manufacturing capacity. External assistance may conceal such imbalances, but only for a limited period.

c) In the phases before industrial development has gained momentum, agricultural exports will be the major source of foreign exchange earnings. In most developing economies, the expansion of agriculture is a precondition for setting in motion an industrialisation process. Industrial development will in most cases start with imports of the equipment required to produce manufactured consumer goods for the domestic market (import substitution). Such "infant industries" are not competitive on the world market, hence only a minor share of their production can be channeled to external markets. For some time, the reproduction and expansion of the manufacturing sector will have to depend upon the ability of agriculture to produce a growing surplus for exports.

d) The expansion of a fledgling manufacturing industry will depend upon the increase in the supply of agricultural and imported capital goods, raw materials, etc., financed through exports of the agricultural surplus. To finance its own imports (internal and external) the industrial sector must "export" some of its own products. Thus an increase in the demand for industrial products cannot be completely self-generated, but will depend primarily upon the increase in agriculture's demand for industrial goods. Accordingly, the growth of the agricultural surplus is a precondition for providing the necessary increase in purchasing power to be able to expand industrial production.

The functions of the agricultural surplus enumerated above indicate the strategic role played by agriculture in economic development. Historical as well as recent studies of economic development show that the growth of an agricultural surplus is conditioned by an increase in the productivity of labour, to some extent subject to autonomous changes that promote innovations within agriculture itself. This implies that agricultural development has a somewhat autonomous character, while industrial expansion depends upon agriculture on both the supply and the demand sides.

Appendix 2

METHODOLOGY OF SURVEY OF NON-AGRICULTURAL PRODUCTION IN RUFIJI DISTRICT

A major survey was carried out by the author of non-agricultural production activities in Rufiji District in the period 1978–80. In the survey, wide coverage was given to recording of the distribution of participants in crafts, fishery and forestry related production. A survey covering all the villages of the district both registered and unregistered, was intended. However, due to road and transport conditions only 80 out of 90 villages were reached. The population of the remaining 10 villages, located mainly in the northern coast and southern delta and hill areas, constituted about 5 per cent of the total population of the district living in villages.[1]

The village survey was based on a questionnaire intending to record the number of villagers participating in the various crafts, forestry and fishing activities, organization of the production units and the division of participation between genders.

In every village the procedure was to call on the village chairman and request a meeting with a group of villagers, including women, with knowledge of non-agricultural activities in the village. The request was always attended to and the size of the groups ranged from 2 to 50 persons, with an average of about 10. In the majority of the meetings, however, women did not attend. The reason was often stated to be their occupation with agricultural cultivation at some distance, or that they were tending to other matters. However, there also seemed to be a general unwillingness among the men to have them attend.[2] In spite of attempts to rectify the bias introduced by having mainly male

---

[1] The 10 villages not reached were: Kivinja A and Mchungu/Msindaji of the agro-economic zone Inner Delta North; Maporoni, Twasalie and Ruma of Delta South; Kilulatambwe of North Hill and Ngarambe, Tawi and Kingupira in the southern hill area. As a consequence of the problems of reaching the villages of the south, the agro-economic zone South Hill was excluded from the survey. The village Mbwara which had been visited was accordingly also excluded.

[2] In those cases where women did attend, the tendency was for men to answer "on behalf of" the women.

informants, the statistics for male participants in non-agricultural activities are seen to be more reliable than those relating to women. The immediate implication was thought to be underestimation of figures for women participation. However, closer investigations indicated this to be relevant mainly for those activities where women participants were relatively few in numbers. For major women activities the tendency was toward overestimation. The net effect is likely to be over- rather than underestimation, as the majority of women participate in few activities in rather large numbers.

To improve the reliability of the data, the informants were asked to name the participants in the various activities. However, name counting was impossible for those activities with large numbers of participants.

In order to check on biases in the obtained statistics, five villages which were visisted in the rainy season were revisited in the dry season and the interviews were reconducted. In three villages selective crafts were scrutinized in order to report on possible inaccurate recordings. In other cases questionable figures were checked and rechecked. In most cases, however, the discrepancies, when found, were tolerable.

The fact that the 1979 flood in Rufiji river was one of the largest ever recorded is seen to have had the effect of causing a shift in participation from agricultural activities to those of fishing and charcoal burning. The impact is however seen to be limited mainly to the Rufiji river plain areas where floods caused major damages to the crops.

My conclusion is hence that the adjusted recordings presented are estimates giving a rather accurate indication of the number of participants in the various non-agricultural production activities. Regarding the reliability of the survey as a complete Rufiji District village survey the conclusion is the same. The exclusion of 5 per cent of the population living in villages, of which only 2.5 per cent are in the age groups relevant for inclusion in the survey, does not affect this conclusion.

Regarding the sampling strategy for obtaining more detailed information about conditions of non-agricultural production it was decided that the main emphasis should be on activities of major importance in the district. A restriction imposed on selection of production lines was that both male and female activities should be included. Based on pilot investigations and increasing knowledge through conducting of the initial phase of the survey, the following activities were selected: carpentry, saw milling, blacksmithery, charcoal production[1], mat making,

---

[1] Charcoal production was the only non-craft activity given main emphasis in the sampling strategy.

pottery and embroidery/clothes making. Sampling within these lines of activities was aimed at including units of different organisational structure in order to trace variations emanating from differences in these structures. Other objectives of the sampling strategy were to include at least one production unit from each of the agro-economic zones and one production unit from each of the lines of activities identified. The three large-scale activities of the district, a cotton ginnery, a sisal estate and an agro-mechanization centre were also included in order to provide a complete picture of production activities in the district.

My judgement is that the actual sample pattern obtained is sufficient to shed light on the economic and organisational aspects of non-agricultural production activities in Rufiji District. In my opinion the broad coverage of villages is seen to make the sample representative, in spite of its size being limited. By covering large areas I was in a good position to detect unusual variations or features, and take account of this in the sampling procedure.

Due to variation in production conditions a differentiated approach was called for in execution of the survey. Different questionnaires were designed, one for small-scale industrial units, one for crafts units and one for individual interviews of producers. In addition specific questionnaires were designed for the survey of charcoal production, blacksmiths and pottery production. Unstructured and informal interviews were employed when neither of the questionnaires were found applicable or suitable. This was mainly the case when particular circumstances existed in the craft or activity in question. Follow-up interviews were conducted in 12 production units.

A major limitation of the sampling strategy was lack of knowledge of the total population of units at the time of its design. The overall survey of non-agricultural production activities which was to provide this information was executed parallel to the survey of the individual units. As the work went on, however, major biases were rectified by adjusting the direction of the sampling.

Selection of units at the village level was also exposed to bias as village representatives showed a tendency to direct attention to good cases. This type of bias was lessened, however, once we had familiarised ourselves in the village and were able to move around freely.

In connection with the survey a number of structured, unstructured and informal interviews were executed in the villages. In addition, a considerable number of district and regional government officials, representatives of promotion organisations such as the Small Industries Development Organisation (SIDO), public institutions and parastatals, were interviewed in order to gain background knowledge and place non-agricultural production activities in Rufiji District in the wider national and international context.

Non-agricultural production activities include mainly craft, fishing and forestry related production lines. My definition of craft is production and technical servicing (products, instruments, maintenance and repair) executed by skilled men or women, working alone or with employees, helpers or apprentices and without extensive division of labour. The skills are acquired through some kind of training, formal or informal. In performing the labour functions skills, but little specialisation is needed. Products are mainly produced one at a time, with individual variation, often to the requirement of a particular customer.[1]

Fishery and the major forestry related activities like charcoal production and wood felling require a lower degree of skills which includes no or very limited training. The producer may work alone, or with employees, helpers or apprentices. Little specialisation and division of labour are needed in performing the labour functions. The products are of standardised character sold on a large and impersonalised market.[2]

---

[1] The definition is similar to that of Schädler, however, differs on some points (Schädler, 1968).
[2] While value added in production is relatively high for crafts, this is not the case for most of the other non-agricultural production lines.

Appendix 3

STUDIES OF THE IMPACT OF THE PROJECTED DAM AT STIEGLER'S GORGE ON THE LOWER RUFIJI

1. Stiegler's Gorge Power and Flood Development Project Planning Report, July 1980. — Hafslund/Norplan (Norwegian)

2. Load Forecast, July 1981. — Tanzania Electrical Supply Co. Ltd. (TANESCO)

3. Mtera Power Plant, Preinvestment Study, 1982. — SWECO (Swedish)

4. Prefeasibility Study of Irrigated Agricultural Development in the Lower Rufiji Valley, 1982. — Agrar und Hydro-technik (West German)

5. Stiegler's Gorge Power and Flood Control Development, Technical Review by a Panel of Experts, June 1982.

6. Tanzania Power Sector Study, February 1981. — Acres International (Canadian)

7. Rufiji River Extended Flood Control Study, October 1980. — Hafslund/Norplan (Norwegian)

8. Study of the Impact of the Stiegler's Gorge Multipurpose Project on Fisheries in the Rufiji Delta and Mafia Channel, 1981. — Atkins Land and Water Management

9. Study of Fisheries in the Proposed Stiegler's Gorge Reservoir and the Kilombero Floodplain, 1981. — Atkins Land and Water Management

10. Survey of Forestry Resources of Stiegler's Gorge Project Impact Area, 1980. — Jaakko Poyry (Finnish)

11. Feasibility Study on Tourism Development, September 1981. — Stokes Kennedy Crowley (Ireland)

12. Study of Bush Clearing for the Stiegler's Gorge Multipurpose Project, 1981. — Harza Engineering Co. International

13. Results of the Three Aerial Surveys of Wildlife in the Immediate Impact Area of the Stiegler's Gorge Dam, 1981. — Ecosystems

14. The Consequences of River Impoundment and Dam Construction on the Wildlife Resources of the Rufiji Basin, 1980. — W.A. Rodgers (University of Dar es Salaam)

15. Stiegler's Gorge Settlement Conceptual Plan and Design Criteria, 1980. — Ardhi Institute (Tanzania)

16. Stiegler's Gorge Sedimentation and Stratifica-   NHL (Norwegian Hyd-
    tion Project, 1979.   rodynamic Laboratories)

17. Identification Study on the Ecological Impacts   Euroconsult/Delft
    of the Stiegler's Gorge Power and Flood Con-
    trol Project, 1980.

18. A report on the Wood Vegetation of the Pro-   Makumbule (University of
    posed Stiegler's Gorge Reservoir, south east   Dàr es Sàlaam)
    Tanzania (no date).

19. Subsurface Drainage of the Lower Rufiji Valley   H. Mtango (RUBADA)
    (no date).

20. Report on Market Place Activity to Rufiji Basin   University of Dar es Salaam
    Development Authority, 1981.   (McKim)

21. Identification Study of Health Problems (no   WHO
    date).

22. Study of the Impacts of the SGMP Project on   Amani Medical Research
    the Incidence of Malaria and Filariasis in the   Centre (Tanzanian)
    Lower Rufiji Valley, 1982.

23. Lower Rufiji Valley Schistosomiasis Survey,   National Institute of
    1982.   Medical Research (Mwanza
                                                         Centre)

24. Paddy Cultivation (no date).   A. Temu (RUBADA)

25. Report on Hydraulic Studies in the Lower   VHL (Norwegian River and
    Rufiji River, 1979.   Harbour Laboratories)

26. Report on the Prawn Fisheries of Rufiji Delta   K.T. Dorsey (FAO)
    with particular reference to possible changes
    resulting from modifications to the environ-
    ment by the proposed dam of Stiegler's Gorge.
    FAO Project Technical Paper No. 2, 1979.

27. Report on the Freshwater Fisheries on the   A.J. Hopson (FAO)
    Lower Rufiji River with particular changes re-
    sulting from modifications to the environment
    by the proposed dam at Stiegler's Gorge. *FAO
    Project TCP/ URT/8806 Paper No. 1, 1979.*

Source: Norplan, 1983: Vol. I, Appendix E. Many of the references to these 27 reports
were imprecise and lacked the date of publication. The list was improved by checking
specific references in the Main Report, Vol. I, Part II and Vol. II, Parts I and II

Index